America Now

Short Readings from Recent Periodicals

TWELFTH EDITION

EDITED BY

Robert Atwan

Series Editor, *The Best American Essays*

EXERCISES PREPARED WITH THE ASSISTANCE OF

Valerie Duff-Strautmann

Gregory Atwan

 bedford/st.martin's
Macmillan Learning
Boston | New York

For Bedford/St. Martin's

Vice President, Editorial, Macmillan Learning Humanities: Edwin Hill
Editorial Director, English: Karen S. Henry
Senior Publisher for Composition, Business and Technical Writing, Developmental Writing: Leasa Burton
Executive Editor: John E. Sullivan III
Senior Developmental Editor: Christina Gerogiannis
Associate Editor: Cara Kaufman
Senior Production Editor: Ryan Sullivan
Media Producer: Rand Thomas
Production Manager: Joe Ford
Executive Marketing Manager: Joy Fisher Williams
Copy Editor: Jennifer Brett Greenstein
Senior Photo Editor: Martha Friedman
Permissions Manager: Kalina K. Ingham
Senior Art Director: Anna Palchik
Cover Design: John Callahan
Cover Art: © Mamadou Cissé, *Untitled*, 2006. Courtesy Galerie Bernard Jordan Paris/Zurich
Composition: Jouve
Printing and Binding: LSC Communications

Manufactured in the United States of America.

2 1 0 9 8 7

f e d c b a

For information, write: Bedford/St. Martin's, 75 Arlington Street, Boston, MA 02116 (617-399-4000)

ISBN 978-1-319-05511-0

Acknowledgments

American Dialect Society. "The Word of the Year Is Singular *They*." From americandialect.org, January 8, 2016. Copyright © 2016. Reprinted by permission of the American Dialect Society.

Lauren Apfel. "Should We Make Our Children Say Sorry? Yes!" From *Brain, Child: The Thinking Magazine for Mothers,* January 5, 2015. Copyright © 2015. Reprinted by permission.

Brett Arends. "The Idea of the 'Gender Pay Gap' Is Mostly Bogus." From *Dow Jones MarketWatch,* April 14, 2016. Reprinted with permission of Dow Jones MarketWatch, copyright © 2016 Dow Jones & Company, Inc. All rights reserved worldwide. License number 3950250858946 and license number 3950251289307.

Desiree Bergstrom. "The Problem with Choosing between BS and BA." From *The Emerald,* April 4, 2016. Copyright © 2016. Reprinted by permission.

Text acknowledgments and copyrights are continued at the back of the book on pages 419–22, which constitute an extension of the copyright page. Art acknowledgments and copyrights appear on the same page as the art selections they cover.

Preface for Instructors

People write for many reasons, but one of the most compelling is to express their views on matters of current public interest. Browse any Web site, newsstand, or library magazine rack, and you'll find an abundance of articles and opinion pieces responding to current issues and events. Too frequently, students see the writing they do in a composition class as having little connection with real-world problems and issues. *America Now*, with its provocative professional and student writing — all very current opinion essays drawn from a range of periodicals — shows students that by writing on the important issues of today, they can influence campus and public discourse and truly make a difference.

The twelfth edition of *America Now* offers a generous sampling of timely material. *America Now* is designed to immerse introductory writing students in the give-and-take of public dialogue and to stimulate thought, discussion, and composition. Its overriding instructional principle — which guides everything from the choice of readings and topics to the design of questions — is that participation in informed discussion will help generate and enrich student writing.

America Now encourages its users to view reading, thinking, discussing, and writing as closely interrelated activities. It assumes that (1) attentive reading and reflection will lead to informed discussion; (2) participation in open and informed discussion will result in a broadening of viewpoints; (3) an awareness of different viewpoints will stimulate further reflection and renewed discussion; and (4) this process in turn will lead to thoughtful papers.

The book's general introduction, "The Persuasive Writer: Expressing Opinions with Clarity, Confidence, and Civility," takes the student through these interrelated processes and offers some useful guidelines for engaging in productive discussion that will lead to effective essays. Two annotated student essays serve as models of persuasive writing. Instructors may also find helpful my essay "Writing and the Art of Discussion," which can be found in the instructor's manual.

New to This Edition

Following is a brief overview of the twelfth edition of *America Now*. For a more in-depth description of the book, see "Using *America Now*" beginning on page v of this preface.

Thirty-two readings — all new and *very* current. Drawn from more than twenty-five recent periodicals, each current professional reading not only is new to this edition but also has appeared within a year or two of the book's publication. With over half of its selections published in 2016, *America Now* is the most current short essay reader available. Some of the readings you will find in the twelfth edition are by college professor Dawn Lundy Martin on the experiences of minority students on campus, columnist Christina Cauterucci on whether women should be required to register for the draft, and the editors at *The Economist* on what it means to be a young person trying to get by in the current economic climate. In addition, four of the book's twelve classic "America Then" selections are new to this edition.

Relevant, compelling student essays. Of the fourteen student essays in the book, twelve are new to this edition, and all are recent works by real student writers from across the nation. Highlights in the twelfth edition include San Diego State University student Maddy Perello on climate change, University of Texas student Adam Hamze on historical symbols on campus, and Wesleyan University student Bryan Stascavage's widely circulated and discussed essay on the Black Lives Matter movement.

Seven unique visual texts cover issues of importance on campuses everywhere — including student activism, the value of a college education, immigration, the criminal justice system, and others.

New issues of current interest. Six of the twelve thematic chapters have been updated to reflect the changing interests of students over the past two years. Sure to spark lively discussion and writing, these topics include the value of a college education, immigration, the criminal justice system, gender, and climate change. In a new chapter on American history, we ask the question "How do we remember our past?"

Expanded use of class-proven features. Popular with instructors and students alike, *America Now*'s "In Brief" feature now leads every chapter in the book, and unique "Spotlight on Data and Research" sections offer more opportunities for discussion and writing than ever before.

Using *America Now*

Professional and Student Writing from a Wide Variety of Sources

The book's selections by professional writers are drawn from recent periodicals, ranging from specialized journals, such as *The Chronicle of Higher Education*, to influential general magazines, such as *Harper's* and *The Atlantic*. As would be expected in a collection that focuses heavily on social trends and current events, *America Now* features several newspapers and news-oriented magazines, including the *Philadelphia Inquirer*, the *New York Times*, and the *Washington Post Magazine*. With its additional emphasis on public discourse, this collection also draws on some of America's leading political magazines, including *The Nation*, *The Federalist*, and *The New Republic*. Also represented are magazines that appeal primarily to specialized audiences, such as *Texas Monthly*, *Forbes*, and *Scientific American*. In general, the selections illustrate the variety of personal, informative, and persuasive writing encountered daily by millions of Americans. The readings are kept short (many under three pages, and some no longer than a page) to hold student interest and to serve as models for the student's own writing. To introduce a more in-depth approach to various topics, the book includes a few longer essays.

America Now also features fourteen published student selections from college newspapers. These recent works reveal student writers confronting in a public forum the same topics and issues that challenge some of our leading social critics and commentators, and they show how student writers can enter into and influence public discussion. In this way, the student selections in *America Now* — many complemented by Student Writer at Work interviews — encourage students to see writing as a form of personal and public empowerment. This edition includes six brief, inspiring interviews in which student authors in the book explain how — and why — they express their opinions in writing. In addition, the book contains two examples of student writing for a classroom assignment.

To highlight models of persuasive writing, each chapter contains an annotated section of a student paper labeled "Looking Closely." The comments point out some of the most effective strategies of the student writers in the book and offer advice for stating a main point, shaping arguments, presenting examples and evidence, using quotations, recommending a course of action, and more.

Timely Topics for Discussion and Debate

Student essays not only make up a large percentage of the readings in this book, but also shape the volume's contents. As we explored the broad spectrum of college newspapers — and reviewed several hundred student essays — we gradually found the most commonly discussed campus issues and topics. Issues such as those mentioned on page iv of this preface have provoked so much recent student response that they could have resulted in several single-topic collections. Many college papers do not restrict themselves to news items and editorial opinion but make room for personal essays as well. Some popular student topics are climate change, gender, ethnic and racial identity, and the economy, all of which are reflected in the book's table of contents.

To facilitate group discussion and in-class work, *America Now* features twelve bite-sized units. These focused chapters permit instructors to cover a broad range of themes and issues in a single semester. Each can be conveniently handled in one or two class periods. In general, the chapters move from accessible, personal topics (language, for example) to more public and controversial issues (the Second Amendment, immigration, and the economy), thus accommodating instructors who prefer to start with personal writing and gradually progress to exposition, analysis, and argument.

Since composition courses naturally emphasize issues revolving around language and the construction of meaning, *America Now* also includes a number of selections designed to encourage students to examine the powerful influence of words and symbols.

The Visual Expression of Opinion

Reflecting the growing presence of advertising in public discussion, among the book's images are opinion advertisements (or "op-ads"). These pieces, which focus on financial responsibility and religious freedom, encourage students to uncover the visual and verbal strategies of an advocacy group trying to influence the consciousness and ideology of a large audience.

Because we live in an increasingly visual culture, the book's introduction offers a section on expressing opinions visually — with striking examples from photojournalism, cartoons, and opinion advertisements.

The Instructional Apparatus: Before, During, and After Reading

To help promote reflection and discussion, the book includes a prereading assignment for each main selection. The questions in "Before You

Read" provide students with the opportunity to explore a few of the avenues that lead to fruitful discussion and interesting papers. A full description of the advantages gained by linking reading, writing, and classroom
discussion can be found in my introduction to the instructor's manual.

The apparatus of *America Now* supports both discussion-based instruction and more individualized approaches to reading and writing.
Taking into account the increasing diversity of students (especially the
growing number of speakers for whom English is not their first language)
in today's writing programs, the apparatus offers extensive help with
college-level vocabulary and features a "Words to Learn" list preceding
each selection. This vocabulary list with brief definitions will allow students to spot ahead of time some of the words they may find difficult;
encountering the word later in context will help lock it in memory. It's
unrealistic, however, to think students will acquire a fluent knowledge of
new words by memorizing a list. Therefore, the apparatus following each
selection includes additional exercises under the headings "Vocabulary/
Using a Dictionary" and "Responding to Words in Context." These sets
of questions introduce students to prefixes, suffixes, connotations, denotations, tone, and etymology.

Along with the discussion of vocabulary, other incrementally structured questions follow individual selections. "Discussing Main Point and
Meaning" and "Examining Sentences, Paragraphs, and Organization"
questions help guide students step-by-step through the reading process,
culminating in the set of "Thinking Critically" questions. As instructors well know, beginning students can sometimes be too trusting of
what they see in print, especially in textbooks. Therefore, the "Thinking
Critically" questions invite students to take a more skeptical attitude
toward their reading and to form the habit of challenging a selection
from both analytical and experiential points of view. The selection apparatus concludes with "Writing Activities," which emphasize freewriting
exercises and collaborative projects.

In addition to the selection apparatus, *America Now* contains end-
of-chapter questions designed to stimulate further discussion and writing. The chapter apparatus approaches the reading material from topical
and thematic angles, with an emphasis on group discussion. The introductory comments to each chapter highlight the main discussion points
and the way selections are linked together. These points and linkages are
then reintroduced at the end of the chapter through three sets of inter-
locking study questions and tasks: (1) a suggested topic for discussion,
(2) questions and ideas to help students prepare for class discussion, and
(3) several writing assignments that ask students to move from discussion
to composition — that is, to develop papers out of the ideas and opinions

expressed in class discussion and debate. Instructors with highly diverse writing classes may find "Topics for Cross-Cultural Discussion" a convenient way to encourage an exchange of perspectives and experiences that could also generate ideas for writing.

Acknowledgments

While putting together the twelfth edition of *America Now*, I was fortunate to receive the assistance of many talented individuals. I am enormously grateful to Valerie Duff-Strautmann and Gregory Atwan, who contributed to the book's instructional apparatus and instructor's manual. Liz deBeer of Rutgers University contributed a helpful essay in the instructor's manual on designing student panels ("Forming Forums"), along with advice on using the book's apparatus in both developmental and mainstream composition classes.

To revise a text is to entertain numerous questions: What kind of selections work best in class? What types of questions are most helpful? How can reading, writing, and discussion be most effectively intertwined? This edition profited immensely from the following instructors who generously took the time to respond to my revision plan for the twelfth edition: Catherine Babbitt, Gateway Community College; Mona Bahouth-Kennedy, Owens Community College; Ingrid Bowman, University of California–Santa Barbara; Tran Chau, Arcadia University; Margaret Cox, Bristol Community College; Brent Griffin, Northeastern University; Sharon Hayes, Community College of Baltimore County; Terrence McNulty, Middlesex Community College; Ann Rivera, Villa Maria College; Andrew Seibert, Ohio State University; Alexis Terrell, Oregon State University; and Eileen Vlcek-Scamahorn, Santa Barbara City College.

Other people helped in various ways. I'm indebted to Barbara Gross of Rutgers University, Newark, for her excellent work in helping to design the instructor's manual for the first edition. Two good friends, Charles O'Neill and the late Jack Roberts, both of St. Thomas Aquinas College, went over my early plans for the book and offered many useful suggestions.

As always, it was a pleasure to work with the superb staff at Bedford/ St. Martin's. Jane Helms and Ellen Thibault, my editors on early editions, shaped the book in lasting ways. I also am indebted to my developmental editor, Christina Gerogiannis. As usual, Christina provided excellent guidance and numerous suggestions, while doing her utmost best to keep a book that depends on so many moving parts and timely material on its remarkably tight schedule. Cara Kaufman, associate editor, took care of many crucial details with grace and skill. Cara is also responsible for the student interviews that are such an important feature of this edition. Kalina Ingham and Martha Friedman managed text and art permissions under a tight schedule. Ryan Sullivan guided the book through production with patience and care, staying on top of many details, and Elise Kaiser managed the production process with great attentiveness. I was fortunate to receive the careful copyediting of Jennifer Brett Greenstein.

I am grateful to Charles H. Christensen, the retired president of Bedford/St. Martin's, for his generous help and thoughtful suggestions throughout the life of this book. I thank Edwin Hill, Karen Henry, Leasa Burton, John Sullivan, and Joy Fisher Williams for their continued support. Finally, I especially want to thank cofounder of Bedford/St. Martin's Joan E. Feinberg, who conceived the idea for *America Now*, for her deep and abiding interest in college composition. It has been a great pleasure and privilege to work with her.

Robert Atwan

With Bedford/St. Martin's, You Get More

At Bedford/St. Martin's, providing support to teachers and their students who use our books and digital tools is our top priority. The Bedford/St. Martin's English Community is now our home for professional resources, including Bedford *Bits*, our popular blog with new ideas for the composition classroom. Join us to connect with our authors and your colleagues at **community.macmillan.com**, where you can download titles from our professional resource series, review projects in the pipeline, sign up for webinars, or start a discussion. In addition to this dynamic online community and book-specific instructor resources, we offer digital tools, custom solutions, and value packages to support both you and your students. We are committed to delivering the quality and value that you've come to expect from Bedford/St. Martin's, supported as always by the power of Macmillan Learning. To learn more about or to order any of the following products, contact your Bedford/St. Martin's sales representative or visit the Web site at **macmillanlearning.com**.

Choose from Alternative Formats of America Now

Bedford/St. Martin's offers a range of affordable formats, allowing students to choose the one that works best for them.

Popular e-book formats. For details about our e-book partners, visit **macmillanlearning.com/ebooks**.

Select Value Packages

Add value to your text by packaging one of the following resources with *America Now*. To learn more about package options for any of the following products, contact your Bedford/St. Martin's sales representative or visit **macmillanlearning.com**.

LaunchPad Solo for Readers and Writers allows students to work on whatever they need help with the most. At home or in class, students learn at their own pace, with instruction tailored to each student's unique needs. *LaunchPad Solo for Readers and Writers* features:

- **Pre-built units that support a learning arc.** Each easy-to-assign unit is comprised of a pre-test check, multimedia instruction and assessment, and a post-test that assesses what students have learned about critical reading, the writing process, using sources, grammar, style, and mechanics. Dedicated units also offer help for multilingual writers.

- **Diagnostics that help establish a baseline for instruction.** Assign diagnostics to identify areas of strength and areas for improvement on topics related to grammar and reading and to help students plan a course of study. Use visual reports to track performance by topic, class, and student, as well as comparison reports that track improvement over time.

- **A video introduction to many topics.** Introductions offer an overview of the unit's topic, and many include a brief, accessible video to illustrate the concepts at hand.

- **Twenty-five reading selections with comprehension quizzes.** Assign a range of classic and contemporary essays, each of which includes a label indicating Lexile level to help you scaffold instruction in critical reading.

- **Adaptive quizzing for targeted learning.** Most units include LearningCurve, game-like adaptive quizzing that focuses on the areas in which each student needs the most help.

- **The ability to monitor student progress.** Use our gradebook to see which students are on track and which need additional help with specific topics.

Order **ISBN 978-1-319-09254-2** to package *LaunchPad Solo for Readers and Writers* with *America Now* at a significant discount. Students who rent or buy a used book can purchase access and instructors may request free access at **launchpadworks.com**.

Writer's Help 2.0 is a powerful online writing resource that helps students find answers, whether they are searching for writing advice on their own or as part of an assignment.

- **Smart search.** Built on research with more than 1,600 student writers, the smart search in Writer's Help 2.0 provides reliable results even when students use novice terms, such as *flow* and *unstuck*.

- **Trusted content from our best-selling handbooks.** Choose *Writer's Help 2.0, Hacker Version*, or *Writer's Help 2.0, Lunsford Version*, and ensure that students have clear advice and examples for all of their writing questions.

- **Diagnostics that help establish a baseline for instruction.** Assign diagnostics to identify areas of strength and areas for improvement on topics related to grammar and reading and to help students plan a course of study. Use visual reports to track performance by topic, class, and student, as well as comparison reports that track improvement over time.

- **Adaptive exercises that engage students.** Writer's Help 2.0 includes LearningCurve, game-like online quizzing that adapts to what students already know and helps them focus on what they need to learn.

Writer's Help 2.0 can be packaged with *America Now* at a significant discount. For more information, contact your sales representative or visit **macmillanlearning.com**.

Macmillan Learning Curriculum Solutions

Curriculum Solutions brings together the quality of Bedford/St. Martin's content with Hayden-McNeil's expertise in publishing original custom print and digital products. Developed especially for writing courses, our ForeWords for English program contains a library of the most popular requested content in easy-to-use modules to help you build the best possible text. Whether you are considering creating a custom version of *America Now* or incorporating our content with your own, we can adapt and combine the resources that work best for your course or program. Some enrollment minimums apply. Contact your sales representative for more information.

Instructor Resources

You have a lot to do in your course. Bedford/St. Martin's wants to make it easy for you to find the support you need — and to get it quickly.

From Discussion to Writing: Instructional Resources for Teaching America Now is available as a PDF that can be downloaded from **macmillanlearning.com**. Visit the instructor resources tab for *America Now*. In addition to chapter overviews and instructor support for the selections in the book, the instructor's manual includes sample syllabi and correlations to the Council of Writing Program Administrators' Outcomes Statement.

Brief Contents

Contents

The Persuasive Writer: Expressing Opinions with Clarity, Confidence, and Civility   1

1

Language: Do Words Matter?   47

Do the words we use matter? Does it make a difference whether we say *girl* or *woman*, *handicapped* or *disabled*? Can words do individual and social harm?

2

Free Speech: Is It Endangered on Campus?   81

Should a university be a hotbed for robust, unflinching dialogue on all sorts of public issues? Or is the old liberal ideal of free and open discussion a thing of the past? Do colleges today need to worry about what content is appropriate and what isn't?

3

U.S. History: How Do We Remember Our Past?   113

Can we hold figures from the past accountable for behavior considered acceptable in their time but not today? For example, should statues of famous people who owned slaves be toppled, even though the practice was legal in their day and even if their national contributions were outstanding? These are difficult questions in any era, but in today's society, with its ideals of diversity and inclusiveness, the debates can grow heated.

5

Race: Does It Still Matter?   181

With the groundbreaking election of the first African American president in 2008 and with his reelection in 2012, it appeared that the United States had finally set its disturbing racial history aside and entered, as many called it, a "postracial society." And yet recent years have witnessed anything but, as spontaneous protests and organized movements — largely provoked by police shootings — constantly called attention to the nation's ongoing racial strife. How deeply has the issue of race affected America's consciousness?

6

Diversity and Identity: How Well Is American Immigration Working?   213

The United States has long been considered a land of immigrants, a country that not only welcomed the foreign-born but offered them the opportunities to thrive. Yet that ideal often falls short, and from time to time — especially during economic downturns and global conflicts — the welcome mat appears to be removed from the nation's doorstep. Today, immigration is one of the country's most controversial issues.

7

Guns: Can the Second Amendment Survive? 243

Given the rate of gun violence in this country, should Americans retain the right to own guns? Does our public safety demand that we curb gun ownership? Or would legislation prohibiting or restricting gun ownership violate the Second Amendment of the Constitution?

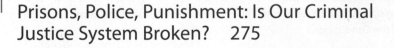

8

Prisons, Police, Punishment: Is Our Criminal Justice System Broken?   275

The United States has the highest incarceration rate in the developed world. How did we reach this point? What have the consequences been for the prison population and society at large? Can anything be done to address the problem?

9

Our Battered Economy: Is the American Dream Over?   305

Is one of America's favorite narratives — the rags-to-riches story of someone who starts
out at the bottom of the social ladder yet manages to make it to the top — a thing of
the past? Such narratives have fueled the American Dream since the days of founder
Benjamin Franklin, one of the first to live and write such a story. For Franklin anyone
could rise here through determination and hard work, no family wealth required.

10

Marriage: What Does It Mean Today?   333

With divorce rates as high as ever, it often looks as if traditional marriage is on its way to extinction. Yet people still keep getting married. Even after several unhappy marriages that end in divorce, many people will marry again, a tendency that the great English essayist Samuel Johnson once called "the triumph of hope over experience."

11

Gender: What Are the Issues Today?   367

Prior to the 1970s, very few people outside of the academic community used the word *gender*, but with the rise of the feminist movement the term took on increasing importance as a way to distinguish between one's biological sex and the sociopolitical construction of that sex. And with the rise of the lesbian, gay, bisexual, and transgender (LGBT) movement, the word has taken on greater significance as society grows more accustomed to a more fluid and less stereotypical way of characterizing people.

12

The Climate Crisis: Have We Reached the Point of No Return?

Are concerns about climate change justified? Can differing views on the issue be attributed to differing levels of education, political affiliation, or economic interests, or is something more complicated going on? Is the science behind climate change "settled"? And assuming that human activity is posing a serious threat to the environment, what can be done?

A Rhetorical Table of Contents

America Now includes numerous examples of rhetorical strategies that aid us in expressing ourselves clearly, cogently, and convincingly. Listed below are eight of the most common rhetorical categories, with a brief account of how they are generally used in both verbal and visual texts. Nearly every selection in the book relies on more than one category, so you will find that several selections appear multiple times. The selections listed are those that most effectively demonstrate — either in whole or in their various segments — a particular strategy.

R.A.

1 Narration

Some uses: telling a story; reporting or summarizing a sequence of events; constructing a historical chronology; recounting a biography or autobiography; detailing how something is done or comes about; breaking down a process into a sequence of events.

2 Description

Some uses: creating a picture in word or image; making information more clear or vivid; reporting objective details.

3 Exemplification

Some uses: providing a "for instance" or "for example"; illustrating ideas; making something abstract more concrete; representing a larger concept or event by a single incident or image.

4 Definition

Some uses: clarifying key terms; reflecting on the significance of a word; enlarging or restricting a term's meaning; eliminating confusion or ambiguity; challenging conventional meanings and euphemisms.

5 Division and Classification

Some uses: dividing a subject into several key parts; organizing material into categories; making distinctions; constructing outlines; arranging ideas in the most appropriate order; viewing an issue from its various sides.

6 Comparison and Contrast

Some uses: finding similarities among different things or ideas; finding differences among similar things or ideas; organizing material through point-by-point resemblance or disparity; forming analogies; expressing a preference for one thing or position over another.

7 Cause and Effect

Some uses: identifying the cause of an event or trend; examining how one thing has influenced another; looking at the consequences of an action or idea; assigning credit, blame, or responsibility.

8 Argument and Persuasion

Some uses: convincing someone that an opinion is correct; defending or refuting a position; gaining support for a course of action; making proposals; resolving conflicts to reach consent or consensus. (At the end of the following list, you will find a collection of the Debates in *America Now*.)

Paired Arguments

About the Editor

Robert Atwan is the series editor of the annual *The Best American Essays,* which he founded in 1985. His essays, reviews, and critical articles have appeared in the *New York Times,* the *Los Angeles Times,* the *Atlantic, Iowa Review, Denver Quarterly, Kenyon Review, River Teeth,* and many other publications. For Bedford/St. Martin's, he has also edited *Ten on Ten: Major Essayists on Recurring Themes* (1992), *Our Times,* Fifth Edition (1998), and *Convergences,* Third Edition (2009). He has coedited (with Jon Roberts) *Left, Right, and Center: Voices from Across the Political Spectrum* (1996), and is coeditor with Donald McQuade of *The Writer's Presence,* Eighth Edition (2015). He lives in New York City.

The Persuasive Writer

Expressing Opinions with Clarity, Confidence, and Civility

It is not possible to extricate yourself from the questions in which your age is involved.

— Ralph Waldo Emerson, "The Fortune of the Republic" (1878)

What Is *America Now*?

America Now collects very recent essays and articles that have been carefully selected to encourage reading, provoke discussion, and stimulate writing. The philosophy behind the book is that interesting, effective writing originates in public dialogue. The book's primary purpose is to help students proceed from class discussions of reading assignments to the production of complete essays that reflect an engaged participation in those discussions.

The selections in *America Now* come from two main sources — from popular, mainstream periodicals and from college newspapers. Written by journalists and columnists, public figures and activists, as well as by professors and students from all over the country, the selections illustrate the types of material read by millions of Americans every day. In addition to magazine and newspaper writing, the book features a number of recent opinion advertisements (what I call "op-ads" for short). These familiar forms of "social marketing" are often sponsored by corporations or nonprofit organizations and advocacy groups to promote policies, programs, and ideas such as gun control, family planning, literacy, civil rights, or conservation. Such advertising texts allow the reader to pinpoint and discuss specific techniques of verbal and visual persuasion that are critical in the formation of public opinion.

I have gathered the selections into twelve units that cover today's most widely discussed issues and topics: gun control, racial identity, gender, incarceration, higher education, environmentalism, and so on. As you respond to the readings in your discussion and writing, you will be actively taking part in some of the major controversies of our time. Although I have tried in this new edition of *America Now* to represent as many viewpoints as possible on a variety of controversial topics, it's not possible in a collection of this scope to include under each topic either a full spectrum of opinion or a universally satisfying balance of opposing opinions. For some featured topics, such as climate change or free expression, an entire book would be required to represent the full range of opinion; for others, a rigid pro-con, either-or format could distort the issue and perhaps overly polarize students' responses to it. Selections within a unit usually illustrate the most commonly held opinions on a topic so that readers will get a reasonably good sense of how the issue has been framed and the public discourse and debate it has generated. But if a single opinion isn't immediately or explicitly balanced by an opposite opinion, or if a view seems unusually idiosyncratic, that in no way implies that it is somehow editorially favored or endorsed. Be assured that questions following *every* selection will encourage you to analyze and critically challenge whatever opinion or perspective is expressed in that selection.

Participation is the key to this collection. I encourage you to view reading and writing as a form of participation. I hope you will read the selections attentively, think about them carefully, be willing to discuss them in class, and use what you've learned from your reading and discussion as the basis for your papers. If you do these things, you will develop three skills necessary for successful work in college and beyond: the ability to read critically, to discuss topics intelligently, and to write persuasively. These skills are also sorely needed in our daily lives as citizens. A vital democracy depends on them. The reason democracy is hard, said the Czech author and statesman Václav Havel, is that it requires the participation of everyone.

America Now invites you to see reading, discussion, and writing as closely related activities. As you read a selection, imagine that you have entered into a discussion with the author. Take notes as you read. Question the selection. Challenge its point of view or its evidence. Compare your experience with the author's. Consider how different economic classes or other groups are likely to respond. Remember, just because something appears in a newspaper or book — in print or online — doesn't make it true or accurate. Form the habit of challenging what you read. Don't be persuaded by an opinion simply because you believe you should accept it. Trust your own observations and experiences. Though logicians never say so, personal experiences and keen observations often form the basis of our most convincing arguments.

Participating in Class Discussion: Six Basic Rules

Discussion is a learned activity. It requires a variety of essential skills: speaking, listening, thinking, and preparing. The following six basic rules are vital to healthy and productive discussion.

1. **Take an active speaking role.** Good discussion demands that everyone participates, not (as so often happens) just a vocal few. Many students remain detached from discussion because they are afraid to speak in a group. This fear is quite common — psychological surveys show that speaking in front of a group is one of our worst fears. It helps to remember that most people will be more interested in *what* you say than in how you say it. Once you get over the initial fear of speaking in public, your confidence will improve with practice.

2. **Listen attentively.** No one who doesn't listen attentively can participate in group discussion. Just think of how many senseless arguments you've had because either you or the person with whom you were talking completely misunderstood what was said. A good listener not only hears what someone is saying but also understands *why* he or she is saying it. Listening carefully also leads to good questions, and when interesting questions begin to emerge, you know good discussion has truly begun.

3. **Examine all sides of an issue.** Good discussion requires that we be patient with complexity. Difficult problems rarely have obvious and simple solutions, nor can they be easily summarized in popular slogans. Complex issues demand to be turned over in our minds so that we can see them from a variety of angles. Group discussion broadens our perspective and deepens our insight into difficult issues and ideas.

4. **Suspend judgment.** To fully explore ideas and issues, you need to be open-minded and tolerant of other opinions, even when they contradict your own. Remember, a discussion is not a debate. Its primary purpose is communication, not competition. The goal of group discussion should be to open up a topic so that everyone is exposed to a spectrum of attitudes. Suspending judgment does not mean you shouldn't hold a strong belief or opinion about an issue; it means that you should be receptive to rival beliefs or opinions. An opinion formed without an awareness of other points of view — one that has

continued

not been tested against contrary ideas — is not a strong opinion but merely a stubborn one.

5. **Avoid abusive or insulting language.** Free and open discussion occurs only when we respect the beliefs and opinions of others. If we speak in ways that fail to show respect for differing viewpoints — if we resort to name-calling or use demeaning and malicious expressions, for example — not only do we embarrass ourselves, but we also close off the possibility for an intelligent and productive exchange of ideas. Some popular radio and television talk shows are poor models of discussion: Shouting insults and engaging in hate speech are usually the last resort of those who have little to say.

6. **Be prepared.** Discussion is not merely random conversation. It demands a certain degree of preparation and focus. To participate in class discussion, you must consider assigned topics beforehand and read whatever is required. Develop the habit of reading with pen in hand, underlining key points, and jotting down questions, impressions, and ideas in your notebook. The notes you bring to class will be an invaluable aid.

When your class discusses a selection, be especially attentive to what others think of it. It's always surprising how two people can read the same article and reach two entirely different interpretations. Observe the range of opinion. Try to understand why and how people arrive at different conclusions. Do some seem to miss the point? Do some distort the author's ideas? Have someone's comments forced you to rethink the selection? Keep a record of the discussion in your notebook. Then, when you begin to draft your paper, consider your essay as an extension of both your imaginary conversation with the author and the actual class discussion. If you've taken detailed notes of your own and the class's opinions about the selection, you should have more than enough information to get started.

What Are Opinions?

One of the primary aims of *America Now* is to help you learn through models and instructional material how to express your opinions in a persuasive, reasonable, civil, and productive fashion. But before we look at effective ways of expressing opinion, let's first consider opinions in general: What are they? Where do they come from?

When we say we have an opinion about something, we usually mean that we have come to a conclusion that something appears true or seems to be valid. But when we express an opinion about something, we are not claiming we are 100 percent certain that something is so. Opinion does not imply certainty and, in fact, is accompanied by some degree of doubt and skepticism. As a result, opinions are most likely to be found in those areas of thought and discussion where our judgments are uncertain. Because human beings know so few things for certain, much of what we believe, or discuss and debate, falls into various realms of probability or possibility. These we call opinions.

Journalists often make a distinction between fact and opinion. Facts can be confirmed and verified and therefore do not involve opinions. We ordinarily don't have opinions about facts, but we can and often do have opinions about the interpretation of facts. For example, it makes no sense to argue whether Washington, D.C., is the capital of the United States since this fact is a matter of record and can be established with certainty. Thus, we don't say we have an opinion that Washington, D.C., is the nation's capital; we know for a fact that it is. But it would be legitimate to form an opinion about whether that city is the best location for the U.S. capital and whether it should permanently remain the capital. In other words:

- *Washington, D.C., is the capital of the United States of America* is a statement of fact.
- *Washington, D.C., is too poorly located to be the capital of a vast nation* is a statement of opinion.

Further, simply not knowing whether something is a fact does not necessarily make it a matter of opinion. For example, if we don't know the capital of Brazil, that doesn't mean we are then free to form an opinion about what Brazilian city it might be. The capital of Brazil is a verifiable fact and can be identified with absolute certainty. There is no conflicting public opinion about which city is Brazil's capital. The answer is not up for grabs. These examples, however, present relatively simple, readily agreed-upon facts. In real-life disputes, a fact is not always so readily distinguished from an opinion; people argue all the time about whether something is a fact. It's therefore a good idea at the outset of any discussion or argument to try to arrive at a mutual agreement of the facts that are known or knowable and those that could be called into question. Debates over abortion, for example, often hinge on biological facts about embryonic development that are themselves disputed by medical experts.

An opinion almost always exists in the climate of other, conflicting opinions. In discourse, we refer to this overall context of competing opinions as public controversy. Every age has its controversies. At any given time, the public is divided on a great number of topics about which it holds a variety of different opinions. Often the controversy is reduced to two opposing positions — for example, we are asked whether we are pro-life or pro-choice; for or against government health care; in favor of or opposed to same-sex marriage; and so on. This book includes many such controversies and covers multiple opinions. One sure way of knowing that something is a matter of opinion is that the public is divided on the topic. We often experience these divisions firsthand as we mature and increasingly come into contact with those who disagree with our opinions.

Some opinions are deeply held — so deeply, in fact, that those who hold them refuse to see them as opinions. For some people on certain issues there can be no difference of opinion; they possess the Truth, and all who differ hold erroneous opinions. This frequently happens in controversies where one side in a dispute is so confident of the truth of its position that it cannot see its own point of view as one of several possible points of view. For example, someone may feel so certain that marriage can exist only between a man and a woman that he or she cannot acknowledge the possibility of another position. If one side cannot recognize the existence of a different opinion, cannot entertain or tolerate it, argues not with the correctness of another's perspective but denies the possibility that there can legitimately be another perspective, then discussion and debate become all but impossible.

To be open and productive, public discussion depends on the capacity of all involved to view their own positions, no matter how cherished, as opinions that can be subject to opposition. There is nothing wrong with possessing a strong conviction, nor with believing our position is the better one, nor with attempting to convince others of our point of view. What is argumentatively wrong and what prevents or restricts free and open discussion is twofold: (1) the failure to recognize our own belief or position as an opinion that could be mistaken; and (2) the refusal to acknowledge the possibility that another's opinion could be correct.

Is one person's opinion as good as another's? Of course not. Although we may believe that everyone has a right to an opinion, we certainly wouldn't ask our mail carrier to diagnose the cause of persistent heartburn or determine whether a swollen gland could be a serious medical problem. In such instances, we respect the opinion of a trained physician. And even when we consult a physician, in serious matters we often seek second and even third opinions just to be sure. An auto mechanic is in a better position to evaluate a used car than someone who's never repaired a car; a lawyer's opinion on whether a contract is valid is more reliable than that of someone who doesn't understand the legal nature of contracts. If an airline manufacturer wants to test a new cockpit instrument design, it solicits opinions from experienced pilots, not passengers. This seems obvious, and yet people continually are persuaded by those who can claim little expert knowledge on a subject or issue: For example, how valuable or trustworthy is the opinion of a celebrity who is paid to endorse a product?

When expressing or evaluating an opinion, we need to consider the extent of our or another person's knowledge about a particular subject. Will anyone take our opinion seriously? On what authority do we base our position? Why do we take someone else's opinion as valuable or trustworthy? What is the source of the opinion? How reliable is it? How biased? One of the first Americans to study the effects of public opinion, Walter Lippmann, wrote in 1925, "It is often very illuminating, therefore, to ask yourself how you get at the facts on which you base your opinion. Who actually saw, heard, felt, counted, named the thing, about which you have an opinion?" Is your opinion, he went on to ask, based on something you heard from someone who heard it from someone else, who in turn heard it from someone else?

How Do We Form Opinions?

How can we possibly have reasonable opinions on all the issues of the day? One of the strains of living in a democracy that encourages a diversity of perspectives is that every responsible citizen is expected to have informed opinions on practically every public question. What do you think about the death penalty? About dependency on foreign oil? About the way the media cover the news? About the extent of racial discrimination? Certainly no one person possesses inside information or access to reliable data on every topic that becomes part of public controversy. Still, many people, by the time they are able to vote, have formed numerous opinions. Where do these opinions come from?

Although social scientists and psychologists have been studying opinion formation for decades, the sources of opinion are multiple and constantly shifting, and individuals differ so widely in experience, cultural background, and temperament that efforts to identify and classify the various ways opinion is formed are bound to be tentative and incomplete. What follows is a brief, though realistic, attempt to list some of the practical ways that Americans come by the opinions they hold.

1. *Inherited opinions.* These are opinions we derive from earliest childhood — transmitted via family, culture, traditions, customs, regions, social institutions, or religion. For example, young people may identify themselves as either Democrats or Republicans because of their family affiliations. Although these opinions may change as we mature, they are often ingrained. The more traditional the culture or society, the more

likely the opinions that grow out of early childhood will be retained and passed on to the next generation.

2. Involuntary opinions. These are opinions that we have not culturally and socially inherited or consciously adopted but that come to us through direct or indirect forms of indoctrination. They could be the customs of a cult or the propaganda of an ideology. Brainwashing is an extreme example of how one acquires opinions involuntarily. A more familiar example is the constant reiteration of advertising messages: We come to possess a favorable opinion of a product not because we have ever used it or know anything about it but because we have been "bombarded" by marketing to think positively about it.

3. Adaptive opinions. Many opinions grow out of our willingness — or even eagerness — to adapt to the prevailing views of particular groups, subgroups, or institutions to which we belong or desire to belong. As many learn, it's easier to follow the path of least resistance than to run counter to it. Moreover, acting out of self-interest, people often adapt their opinions to conform to the views of bosses or authority figures, or they prefer to succumb to peer pressure rather than oppose it. An employee finds himself accepting or agreeing with an opinion because a job or career depends on it; a student may adapt her opinions to suit those of a professor in the hope of receiving a better grade; a professor may tailor his opinions in conformity with the prevailing beliefs of colleagues. Adaptive opinions are often weakly held and readily changed, depending on circumstances. But over time they can become habitual and turn into convictions.

4. Concealed opinions. In some groups in which particular opinions dominate, certain individuals may not share the prevailing attitudes, but rather than adapt or "rock the boat," they keep their opinions to themselves. They may do this merely to avoid conflict or out of much more serious concerns — such as a fear of ostracism, ridicule, retaliation, or job loss. A common example is seen in the person who by day quietly goes along with the opinions of a group of colleagues but at night freely exchanges "honest" opinions with a group of friends. Some individuals find diaries and journals to be an effective way to express concealed opinions, and many today find online forums a space where they can anonymously "be themselves."

5. Linked opinions. Many opinions are closely linked to other opinions. Unlike adaptive opinions, which are usually stimulated by convenience and an incentive to conform, these are opinions we derive from an enthusiastic and dedicated affiliation with certain groups, institutions, or parties. For example, it's not uncommon for someone to agree with every position his or her political party endorses — this phenomenon is usually called "following a party line." Linked opinions may not be well thought out on every narrow issue: Someone may decide to be a Republican or a Democrat or a Green or a Libertarian for a few specific reasons — a position on war, cultural values, the environment, civil liberties, and so forth — and then go along with, even to the point of strenuously defending, all of the other positions the party espouses because they are all part of its political platform or system of beliefs. In other words, once we accept opinions A and B, we are more likely to accept C and D, and so on down the chain. As Ralph Waldo Emerson succinctly put it, "If I know your sect, I anticipate your argument."

6. Considered opinions. These are opinions we have formed as a result of firsthand experience, reading, discussion and debate, or independent thinking and reasoning. These opinions are formed from direct knowledge and often from exposure and consideration of other opinions. Wide reading on a subject and exposure to diverse views help ensure that our opinions are based on solid information and tested against competing opinions. One simple way to judge whether your opinion is carefully thought out is to list your reasons for holding it. Some people who express opinions on a topic are not able to offer a single reason for why they have those opinions. Of course, reasons don't necessarily make an opinion correct, but people who can support their opinions with one or more reasons are more persuasive than those who cannot provide any reasons for their beliefs (see "How to Support Opinions," p. 15).

This list is not exhaustive. Nor are the sources and types above mutually exclusive; the opinions of any individual may derive from all six sources or represent a mixture of several. As you learn to express your opinions effectively, you will find it useful to question yourself about the origins and development of those opinions. By tracing the process that led to the formation of our present opinions, we can better understand ourselves — our convictions, our inconsistencies, our biases, and our blind spots.

From Discussion to Writing

As this book amply demonstrates, we live in a world of conflicting opinions. Each of us over time has inherited, adopted, and gradually formed many opinions on a variety of topics. Of course, there are also a good number of public issues or questions about which we have not formed opinions or have undecided attitudes. In many public debates, members have unequal shares at stake. Eighteen-year-olds, for example, are much more likely to become impassioned over the government's reviving a military draft or a state's raising the legal age for driving than they would over Medicare cuts or Social Security issues. Some public questions personally affect us more than others.

Thus, not all the issues covered in this book will at first make an equal impact on everyone. But whether you take a particular interest in a given topic or not, this book invites you to share in the spirit of public controversy. Many students, once introduced to the opposing sides of a debate or the multiple positions taken on a public issue, will begin to take a closer look at the merits of different opinions. Once we start evaluating these opinions, once we begin stepping into the shoes of others and learning what's at stake in certain positions, we often find ourselves becoming involved with the issue and may even come to see ourselves as participants. After all, we are all part of the public, and to a certain extent all questions affect us: Ask the eighteen-year-old if he or she will be equipped to deal with the medical and financial needs of elderly parents, and an issue that appears to affect only those near retirement will seem much closer to home.

As mentioned earlier, *America Now* is designed to stimulate discussion and writing grounded in response to a variety of public issues. A key to using this book is to think about discussion and writing not as separate activities but as interrelated processes. In discussion, we hear other opinions and formulate our own; in writing, we express our opinions in the context of other opinions. Both discussion and writing require articulation and deliberation. Both require an aptitude for listening carefully to others. Discussion stimulates writing, and writing in turn stimulates further discussion.

Group discussion stimulates and enhances your writing in several important ways. First, it supplies you with ideas. Let's say that you are participating in a discussion on the importance of ethnic identity. One of your classmates mentions some of the problems a mixed ethnic background can cause. But suppose you also come from a mixed background, and when you think about it, you believe that your mixed heritage has given you more advantages than disadvantages. Hearing her viewpoint may inspire you to express your differing perspective on the issue. Your perspective could lead to an interesting personal essay.

Suppose you now start writing that essay. You don't need to start from scratch and stare at a blank piece of paper or computer screen for hours. Discussion has already given you a few good leads. First, you have your classmate's opinions and attitudes to quote or summarize. You can begin your paper by explaining that some people view a divided ethnic identity as a psychological burden. You might expand on your classmate's opinion by bringing in additional information from other student comments or from your reading to show how people often focus on only the negative side of mixed identities. You can then explain your own perspective on this topic. Of course, you will need to give several examples showing *why* a mixed background has been an advantage for you. The end result can be a first-rate essay, one that takes other opinions into account and demonstrates a clearly established point of view. It is personal, and yet it takes a position that goes beyond one individual's experiences.

Whatever the topic, your writing will benefit from reading and discussion, activities that will give your essays a clear purpose or goal. In that way, your papers will resemble the selections found in this book: They will be a *response* to the opinions, attitudes, experiences, issues, ideas, and proposals that inform current public discourse. This is why most writers write; this is what most newspapers and magazines publish; this is what most people read. *America Now* consists entirely of such writing. I hope you will read the selections with enjoyment, discuss the issues with an open mind, and write about the topics with purpose and enthusiasm.

The Practice of Writing

Suppose you wanted to learn to play the guitar. What would you do first? Would you run to the library and read a lot of books on music? Would you then read some instructional books on guitar playing? Might you try to memorize all the chord positions? Then would you get sheet music for songs you liked and memorize them? After all that, if someone handed you an electric guitar, would you immediately be able to play like Jimi Hendrix or Eric Clapton?

I don't think you would begin that way. You probably would start out by strumming the guitar, getting the feel of it, trying to pick out something familiar. You probably would want to take lessons from someone who knows how to play. And you would practice, practice, practice. Every now and then your instruction book would come in handy. It would give you basic information on frets, notes, and chord positions, for example. You might need to refer to that information constantly in the beginning. But knowing the chords is not the same as knowing how to manipulate your fingers correctly to produce the right sounds. You need to be able to *play* the chords, not just know them.

Learning to read and write well is not that much different. Even though instructional books can give you a great deal of advice and information, the only way anyone really learns to read and write is through constant practice. The only problem, of course, is that nobody likes practice. If we did, we would all be good at just about everything. Most of us, however, want to acquire a skill quickly and easily. We don't want to take lesson after lesson. We want to pick up the instrument and sound like a professional in ten minutes.

Wouldn't it be a wonderful world if that could happen? Wouldn't it be great to be born with a gigantic vocabulary so that we instantly knew the meaning of every word we saw or heard? We would never have to go through the slow process of consulting a dictionary whenever we stumbled across an unfamiliar word. But, unfortunately, life is not so easy. To succeed at anything worthwhile requires patience and dedication. Watch a young figure skater trying to perfect her skills and you will see patience and dedication at work; or watch an accident victim learning how to maneuver a wheelchair so that he can begin again an independent existence; or observe a new American struggling to learn English. None of these skills are quickly or easily acquired. Like building a vocabulary, they all take time and effort. They all require practice. And they require something even more important: the willingness to make mistakes. Can someone learn to skate without taking a spill? Or learn a new language without mispronouncing a word?

What Is "Correct English"?

One part of the writing process may seem more difficult than others — correct English. Yes, nearly all of what you read will be written in relatively correct English. Or it's probably more accurate to say "corrected" English, because most published writing is revised or "corrected" several times before it appears in print. Even skilled professional writers make mistakes that require correction.

Most native speakers don't actually *talk* in "correct" English. There are numerous regional patterns and dialects. As the Chinese American novelist Amy Tan says, there are "many Englishes." What we usually consider correct English is a set of guidelines developed over time to help standardize written expression. This standardization — like any agreed-upon standards such as weights and measures — is a matter of use and convenience. Suppose you went to a vegetable stand and asked for a pound of peppers and the storekeeper gave you a half pound but charged you for a full one. When you complained, he said, "But that's what *I* call a pound." Life would be very frustrating if everyone had a different set of standards: Imagine what would happen if some states used a red light to signal "go" and a green one for "stop." Languages are not that different. In all cultures, languages — especially written languages — have gradually developed certain general rules and principles to make communication as clear and efficient as possible.

You probably already have a guidebook or handbook that systematically sets out certain rules of English grammar, punctuation, and spelling. Like our guitar instruction book, these handbooks serve a very practical purpose. Most writers — even experienced authors — need to consult them periodically. Beginning writers may need to rely on them far more regularly. But just as we don't learn how to play chords by merely memorizing finger positions, we don't learn how to write by memorizing the rules of grammar or punctuation.

Writing is an activity, a process. Learning how to do it — like learning to ride a bike or prepare a tasty stew — requires *doing* it. Correct English is not something that comes first. We don't need to know the rules perfectly before we can begin to write. As in any activity, corrections are part of the learning process. You fall off the bike and get on again, trying to "correct" your balance this time. You sample the stew and "correct" the seasoning. You draft a paper about the neighborhood you live in, and as you (or a classmate or instructor) read it over, you notice that certain words and expressions could stand some improvement. And step by step, sentence by sentence, you begin to write better.

Writing as a Public Activity

Many people have the wrong idea about writing. They view writing as a very private act. They picture the writer sitting all alone and staring into space waiting for ideas to come. They think that ideas come from "deep" within and reach expression only after they have been fully articulated inside the writer's head.

These images are part of a myth about creative writing and, like most myths, are sometimes true. A few poets, novelists, and essayists do write in total isolation and search deep inside themselves for thoughts and stories. But most writers have far more contact with public life. This is especially true of people who write regularly for magazines, blogs, newspapers, and professional journals. These writers work within a lively social atmosphere in which issues and ideas are often intensely discussed and debated. Nearly all the selections in this book illustrate this type of writing.

As you work on your own papers, remember that writing is very much a public activity. It is rarely performed alone in an "ivory tower." Writers don't always have the time, the desire, the opportunity, or the luxury to be all alone. They may be writing in a newsroom with clacking keyboards and noise all around them; they may be writing at a kitchen table, trying to feed several children at the same time; they may be texting on subways or buses. The great English novelist D. H. Lawrence (1885–1930) grew up in a small impoverished coal miner's cottage with no place for privacy. It proved to be an enabling experience. Throughout his life, he could write wherever he happened to be; it didn't matter how many people or how much commotion surrounded him.

There are more important ways in which writing is a public activity. Writing is often a response to public events. Most of the articles you encounter every day in newspapers and magazines respond directly to timely or important issues and ideas, topics that people are currently talking about. Writers report on these topics, supply information about them, and discuss and debate the differing viewpoints. The units in this book all represent topics now regularly discussed on college campuses and in the national media. In fact, all of the topics were chosen because they emerged so frequently in college newspapers.

When a columnist decides to write on a topic like the impact of today's economy on young people, she willingly enters an ongoing public discussion about the issue. She hasn't just made up the topic. She knows that it is a serious issue, and she is aware that a wide variety of opinions have been expressed about it. She has not read everything on the subject but usually knows enough about the different arguments to state her own position or attitude persuasively. In fact, what helps make her writing persuasive is that she takes into account the opinions of others. Her own essay, then, becomes a part of the continuing debate and discussion, one that you in turn may want to join.

Such issues are not only matters for formal and impersonal debate. They also invite us to share our *personal* experiences. Many of the selections in this book show how writers participate in the discussion of issues by drawing on their experiences. For example, the essay by Wendy Wilson, "Come See What Mass Immigration Looks Like in My School," is based largely on the author's personal observations and experience, though the topic — immigration — is one widely discussed and debated by countless Americans. You will find that nearly every unit of *America Now* contains a selection that illustrates how you can use your personal experiences to discuss and debate a public issue.

Writing is public in yet another way. Practically all published writing is reviewed, edited, and re-edited by different people before it goes to press. The author of a magazine article has most likely discussed the topic at length with colleagues and publishing professionals and may have asked friends or experts in the field to look over his or her piece. By the time you see the article in a magazine, it has gone through numerous readings and probably quite a few revisions. Although the article is credited to a particular author, it was no doubt read and worked on by others who helped with suggestions and improvements. As a beginning writer, you need to remember that most of what you read in newspapers, magazines, and books has gone through a writing process that involves the collective efforts of several people besides the author. Students usually don't have that advantage and should not feel discouraged when their own writing doesn't measure up to the professionally edited materials they are reading for a course.

How to Support Opinions

In everyday life, we express many opinions, ranging from weighty issues such as race relations or the environment to personal matters such as our Facebook profile. In conversation, we often express our opinions as assertions. An assertion is merely an opinionated claim — usually of our likes or dislikes, agreements or disagreements — that is not supported by evidence or reasons. For example, *"Amnesty for illegal immigrants is a poor idea"* is merely an assertion about public policy — it states an opinion, but it offers no reason or reasons why anyone should accept it.

When entering public discussion and debate, we have an obligation to support our opinions. Simple assertions — *"Men are better at math than women"* — may be provocative and stimulate heated debate, but the discussion will go nowhere unless reasons and evidence are offered to support the claim. The following methods are among the most common ways you can support your opinions.

1. **Experts and authority.** You support your claim that the earth is growing warmer by citing one of the world's leading climatologists; you support your opinion that a regular diet of certain vegetables can drastically reduce the risk of colon cancer by citing medical authorities.

2. **Statistics.** You support the view that your state needs tougher drunk driving laws by citing statistics that show that fatalities from drunk driving have increased 20 percent in the past two years; you support the claim that Americans now prefer smaller, more fuel-efficient cars by citing surveys that reveal a 30 percent drop in SUV and truck sales over the past six months.

3. **Examples.** You support your opinion that magazine advertising is becoming increasingly pornographic by describing several recent instances from different periodicals; you defend your claim that women can be top-ranked chess players by identifying several women who are. Note that when using examples to prove your point, you will almost always require several; one example will seldom convince anyone.

4. **Personal experience.** Although you may not be an expert or authority in any area, your personal experience can count as evidence in

continued

support of an opinion. Suppose you claim that the campus parking facilities are inadequate for commuting students, and, a commuter yourself, you document the difficulties you have every day with parking. Such personal knowledge, assuming it is not false or exaggerated, would plausibly support your position. Many reporters back up their coverage with their eyewitness testimony.

5. **Possible consequences.** You defend an opinion that space exploration is necessary by arguing that it could lead to the discovery of much-needed new energy resources; you support an opinion that expanding the rights of gun ownership is a mistake by arguing that it will result in more crime and gun-related deaths.

These are only a few of the ways opinions can be supported, but they are among the most significant. Note that providing support for an opinion does not automatically make it true or valid; someone will invariably counter your expert with an opposing expert, discover conflicting statistical data, produce counterexamples, or offer personal testimony that contradicts your own. Still, once you've offered legitimate reasons for what you think, you have made a big leap from "mere opinion" to "informed opinion." In each chapter of *America Now*, you will find a "Spotlight on Data and Research" feature that demonstrates how opinions can be supported by statistical data, surveys, polls, scientific studies, and laboratory experiments.

The American Political Spectrum: A Brief Survey

It's almost impossible to engage in public discourse today without immediately encountering terms like *liberal* and *conservative, right wing* and *left wing, libertarian* and *progressive.* Our discussion on public issues is largely framed by these affiliations, as well as by the big political parties (Republicans and Democrats) and the smaller ones (Tea Party, Green, and others) that are formed to advance the causes of those affiliations in government.

These terms don't necessarily account for how complex the spectrum of public opinion actually is. But for the most part, the distinctions revolve around two key questions: *What role should government play in regulating our behavior?* and *What role should government play in controlling the economy and our economic lives?* Most Americans agree on having a representative government that is elected (and can be removed) and is responsible to the people. Commentators and op-ed columnists on all stretches of the spectrum more or less take this for granted. We also pretty much agree that the government should intervene in our lives at times, and should be restrained at other times. Our debates are nearly always about exactly how much the state should intervene *socially* and *economically.*

In general, American liberals believe the government has a major role in regulating the economy, providing services that are available to everyone, and promoting economic equality among citizens. Conservatives often quote President Ronald Reagan's remark that "government is not the solution to our problem; government is the problem." Most conservatives believe that government mismanages money, that taxes should be lower, and that liberal social programs are wasteful and should be reduced or eliminated. Liberals gravitate toward government as the economic engine, while conservatives believe that engine is the private sector.

Socially, conservatives tend to believe that individuals should be held to a standard of conduct consistent with past tradition. Many mainstream conservatives disapprove of same-sex marriage and abortion, think criminals should be punished harshly, and want religion to be a part of public life to some degree. Liberals mistrust government in the social sphere, and they tend to promote extended liberties, such as legalized protections for transgender people, and consider bans on abortion or severe penalties for drug use an invasion of personal privacy. A liberal is more likely to defend a newspaper's claim to free speech against a conservative claim that speech may be unpatriotic or harmful.

Of course, that's only the beginning of the story. Other points of view hover between these ideological pillars. Libertarians dislike the power of government in both the economic and social spheres. They argue government should stay out of both the bedroom and the boardroom, advocating for much less intervention in the economy but often maintaining traditionally liberal positions on social issues. Many libertarians go further than both mainstream liberals and conservatives, arguing, for instance, that drugs should be legalized and the government should not deliberately manipulate the money supply. Opposite the libertarians are statists, believers in big government, who are economically liberal but socially conservative — this ideology is rather rare in the recent American political climate and the term is rarely used with positive connotations.

Centrists, on the other hand, are common but difficult to analyze. They either hold to a variety of positions too inconsistent with any one group to affiliate with it, or take positions that fall in between those of liberals and conservatives, or libertarians and statists. For instance, a centrist position on gun control might be that government should be allowed to ban assault and automatic weapons, but individuals should have the right to keep handguns. Many centrists feel that the economy should shift to be more equitable, but very gradually. Centrists are not, of course, lethargic or dispassionate in their beliefs — their beliefs are simply in the middle. Politicians who are called moderate Democrats or moderate Republicans tend to be centrists.

There are quite a few other political positions in addition to these five groups. Progressives, for instance, believe that it's government's task to advance the human condition in a substantial way. Progressives are a great deal like liberals, but focus more on using the levers of government to check the power large institutions like corporations have in the public sphere. They often believe that society should aspire to something like total economic parity between people, a goal of which many liberals feel wary. Recently, progressives have often attacked mainstream liberal positions, and a number of politicians now call themselves progressives instead of liberals.

Populists, meanwhile, believe in the power of the people collectively, and desire the outcome that provides the most benefit to the most people. However, populists are typically antagonistic to government itself, which they believe to be part of a privileged elite.

Despite the many ideologies in the American political landscape, conversation is most often framed by the division between the two major political parties. It is oversimplified to say that Democrats are liberals and Republicans are conservatives, but it is a convenient place to start. You'll often hear references to "conservative Republicans" and "liberal Democrats," who take more extreme stances on some issues. In recent years, the Tea Party has made a significant impact with an ideology that focuses on economic libertarianism. Analysts debate whether Tea Party members are just conservative Republicans (most elected Tea Party officials actually run as Republicans) or a libertarian party. Though the Tea Party's focus is on the economy, polls show that most Tea Party members are socially conservative. Some progressives and populists vote for the Green Party, which emphasizes the environment but also advocates for high taxes on the rich and wealth redistribution.

Some issues, however, throw the Republican-conservative-Democratic-liberal equation off entirely. Consider military action, such as America's invasion of Iraq and Afghanistan. Not knowing any better, one might imagine Democrats would approve more of foreign wars, which cost money, create government jobs, and enhance the power of the government. However, those wars have, until recently, found more support from Republicans. Gun control is another issue in which conservatively aligned people tend to take the more socially liberal position: Government shouldn't make laws against guns in the name of maintaining law and order.

In response to these complications, many sociologists have developed a more geographical approach to the origin of American opinion.

They point out that most American conservatives statistically live and vote more in rural and suburban areas. Their conservative opinions, these theorists argue, is a result of the landscape in which they live, where people are more isolated from each other, need and use government services less, and see fewer changes occurring around them. In these areas, religion, gun culture, and the military are traditional forces of social cohesion, perhaps explaining some of the anomalies listed above.

Liberals, on the other hand, are far more heavily concentrated in cities, where they are close to their neighbors, rely more heavily on government services like police and sanitation, and have more contact with people on all parts of the economic ladder. Tea Party member and former congresswoman Michele Bachmann once lampooned liberal Democrats by saying that their vision was for all Americans to "move to the urban core, live in tenements, [and] take light rail to their government jobs." Her joke contains a truth — many liberal positions seem concordant with urban life. Of course, in an age of unprecedented geographical mobility, it's an open question whether the places liberals and conservatives tend to live are the cause or the *result* of their opinions.

Free, Open, and Civil Discussion: The Challenges Today

As should be clear by now, *America Now* is intended to advance the ideal of free, open, and civil discussion as a way to both express our opinions and evaluate those of others in our conversation and writing. This ideal of discussion has been honored for centuries and is considered one of the foundations for the practice of democratic governments such as our own. It has not been a worldwide ideal, however, as many dictatorships and authoritarian regimes throughout the world remain in existence even today by suppressing the free discussion of ideas and punishing — at times by death — attempts to participate in such dialogue.

Yet how free and open can discussion be? Are there — even in free societies — limits and justifiable challenges to what someone can express? As many students are well aware, we are daily exposed to speech and opinions that are considered objectionable, unacceptable, offensive, inappropriate, insensitive, or inexcusable. Not a news cycle goes by where someone isn't vehemently attacking someone else's opinions with these very words. In a cover story, "Free Speech under Attack" (June 4, 2016), the *Economist* magazine observed "the swelling range of opinion deemed to fall outside civilized discourse." If free and open discussion has long been an ideal of modern democracy, why is so much expression now attacked and considered worthy of censorship? In summarizing eighteenth-century French philosopher Voltaire's passionate defense of free speech, British author Evelyn Beatrice Hall famously wrote: "I wholly disapprove of what you say, but I will defend to the death your right to say it." Have we reached an opposite position ("I wholly disagree with what you say and therefore you have no right to say it")? Has the once-lofty ideal of free expression been abandoned? Did it ever truly exist?

Democracies can often be tempestuous, and America has had its share of bitter conflicts, but many commentators believe that in the past twenty-five years the situation has worsened. For one thing, the nation has become increasingly polarized and fragmented (see "The American Political Spectrum: A Brief Survey" on p. 16). This state of affairs has largely been blamed on a lack of a collegial and cooperative spirit in government and a determination of elected officials to defend their party's beliefs with no willingness to take into account opposing views. In other words, party becomes more important to politicians than the nation's welfare (though of course each party claims to be on the side of the people). Compromise — long considered the glue of representative democracy — is too often regarded as capitulation. So an overall turbulent political climate, in which opposing views are frequently demonized, has undeniably affected the ideals of free and open discourse.

Yet other factors are also at play. At the end of the twentieth and the turn of the twenty-first century, social media as we now know it barely existed. Today, political candidates tweet messages routinely, and everyone who cares to can voice opinions, no matter how crudely or offensively worded. More political opinion comes across the Internet unsupervised or uncurated than anyone living in 1993 (when this book first appeared) would ever have imagined. Researchers have shown that when news sources become so fragmented, opinion becomes less diverse, not more, as audiences prefer to look at only the sources they agree with and have little patience or tolerance to see the other side's perspective or view all sides of an issue. A 2016 Pew study showed that 62 percent of Americans get their news from social media, a format that rarely strives for balance of viewpoints and that tends to isolate readers in echo chambers of opinion.

So free, open, and civil discussion today meets more challenges than it did, say, a quarter of a century ago. To complicate matters, social media also introduced concepts that over the past few years have played a large role in affecting discussion on the campus and in the classroom. Two of these concepts — "trigger warnings" and "safe spaces" — have been widely publicized in the news media and are covered in the chapters that follow. They are concepts designed to protect students from potentially traumatizing material and hostile environments, but they can be easily caricatured as methods of coddling an overprotected younger generation incapable of confronting disagreeable ideas. Analysis and appraisal of these concepts will be taken up more fully in various selections throughout the book.

Perhaps the greatest advocate of free and open discussion was nineteenth-century British philosopher John Stuart Mill (1806–1873). In his once-classic but now little-read book, *On Liberty*, Mill took what could be called an extreme view of free discussion, which he considered a moral imperative. For example, in one famous statement he argues that "if all mankind minus one were of one opinion, and only one person were of the contrary opinion, mankind would be no more justified in silencing that one person, than he, if he had the power, would be justified in silencing mankind." Another statement demonstrates how seriously he took the stifling of opinion as a moral issue: "We can never be sure," he maintains, "that the opinion we are attempting to stifle is a false opinion; and, if we were sure, stifling it would be an evil still." Though it had its opponents, Mill's view of discussion was highly influential and helped form the groundwork of what used to be called classic liberalism.

We can wonder how a philosopher like John Stuart Mill might respond to the way issues are handled today, when certain topics are considered off limits, inappropriate, or simply problematic. His views have been challenged by some contemporary philosophers and social activists as examples of an elite reinforcement of power. Free and open discussion means nothing to people who aren't invited to the discussion nor to those who are, through various means, eliminated from the discussion — nor to those who had no role in framing the terms or boundaries of the discussion. Whose voices get heard? The ideals of free and open discussion may be, some argue, an insidious way of making sure the public discussion of ideas is actually confined and restricted. And promoting the ideal of civility may be a way of preventing more urgent and less mannerly voices from being heard.

Mill's radical view of open discussion poses another problem, one highly relevant today. As can be easily inferred from the two quotations above, Mill regarded no issue or problem as "settled." For him, an opinion must be constantly and vigilantly tested, even though we are positive it is wrong. Should we then spend hour upon hour debating whether the earth is truly flat? It's unclear what Mill would have thought of those who, despite all hard evidence and testimony, deny that the Holocaust occurred. And as the book's final chapter shows, a large part of the climate change debate is not about the facts that confirm or disconfirm manmade global warming, but about whether the matter is so "settled" scientifically that it is unethical to debate it at all. Thus, Mill's moral obligation that we must examine and weigh all opinions on a subject becomes in some cases an *immoral* imperative. For many, the patient sifting through of dubious opinion after dubious opinion just to be fair and open-minded may be a luxury our society can no longer afford.

The ideal of free, open, and civil discussion — as well as the many contemporary challenges to it — will play a large role in nearly all the chapters that make up this new edition of *America Now*.

Writing for the Classroom: Two Annotated Student Essays

The following student essays perfectly characterize the kind of writing that *America Now* features and examines. Written by Kati Mather, a student at Wheaton College in Massachusetts, and Erika Gallion, a student at Ashland University in Ohio, the essays will provide you with a convenient and effective model of how to express an opinion on a public issue in a concise and convincing manner.

The essays also embody the principles of productive discussion outlined throughout this introduction. In fact, each essay was especially commissioned to perform a double service: to show a writer clearly expressing opinions on a timely topic that personally matters to her and, at the same time, demonstrate how arguments can be shaped to advance the possibility of further discussion instead of ending it.

The two essays demonstrate two different ways of handling a topic, in this case the values of a college education. (For more on this topic, see Chapter 4.) In the first, Kati Mather's "The Many Paths to Success — with or without a College Education," a student expresses an opinion based on personal experience alone. In the second, Erika Gallion's "What's in a Major?," a student expresses an opinion by responding to an opposing opinion. In addition, the second example shows how opinions can be expressed with references to reading and research.

Although there are many other approaches to classroom writing (too many to be fully represented here), these two should provide you with accessible and effective models of the types of writing you will most likely be required to do in connection with the assignments in *America Now*.

Each essay is annotated to help you focus on some of the most effective means of expressing an opinion. First, read through each essay and consider the points the writer is making. Then, return to the essays and analyze more closely the key parts highlighted for examination. This process is designed to help you see how writers construct arguments to support their opinions. It is an analytical process you should begin to put into practice on your own as you read and explore the many issues in this collection. A detailed explanation of the highlighted passages follows each selection.

Expressing an Opinion Based on Personal Experience Alone

The first essay, Kati Mather's "The Many Paths to Success — with or without a College Education," expresses an opinion that is based almost entirely on personal experience and reflection. In her argument that Americans have grown so predisposed to a college education that they dismiss other forms of education as inferior, Mather shows how this common attitude can lead to unfair stereotypes. Her essay cites no formal evidence or outside sources — no research, studies, quotations, other opinions, or assigned readings. Instead, she relies on her own educational experience and the conclusions she draws from it to support her position.

Kati Mather wrote "The Many Paths to Success — with or without a College Education" when she was a senior at Wheaton College in Massachusetts, majoring in English and Italian studies.

Kati Mather

The Many Paths to Success — with or without a College Education

1

Opens with personal perspective

(1) I always knew I would go to college. When I was younger, higher education was not a particular dream of mine, but I understood that it was the expected path. Even as children, many of us are so thoroughly groomed for college that declining the opportunity is unacceptable. Although I speak as someone who could afford such an assumption, even my peers without the same economic advantages went to college. Education is important, but I believe our common expectations — that everyone can and should go to college, and that a college education is necessary to succeed — and the stigmas attached to those who forgo higher education, are false and unfair.

1

2
*Establishes main
point early*

(2) In the past, only certain fortunate people could attain   2
a college education. But over time, America modernized
its approach to education, beginning with compulsory
high school attendance in most states, and then evolving
into a system with numerous options for higher learning.
Choices for postsecondary education today are overwhelming, and — with full- and part-time programs offered
by community colleges, state universities, and private
institutions — accessibility is not the issue it once was. In
our frenzy to adhere to the American dream, which means,
among other things, that everyone is entitled to an education, the schooling system has become too focused on the
social expectations that come with a college education. It
is normally considered to be the gateway to higher income
and an upwardly mobile career. But we would all be better
served if the system were instead focused on learning, and
on what learning means to the individual.

3
*Supports main
point*

(3) It is admirable that we are committed to education   3
in this country, but not everyone should be expected to
take the college track. Vocational education, for instance,
seems to be increasingly a thing of the past, which is regret-
table because careers that do not require a college degree
are as vital as those that do. If vocational schooling were
more widely presented as an option — and one that everyone should take the time to consider — we would not be
so quick to stereotype those who do not attend traditional
academic institutions. Specialized labor such as construction, plumbing, and automobile repair are crucial to a
healthy, functioning society. While a college education can
be a wonderful thing to possess, we need people to aspire
to other forms of education, which include both vocational
schooling and learning skills on the job. Those careers
(and there are many others) are as important as teaching,
accounting, and medicine.

Despite the developments in our educational system that   4
make college more accessible, financial constraints exist for
many — as do family pressures and expectations, intellectual
limitations, and a host of other obstacles. Those obstacles
warrant neither individual criticism nor far-reaching stereotypes. For example, a handful of students from my high
school took an extra year or two to graduate, and I sadly
assumed that they would not be as successful as those who
graduated on time. I did not stop to consider their situations,
or that they might simply be on a different path in life than I
was. Looking back, it was unfair to stereotype others in this

4
Provides examples of alternatives to college

way. Many of them are hardworking and fulfilled individuals today. (4) <u>There is no law that says everyone has to finish high school and go to college to be successful.</u> Many famous <u>actors, musicians, artists, and professional athletes will freely admit that they never finished high school or college, and these are people we admire, who could very well be making more money in a year than an entire graduating class combined.</u> Plus, we applaud their talent and the fact that they chose their own paths. But banking on a paying career in the arts or sports is not a safe bet, which is why it is so important to open all practical avenues to young people and to respect the choices they make.

We should focus on this diversity instead of perpetuating the belief that everyone should pursue a formal college education and that those who do not are somehow inadequate. There are, of course, essential skills learned in college that remain useful throughout life, even for those who do not pursue high-powered careers. As a student myself, I will readily admit that a college education plays an important role in a successful life. (5) <u>The skills we have the opportunity to learn in college are important in "real" life, and some of these can be used no matter what our career path.</u> Among other things, I've learned how to interact with different people, how to live on my own, how to accept rejection, how to articulate what I want to say, and how to write. Writing is one of the most useful skills taught in college because written communication is necessary in so many different aspects of life.

5
Offers balanced view of alternatives

I hope that my college education will lead to success and upward mobility in my career. But I can also allow that, once out of college, most students want to find a job that relates to their studies. In these hard times, however, that may not always be the case. I know from my own experience that other jobs — including those that do not require a college education — can be meaningful to anyone with the will to work and contribute. I'm grateful for the opportunities I've had that led to my college education, and though I do think we have grown too rigid in our thinking about the role of education, I also think we have the chance to change our attitudes and approaches for everyone's benefit.

6
Closes by summarizing position

(6) <u>The widespread belief that everyone must go to college to be a success, and that everyone *can* go to college, is not wholly true.</u> Of course, many people will benefit greatly from a quality education, and a quality education is more accessible today than ever before. But college is not the only option.

5

6

7

Hardworking people who do not take that path can still be enormously successful, and we should not think otherwise. We can all disprove stereotypes. There are countless accomplished people who are not formally educated.

This country offers many roads to success, but we must remember that embracing diversity is essential to all of us. While I will not deny that my education has helped me along my chosen path, I firmly believe that, had I taken a different one, it too would have enabled me to make a valuable contribution to our society.

8

Comments

The following comments correspond to the numbered annotations that appear in the margins of Kati Mather's essay.

1. Opens with personal perspective. Mather begins her essay with an effective opening sentence that at once identifies her background and establishes the personal tone and perspective she will take throughout. The word *always* suggests that she personally had no doubts about attending college and knew it was expected of her since childhood. Thus, she is not someone who opted to skip college, and she is writing from that perspective. As a reader, you may want to consider how this perspective affects your response to arguments against attending college; for example, would you be more persuaded if the same argument had been advanced by someone who decided against a college education?

2. Establishes main point early. Mather states the main point of her essay at the end of paragraph 1. She clearly says that the "common expectations" that everyone should attend college and that only those who do so will succeed are "false and unfair." She points out that those who don't attend college are stigmatized. These general statements allow her to introduce the issue of stereotyping in the body of her essay.

3. Supports main point. Although Mather does not offer statistical evidence supporting her assumption that a college education is today considered a necessity, she backs up that belief with a brief history of how the increasing accessibility of higher education in the United States has evolved to the point that a college degree now appears to be a universal entitlement.

4. Provides examples of alternatives to college. In paragraph 3, Mather introduces the subject of vocational education as an alternative to college. She believes that vocational training is not sufficiently presented to students as an option, even though such skills are as "vital" to society as are traditional college degrees. If more students carefully considered vocational schooling, she maintains, we would in general be less inclined to "stereotype" those who decide not to attend college. In paragraph 4, she acknowledges how she personally failed to consider the different situations and options faced by other students from her high school class.

5. Offers balanced view of alternatives. In paragraph 5, Mather shows that she is attempting to take a balanced view of various educational options. She thus avoids a common tendency when forming a comparison — to make one thing either superior or inferior to the other. At this point in the argument, some writers might have decided to put down or criticize a college education, arguing that vocational training is even better than a college degree. By stating how important college can be to those who choose to attend, Mather resists that simplistic tactic and strengthens her contention that we need to assess all of our educational options fairly, without overvaluing some and undervaluing others.

6. Closes by summarizing position. In her concluding paragraphs, Mather summarizes her position, claiming that "college is not the only option" and reminding readers that many successful careers were forged without a college degree. Her essay returns to a personal note: Had she decided not to attend college, she would still be a valuable member of society.

Expressing an Opinion in Response to an Opposing Opinion

As mentioned earlier in this introduction, most of our opinions develop as a response to the opinions of others. It is difficult to imagine having an opinion in a complete vacuum. Much of the writing we encounter takes the form of a response to opinions that currently circulate in the media. In this case, the student essay is a response to a specific opinion piece that the *Washington Post* published in 2012: Michelle Singletary's "Not All College Majors Are Created Equal." The general topic — the value of a college education — has been covered frequently in the news ever since the economic downturn combined with a student loan crisis stimulated a broad discussion about the financial advantages of attending college. Singletary herself was responding to the general issue by arguing that college was worthwhile but only if one selected a major that paid off with high employment and competitive salaries.

We asked Gallion to read Singletary's essay carefully and take notes on her responses, to note points she agreed with and others she didn't, to research other relevant material, and then to shape those responses and additional information into a short essay that presented her considered opinion on the issue. Note that Gallion, an English major, doesn't respond by recounting her own experiences and defending her career choice. Instead, she follows two of the most effective methods of composing an opinion essay: (1) she forms her opinion as a response to an opposing opinion, and (2) she supports her response with additional reading and research that she discovered independently. These represent two common methods of learning to write for the classroom.

Erika Gallion (student essay)

What's in a Major?

1
Cites opposing view concisely

In January of 2012, columnist Michelle Singletary wrote   1
a piece for the *Washington Post* titled "Not All College Majors Are Created Equal." (1) <u>In it, Singletary discusses the importance of choosing a major that leads to a career after graduation — with the view that job preparation is the greatest benefit of a college education and, without it, the other benefits aren't worth the price. In fact, her essay implies that if a student selects a major that does *not* lead to a well-paying career right away, then attending college may not have been worth it.</u> Although Singletary makes a good case for the importance of career planning, her essay fails to describe fully the meaning of a college education.

2
Establishes main point early

(2) <u>Colleges exist as more than preparatory schools for the job market and, despite the major students choose, we all generally benefit from attending college.</u>

Singletary begins her argument by explaining a "game"   2
she plays with college students in which she asks them their majors. She suggests that an English major, for example, without an internship will have no job after graduation, whereas an engineering major with three internships will find a job. Her argument that these majors are unequal is weakened because her example proves only that having one or more internships will benefit a student in a job search, regardless of the major. Of course an engineering major with three internships will find a job, but what about an English

3
Challenges opponent's claim

major who also took advantage of internships? Would she also have an equal chance of finding a job? (3) <u>Singletary's scenario privileges engineering majors because it does not</u>

give students in the humanities, arts, and social sciences equal credentials.

Despite Singletary's argument that college is best taken advantage of by students who enroll in a highly paid major, (4) there are many students today who simply want to pursue a certain subject because they love it. Singletary makes it seem as if students who choose to study the arts, humanities, or social sciences do not consider the worth of their major. But college is a serious investment, and it's safe to say that most of these students are completely aware of the extra schooling or work it will take to succeed in their area of interest. (5) Academic courses are more than simply strategy-sessions for a future career. As *Reason* editor Nick Gillespie writes in his article "Humanities Under Siege," "You should be going to college to have your mind blown by new ideas." If students feel truly passionate about their majors, their academic experiences will be much more interesting and desirable. The majors that Singletary views as unimportant because of the job market "will give you the tools to figure out who you are and what you want to be" (Gillespie). Career options represent only one aspect of a college education. And it's worth considering that if every prospective student were to major in engineering merely because of a more easily attainable career after graduation, those jobs would soon be all taken.

Most importantly, Singletary overlooks how much students learn and grow outside of the academic curriculum. (6) As a result of a survey, the U.K's *Daily Mail* published a list of the top fifty lessons students actually learn during their time in college. The top three results are: budgeting and prioritizing, living with others, and doing a weekly food shop. Interestingly enough, only ten of these top fifty lessons have anything to do with academics at all. Most of these lessons involve cleaning, socializing, and making time for relaxation. The college years are a prime time for learning important and practical life lessons. College teaches more than just academics: In this sense, college majors *are* created equal.

Although Singletary's concerns are understandable and make perfect sense in this day and age, her desire for prospective students to major in only those areas that guarantee an immediate high-paying career is disappointing. (7) College benefits any student with an academic passion, whether it's English or engineering. As long as a student remains dedicated and determined, a major in any subject can be rewarding and worthwhile.

4
Offers an alternative argument

5
Supports alternative view with apt quotations

6
Offers another view with support

7
Summarizes her position

3

4

5

8
*Demonstrates
sources*

(8) **Works Cited**

Gillespie, Nick. "Where Higher Education Went Wrong." *Reason*, Apr. 2013, www.reason.com/archives/2013/03/19/where-higher-education-went-wrong/3.

Singletary, Michelle. "Not All College Majors Are Created Equal." *Washington Post*, 14 Jan. 2012, www.washingtonpost.com/business/not-all-college-majors-are-created-equal/2012/01/12/gIQAfz4XzP_story.html.

Smith, Jennifer. "Making Spaghetti Bolognese, Building Flat Pack Furniture and Going Three Nights without Sleep: What Students REALLY Learn at University." *Mail Online*, 12 Nov. 2013, www.dailymail.co.uk/news/article-2502847/What-students-REALLY-learn-university.html.

Comments

The following comments correspond to the numbered annotations that appear in the margins of Erika Gallion's essay.

1. Cites opposing view concisely. Because her readers may be unfamiliar with Singletary's position, Gallion needs to offer a brief summary. With little space for a detailed summary, she provides the gist of Singletary's argument in two sentences. Gallion's concision allows her to move straight into her own argument. But note that she will refer to various other points made by Singletary throughout the essay. Had she started with a full summary of Singletary's argument, including long quotations, the reader might feel burdened with too much extraneous information.

2. Establishes main point early. With little space to waste, Gallion clearly establishes her main point at the end of her first paragraph. As opposed to Singletary's view, she sees colleges to be "more than preparatory schools for the job market." One doesn't attend college simply for the purpose of finding a job. No matter what major students select, they will "all generally benefit from attending college." These comments show her dominant point of view, and the body of her essay will support and reinforce it.

3. Challenges opponent's claim. In crafting an opinion essay that takes an opposing view of another opinion, the writer should examine weaknesses in the opposing argument. Here, Gallion objects to an argument Singletary makes to support her point that all majors are not created equal. She points out that Singletary creates an unfair scenario in which an engineering major with several internships easily finds a job, and she contrasts this with an English major without internships who finds no job. Gallion argues that this argument is unfair because it "privileges" one major over another.

4. Offers an alternative argument. In effective arguments, it is usually not enough to discredit or refute an opponent's reasoning or claims. The writer ought to offer alternative arguments, other ways of viewing an issue. Note how Gallion accomplishes this by suggesting that many students attend college to study something they "love," and that this is sufficient motivation outside of selecting a major simply because it would make one more employable.

5. Supports alternative view with apt quotations. Gallion enhances her own point that students often select certain majors because they "love" them by citing remarks written by the political writer Nick Gillespie, who offers reasons for attending college that have nothing to do with the job market. Note that such quotations do not "prove" one's point, but they have the important effect of showing readers that other people, sometimes significant writers and experts, agree with your position and disagree with your opponent's. It is also important to note that the author she cites did not appear in Singletary's essay but that Gallion found the quotation independently, thus broadening the range of opinion.

6. Offers another view with support. Gallion develops her argument in opposition to Singletary's view by citing another source she found independently. Note that this source offers more objective data in the form of a survey that examined what students actually learn in college. As Gallion reports, these lessons have little to do with academics and more to do with practical skills. This information allows her to directly reverse Singletary's central claim. Since the lessons learned in college have little to do with the classroom and course work, majors are irrelevant. Or as Gallion points out: "In this sense, college majors *are* created equal."

7. Summarizes her position. In her concluding paragraph, Gallion summarizes her position. She concedes Singletary's concern about jobs, especially in today's world, but ends by saying she finds that point of view disappointing. Her final sentences restate the opinion she has expressed throughout her essay: that the benefits of a college education can apply to all majors.

8. Demonstrates sources. Gallion provides a "Works Cited" list to indicate the precise sources of her quotations. This list, arranged in alphabetical order by the authors' last names (not in the order that the citations appear in the essay), allows readers to find the works she cites.

STUDENT WRITER AT WORK
Erika Gallion

R.A. What inspired you to write this essay?

E.G. Reading Michelle Singletary's "Not All College Majors Are Created Equal" made me think about the true worth of a college education. Singletary's focus on finding a career and making money made me want to respond with something about what the "nonmaking money" majors do. I wanted to stress the importance of learning about something an individual loves and show the positives of majoring in things like the arts or humanities.

R.A. Are your opinions unusual or fairly mainstream given the general climate of discourse on campus?

E.G. I think there are a few who would agree with me, especially since I'm living on a liberal arts campus. But in the world of research, I think there's been much discourse about Singletary's view. More and more parents are stressing career-driven majors instead of valuing the education classes within the humanities (for example). And that worries me.

R.A. Who was your prime audience?

E.G. I wanted to specifically write this for potential students thinking or worrying about what to major in. I think it is important to advocate for things like true education and/or true passion. I also wanted to write to the current students majoring within the majors that Singletary views as unnecessary. I think it is empowering and comforting to see someone advocate for the opinions you have.

R.A. How long did it take for you to write this piece? Did you revise your work? What were your goals as you revised?

E.G. I drafted this about three times. It took me about two and a half weeks to completely finish it. The revision process included using more action verbs instead of using *is* a lot. I also focused on cutting things out that were unnecessary to the piece as a whole.

R.A. What do you like to read?

E.G. I love reading novels, short stories, essay collections, memoirs, poetry. Anything, really. As far as magazines go, I love reading *Time* and *National Geographic*. There are multiple blogs on tumblr that I frequently read. My heart lies in the literature realm.

R.A. What topics most interest you as a writer?

E.G. Issues surrounding multiculturalism and diversity. I love reading about different cultures and/or religions and the issues that surround them. As a writer,

I like to attempt to tackle these issues because of how important they are in today's connected world.

R.A. Are you pursuing a career in which writing will be a component?

E.G. Yes. I'm going to graduate school for higher education administration, and afterward I hope to pursue a career at the university level helping with international student services. Being able to write well is essential in any career.

R.A. What advice do you have for other student writers?

E.G. Make time for it! I know how busy being a student is, but in order to develop writing skills, you have to sit down and spend time writing.

The Visual Expression of Opinion

Public opinions are expressed in a variety of ways, not only in familiar verbal forms such as persuasive essays, magazine articles, or newspaper columns. In newspapers and magazines, opinions are often expressed through photography, political cartoons, and paid opinion advertisements (or op-ads). Let's briefly look at these three main sources of visual opinion.

Photography

At first glance, a photograph may not seem to express an opinion. Photography is often considered an "objective" medium: Isn't the photographer simply taking a picture of what is actually there? But on reflection and careful examination, we can see that photographs can express subjective views or editorial opinions in many different ways.

1. A photograph can be deliberately set up or "staged" to support a position, point of view, or cause. For example, though not exactly staged, the renowned World War II photograph of U.S. combat troops triumphantly raising the American flag at Iwo Jima on the morning of February 23, 1945, was in fact a reenactment. After a first flag raising was photographed, the military command considered the flag too small to be symbolically effective (though other reasons are also cited), so it was replaced with a much larger one and the event was reshot. The 2006 Clint Eastwood film *Flags of Our Fathers* depicts the reenactment and the photograph's immediate reviving effect on a war-weary public's patriotism. The picture's meaning was also more symbolic than actual, as the fighting on the island went on for many days after the flag was raised. Three of the six Americans who helped raise the famed second

AP Photo / Joe Rosenthal

"Flag Raising at Iwo Jima," taken by combat photographer Joe Rosenthal on
February 23, 1945

flag were killed before the fighting ended. The photograph, which was also cropped, is considered the most reproduced image in photographic history.

2. A photographer can deliberately echo or visually refer to a well-known image to produce a political or emotional effect. Observe how the now-famous photograph of firefighters raising a tattered American flag in the wreckage of 9/11 instantly calls to mind the heroism of the Iwo Jima marines. (See photograph on p. 35.)

3. A photographer can shoot a picture at such an angle or from a particular perspective to dramatize a situation, to make someone look less or more important, or to suggest imminent danger. A memorable photograph taken in 2000 of Cuban refugee Elián González, for example, made it appear that the boy, who was actually in no danger whatsoever, was about to be shot. (See photograph on p. 36.)

4. A photographer can catch a prominent figure in an unflattering position or embarrassing moment, or in a flattering and lofty fashion. Newspaper or magazine editors can then decide based on their political

"Three Firefighters Raising the Flag," taken by Thomas E. Franklin,
staff photographer for the *Record* (Bergen County, NJ), on
September 11, 2001

or cultural attitudes whether to show a political figure in an awkward or
a commanding light.

5. A photograph can be cropped, doctored, or digitally altered to
show something that did not happen. For example, a photo of a young
John Kerry was inserted into a 1972 Jane Fonda rally to misleadingly
show Kerry's association with Fonda's anti–Vietnam War activism. Dart-
mouth College has created a Web site that features a gallery of doctored
news photos. (See fourandsix.com.)

AP Photo / Alan Diaz

6. A photograph can be taken out of context or captioned in a way that is misleading.

These are only some of the ways the print and online media can use photographs for editorial purposes. Although most reputable news sources go to great lengths to verify the authenticity of photographs, especially those that come from outside sources, and enforce stiff penalties on photographers who manipulate their pictures, some experts in the field maintain that doctoring is far more common in the media than the public believes.

"We can no longer afford to accept news photography as factual data," claims Adrian E. Hanft III, a graphic designer, in an August 2006 photography blog. "If we are realistic," he continues, "we will come to the conclusion that much of the photography in the news is fake — or at least touched up to better tell the story. It is relatively simple to doctor a photo and everybody knows it. The fact that the term 'Photoshop it' is a part of the English vernacular shows just how accustomed to fake photography we have become. The interesting thing is that in the face of the massive amounts of doctored photos, most people still expect photos in the news to be unaltered. I think this has something to do with a human desire for photographs to be true. We know the cover photo of Teri Hatcher (of 'Desperate Housewives' fame) is touched up but we don't question it because we *want* her to look like that. Likewise when we see news stories that confirm our beliefs we want them to be true.

As photo manipulation becomes easier and easier, there is an increase in the demand for photographs that confirm what people want to believe. The market responds by flooding the world with 'fake' photography. Today people can believe almost anything they want and point to photography that 'proves' their beliefs."

Political Cartoons

The art of American political cartoons goes back to the eighteenth century; Benjamin Franklin was allegedly responsible for one of the nation's earliest cartoons. Almost from the start, political cartoonists developed what would become their favored techniques and conventions. Because cartoonists hoped to achieve an immediate intellectual and emotional impact, usually with imagery and a brief written message, they soon realized that exaggeration worked better than subtlety and that readily identified symbols were more quickly comprehended than nuanced or unusual imagery. The political cartoon is rarely ambiguous — it takes a decided position that frequently displays enemies negatively and friends positively. Rarely does a political cartoonist muddy the waters by introducing a mixed message or entertaining an opposing view. A cartoonist, unlike a columnist, cannot construct a detailed argument to support a position, so the strokes applied are often broad and obvious.

The humorous impact of most political cartoons depends on a combination of elements. Let's look at two relatively recent cartoons and examine the role of **context, iconography, exaggeration, irony, caption**, and **symbol**. Please note that the following cartoons are included for illustrative purposes only. They were selected not for their political and social opinions or for their artistic skill but primarily because they conveniently demonstrate the major elements and techniques of the political cartoon. Many other recent cartoons could just as easily have been selected.

First, a note about **context**. Chances are that if you don't know the political situation the cartoonist refers to, you won't "get" the cartoon's intended message. So it's important to remember that the cartoon's meaning depends on previously received information, usually from standard news sources. In other words, most cartoonists expect their audience to know a little something about the news story the cartoon refers to. Unlike the essayist, the cartoonist works in a tightly compressed verbal and visual medium in which it is unusually difficult to summarize the political context or the background the audience requires for full comprehension. This is one reason that cartoonists often work with material from headlining stories that readers are likely to be familiar with. In many cases, the audience needs to supply its own information to grasp the cartoon's full meaning.

Let's examine the context of the cartoon "Government Listens to Its Citizens" (see p. 39). The cartoonist expects his audience to be familiar with an ongoing news story: Documents leaked in the summer of 2013 showed that the National Security Administration (NSA) conducts extensive telephonic surveillance of people, including U.S. citizens, to an extent that made many Americans uncomfortable. The cartoon also plays on another, more perennial, complaint about the U.S. government — namely, that it is unresponsive to the needs and demands of its public. The cartoonist depicts the Capitol dome, seat and symbol of the U.S. legislature, literally flipped over to reveal a giant surveillance satellite dish. The message is clear — government *is* in fact listening to you, but maybe not in the ways you'd choose to have it do so. Notice how much the cartoonist expects the audience to bring to his cartoon, however. If you hadn't heard of the NSA spying scandal, the cartoon would be far more confusing. Imagine how you'd interpret the imagery if you didn't know the context of the cartoon.

Note the elements of **iconography**. Iconography is the use of shorthand images that immediately suggest an incident, idea, era, institution, and so on. Such images are intended to reflect immediately and clearly what they stand for. For example, a teenager with a pack of cigarettes rolled up inside the sleeve of his T-shirt is iconographic of the 1950s; a cap and gown indicates an academic; a briefcase represents a businessperson or a public official; a devil is traditionally represented with horns and a pitchfork. In this cartoon, the Capitol dome immediately suggests not only Washington, but also all that American government is supposed to stand for: democracy, inclusiveness, openness, and justice for everyone. In the cartoon, this symbol of a people's government is turned on its head. On the other side is another icon — the parabolic dish that immediately conjures up thoughts of espionage, secrecy, and invasion of privacy.

Note, too, the cartoon's use of **exaggeration** and unrealistic depiction: We are not meant to think that the Capitol dome actually conceals a spy satellite, or — what would be equally ridiculous — that the controversial phone monitoring is going on in the Capitol building itself. The image is an extreme, hyperbolic representation of the frustrations its cartoonist wants to express. In expressing it as a cartoon, of course, he takes obvious liberties for the sake of demonstrating how big a problem he thinks the alleged spying is.

To "get" the cartoon's full meaning is to understand its clever use of **visual irony**. Although it's a large literary subject, irony can be understood

WHO SAYS GOVERNMENT DOESN'T LISTEN TO WHAT ITS CITIZENS HAVE TO SAY?

NSA

© R. J. Matson, Roll Call 2013

"Government Listens to Its Citizens," by *Roll Call* cartoonist R. J. Matson, published on June 17, 2013

simply as a contrast between what appears to be expressed and what is actually being expressed. The contrast is often humorous and could be sarcastic, as when someone says after you've done something especially dumb, "Nice work!" What appears to be expressed (verbally) in the cartoon is that the government is finally "listening" to its citizens, something many of those citizens have claimed it has failed to do. What is actually expressed (visually) is that this statement is literally true, because it is "listening" to those citizens in a questionably legal way. Note also that this cartoon's irony is almost entirely dependent on its **caption**—without the apparently ordinary citizen delivering the line, with its telling double meaning of the word *listens*, the cartoon would have far less impact and meaning.

However, cartoons can be equally effective without a caption, and with few or little words to push their messages. Let's look at another cartoon from 2013, Nate Beeler's "Gay Marriage" (see p. 40). This cartoon comes on the heels of a decision by the U.S. Supreme Court striking down key aspects of the Defense of Marriage Act (DOMA), a 1996 law that refused gay and lesbian couples federal recognition for their marriages, even when states recognized them. The DOMA decision was seen as a major victory for gay rights, especially prior to the 2015 Supreme Court decision that made same-sex marriage legal in all states. In the cartoon, a gay couple celebrates the decision with a warm embrace, but it's an unexpected couple: Lady Justice, the personification of blind justice familiar from courthouses, and the Statue of Liberty.

"Gay Marriage," by *Columbus Dispatch* cartoonist Nate Beeler, published on June 26, 2013

© Nate Beeler, Cagle Cartoons, Inc.

Notice how the cartoonist tells a story with only one static image, rich in **symbol**. Justice appears to have dropped her iconic sword and scales as she's rushed into Liberty's arms, though she's still in her traditional blindfold. She carries the DOMA ruling with her, as if it's coming straight from the Supreme Court. Both characters look far more relaxed and joyous than they do in the well-known poses of the statues, signaling that this is a moment of jubilation for both. The image makes a conventional case for gay marriage to those who oppose it: These two women appear to be in love in the sense of the love that marriage exists to acknowledge. It's their symbolism, however, that makes this cartoon complete: The Supreme Court ruling has not only made the path for gay marriage easier, but also is itself a kind of "marriage" between liberty and justice — a pair of words that immediately makes us think "for all."

Opinion Ads

Most of the ads we see and hear daily try to persuade us to buy consumer goods like cars, cosmetics, and cereal. Yet advertising does more than promote consumer products. Every day we also encounter numerous ads that promote not things but opinions. These opinion advertisements (op-ads) may take a variety of forms — political commercials, direct mail from advocacy groups seeking contributions, posters and billboards, or paid newspaper and magazine announcements. Sometimes the ads are released by political parties and affiliated organizations, sometimes by large corporations hoping to influence policy, and sometimes by public advocacy groups such as Amnesty International, the National Association for the Advancement of Colored People, the National Rifle Association, or — as we see on page 42 — the Ad Council, a nonprofit organization that distributes and promotes public service campaigns on a wide variety of important issues.

One of the Ad Council's recent campaigns attempted to promote financial literacy — that is, to advise people on how to think about the ways they waste money and to encourage them to save. These ads were prompted by the economic woes facing the nation over the past several years. Teaming up with the American Institute of Certified Public Accountants (AICPA), the Ad Council began targeting messages to those younger Americans who were feeling the financial pinch most severely. The ads used an image and text to persuade people to pay closer attention to the way they spend and directed them to an interactive site called "Feed the Pig," which offered practical tips on how to develop better spending habits and save money over time.

These three ads, which first appeared in magazines and newspapers, represent only a tiny sample of the hundreds of such print ads readers come across daily. Carefully examining their verbal and visual techniques — whether you agree with the message or not — will help you become better acquainted with the essentials of rhetorical persuasion.

In print advertising, an ad's central argument is known as body copy, body text, or simply copy to distinguish it from the headline, illustrations, and other visuals. Note that all three ads reproduced here consist of three main elements: a visual image, a headline, and a body text in smaller type. This is typical of all kinds of advertising campaigns — whether print or new media — which try for a uniformity of design and message, though each particular ad may appear different. Let's look at these three elements — image, headline, and copy — more closely.

1. Image. Each advertisement features an arresting image that reinforces the ad's overall message. The creators of the ads clearly expect that readers will look first at the images, and therefore the creators want these images to be intriguing: A common french fry container stuffed not with fries but with rolled-up ten- and twenty-dollar bills visually makes the point that the food you may order for lunch is equivalent to money; familiar takeout containers strikingly packed into a safe like gold bars also visually make the connection between food and money; and a young man searching a beach with a metal detector that is hovering over a buried pirate's chest drives home the notion of unrealistic financial dreams.

Ads are usually addressed to a particular audience, known in the advertising profession as the "target audience." This audience may be defined by sex, income, age, race, educational level, hobbies, or other characteristics. When an individual or a group is featured in an ad, it often signals that a particular audience is being targeted. Note that the only character that appears in these three ads is someone young. This suggests that the ad's creators are hoping to appeal to those in a younger age bracket, those who are still in a financial planning stage.

2. Headline. An effective headline needs to capture the audience's attention in a few words.

Though brief, headlines can be difficult to write since writers need to compress large amounts of content while still engaging the audience's interest. Each of the headlines reprinted here demonstrates some common feature of an effective headline:

Puns: When appropriate, headline writers like to use puns, such as "Takeout can *eat up* your savings." Puns are words or expressions that have two different meanings in the same context. "Eat up" can mean literally to devour food as well as to rapidly devour any commodity ("SUVs eat up a lot of gas").

Questions: Effective ads often use questions in their headlines. The questions are usually known as "rhetorical questions," meaning that the answer is obvious: "Would you rather have $46,000 or a whooooole lotta take-out?"

Image references: Some headlines like to refer the reader directly to the image. Images can only do so much persuasive work. Imagine how you would respond to the image of the young man with a metal detector if you had no verbal copy whatsoever. You would have no clue about what the image is intended to mean. The headline tells us how to "read" the image: "Until this happens, start a savings plan." Note that the key word in the headline is "this." The ad invites you to verbalize the image. We may all come up with different ways of saying it, but "this" will invariably refer to "luckily finding buried treasure."

3. Copy. Those writing and designing ads usually place the central argument in the body copy, which, as we can see from the financial literacy ads, constitutes the main text. Ads differ significantly in the amount of text used. Sometimes the persuasive elements can be simply an image and a headline. But often some verbal argument is employed to support the ad's message. The body copy will usually pick up details from the image and headline but will also supply new information. Two of the three ads encourage their audience to save money by packing their own lunch or cooking their own dinner and avoiding expensive takeout. The third ad encourages broader changes in habits.

Do the math: The first and last ads argue their point with simple arithmetic. If you pack your own lunch or cook your own dinner five times a week, then over a ten-year period you will be ahead $19,592 in lunches and $46,694 in dinners. Yes, that's an impressive $66,286 total. But where, an attentive reader might ask, are these numbers coming from? If we pack our own lunches and cook our own dinners, won't that cost something as well? We can't make lunch or dinner for nothing. Food may cost less at the supermarket than at a restaurant, but it still costs something. The ads claim that we will save $6 by packing our lunch and $9 by cooking dinner, but they don't say (a) how those costs are arrived at or (b) whether those amounts take into account what it costs to buy the food we prepare ourselves.

There's another bit of mystery in the math: Where does 6 percent interest come from? Most savings and checking accounts today offer interest rates that barely reach 1 percent. Are the ads suggesting that readers invest the money they are saving in other ways (the stock market?) and that this would be the average gain over ten years? And that there is no risk? This figure also remains unexplained.

Tag lines: In advertising and marketing, a tag line is a memorable phrase closely associated with the brand or message that is repeated often in a campaign. Note that all three ads repeat (in addition to other language) the phrase "Small changes today. Big bucks tomorrow." The pun on "changes" is of course intentional. Small change now can accumulate into big bucks in the future. But in this case the word *changes* suggests not just coins but also a change in one's lifestyle.

Taking action: Most opinion ads often conclude with a call to take some direct action — vote, write, call, redeem a coupon, register a complaint, and so on. The financial literacy ads not only suggest that readers act to change their sloppy and wasteful economic habits, but also invite them to visit a Web site called "feedthepig.org" for more savings tips. The pig stands for an old-fashioned piggy bank (and "feeding" again reinforces the connection between money and eating). Because of the Internet, an ad today is able to continue and expand its message in ways that could never have been done in earlier times.

Writing as Empowerment

Writing is one of the most powerful means of producing social and political change. Through their four widely disseminated gospels, the first-century evangelists helped propagate Christianity throughout the world; the writings of Adam Smith and Karl Marx determined the economic systems of many nations for well over a century; Thomas Jefferson's

Declaration of Independence became a model for countless colonial liberationists; the carefully crafted speeches of Martin Luther King Jr. and the books and essays of numerous feminists altered twentieth-century consciousness. In the long run, many believe, "The pen is mightier than the sword."

Empowerment does not mean instant success. It does not mean that your opinion or point of view will suddenly prevail. It does mean, however, that you have made your voice heard, that you have given your opinions wider circulation, and that you have made yourself and your position a little more visible. And sometimes you get results: A newspaper prints your letter; a university committee adopts your suggestion; people visit your Web site. Throughout this collection, you will encounter writing specifically intended to inform and influence a wide community.

Such influence is not restricted to professional authors and political experts. This collection features a large number of student writers who are actively involved with the same current topics and issues that engage the attention of professionals — the environment, racial and ethnic identity, gender differences, and so on. The student selections, all of them previously published and written for a variety of reasons, are meant to be an integral part of each unit, to be read in conjunction with the professional essays, and to be criticized and analyzed on an equal footing.

America Now urges you to voice your ideas and opinions — in your notebooks, in your papers, in your classrooms, and, most important, on your campus and in your communities. Reading, discussing, and writing will force you to clarify your observations, attitudes, and values, and as you do, you will discover more about yourself and the world. These are exciting times. Don't sit on the sidelines of controversy. Don't retreat into invisibility and silence. Jump in and confront the ideas and issues currently shaping America.

1

Language: Do Words Matter?

How do the words we use in everyday conversation matter? Does it make any difference if we say *girl* instead of *woman* or *colored people* instead of *people of color*? Do some words indicate a hostile attitude? Do some words inflict harm? Our chapter begins with an "In Brief" feature introducing a number of "sound bites" that focus on a controversy that has been in the news for decades: the name of the Washington football team. *Redskins* is a word that many Americans, both native and nonnative, find hostile, insulting, and racist. Is the term an ethnic slur from the past that is no longer appropriate, or is it simply a part of American sports tradition that was never intended to cause offense? A series of brief quotations demonstrates the range of opinion about this ongoing and often-heated controversy.

For many Americans, words may be not only offensive but also politically damaging, which is why in 2015 California removed the sensitive word *alien* from the state's labor code. "How did 'alien' come to be a term for immigrants in the first place?" asks Francie Diep in "Why Did We Ever Call Undocumented Immigrants 'Aliens'?," a short essay that explains the origins of the term in U.S. history — and goes on to note its eventual "science-fiction definition" along with the term's dehumanizing connotations.

Yet, even the most ordinary of words can become a subject of controversy. The magazine *Brain, Child* invited two mothers to debate the topic: "Should We

Make Our Children Say Sorry?" "Yes!" argues Lauren Apfel, who is "convinced that language is a formative bridge to emotion, and that routinely using the right words paves the way for young kids to feel the right feelings." But Carinn Jade says "No!" and maintains that the word is overused to the point of being meaningless—and states that she doesn't want her "children repeatedly hearing they should be sorry for what they have done." Pepperdine University student Sarah Elliott takes the argument to another level. In "Women: Stop Apologizing; Be Confident," Elliott argues that women are too inclined to apologize needlessly, a habit that hurts their chances at success. "Every day," she writes, "I sit in my classes and listen to girls apologize for speaking, for taking up too much time in discussion, for having an opinion."

Words are often in the news because of their ability to offend (*Redskins*) or their political implications (*illegal alien*). But words also provide the public with convenient labels, a way to describe something like a musical genre (*metal*), a doctrine of belief (*veganism*), or a social type (*hipster*). Lately, as the millennial generation grows older, social commentators are looking for a word that will capture the new generation of young people. This chapter's "Spotlight on Data and Research" takes a look at some characteristics of the generation born in the late 1990s to the present. In "The Perfect Name for the Next Generation of Americans," research consultant Mary Meehan considers how we will refer to these youngest Americans. For example, will they be known as the "We Generation"?

Certain words attract attention because a thinker or writer decides that they have become detached from their true or conventional meaning and are now being loosely substituted for clearer and more useful terms. As scholar Robert F. Wilson Jr. suggests in "I Have a Problem with 'Issues,'" such words are often pretentious, redundant, and clichéd. As Wilson sees it, "the 'issues' virus has gone viral and shows no signs of abating." He offers several examples: "Schoolchildren struggle with 'homework issues'; super-sized citizens are fighting 'food issues' (which issue in 'weight issues'); slumping basketball players face 'scoring issues'; and troubled couples are dealing with 'relationship issues.'" In all of these instances, the old-fashioned word *problem* could be substituted with greater clarity.

The chapter ends as it began. In "America Then . . . 1951," we look at another word with racist overtones: *black*. In his short classic dialogue essay "That Word *Black*," writer and poet Langston Hughes ponders the word *black* (an insulting term at a time when *Negro* was the preferred designation) and shows how it can be rescued from centuries of negative connotations.

What's in a Name?

Native American images and logos have long been a part of the cultural history of the United States: A profile of an American Indian began appearing on the U.S. penny in 1859, and tobacco stores often featured a carved wooden statue of what became known as a "cigar store Indian" to attract customers. In 1912 the Boston baseball team (now in Atlanta) named themselves the Braves, and three years later the Cleveland team began calling themselves the Indians. The current Washington football team, which dates back to 1932, was soon after its founding renamed the Boston Redskins.

The controversy over the Redskins' name is not new but rather has been alive for decades, and every now and then it is reignited by a comment, demonstration, or newsworthy event. The main spark for the current heated controversy was the Washington team owner's categorical statement that he would never change the name. This prompted many media outlets to weigh in, and that led to a national debate on whether the word *Redskins* is a racial slur or an innocent label. A great deal of the debate was fueled by leading sports personalities. In October 2013, during a nationally televised game between the Redskins and the Dallas Cowboys (one of the biggest rivalries in sports, as their names indicate), NBC commentator Bob Costas called the word "an insult, a slur, no matter how benign the present-day intent." On the other side of the issue, former player, coach, and now ESPN commentator Mike Ditka had defended the name a few months earlier, calling the debate over it "so stupid it's appalling." His position was backed up by former vice-presidential candidate and news personality Sarah Palin.

As you'll see in the following assorted "sound bites," a number of people — despite what the team's owner declares — think the change of name is inevitable, that eventually enough political, economic, and social pressure will be put on the franchise so that a new name will be found. A large number of media outlets have stated that they will no longer use the word in print and on their broadcasts. The team also faces legal pressure from the government's trademark office, which decided the word was "disparaging" to Native Americans and therefore no longer eligible for trademark registration and protection. The controversy remains heated, and the case appears to be headed to the Supreme Court. As you read the following comments, consider your position: Do you think the Redskins' name should be changed? If not, why not? And if you do, what name would you change it to?

Off in the distance the wheels of change are grinding. You may not be able to hear them yet. But it's only a matter of time until "Redskins" is gone.

— Sports columnist Tony Kornheiser
(*The Washington Post*, March 5, 1992)

The owners of professional sports franchises like the Cleveland Indians, the Atlanta Braves and the Washington Redskins continue to disrespect the heritage of Native American people with mascots and logos that insultingly portray aspects of our culture as a cheap cartoon — and nothing more.

— Ray Halbritter, Oneida Nation Representative
(*Daily News*, February 22, 2013)

We'll never change the name. It's that simple. NEVER — you can use caps.

— Dan Snyder, owner of the Washington football
team since 1999, to reporters in May 2013
(*USA Today*, May 10, 2013)

If I were the owner of the team and I knew that there was a name of my team — even if it had a storied history — that was offending a sizeable group of people, I'd think about changing it.

— President Barack Obama
(in an interview published by the Associated Press,
October 5, 2013)

The Redskins name will change sooner than you think — two or three years, tops.

— Sports columnist Chris Chase
(*USA Today*, October 8, 2013)

No one picks a team name as a means of disparagement. San Francisco didn't choose the name "49ers" because it wanted to mock the foolish desperation of people panning for gold in the mid-19th century. . . . Team nicknames and logos invariably denote fierceness and strength, which in the context of the NFL are very good things.

— Rich Lowry
(*National Review Online*, October 8, 2013)

Cool down, Dan [Snyder]. It is not that big a deal as long as you find a good name to replace the old one. I'd even prefer that you keep the Native American reference since this area of the country was home to several tribes. So here are my suggestions for new names: "Tribe"; "Nation"; "Rebels"; "Potomacs" and "Native Americans."
— Author and news commentator Juan Williams
(*FoxNews.com*, October 13, 2013)

This page has for many years urged the local football team to change its name. . . . But the matter seems clearer to us now than ever, and while we wait for the National Football League to catch up with thoughtful opinion and common decency, we have decided that, except when it is essential for clarity or effect, we will no longer use the slur ourselves. That's the standard we apply to all offensive vocabulary.
— *The Washington Post* Editorial Board
(May 22, 2014)

POINTS TO CONSIDER

1. After reading the various sound bites, do you think the change of the Redskins' name is inevitable? Explain why or why not.

2. What do you think of Juan Williams's suggestions of alternative team names? Assuming you find the name Redskins inappropriate, what names would you suggest? Would you approve of "Washington Tomahawks"?

3. How do you respond to Rich Lowry's point that teams select names that indicate positive traits in the context of sports? In other words, is the name Redskins meant to honor Native Americans? If it is, is that a sufficient reason to keep the name?

Francie Diep

Why Did We Ever Call Undocumented Immigrants "Aliens"?

[*Pacific Standard*, August 12, 2015]

BEFORE YOU READ
Is there a difference between calling someone an immigrant and calling someone an alien? How might the words we use shape our perceptions of people?

WORDS TO LEARN

derogatory (para. 1): uncomplimentary
or disparaging (adjective)
denote (para. 2): to indicate or mean
(verb)
emergence (para. 3): the process of
coming into view (noun)
cite (para. 3): to quote (verb)

unreliable (para. 3): undependable
(adjective)
undocumented (para. 4): lacking
proper legal papers (adjective)
implications (para. 4): associations, or
things implied (noun)
potentially (para. 4): possibly (adverb)

Yesterday [April 11, 2015], California Governor Jerry Brown 1
signed a law that removes the word "alien" from the state's labor
code. It's a change that's largely symbolic — Brown signed other
laws yesterday that make a more concrete difference — but the vocabulary shift is still important to many. "Alien is now commonly considered a
derogatory term for a foreign-born person and has very negative connotations," as California Senator Tony Mendoza, who introduced the bill,
told the *Los Angeles Times*.

How did "alien" come to be a term for immigrants in the first 2
place? American politicians have actually used the word to denote foreign nationals for more than 200 years. Legally speaking, it doesn't
have anything to do with an immigrant's documentation status. You
can be an alien whether you entered the United States with or without
papers.

Francie Diep is a science journalist and staff writer for Pacific Standard. *She has
contributed pieces to* Popular Science, Scientific American, *and* Smithsonian, *among others.*

Between the 1950s and the '90s, however, newspapers began using   3
the phrase "illegal alien" more frequently, as sociology student Edwin
Ackerman documents in a paper published in the journal *Ethnic and
Racial Studies* in 2012. The rise in the phrase's popularity paralleled the
emergence in the American political consciousness that *how* an immigrant entered the U.S. mattered, Ackerman argues. In other words,
before the 1970s or so, most Americans didn't much care whether
people entered the country legally or illegally. They found other reasons
to worry about, and discriminate against, immigrants. But in the 1970s,
federal agencies in charge of immigration played up illegality in hopes
of increasing their budgets, Ackerman argues. He cites an analysis of
Los Angeles Times articles from that period, which found that more than
one in five border officials quoted in news stories talked about how
agencies needed more money, and how a greater number of undocumented immigrants were entering the U.S. than ever. Meanwhile,
official estimates of the number of undocumented immigrants varied
wildly, Ackerman writes, suggesting the numbers were unreliable.

At the same time, labor-union leaders saw undocumented work-   4
ers as strike-breakers, and ethnicity-based organizations sought to reduce
discrimination against their members by
separating themselves from undocumented | By 1994, 90 per-
immigrants, Ackerman writes. The combi- | cent of newspaper
nation of all of these forces — which weren't | articles addressed
trying to work together — made the idea of | undocumented
undocumented immigrants being a prob- | immigrants as
lem a particularly powerful cultural force. | "illegal aliens."
By 1994, 90 percent of newspaper articles
addressed undocumented immigrants as
"illegal aliens." Coincidentally, "alien" gained its science-fiction definition
with the Space Age in the 1950s. So now we have a word that once meant
foreign national, but has taken on implications of being criminal, potentially
even less than human.

Does it matter what we call immigrants? One recent study found that   5
what terms news media use to refer to immigrants doesn't affect what
immigration policies readers support. Maybe banning words doesn't
cause changes in policy, but it is a reflection of shifting public perception.
After all, California laws are among the most inclusionary of immigrants,
as *Pacific Standard* recently reported. The "California Package" of laws
offers immigrants of all stripes unique freedom of movement and opportunity. It's no wonder the Golden State should pioneer symbolic, cultural
changes as well as legal, material ones.

VOCABULARY/USING A DICTIONARY

1. What do you think *inclusionary* (para. 5) means? How is it different from being *exclusionary*? What root words do these two terms contain?

2. What are *connotations* (para. 1) of a word? In your own words, explain the difference between a word's *connotations* and *denotations*.

3. If a change made to a law is *symbolic* (para. 1), what is its value?

RESPONDING TO WORDS IN CONTEXT

1. What part of speech is the word *pioneer* (para. 5) as it's used in this essay?

2. Define the word *discriminate* (para. 3) in this context. What do we do when we *discriminate* between two items? What are the connotations of the word *discrimination*?

3. What comes to mind when you hear the word *alien* (para. 1)? What has the word come to mean?

DISCUSSING MAIN POINT AND MEANING

1. Why did the terminology used for immigrants shift after 1950? How did we refer to immigrants before that time?

2. What issue, faced by federal agencies in the 1970s, added to negative feelings about undocumented workers? How did the focus on undocumented workers help federal agencies?

3. In addition to federal agencies, what other groups have called attention to the distinctions between illegal and legal immigrants in order to cope with issues of their own?

EXAMINING SENTENCES, PARAGRAPHS, AND ORGANIZATION

1. Think about how the essay begins and ends with references to California law. How does this particular beginning and ending affect our experience of the essay? Would the essay be different without these bookends?

2. California senator Mendoza is quoted in paragraph 1. What would the effect be of *not* including a direct quotation in the first paragraph? How does the use of the quotation create a more effective paragraph?

3. What is the effect of starting the last paragraph with a question? Does the question influence the final (concluding) paragraph?

THINKING CRITICALLY

1. How do you view the nation's immigrants? Do your feelings about immigration change when you are thinking about documented immigrants rather than undocumented immigrants? Explain.

2. Do you think the changes made by Jerry Brown are important or not? Is there anything in the essay that supports your position?

3. In paragraph 4, Diep writes, "Now we have a word that once meant foreign national, but has taken on implications of being criminal, potentially even less than human." Does the word *alien* have these connotations for you? Are there other words you can think of that are used to label people, creating similar negative implications?

WRITING ACTIVITIES

1. Diep writes, "Maybe banning words doesn't cause changes in policy, but it is a reflection of shifting public perception" (para. 5). Write a defense of this statement that considers how the change may shift perception of these immigrants in California and/or have a trickle-down effect in other states. Try to bring in examples of other words that are "banned" or changed in order to shift public perception of a group of people who face or have faced discrimination.

2. Write a short op-ed from the point of view of a labor-union leader, ethnicity-based organization worker, or federal agency worker who views undocumented immigrants as a problem that needs to come to the country's attention. Consider *why* illegal immigration is a problem for the person you are speaking for: What are the issues that affect you in particular, and how do you see undocumented immigrants as a problem in general?

3. Diep points out that California is already a leader in inclusive immigration policy. In a few paragraphs, explain how a change in terminology could benefit immigrants in California as much as supportive laws do. How might Brown's removal of the word *alien* affect future policies? Do you think the two factors—laws that provide opportunity for immigrants without distinction *and* words that are chosen carefully to describe immigrants in a positive light—are necessary and build on each other? Explore how that might work in your paragraphs as you write.

Lauren Apfel

Should We Make Our Children Say Sorry? Yes!

[*Brain, Child*, January 5, 2015]

Carinn Jade

Should We Make Our Children Say Sorry? No!

[*Brain, Child*, January 5, 2015]

BEFORE YOU READ
Should a child be taught to say "sorry"? Is it important for children to know how to apologize? If so, why? If not, why not?

WORDS TO LEARN

inconvenience (Apfel, para. 2): an annoyance or difficulty (noun)

unwittingly (Apfel, para. 2): unintentionally (adverb)

formative (Apfel, para. 3): relating to development or growth (adjective)

reciprocity (Apfel, para. 4): mutual exchange (noun)

transactional (Apfel, para. 4): having to do with an exchange (adjective)

empathy (Apfel, para. 4): ability to identify with the feelings of others (noun)

salve (Apfel, para. 4): an ointment used to soothe (noun)

retaliate (Apfel, para. 6): to return a wrong for a wrong (verb)

reliance (Apfel, para. 8): dependence (noun)

stereotypical (Apfel, para. 9): having to do with general beliefs about someone or something that are often unfair or untrue (adjective)

chronic (Apfel, para. 9): habitual; recurring frequently (adjective)

dissipate (Apfel, para. 10): to scatter or disappear (verb)

oblivious (Jade, para. 2): unaware (adjective)

remorse (Jade, para. 3): regret (noun)

permutation (Jade, para. 5): a change or alteration (noun)

Lauren Apfel is the debate editor at Brain, Child. *She is also the cofounder and executive editor of* Motherwell, *a publication about parenting. Carinn Jade is an attorney and a writer. Her work has appeared in the* New York Times, Brain, Child, *and* DailyWorth, *among other publications.*

Lauren Apfel

Should We Make Our Children Say Sorry? Yes!

[*Brain, Child*, January 5, 2015]

A ccidents happen, they sometimes happen. There's only one thing to   1
say: "Sorry, my friend . . . Sorry again."
    So claim the Wiggles, at least, that iconic children's rock band   2
whose morality-tinged music formed the soundtrack to my early experience of motherhood. My kids learned many lessons from watching the
Australian fab four. Apologizing when you have caused harm and/or
inconvenience to another person, even if unwittingly, might have been
the most important. There's one thing we always like to say, Captain
Feathersword croons, when something spills or gets in the way. That
word is "sorry," and I have taught my kids — and will continue to impress
it upon them — that it is a powerful word indeed.

    When children are young, manners are always by rote. I used to   3
think this was a reason to let them slide. That niceties such as "please"
and "thank you" are no more than empty tents, if not propped up by a
true understanding of meaning. But having watched my first son, the one
who was never made to say sorry, turn into a school-aged boy who was
still slow to apologize or express an appropriate amount of remorse for
his actions, I changed my tune. Now I am convinced that language is a
formative bridge to emotion, and that routinely using the right words
paves the way for young kids to feel the right feelings.

    Manner words are especially significant bridges because they are sym-   4
bols of reciprocity, which I consider a cornerstone of human interaction.
"Sorry" is in a class by itself here. It is not transactional like "please" or
"thank you." Nor is it a filler like "excuse me" or "pardon." It is a term that
grows from the soil of empathy. And isn't empathy one of the most salient
qualities we seek to foster in our children? Apologizing has an amazing
and multifaceted capacity in this respect. It can act as either a salve or a
white flag or an acknowledgment of responsibility, depending on its use.

    My three-year-old spills his juice, spectacularly, all over the floor.   5
"Sorry" = this was completely an accident and it's not the end of the world,
but I realize you still have to clean it up, which takes time and effort.

    My six-year-old elbows his brother in the face, bringing their game   6
of football to a grinding halt. "Sorry" = I didn't mean to do that, of course

it was in the rough and tumble of play, but I recognize that I hurt you and please don't retaliate.

My nine-year-old has an attitude, he's speaking in a tone and holding   7
a posture that is not very pleasant. "Sorry" = I understand how I act can have unintended consequences for other people I care about. I might not think I did anything wrong per se, but I see that my behavior has upset you and that matters to me.

> In the heat of the moment, an apology, voiced genuinely, takes so much sting from the wound.

Clearly, in the context of children,   8
sorry is a shorthand. And one could argue that we are better off prompting our kids to find the more specific words. But reliance on verbal shortcuts and the conventions they signify is the oil that helps spin the great wheel of social dynamics, especially in the early years. It's not that we shouldn't encourage further exploration of the issues and emotions involved. It's that in the heat of the moment, an apology, voiced genuinely, takes so much sting from the wound. It is an instant, universal indication that the wrongdoer accepts his actions have had an unwanted impact on somebody else. And that is no small thing.

My kids say sorry a lot. Sometimes it is done imploringly, to stave   9
off punishment. Sometimes it is done in a knee-jerk way, stereotypical of where we live in the UK, the land of chronic apologies. I am aware of the pitfalls of apologizing too much, that it can make one look weak and overly self-deprecating. And yet, I would rather them err on the side of overdoing it than under-doing it. Common courtesy should not be sacrificed unnecessarily in the name of self-esteem.

Every single time my children apologize, whether to me or to some-   10
one else, my disappointment at whatever misstep they have made starts to dissipate. With one simple word. Not merely because that word is a Band-Aid on the graze of hurt feelings, though it is certainly that. But because it shows me — and it shows me quickly — that they have grasped, even at this inherently self-centered stage of their life, the crucial truth that one's behavior never exists in a vacuum.

Carinn Jade

Should We Make Our Children Say Sorry? No!

[*Brain, Child*, January 5, 2015]

My daughter was born, it seems, with "I'm sorry" on her lips. 1
At the age of three, I started hearing the words tumble from
her mouth a dozen times a day. There were occasions when
her apology was appropriate, but those times were the exception. More
often than not, she was saying sorry for things that pierced my gut — her
brother getting angry, her mother (me) crying, not knowing how to spell
"Brooklyn." Why should she feel responsible for those things? What
exactly was she sorry for anyway? Since I couldn't very well get the kind
of answers I needed from a toddler, I made a bright-line rule: "No more
sorry," I told my three-year-old daughter and my five-year-old son.

It's not that I want my children to be rude or oblivious. I value cour- 2
tesy, empathy, and responsibility highly. However, teaching them those
important lessons with the word "sorry" is reactive rather than proactive;
and often the point is missed, by adults and children alike.

Courtesy. Good manners are important. My children ask for things 3
politely and say "thank you" to express their gratitude. But I have trouble
understanding the mother who responds to her child's screaming, whin-
ing demands with the request to "say please." Yelling is not a nice way to
ask for something, no matter if you've added the word "please." It follows
that the word "sorry" is not critical to a good apology. The key is that a
child takes responsibility for her actions and expresses remorse for negative consequences. It's not what you say, but how you say it.

Empathy. Some argue that apologizing teaches empathy. It doesn't. 4
Understanding one another's emotions and reactions does. When my children have thrown their legs up to swing on the monkey bars, accidentally
kicking someone in the process, I guide them to ask how the other child feels
(Are you hurt? Were you scared?). Then, after assessing that child's state of
mind, they are told to ask if there is anything they can do to help (Can I get
you some ice?) or make the other person feel better (Do you want a hug?).
These actions are far more powerful and healing than an empty "I'm sorry."

Responsibility. I want my children to take responsibility for their 5
actions, but I don't want them to carry the weight of guilt or culpability
for every permutation of consequences that could result from their decisions. Actions have repercussions, yes. And yet, my kids must also know

that they can control only themselves, they cannot control another's response. Nor should they have to anticipate possible reactions before they make their own choices.

We've all seen the common playground collision where someone   6
wanders into the path of the swing and gets knocked down. To say the swinging child should have to apologize for bumping the other is confusing. Must they have known someone could walk by and therefore never swing as high or as fast as they can? If they aren't granted that kind of freedom as children on a swing set, where is it possible at all? Of all the things a kid should say in this situation, "I'm sorry" does not suit the action.

The word "sorry" should be limited to   7
few occasions in life. It should not mean "excuse me" or "I didn't realize" or "I need to ask a question." Sorry is more powerful if used in the context it was intended — to show remorse for something a child meant to do that had a negative effect on someone

> The word "sorry" should be limited to few occasions in life.

else. Instead, when used as a placeholder for all sorts of other words, it robs the person using it of its true power. Studies show that people hear weakness when they hear "I'm sorry," even if it isn't present or intended. Therefore those who use an apology to simply express compassion are being misunderstood by those who take the word literally.

At best, the word is insufficient shorthand. But it can also be down-   8
right harmful in the way it causes others to perceive the people who use it, which can then magnify their own self-doubt. I don't want my children repeatedly hearing they should be sorry for what they have done. Instead, I want them to be proud of their decisions. I hope they will act in accordance with their moral and ethical code and rarely have to apologize for it. Yet they miss that lesson — or truly knowing the meaning of an apology — when we teach them to say sorry for every little thing that happens on the playground.

VOCABULARY/USING A DICTIONARY

1. What does it mean to be *culpable*? What part of speech is *culpability* (Jade, para. 5)?

2. If something is learned *by rote* (Apfel, para. 3), how is it learned?

3. What is *shorthand* (Jade, para. 8)?

RESPONDING TO WORDS IN CONTEXT

1. Given how Jade feels about saying "sorry," what do you think *insufficient* means in paragraph 8 ("At best, the word is *insufficient* shorthand")? If you know what *sufficient* means, what does the prefix *in-* do to the word?

2. In paragraph 2, Jade writes, "Teaching . . . those important lessons with the word 'sorry' is *reactive rather than proactive*; and often the point is missed." Do you think *reactive* and *proactive* share a root word? How would you define each word?

3. Apfel ends by saying she wants her children to say "sorry" because "one's behavior never exists in a *vacuum*" (para. 10). What do you think this means?

DISCUSSING MAIN POINT AND MEANING

1. In one sentence for each essay, can you summarize the main point of Apfel's and Jade's arguments?

2. Why does Apfel not mind that her kids "say sorry a lot" (para. 9)? What social skill are they demonstrating, even if the apology is unnecessary or unfelt?

3. Why does Jade feel her daughter is saying "sorry" too much? In her opinion, what is the drawback of a toddler's saying that all the time?

EXAMINING SENTENCES, PARAGRAPHS, AND ORGANIZATION

1. Do Apfel's personal examples provide convincing evidence for her argument? Would more distanced research add or detract from her essay? Why?

2. How does Jade's method of organizing her paragraphs clarify her argument?

3. Where in these essays do you notice the writer's attention to sound, rhyme in particular? When the essayists use rhyme in their sentences or paragraphs, what happens to your experience of the writing?

THINKING CRITICALLY

1. Courtesy, empathy, and responsibility are a big focus in these essays. Are there other important things that saying "sorry" or not saying "sorry" teaches children? Did the writers include the most important lessons?

2. Apfel describes manner words as "a cornerstone of human interaction" (para. 4). Do you agree with this statement? Why or why not?

3. Both of these essays are written by mothers. Would you be interested in hearing what someone who is not a parent has to say about children's saying "sorry"? Why or why not? How might such an essay be different?

WRITING ACTIVITIES

1. Consider the power of words you use every day, from manner words to snark, from how you say hello to how you say good-bye. Write a reflection on your daily language, noting particular words you use and their effects on those around you. Is there anything you want to change in or add to your typical vocabulary?

2. Outline both of these essays. The essayists hold opposing viewpoints, but both are writing about how their children use the same word and how they want their children to use it. Given what you see in your outlines, do the writers approach the material from different angles? Where are they hitting the same points — and where does their material diverge?

3. Write a defense of one of these arguments, either Apfel's support of saying "sorry" or Jade's wariness of oversaying it. Explain where you find the author's arguments persuasive. Briefly add personal evidence or support to the author's claims: Where in your own life have you experienced this particular truth about the word *sorry*?

Sarah Elliott (student essay)

Women: Stop Apologizing; Be Confident

[*Graphic*, Pepperdine University, October 28, 2015]

BEFORE YOU READ
Do women "cloak . . . thoughts" in ways that make them seem less powerful and educated than they are? Would women and men say the same things differently?

WORDS TO LEARN
insurmountable (para. 1): incapable of being overcome (adjective)
proficient (para. 1): skilled (adjective)
aspiration (para. 2): goal (noun)
linguistic (para. 4): belonging to language (adjective)
iconic (para. 5): relating to someone who is idolized (adjective)

audacity (para. 9): daring (adjective)
barrage (para. 9): an overwhelming quantity (noun)
simultaneously (para. 10): happening at the same time (adverb)
superfluous (para. 12): excessive; needless (adjective)

I was four years old during the 2000 presidential election, and quite fascinated with the concept of becoming a U.S. president. At four, it doesn't seem like such an insurmountable task to run a country, as I was perfectly proficient running the country of Beanie Babies in my bedroom.

1

Sarah Elliott is a student at Pepperdine University.

It wasn't more than two seconds after I told my kindergarten teacher   2
my new career aspiration when some boy sitting next to me piped up to
say, "You can't be the president — you're a girl!"

If I had a dollar for every time I've heard those words, I could gradu-   3
ate debt-free. Too bad my dollar would only be worth 79 cents, according
to a 2014 report on the current pay gap from the Association of American
University Women.

As a communication major and a woman, it's become apparent to   4
me that social expectations set by a male-dominated society have driven
women to code their communication to mask expressions of power or
opinions. There's a reason why even a boy in a kindergarten class knew
that girls aren't "allowed" to be president. Alexandra Petri illustrated
this careful act of linguistic acrobatics perfectly in her October 13,
2015, opinion piece in the *Washington Post*, "Famous Quotes, the Way a
Woman Would Have to Say Them during a Meeting."

"Give me liberty or give me death," Patrick Henry's iconic phrase   5
from the American Revolution, becomes "Dave, if I could, I could just — I
just really feel like if we had liberty it would be terrific, and the alternative
would just be awful, you know? That's just how it strikes me. I don't know."

Try a more modern quote, such as FDR's "The only thing we have   6
to fear is fear itself." Our friendly woman-in-meeting's version: "I have to
say — I'm sorry — I have to say this. I don't think we should be as scared
of non-fear things as maybe we are? If that makes sense? Sorry, I feel like
I'm rambling."

If these translations sound familiar, it's because they are. You don't   7
have to be in a meeting to hear a girl spin a turn of phrase like this; you
could simply walk into a college classroom and wait.

Every day I sit in my classes and listen   8
to girls apologize for speaking, for taking
up too much time in discussion, for having
an opinion. And if an opinion is expressed,
half the time it comes with a disclaimer,
mentioning how it's "probably not right" or
finishing off with an "I don't know."

> Every day I sit in
> my classes and lis-
> ten to girls apolo-
> gize for speaking,
> for taking up too
> much time in dis-
> cussion, for having
> an opinion.

In the academic setting, much like the   9
workplace, women are conditioned to say
"I'm sorry" for everything: taking up their
professors' time, asking questions, offer-
ing help — even reporting sexual harassment has become somewhat of
an apologetic practice. We can never be too careful, because dropping
the meek, gentle facade leaves us vulnerable to labels such as "bossy"

or "feisty" or everyone's favorite b-word. Just look at Hillary Clinton, a woman who has the audacity to run for the presidency — like hundreds of men before her — only to be stoned by the media with a barrage of these misogynistic words.

Because our female role models are treated like this in the pub-   10
lic eye, it follows quite logically that women shy away from creating spaces for themselves in powerful roles. According to statistics from the *Washington Post* and the Pew Research Center, respectively, only 4.6 percent of Fortune 500 CEOs are women, and only 19 percent of our current Congress is female (which is, sadly, the largest number we've ever had). Those who do manage to break gender barriers suffer from criticisms in areas men don't receive: We are simultaneously too fat and too skinny, too ugly and too pretty, too smart and too stupid.

There's no middle ground for a powerful woman. The higher women   11
get on the totem pole of accomplishment, the more they suffer from the sinking realization that the patriarchy of their own society does not want them there.

So here's the challenge for all my Pepperdine ladies: Let's stop cloak-   12
ing our thoughts in superfluous disclaimers and start speaking like we deserve to be where we are, because we do. Our aspirations do not have to be limited to future first ladies, so we shouldn't have to be afraid of speaking like the educated, powerful and influential women we are.

During a discussion at Georgetown University in February, Supreme   13
Court Justice Ruth Bader Ginsburg was asked when she thinks there will be enough women on the Supreme Court. She said, "My answer is when there are nine."

When do I think there will be enough women in the White House?   14
When kindergarten boys stop telling four-year-old girls who gets to run the country.

VOCABULARY/USING A DICTIONARY

1. What does it mean if one is *debt-free* (para. 3)?

2. What happens when one performs *acrobatics* (para. 4)?

3. What part of speech is *misogynistic* (para. 9)? What is its root word?

RESPONDING TO WORDS IN CONTEXT

1. If "it's probably not right" or "I don't know" is a *disclaimer* (para. 8), how would you define the word?

2. If someone is *conditioned* (para. 9) to do something, what is controlling his or her choices?

3. What is a *facade* (para. 9)? What does it mean in this context?

DISCUSSING MAIN POINT AND MEANING

1. Why, according to Elliott, do women tend to apologize?

2. Elliott brings Hillary Clinton in as an example of what happens to women when they present themselves as strong and unapologetic. What has happened to Clinton, according to Elliott?

3. Elliott offers a challenge at the end of her essay. What is it? Why does she offer it?

EXAMINING SENTENCES, PARAGRAPHS, AND ORGANIZATION

1. Why do you think Elliott introduces information about her college major in the fourth paragraph? Is there a benefit to knowing her major?

2. Explain the differences between the famous phrases Elliott introduces and the women's versions she imagines. Choose an aspect of the examples to focus on, such as the sound or the length of the statement.

3. Elliott begins one of her sentences with "If I had a dollar for every time I've heard those words." How does she turn that trite phrase into something meaningful and to the point?

THINKING CRITICALLY

1. Why would a boy in kindergarten think a girl couldn't be president in 2000?

2. What are the differences between the famous quotations (by men) and the reworkings of these statements by women? Based on what you see, what else could Elliott ask women to stop saying, besides "sorry"?

3. Elliott writes, "The higher women get on the totem pole of accomplishment, the more they suffer from the sinking realization that the patriarchy of their own society does not want them there" (para. 11). What gains have women made in terms of the totem pole of accomplishment, given what you learn in this article?

WRITING ACTIVITIES

1. Do you notice differences in the way men and women speak in the classroom, workplace, or public places? Try to identify a difference in words, tone, or style, and write about how men and women communicate differently.

2. With whom does Elliott begin the essay? With whom does she end it? Describe the arc of the essay, with an eye on the women mentioned throughout. How do her examples of women at the beginning and the end underscore her point?

3. Think about the labels Elliott mentions in the essay ("bossy," "feisty," "b-word"). What sort of labels do all of us — men and women — encounter every day? Are these based on stereotypes? Describe, in a short freewriting exercise, labels you've encountered (for yourself or others), what they are based on, and your reaction to them.

Establishing Your Main Point

As you learn to express opinions clearly and effectively in writing, you need to ask yourself a relatively simple question: What is my main point? In composition, a main point is sometimes called a thesis or a thesis statement. It is often a sentence or two that summarizes your central idea or position. It need not include any factual proof or supporting evidence — that can be supplied in the body of your essay — but it should represent a general statement that clearly shows where you stand on an issue, what you are attacking or defending, and what exactly your essay is about. Although main points are often found in opening paragraphs, they can also appear later on in an essay, especially when the writer wants to set the stage for his or her opinion by opening with a topical reference, an emotional appeal, a personal experience, or a general observation.

For instance, Pepperdine University student Sarah Elliott begins her essay on the ways women are conditioned to apologize for expressing opinions by recounting a relevant childhood experience. But in her fourth paragraph she states the main point of her essay explicitly. Note that she then immediately refers to her opening paragraphs to show their significance.

1 *States the main point of her essay*	As a communication major and a woman, (1) <u>it's become apparent to me that social expectations set by a male-dominated society have driven women to code their communication to mask expressions of power or opinions.</u>
2 *Ties her opening to the main point*	(2) <u>There's a reason why even a boy in a kindergarten class knew that girls aren't "allowed" to be president.</u>

STUDENT WRITER AT WORK
Sarah Elliott

R.A. What inspired you to write this essay? And publish it?

S.E. I read a piece in the *Washington Post* by Alexandra Petri that touched on the way professional settings limit the communication of women by enforcing socially constructed speech barriers. That piece resonated deeply with me because, as a young woman in college, I see examples of these barriers used nearly every day in my classes. I felt that it would be interesting to explore this subject at the classroom level instead of just at the professional level.

R.A. What response have you received to this piece?

S.E. The response to this piece has been very positive for me. I have had both faculty and students talk with me about the message and how it caused them to rethink the way they communicate or encourage others to communicate.

R.A. What do you like to read?

S.E. I love to read, and the first thing I do every morning is spend a couple minutes in bed catching up on current events with my news app or *theSkimm*, an e-mail newsletter I subscribe to. I tend to read a lot of online publications like the *Huffington Post* or *BuzzFeed*, but I also subscribe to the *New Yorker* (student discount!), so I have my physical publications, too. Honestly, I think I get most of my news from Twitter, which is a very millennial thing to say, but it's a great source of live updates on the world around me, and I love the bite-sized humor.

R.A. What topics most interest you as a writer?

S.E. I am very passionate about women's issues, feminism, and youth-focused topics. I also like to write about religion, specifically Christianity, and politics. I know those are the two topics you're never supposed to bring up (oops), so I try to balance it out with humor and fiction, which are some of my favorite things to write.

R.A. Do you plan to continue writing for publication?

S.E. I would love to publish a novel someday; it's been my dream ever since I learned how to talk, so I know that I will always keep pursuing publication in that regard. Once I graduate, I'm not sure how much opportunity I'll have to publish pieces like this, but I'm certainly going to go out of my way to try.

R.A. What advice do you have for other student writers?

S.E. I think the best thing any writer can do is just write consistently, whether it be for class, in a journal, for a student publication, for a blog, or even just for yourself. Sometimes it can be hard to think of something to write about, so I'd encourage you to try blogging or journaling about your life as a way to at least get pen to paper (or hand to keyboard) and start practicing. And then once you've written, share it. There are so many ways to engage with an audience through the Internet, and that kind of feedback and exposure is so valuable to us young writers, especially when there are so many communities that are specifically geared for people our age.

Spotlight on Data and Research

Mary Meehan

The Perfect Name for the Next Generation of Americans

[*Forbes*, April 15, 2014]

For many years the media, along with many historians and sociologists, have liked to think of particular generations as distinct entities that also possess a cultural identity. One of the earliest generations to be named is the "Baby Boomers," a name intended to describe a spike in the birthrate immediately after World War II and that included people born between 1946 and 1964. Although such designations include many millions of people and are therefore generalities, particular generations are thought to share certain traits and values. Given the growth in America's postwar economy, Baby Boomers, for example, would inherit a more affluent world than any generation before them and would permanently alter the consumer society. Understanding the dynamics and demographics of generations is important for marketing experts who want to be able to identify dominant trends and characteristics of large groups and subgroups and find ways to match products to collective tastes. As America's latest named generation (those born between approximately 1978 and 1995), usually termed Millennials, has grown older, with many reaching their early thirties, some of the attention has shifted to the next generation, the oldest of which will be in their early teens by 2017. Demographers are now publishing research characterizing the traits and habits of this generation, which has not yet received a convenient name or label. You may want to see if you can come up with one as you read the following item on this new generation from Forbes magazine.

Baby Boomers. Gen X. Millennials. These cohort names get thrown   1
around a lot. That's because generational marketing is big business.
And it makes for simpler discussions to have large groups of people
grouped together in big chunks. It's simplistic, but it's also a helpful way
to understand consumers and your customers. But what do the names
of generations mean, really? How do generations get named? And what

should we be calling kids today? What does the generation that's coming up look like?

THE NAME GAME

Talking about Baby Boomers, Gen Xers, or Millennials leads to an inevitable question: What should we call the generational group coming up after the Millennials? Before jumping into what the youngest generation should be named, it's worth a review of how and why other generations got their names. 2

Generational profiles are generalized looks at a population of the same age cohort, and they're helpful in understanding consumer groups from a very broad perspective. Each cohort came of age during a particular period in our cultural history — they shared major societal events and cultural mores — and that shared societal background shapes their attitudes, behaviors, and worldview. In the marketing world, generations are typically delineated every 20 or so years, a span that covers a meaningful phase of life stretching from early childhood into young adulthood. Each generation carries the values, experiences, and moniker throughout ensuing life stages. Not everyone agrees on the exact years that mark the generations or the names used to describe them, but most people are in the same ballpark. 3

Generational Profile: Major Consumer Groups in U.S.

	Matures	Boomers	Gen Xers	Millennials
Years born	1945 and before	1946–1964	1965–1977	1978–1995
Age in 2014	69+ years old	50–68 years old	37–49 years old	19–36 years old
Cultural ethos	Uncertainty; conformity	Prosperity; counterculture	Disillusionment; information	Globalization; social responsibility
Population	33.0 million	74.6 million	53.4 million	78.3 million
Median income	$36,743	$57,844	$58,271	$44,946
Outlook	Practical	Optimistic	Skeptical	Hopeful

Population source: Census Population Estimates, December 2013

Income Source: Estimate based on Census Population Estimates, December 2013, U.S. Census Bureau 2012 American Community Survey

Global Panoramix

continued

MILLENNIALS, GEN XERS, BABY BOOMERS, AND MATURES

Let's start with our oldest group, the **Matures**. Born in or before 1945,   4
Matures lived through the Depression and WWII, events that marked
all who lived through the '30s and '40s with an outlook of uncertainty.
But post-WWII, America experienced an economic and industrial
boom like the country hasn't ever seen, before or since. Matures were
happy to have life return to "normal," to contribute to the growth of
the nation, and to just plain fit in. This experience helped define them
as loyal, patriotic, and responsible. The name Matures wasn't assigned
until after generational marketing came of fashion, but it does resonate
for a generation who grew up very early due to great sacrifice.

Baby Boomers. Born between 1946 and 1964, the '50s postwar era   5
of Baby Boomers' youth was a time of massive growth and prosperity.
Couples could get married, own a home, and have kids. Lots of kids. The
Matures wanted a better life for the generation that followed them, and
they sacrificed to provide it. Baby Boomers were the first generation to be
marketed to as children, and the advent of television made that more than
possible on a mass scale. As they grew up, especially in the '60s, this huge
age cohort took part in a massive rebellion against all the rules and regulations their parents struggled hard for. Known for individuality, aspiration,
and idealism, they fought to make the world more just and fair.

Gen Xers were born between 1965 and 1977. There were fewer of   6
them than there were Baby Boomers, and while living in the shadow
of Boomers, it felt harder to know or understand them. Hence the
name that caught on for this group has an X, signifying an unknown.
Douglas Coupland popularized the term Generation X in his 1991
book *Generation X: Tales for an Accelerated Culture*, and the name stuck.
Gen Xers came of age during a time of disillusionment marked by the
Challenger disaster, skyrocketing divorce rates, the Iran hostage crisis,
institutional fraud, and the first cases of AIDS. Naturally, this group
became suspicious of what they saw as phony values and the corporate
greed of the '80s. But they also lived through an age of innovation that
will alter history, as "information" became powerful and Gen X took to
an info-rich world naturally. Long known derisively as slackers, nothing
could be further from the truth; Gen Xers are recognized for their independence, authenticity, thrift, and balanced outlook on life.

Millennials. Our Millennial cohort was born between 1978 and 1995,   7
as a new millennium was dawning. The world flattened and globalization exploded. As a result, Millennials have had more exposure to the
rest of the world and feel a responsibility to take care of it — and they
often hold companies and other institutions to the same standards.

Their early lives are marked by foreign and homegrown terrorism of 9/11, the Oklahoma City bombing, and the Columbine shooting. But they also had the first helicopter parents to make them feel valued, secure, and hopeful. As socially responsible, diverse, and always-on tech natives, these traits are shaping the culture of the early 2000s.

SO WHO'S NEXT?

Our youngest generation, those born after 1995, may not have lived   8
long enough for us to get a full picture of what will define them. But what we know so far is that they are coming of age during the worst economic downturn since the Great Depression. Further, the U.S. engaged in an unpopular and protracted war for much of their lives. However, this cohort will be the most diverse generation ever. Their whole world is 3-D, with technology in the palm of their hand (and the outside of their wrist or the back of their eyeglasses). Some of the names that have already been suggested and used are Digitals, iGen, Selfies, Tweenials, Hashtagers, Homelanders, Evernets, Plurals, Globalists, and 20firsters.

Who is the final arbiter, though? Ultimately, generations get named   9
because a certain phrase gains influence, and shows enough utility to the people talking about big groups of people, that everyone can use the term as shorthand. There are many names of previous generations that didn't ever quite make it to popularity – Generation Jones, Generation Y — and right now what to call the youngest generation isn't quite clear yet.

I, for one, suggest we call this group **Gen We**. When I worked at   10
Iconoculture, my colleagues and I believed this was the We Generation for many reasons: Many generational attitudes come as backlashes against the values of previous generations — emphasizing the WE turns ideas about the Me Generation on their head. Additionally, due to technological advances, this cohort is wired and constantly connected. They're rarely alone, even if they're hanging out with buddies via text message, through gaming consoles, or on social network sites. Their every moment is a We moment. I'll be watching to see what other names emerge as the cohort continues to grow.

DRAWING CONCLUSIONS

1. What is your response to some of the names suggested for the new generation? Do you agree with the author that the "We Generation" might be the best name? Can you think of a better one?

2. What appear to be the most dominant characteristics of the next generation? How do you think this generation will help define future American culture?

3. Why are marketers and academics so interested in the next generation? What motives might they have to study it?

Robert F. Wilson Jr.

I Have a Problem with "Issues"

[*New Letters*, Fall 2015]

BEFORE YOU READ

Does the word *issue* refer to a real issue? Has the word lost its meaning? If so, is it possible to get it back?

WORDS TO LEARN

eulogy (para. 1): a speech for someone who has died (noun)

serviceable (para. 1): useful (adjective)

profound (para. 1): deep; intense (adjective)

locution (para. 2): the way words are used (noun)

mundane (para. 4): ordinary (adjective)

ubiquitous (para. 5): seemingly everywhere (adjective)

senselessly (para. 6): foolishly or unthinkingly (adverb)

modify (para. 7): to change or limit (verb)

revive (para. 8): to bring back (verb)

What I'm about to write is a eulogy for nouns like "problem," "concern," and "question." These were once serviceable words, carrying specific meanings and capable of being "solved," "addressed," and "answered." They were unpretentious terms, too, never claiming to be more profound than they are. Let us now bow our heads in silence as they enter the land of the No. 2 pencil, the typewriter, and the handwritten thank-you note.   1

In our brave new world of instant communication, these once-popular words have been replaced by an upstart locution that used to have specific meanings. When someone referred to an "issue," we understood that the speaker was talking about a copy of a newspaper, magazine, or periodical. Political "issues" were things that politicians argued about — taxation, voting rights, and military preparedness. Offspring were said to be the "issue" of a particular family; proceeds from an estate were also identified as "issue."   2

Robert F. Wilson Jr. is a professor emeritus of English at the University of Missouri–Kansas City. He has published five volumes of criticism on Shakespeare, as well as numerous articles and notes.

Somewhere along the usage highway, however, we took the wrong   3
exit and started labeling any problem or question an "issue." I suspect
that this usage might have been born during the age of psychobabble,
when a Dr. Phil's[1] clinical approach required the employment of neutral
language to avoid placing blame on anyone. Thus, when some lost soul
announced to a TV audience that he hated his mother, he was told that
he must find a way to deal with his "anger issues." Suddenly, athletes were
described as having "injury issues," and people struggling to pay bills
were facing "financial issues."

It somehow now seemed mundane to be angry or injured or broke;   4
adding "issues" to these conditions made them more dramatic and in
need of therapy or counseling.

With the birth of the 24-hour news   5
cycle, proliferating talk and reality shows,
and ubiquitous ESPN commentators, the
"issues" virus has gone viral and shows no
signs of abating. Schoolchildren struggle
with "homework issues"; super-sized citizens are fighting "food issues" (which

> It somehow now
> seemed mundane
> to be angry or
> injured or broke.

issue in "weight issues"); slumping basketball players face "scoring
issues"; and troubled couples are dealing with "relationship issues."

It seems that we so strongly desire to characterize our daily chal-   6
lenges as symptoms that we've senselessly latched on to a word that
sounds cool (or clinical) but requires an adjective to give it any kind of
meaning. "Issues" is now so deeply embedded in our discourse that we
don't even question its euphemistic quality or how quickly it has become
a cliché.

As we scatter dirt on the coffins of "problem," "question," and "con-   7
cern," let's remember for a moment why they were once valued. We didn't
have to add an adjective to modify them; "anger" was clearly a "problem"
and didn't become an even greater one by linking it to "issue." It could
often be solved by counting to ten or leaving the room until one cooled
down. It was not something in need of extended professional therapy.
Let's face it, we all have problems that are serious but not unique; when
we use the word "problems," we tend to send a signal that we acknowledge that others face them, too.

---

[1] Dr. Phil (para. 3): Dr. Phil McGraw first appeared on *The Oprah Winfrey Show*,
offering psychological advice to guests in a regular segment. The spin-off television show, *Dr. Phil*, premiered in 2002 and was very popular with *Oprah*
audiences and others.

Perhaps if we revived "problems" instead of embracing "issues," we'd   8
begin to talk (not text or tweet) to one another about them and come to
realize that ours aren't such an "issue" after all.

VOCABULARY/USING A DICTIONARY

1. *Proliferate* is a term used frequently in biology. When cells are *proliferating* (para. 5), what are they doing?
2. What happens when something is *abating* (para. 5)?
3. What part of speech is *euphemistic* (para. 6)?

RESPONDING TO WORDS IN CONTEXT

1. If someone is *pretentious*, what is he or she like? What is an *unpretentious* (para. 1) person like? What does the prefix *un-* mean?
2. What does Wilson mean by "the usage highway" (para. 3)?
3. Wilson speaks of the word *issues* as *embedded* (para. 6) in our discourse. Reporters are often spoken of as being *embedded* in the military, or a tutor might be *embedded* in a classroom. What do you think this word means?

DISCUSSING MAIN POINT AND MEANING

1. How are words changing, according to Wilson?
2. What word in particular has lost meaning, in Wilson's opinion? What has it come to mean?
3. When Wilson writes that "we so strongly desire to characterize our daily challenges as symptoms" (para. 6), what does he mean? From this perspective, what have our daily challenges become?

EXAMINING SENTENCES, PARAGRAPHS, AND ORGANIZATION

1. Identify examples of figurative language, analogies in particular, in Wilson's essay.
2. What pronouns does Wilson use in this essay? Is his choice effective? How would the essay be different from a different point of view?
3. Where does Wilson bring references to technology into the essay? How do those remarks shape the essay?

THINKING CRITICALLY

1. Do you agree with Wilson's suggestion that the meaning of the word *issue* began to change in what he calls "the age of psychobabble" (para. 3)? Do you think the word *issue* has lost its meaning or gained in meaning?

2. In paragraph 7, Wilson claims that at one time "anger . . . could often be solved by counting to ten or leaving the room until one cooled down. It was not something in need of extended professional therapy." Do you think the idea of "issues" is overblown? Does everyone with "issues" need counseling?

3. How does the age of "instant communication" (para. 2) add to the problem of words' changing definitions or losing meaning?

WRITING ACTIVITIES

1. How has the world changed over the years since the "No. 2 pencil, the type-writer, and the handwritten thank-you note" (para. 1) were largely replaced? Write a report that outlines the changes that have taken place in communication since the rise of the computer and the Internet. Then consider changes that are currently taking place in how we communicate.

2. What are some of the "issues" we face in today's world? List the "issues" mentioned by Wilson and then come up with your own list, using the earlier definition cited by Wilson in paragraph 2 ("things that politicians argued about"). Compare lists. Does Wilson have a point when he suggests that some of the things labeled "issues" these days are simply "problems" faced by most people? Do you want to see a return to a weightier definition of "issues"? Why or why not?

3. In a three- to four-paragraph essay, write about a word that bothers you. It can be one that's overused or that seems to have lost its meaning (like the words in Wilson's essay). It can be one that people consistently misuse. Try to imitate some of Wilson's style. For example, you may choose to use the first-person plural ("we" and "our") throughout, include some allusions or figurative language, or suggest a possible solution in your conclusion.

Langston Hughes

That Word *Black*

[*The Chicago Defender*, November 3, 1951]

Getty Images / Hulton Archive

Author Langston Hughes, photographed in 1943

When the following short essay first appeared in 1951, it was considered an insult to call an African American "black." The acceptable and respectful word at the time — the one Langston Hughes himself would have used — was Negro. But by August 1963, when Martin Luther King Jr. delivered his famous "I Have a Dream" speech, the terms used to describe African Americans were changing. King favored the term Negro, but in a speech that preceded his that historic day, the twenty-three-year-old John Lewis (now a congressional leader) repeatedly used the word black instead of Negro. By the late 1960s, the word black had grown more popular, a result of movements like the Black Panthers and such expressions as "black is beautiful," a sentiment Hughes anticipates at the conclusion of the essay.

One of the nation's most prolific writers, Langston Hughes (1902–1967) was born in Joplin, Missouri, but traveled east as a young man and became a leading, multitalented figure of the Harlem Renaissance. A poet, novelist, essayist, dramatist, short story writer, and journalist who also wrote many children's books, Hughes is still widely read today. In 1943, he created in his newspaper columns for the Chicago Defender the memorable character Jesse B. Semple ("Simple"), a plain-speaking, working-class man from Harlem. The character was so engaging that Hughes went on to publish five collections of sketches: Simple Speaks His Mind (1950), Simple Takes a Wife (1953), Simple Stakes a Claim (1957), The Best of Simple (1961), and Simple's Uncle Sam (1965). Hughes said he based "Simple" on an actual factory worker he met in a Harlem bar in 1942.

"This evening," said Simple, "I feel like talking about the word *black*."   1

"Nobody's stopping you, so go ahead. But what you really ought to   2
have is a soap-box out on the corner of 126th and Lenox where the rest
of the orators hang out."

"They expresses some good ideas on that corner," said Simple,   3
"but for my ideas I do not need a crowd. Now, as I were saying, the
word *black*, white folks have done used that word to mean something
bad so often until now when the N.A.A.C.P. asks for civil rights for the
black man, they think they must be bad. Looking back into history, I
reckon it all started with a *black* cat meaning bad luck. Don't let one
cross your path!

"Next, somebody got up a *black-list* on which you get if you don't   4
vote right. Then when lodges come into being, the folks they didn't want
in them got *black-balled*. If you kept a skeleton in your closet, you might
get *black-mailed*. And everything bad was *black*. When it came down to
the unlucky ball on the pool table, the eight-rock, they made it the *black*
ball. So no wonder there ain't no equal rights for the *black* man."

"All you say is true about the odium attached to the word *black*," I   5
said. "You've even forgotten a few. For example, during the war if you
bought something under the table, illegally, they said you were trading
on the *black* market. In Chicago, if you're a gangster, the *Black Hand
Society* may take you for a ride. And certainly if you don't behave yourself, your family will say you're a *black* sheep. Then if your mama burns a
black candle to change the family luck, they call it *black* magic."

"My mama never did believe in voodoo so she did not burn no   6
black candles," said Simple.

"If she had, that would have been a *black* mark against her."   7

"Stop talking about my mama. What I want to know is, where do   8
white folks get off calling everything bad *black*? If it is a dark night, they
say it's *black* as hell. If you are mean and evil, they say you got a *black*
heart. I would like to change all that around and say that the people who
Jim Crow me have got a *white* heart. People who sell dope to children
have got a *white* mark against them. And all the white gamblers who
were behind the basketball fix are the *white* sheep of the sports world.
God knows there was few, if any, Negroes selling stuff on the black market during the war, so why didn't they call it the *white* market? No, they
got to take me and my color and turn it into everything *bad*. According
to white folks, black is bad."

"Wait till my day comes! In my language, bad will be *white*.   9
Blackmail will be *white* mail. Black cats will be good luck, and *white*
cats will be bad. If a white cat crosses your path, look out! I will take
the black ball for the cue ball and let the *white* ball be the unlucky eight-
rock. And on my blacklist — which will be a *white* list then — I will put
everybody who ever Jim Crowed me from Rankin to Hitler, Talmadge
to Malan, South Carolina to South Africa.

"I am black. When I look in the mirror, I see myself, daddy-o, but   10
I am not ashamed. God made me. He did not make us no badder than
the rest of the folks. The earth is black and all kinds of good things
comes out of the earth. Everything that grows comes up out of the
earth. Trees and flowers and fruit and sweet potatoes and corn and all
that keeps mens alive comes right up out of the earth — good old black
earth. Coal is black and it warms your house and cooks your food. The
night is black, which has a moon, and a million stars, and is beautiful.
Sleep is black which gives you rest, so you wake up feeling good. I am
black. I feel very good this evening.

"What is wrong with black?"   11

BACKGROUND AND CONTEXT

1. Words have denotations (their literal, explicit meanings) and connotations
   (their range of associations). For example, to call something "cool" doesn't
   necessarily mean that it's cold or chilly. What connotations does Hughes use
   to characterize the word *black*? How embedded are these expressions in the
   English language? Would a foreign speaker know these connotations?

2. What does the essay tell you about how "black" was thought of sixty years
   ago? What is Hughes saying about the use of the word through his invented
   character Simple? Within twenty years the word *black* became accepted
   usage and the word *Negro* was considered unacceptable. What do you think
   caused this change?

STRATEGY, STRUCTURE, AND STYLE

1. Note that the essay takes the form of a dialogue and that both characters are
   "black." But in what ways do the characters differ in speech and style of address?
   What advantages does Hughes gain through the use of dialogue? What would
   the essay be like if it took the form of an address by a single speaker?

2. How would you describe Simple's basic argument? How does he arrive at his
   conclusion? How important are examples to his point of view? Would you
   argue that these are all just words and common expressions, or that these
   words have an impact on ways we think and feel?

COMPARISONS AND CONNECTIONS

1. Compare the way Hughes explores the word *black* to the way Robert F. Wilson Jr. writes about *issues* (p. 72). Does the word *issues* have only negative connotations? Which essay do you think does a better job of helping readers understand the power of certain words?

2. Try doing what Hughes does. Take a common word (such as *boy* or *girl*), and in a short essay examine its various connotations, looking at both negative and positive aspects of its use. You might look at the word from the perspective of different cultures and ethnic groups.

Discussing the Unit

SUGGESTED TOPIC FOR DISCUSSION

What's in a word? The authors in this chapter explore situations when a word is appropriate and when it is not — and all that a word comes to stand for. After reading these essays, consider the various choices we all make when we use certain words.

PREPARING FOR CLASS DISCUSSION

1. Do words matter? The authors in this chapter write about their unique power. As you reflect upon the essays you've read, think about how words shape the thought and experience of both the individual and our society.

2. Do you habitually use words without considering their connotations? What associations do you have with words like *sorry*, *alien*, and *black*? What about with a team name like the Washington Redskins? Under what circumstances might you begin to examine words and their associations more closely?

FROM DISCUSSION TO WRITING

1. As the authors in this chapter point out, some words say too much, some say too little, and some are in the Goldilocks zone of just right. Discuss which essays in this chapter are particularly compelling in showing when a word is illuminating and which essays are particularly convincing in pointing out when a word is meaningless. Use examples from the essays to illustrate your point.

2. What are some of the reasons that we say the word *sorry*? What thoughts and impulses lie behind that word? Does Sarah Elliott's essay (p. 62) touch on any common points made in the debate between Lauren Apfel and Carinn Jade (p. 56)? Explain in a brief comparison and contrast essay.

TOPICS FOR CROSS-CULTURAL DISCUSSION

1. Does your race or gender influence how you use words or what words you use? Explain your answer, citing examples from at least two of the essays in this chapter that bring gender and race into the discussion.

2. What happens when one particular group has control over the names of other people or things? What happens when it does not? Did any of the essays in this chapter change your perspective? Why or why not?

2

Free Speech: Is It Endangered on Campus?

Free expression is such a fundamental liberty that many national charters, including the U.S. Constitution, have made it among the first rights they've expressly numbered. On college campuses, the right to hold and express dissenting views has always been considered not only an important personal freedom but also a critical component of healthy academic discourse and diversity. What happens, though, when one student's right starts to infringe on another student's well-being? Where should we draw the line?

A major battlefield in the academic free-speech wars has been what to do about content that, while it might be important to understanding a particular field or discipline, upsets students exposed to it. Some students have recently called for professors to confront this problem head-on by adopting the Internet trend of appending their courses with trigger warnings, explicit alerts that certain material on a syllabus may be upsetting, or "triggering," especially to students with past traumas.

Although it may seem from many news reports that colleges across the nation are contributing to the suppression of free speech, some schools are reacting against this perceived trend. Over the summer of 2016, the prestigious University of Chicago sent a letter to the incoming freshman class informing students in no uncertain terms that the school remains dedicated to academic freedom. "Our commitment to academic freedom," the letter said in part, "means that we do not support so-called trigger warnings, we do not cancel invited speakers because their topics might prove controversial, and we do not condone the creation of intellectual 'safe spaces' where individuals can retreat from ideas and perspectives at odds with their own."

This chapter examines that trigger warning debate in the larger context of freedom of expression, and it opens with an "In Brief" newspaper editorial that criticizes recent intolerance on campus and claims that "of all places, a university should foster an environment where students, rather than being shielded from opposing views, are exposed to the widest variety of thought."

This may be a noble view of a college education, but in a widely discussed *Atlantic* article, researchers Greg Lukianoff and Jonathan Haidt found that free and open discussion on campus is becoming increasingly threatened. In "The Coddling of the American Mind," they point to two campus trends they consider alarming: trigger warnings and microaggressions. They view both of these trends as dangerously overprotective and believe they are "creating a culture in which everyone must think twice before speaking up, lest they face charges of insensitivity, aggression, or worse."

Yet, others are not so sure that these campus trends are simply political correctness spun out of control or an overprotective form of "coddling." To some professors, certain forms of preemptive protection and warning make sense. In a *New York Times* opinion essay that directly refers to the Lukianoff and Haidt article, Kate Manne, a philosophy professor, offers a defense of trigger warnings and explains how and why she uses them. "It's not about coddling anyone," she argues. "It's about enabling everyone's rational engagement."

Students, too, have weighed in on a subject that especially concerns them. Two student essays from the University of Iowa debate the merits of these warnings. In "Colleges Should Adopt Trigger Warnings," Brianne Richson argues that the issue is not freedom versus repression, but the protection of people suffering from severe traumas, who have every right to share a classroom with the majority. She focuses on victims of post-traumatic stress disorder, who may be especially upset by course material that touches on their traumas, while there's little benefit to teaching it.

These victims, Richson writes, "do not have more to learn about the academic subject matter that is traumatic for them; they have lived it." In a rebuttal, Jon Overton asserts the importance of absolutely unrestrained conversation. Trigger warnings threaten to turn the classroom into "a horrific nightmare in which political correctness on steroids allows students to avoid any information with which they disagree," he writes in "Beware the Trigger Warning."

In another response to Lukianoff and Haidt's notion of "coddling" — this one a supportive response — columnist Lenore Skenazy wonders why college students today are "being treated as so supremely fragile that they can't read a disturbing book, and must be constantly on the lookout for any remarks or attitudes that could somehow be labeled aggressive." In "How Helicoptered Kids Grow Up to Become Hypersensitive College Students," she partly blames the recent generation of overly protective parents who raised their now college-age kids as though they were helpless and vulnerable infants.

In the chapter's "Spotlight on Data and Research" feature, we look at a recent poll conducted by the prominent Pew Research Center that shows that younger people may be more inclined to censor offensive speech than older generations are. The poll's data indicate that "American Millennials are far more likely than older generations to say the government should be able to prevent people from saying offensive statements about minority groups."

This chapter's "America Then" comes from a liberal academic, law professor Wendy Kaminer, who, over twenty years ago, reacted to what she saw as the problem of coddled students (long before the trigger warning trend), who demanded comfort at the expense of the rights of others. In "A Civic Duty to Annoy," she reminds us that "everyone is bound to feel silenced, invisible, or unappreciated at least once in a while." But is Kaminer's outlook fading as the university becomes ever more diverse? Can we, and should we, sacrifice a bit of our ability to say whatever we want for the sake of others' well-being?

Staff, *Jacksonville Daily News*

Intolerance Doesn't Belong on Campus

[*Jacksonville Daily News*, June 2, 2015]

*E*ach year, it appears, as they prepare for graduation ceremonies, college campuses are divided by highly polarized views about commencement speakers — who is acceptable to the campus community and who isn't. And just about every year protests arise and speakers are disinvited because their presence will cause distraction and commotion at an occasion that should be celebratory. As the editorial from the Jacksonville Daily News notes with regret, in 2014 former secretary of state Condoleezza Rice was forced to decline her invitation to speak at Rutgers University because students and faculty objected to her role in the Iraq War. The newspaper, however, points out that the year 2015 didn't see a similar number of canceled speakers and its editorial reminds students and educators that a "campus should be a place where students are challenged to examine and defend their own points of view and consider the strengths and shortcomings of opposing points of view."*

It's that time of year when new college graduates head out into the world with high hopes of making their mark on the future. 1

It's also the time of year when advice abounds from those with experience in the world awaiting the grads. Some wise and worthwhile. Some frivolous and soon forgotten. And some, like Michelle Obama's recent graduation address at Tuskegee University in Alabama, a topic of controversy. 2

This year, however, it appears that free speech and the open exchange of ideas at the country's institutions of higher learning isn't quite as dead as was the case a year ago, when college graduations seemed to foster and celebrate closed minds — the enemy of education. 3

Last year, student and faculty protests succeeded in barring persons of prominence and distinction from the graduation speaker's podium. 4

Most notable was former Secretary of State Condoleezza Rice, who said no to an invitation from Rutgers. A contingent of students and faculty urged the school to "disinvite" Rice for her role in the Iraq war. The highly accomplished Rice declined Rutgers' invitation, saying it had 5 become a "distraction" from what rightly should be a joyous celebration for the graduates and their families.

The number of canceled speeches set a worrisome tone for gradu-   6
ation 2014 that, thankfully, appears missing across the nation this year.

To close one's mind to opposing ideas is to close one's eyes to the   7
ways of the world after graduation.

Faculty may be able to shut out differences of thought in their ivory-   8
tower existence; but students will find that impossible once they have
left the hallowed halls of their alma mater.

Of all places, a university should foster an environment where stu-   9
dents, rather than being shielded from opposing views, are exposed to
the widest variety of thought. The campus should be a place where students are challenged to examine and defend their own points of view
and consider the strengths and shortcomings of opposing points of view.

Most worrisome about insisting upon graduation speakers with only   10
certain ideas and thoughts is that such notions contradict the essence of
America's freedoms.

The Founders understood the relationship of free speech to a free   11
society and protected the right of every American in the First Amendment. It is a right not to be taken lightly, and certainly a right not to be
dismissed by a protesting faculty.

As educators, faculty members have an obligation to encourage   12
learning, and the best way to learn is with an open mind.

Intolerance does not belong on a university campus. That is a lesson   13
that appears to have been learned for Graduation 2015.

POINTS TO CONSIDER

  1. The editorial declares that "of all places, a university should foster an environment where students, rather than being shielded from opposing views,
  are exposed to the widest variety of thought." Do you agree with this statement? Do you think that most people would agree? Can you think of people
  or groups who would not agree?

  2. The editorial often refers to "faculty." What does the writer seem concerned
  that faculty will do? Do you share these concerns?

  3. What is your opinion about tolerance and intolerance when it comes to
  speech and ideas? Is it always possible to be tolerant? Do you think there
  could be issues that are best met with intolerance?

Greg Lukianoff and Jonathan Haidt

From The Coddling of the American Mind

[*The Atlantic*, September 2015]

BEFORE YOU READ

How do you feel about attempts on college campuses to block words and ideas that might cause offense to someone? Is the new protectiveness on campus helping or hurting students?

WORDS TO LEARN

violate (para. 1): to transgress (verb)

paranoia (para. 1): mental disorder involving extreme suspicion of others (noun)

pseudonym (para. 1): made-up name used by an author; pen name (noun)

gingerly (para. 1): with great caution (adverb)

parlance (para. 2): way of speaking (noun)

misogyny (para. 2): hatred of women (noun)

recurrence (para. 2): a return of something, or to a previous condition (noun)

installation (para. 3): something erected or installed in a certain place (noun)

tenets (para. 4): beliefs (noun)

misguided (para. 4): mistaken (adjective)

collegiate (para. 6): relating to college and college students (adjective)

uncongenial (para. 9): disagreeable (adjective)

pathologically (para. 9): in terms of disease (adverb)

S omething strange is happening at America's colleges and universi-   1
ties. A movement is arising, undirected and driven largely by students, to scrub campuses clean of words, ideas, and subjects that

Greg Lukianoff is a lawyer who serves as the president and CEO of the Foundation for Individual Rights in Education. He is the author of Unlearning Liberty: Campus Censorship and the End of American Debate *(2014). Jonathan Haidt, a social psychologist, is a professor of ethical leadership at New York University's Stern School of Business. He has written two books,* The Happiness Hypothesis: Finding Modern Truth in Ancient Wisdom *(2006) and* The Righteous Mind: Why Good People Are Divided by Politics and Religion *(2012).*

might cause discomfort or give offense. Last December, Jeannie Suk wrote in an online article for *The New Yorker* about law students asking her fellow professors at Harvard not to teach rape law — or, in one case, even use the word *violate* (as in "that violates the law") lest it cause students distress. In February, Laura Kipnis, a professor at Northwestern University, wrote an essay in *The Chronicle of Higher Education* describing a new campus politics of sexual paranoia — and was then subjected to a long investigation after students who were offended by the article and by a tweet she'd sent filed Title IX[1] complaints against her. In June, a professor protecting himself with a pseudonym wrote an essay for *Vox* describing how gingerly he now has to teach. "I'm a Liberal Professor, and My Liberal Students Terrify Me," the headline said. A number of popular comedians, including Chris Rock, have stopped performing on college campuses. Jerry Seinfeld and Bill Maher have publicly condemned the oversensitivity of college students, saying too many of them can't take a joke.

Two terms have risen quickly from obscurity into common campus parlance. *Microaggressions* are small actions or word choices that seem on their face to have no malicious intent but that are thought of as a kind of violence nonetheless. For example, by some campus guidelines, it is a microaggression to ask an Asian American or Latino American "Where were you born?" because this implies that he or she is not a real American. *Trigger warnings* are alerts that professors are expected to issue if something in a course might cause a strong emotional response. For example, some students have called for warnings that Chinua Achebe's *Things Fall Apart* describes racial violence and that F. Scott Fitzgerald's *The Great Gatsby* portrays misogyny and physical abuse, so that students who have been previously victimized by racism or domestic violence can choose to avoid these works, which they believe might "trigger" a recurrence of past trauma.

Some recent campus actions border on the surreal. In April, at Brandeis University, the Asian American student association sought to raise awareness of microaggressions against Asians through an installation on the steps of an academic hall. The installation gave examples of microaggressions such as "Aren't you supposed to be good at math?" and "I'm color-blind! I don't see race." But a backlash arose among other Asian American students, who felt that the display itself was a microaggression. The association removed the installation, and its president

2

3

---

[1] Title IX (para. 1): A federal law that forbids discrimination on the basis of sex in any educational setting that is federally funded

wrote an e-mail to the entire student body apologizing to anyone who was "triggered or hurt by the content of the microaggressions."

According to the most basic tenets of psychology, helping people   4
with anxiety disorders avoid the things they fear is misguided.

This new climate is slowly being institutionalized, and is affect-   5
ing what can be said in the classroom, even as a basis for discussion.
During the 2014–15 school year, for instance, the deans and department
chairs at the 10 University of California system schools were presented
by administrators at faculty leader-training sessions with examples of
microaggressions. The list of offensive statements included: "America is
the land of opportunity" and "I believe the most qualified person should
get the job."

The press has typically described these developments as a resur-   6
gence of political correctness. That's partly right, although there are
important differences between what's happening now and what happened in the 1980s and '90s. That movement sought to restrict speech
(specifically hate speech aimed at marginalized groups), but it also
challenged the literary, philosophical, and historical canon, seeking to
widen it by including more diverse perspectives. The current movement
is largely about emotional well-being. More than the last, it presumes
an extraordinary fragility of the collegiate
psyche, and therefore elevates the goal
of protecting students from psychological
harm. The ultimate aim, it seems, is to turn
campuses into "safe spaces" where young
adults are shielded from words and ideas
that make some uncomfortable. And more
than the last, this movement seeks to pun-
ish anyone who interferes with that aim, even accidentally. You might
call this impulse *vindictive protectiveness*. It is creating a culture in which
everyone must think twice before speaking up, lest they face charges of
insensitivity, aggression, or worse.

> It is creating a
> culture in which
> everyone must
> think twice before
> speaking up.

We have been studying this development for a while now, with   7
rising alarm. The dangers that these trends pose to scholarship and
to the quality of American universities are significant; we could write
a whole essay detailing them. But in this essay we focus on a different question: What are the effects of this new protectiveness *on the
students themselves*? Does it benefit the people it is supposed to help?
What exactly are students learning when they spend four years or
more in a community that polices unintentional slights, places warning labels on works of classic literature, and in many other ways conveys the sense that words can be forms of violence that require strict

control by campus authorities, who are expected to act as both protectors and prosecutors?

There's a saying common in education circles: Don't teach students   8 *what* to think; teach them *how* to think. The idea goes back at least as far as Socrates. Today, what we call the Socratic method is a way of teaching that fosters critical thinking, in part by encouraging students to question their own unexamined beliefs, as well as the received wisdom of those around them. Such questioning sometimes leads to discomfort, and even to anger, on the way to understanding.

But vindictive protectiveness teaches students to think in a very   9 different way. It prepares them poorly for professional life, which often demands intellectual engagement with people and ideas one might find uncongenial or wrong. The harm may be more immediate, too. A campus culture devoted to policing speech and punishing speakers is likely to engender patterns of thought that are surprisingly similar to those long identified by cognitive behavioral therapists as causes of depression and anxiety. The new protectiveness may be teaching students to think pathologically.

VOCABULARY/USING A DICTIONARY

1. What does the prefix *over-* add to the definition of the word *sensitivity* (para. 1)?

2. What is *backlash* (para. 3)?

3. What part of speech is *engender* (para. 9), and what does it mean?

RESPONDING TO WORDS IN CONTEXT

1. What does it mean to *give offense* (para. 1)?

2. Paragraph 6 mentions "the literary, philosophical, and historical *canon.*" How is that type of *canon* different from a *cannon*?

3. What do you think the essayists mean by the term *vindictive protectiveness* (para. 6)?

DISCUSSING MAIN POINT AND MEANING

1. Why would trigger warnings be placed on some material found in college classes?

2. What do Lukianoff and Haidt fear will be the consequence of this increased sensitivity to how students react to what they read and to what is said to them on college campuses today?

3. Which two terms do Lukianoff and Haidt focus on in their argument? What do these terms mean?

EXAMINING SENTENCES, PARAGRAPHS, AND ORGANIZATION

1. Lukianoff and Haidt give an indication of their position on campus free speech early in their essay. How do they communicate their feelings on the matter in the first two sentences?

2. Based on what you read in the second paragraph of the essay, do you think you have a good idea of what a microaggression is or what a trigger warning is for? How do Lukianoff and Haidt clarify their terms?

3. The essay ends with claims about how vindictive protectiveness is harmful to students. Are you convinced by these claims? If so, why? If not, what would make the claims more convincing?

THINKING CRITICALLY

1. Do you believe you go to college to learn *what* to think or *how* to think? Explain.

2. Would you call the impulse behind the new environment on college campuses *protectiveness*? Who exactly is being protected? Who might not be protected?

3. Do you think the new protectiveness leaves students and faculty feeling confused about what can and can't be said on campus?

WRITING ACTIVITIES

1. How are you affected by trigger warnings and your awareness of the possibility of microaggression? Write briefly about your experience. If you have not met with these debates on your campus, do you believe that their absence is a result of an already-heightened awareness and protectiveness? Why or why not?

2. Should colleges be invested in students' emotional well-being? Write a brief persuasive essay that argues why they should or should not be.

3. Lukianoff and Haidt write that they want to answer the question about the effects of this new protectiveness on the students themselves. What do you think the effects are on students? List possible good and possible troubling results. Try to generate as many possible good effects as bad for a balanced list, even if you feel strongly that there is a more positive or negative consequence.

Kate Manne

Why I Use Trigger Warnings

[*The New York Times*, September 19, 2015]

BEFORE YOU READ

How and when should trigger warnings be used in the classroom? Are they effective in helping some students interact with material that otherwise would be too emotionally difficult for them to encounter?

WORDS TO LEARN

pushback (para. 1): opposition (noun)

depict (para. 3): portray (verb)

subsequent (para. 4): happening after something else (adjective)

induce (para. 8): to bring about (verb)

sensitize (para. 11): to make sensitive (verb)

implausible (para. 11): not credible (adjective)

efficacy (para. 12): effectiveness (noun)

eerily (para. 13): uncannily (adverb)

rein (para. 14): to curb or control (verb)

pedagogical (para. 15): having to do with teachers or teaching (adjective)

mandatory (para. 15): required (adjective)

Trigger warnings have been getting a lot of pushback lately. Professors who have adopted the practice of alerting their students to potentially disturbing content in a text or class are being accused of coddling millennials. And the students who request them are being called "infantile," or worse. In a recent story in *The Atlantic*, the authors Greg Lukianoff and Jonathan Haidt describe them as part of a movement, "undirected and driven largely by students, to scrub campuses clean of words, ideas, and subjects that might cause discomfort or give offense." 1

I happen to be both a millennial and, for the past two years, an assistant professor of philosophy. I've been using trigger warnings in my teaching — in cases when they seem appropriate — since I began to lecture. 2

Trigger warnings are nothing new. The practice originated in Internet communities, primarily for the benefit of people with post-traumatic stress disorder. The idea was to flag content that depicted or discussed 3

Kate Manne is an assistant professor of philosophy at Cornell University. Her areas of interest include moral philosophy, feminist philosophy, and social philosophy. She is currently at work on a book about misogyny.

common causes of trauma, like military combat, child abuse, incest and sexual violence. People could then choose whether or not to engage with this material.

But trigger warnings have been adapted to serve a subtly different   4
purpose within universities. Increasingly, professors like me simply give students notice in their syllabuses, or before certain reading assignments. The point is not to enable — let alone encourage — students to skip these readings or our subsequent class discussion (both of which are mandatory in my courses, absent a formal exemption). Rather, it is to allow those who are sensitive to these subjects to prepare themselves for reading about them, and better manage their reactions. The evidence suggests that at least some of the students in any given class of mine are likely to have suffered some sort of trauma, whether from sexual assault or another type of abuse or violence. So I think the benefits of trigger warnings can be significant.

Criticisms of trigger warnings are often based on the idea that col-   5
lege is a time for intellectual growth and emotional development. In order for this to happen, students must be challenged. And they need to learn to engage rationally with ideas, arguments and views they find difficult, upsetting or even repulsive. On this count, I agree with the critics, and it is in fact the main reason that I do issue warnings.

In philosophy, we often draw a distinction between responses based   6
on reasons and those that are merely *caused*. In the first case, our response has a basis in rational reflection. We can cite reasons that we think justify our opinion. But in the latter case, we find ourselves involuntarily caused — or triggered — to have a certain reaction.

Triggered reactions can be intense and unpleasant, and may even   7
overtake our consciousness, as with a flashback experienced by a war veteran. But even more common conditions can have this effect. Think, for example, about the experience of intense nausea. It comes upon a person unbidden, without rational reflection. And you can no more reason your way out of it than you reasoned your way into it. It's also hard, if not impossible, to engage productively with other matters while you are in the grip of it. You might say that such states temporarily eclipse our rational capacities.

For someone who has experienced major trauma, vivid reminders   8
can serve to induce states of body and mind that are rationally eclipsing in much the same manner. A common symptom of PTSD is panic attacks. Those undergoing these attacks may be flooded with anxiety to the point of struggling to draw breath, and feeling disoriented, dizzy and nauseated. Under conditions such as these, it's impossible to think straight.

The thought behind trigger warnings isn't just that these states are   9
highly unpleasant (although they certainly are). It's that they temporarily

render people unable to focus, regardless of their desire or determination to do so. Trigger warnings can work to prevent or counteract this.

As teachers, we can't foresee every instance of potentially trigger-   10 ing material; some triggers are unpredictable. But others are easy enough to anticipate, specifically, depictions or discussions of the very kinds of experiences that often result in post-traumatic stress and even, for some, a clinical disorder. With appropriate warnings in place, vulnerable students may be able to employ effective anxiety management techniques, by meditating or taking prescribed medication.

To me, there seems to be very little reason not to give these warn-   11 ings. As a professor, it merely requires my including one extra line in a routine e-mail to the class, such as: "A quick heads-up. The reading for this week contains a graphic depiction of sexual assault." These warnings are not unlike the advisory notices given before films and TV shows; those who want to ignore them can do so without a second thought. The cost to students who don't need trigger warnings is, I think, equally minimal. It may even help sensitize them to the fact that some of their class-mates will find the material hard going. The idea, suggested by Professor Haidt and others, that this considerate and reasonable practice feeds into a "culture of victimhood" seems alarmist, if not completely implausible.

> To me, there seems to be very little reason not to give these warnings.

Mr. Lukianoff and Professor Haidt also argue in their article that   12 we shouldn't give trigger warnings, based on the efficacy of exposure therapy — where you are gradually exposed to the object of a phobia, under the guidance of a trained psychotherapist. But the analogy works poorly. Exposing students to triggering material without warnings seems more akin to occasionally throwing a spider at an arachnophobe.

Of course, all this still leaves the questions of how and when to give   13 trigger warnings, and where to draw the line to avoid their overuse. There is no formula for this, just as there is no formula for designing classes, for successful teaching and meaningful communication with students. As teachers we use our judgment and experience to guide our words and actions in the entire act of teaching. We should be trusted, without leg-islation from college administrators, to decide, ideally in dialogue with our students — whose voices are eerily silent in these discussions in the media — when (and when not) to use these warnings.

Common sense should tell us that material that is merely offensive to   14 certain people's political or religious sensibilities wouldn't merit a warn-ing. True, politics and religion can make people irrationally angry. But unlike a state of panic, anger is a state we are able to rein in rationally — or at least we should be able to.

There are several difficult issues that still need to be hashed out. For   15
example, although I see a willingness to use trigger warnings as part of
pedagogical best practices, I don't believe their use should be mandatory.
There is already too much threat to academic freedom at the moment
because of top-down interference from overreaching administrators.
But when it comes to the bottom-up pressure from students on professors to adopt practices like giving trigger warnings, I am sympathetic.
It's not about coddling anyone. It's about enabling everyone's rational
engagement.

VOCABULARY/USING A DICTIONARY

1. How does the word *eclipse* (para. 7), used here as a verb, relate to the word
   eclipse when used as a noun?

2. What language does the word *arachnophobe* (para. 12) come from? What
   does it mean?

3. What is the opposite of the word *minimal* (para. 11)?

RESPONDING TO WORDS IN CONTEXT

1. Professors who use trigger warnings are accused by some of *coddling*
   (para. 1) students. What does this mean?

2. What part of speech is the word *flag* (para. 3) in this essay? How is it different
   from other meanings of the word *flag*?

3. If an idea is *alarmist* (para. 11), what sort of response might it evoke?

DISCUSSING MAIN POINT AND MEANING

1. Manne writes that she uses trigger warnings when they are appropriate.
   When does she use them?

2. What distinctions does Manne, a philosophy professor, draw between different kinds of responses (para. 3)?

3. When people have "triggered" reactions, what is their experience? How do
   warnings help them?

EXAMINING SENTENCES, PARAGRAPHS, AND ORGANIZATION

1. How does Manne use personal experience and objective information in her
   essay?

2. Describe Manne's concluding paragraph. Does it provide an accurate reflection of what she has covered in the essay?

3. Manne writes, "I've been using trigger warnings in my teaching — in cases
   when they seem appropriate — since I began to lecture" (para. 2). What is the

effect of using dashes in this sentence? How would the sentence be different without the dashes?

THINKING CRITICALLY

1. Do you think a person having a "triggered" reaction is capable of learning material presented in a course? Why or why not? Do you believe Manne's analogy of someone having a triggered reaction to someone experiencing intense nausea is valid? Why or why not?

2. Manne mentions that we get advisory notices before television shows and films. How is our experience of these shows different if we are not given a warning? Why are these warnings given?

3. "There is no formula" (para. 13) for teachers who use trigger warnings, according to Manne. When should trigger warnings be given? How can teachers adopt a balanced approach and use trigger warnings as necessary without tipping into overuse?

WRITING ACTIVITIES

1. Think of a novel, article, or lecture you've read or heard recently for class. How did you react to the information you were learning? Was your response "based on reasons," or was it "merely *caused*" (see Manne's distinction in para. 6)? Was your response a blend of the two? Consider how you respond to material and whether or not a trigger warning adds or detracts from your response, based on the example you've chosen.

2. How do you experience trigger warnings in your college education? Do you think they are intrusive to your learning, or are they a "quick heads-up" (para. 11), as Manne uses them? Do you encounter them routinely, or have you never encountered them in the classroom? In a short report, discuss your experience with trigger warnings — how frequently they are used, how they affected your experience of material, and whether or not you think their use is an issue worth debating. Discuss your experience, using as many specific details as possible. For example, were you assigned readings that had warnings? If so, name the readings, and discuss their content. Were there other readings that you felt *should* have had warnings but didn't?

3. For Manne, trigger warnings allow students to engage with material they might not have been able to process otherwise, rather than allowing them to avoid that material. Explain Manne's viewpoint, and then explain how a student might use trigger warnings to avoid such material or to pressure teachers to avoid controversial material. Present both perspectives in writing, and then, in your conclusion, decide which perspective persuades you more — whether you think trigger warnings help students process material or steer them away from it.

Brianne Richson

Colleges Should Adopt Trigger Warnings

[*The Daily Iowan*, University of Iowa, May 6, 2014]

Jon Overton

Beware the Trigger Warning

[*The Daily Iowan*, University of Iowa, May 7, 2014]

BEFORE YOU READ

What sort of precautions should we take to protect people suffering from post-traumatic stress disorder (PTSD) from reexperiencing their trauma? Should our concern for them extend into the classroom? Is it the responsibility of a student with PTSD to discuss that condition with his or her professor?

WORDS TO LEARN

adverse (Richson, para. 2): unfavorable in effect (adjective)

prominent (Richson, para. 2): standing out (adjective)

affinity (Richson, para. 3): attraction to a person or thing (noun)

sensory (Richson, para. 5): relating to the senses (adjective)

antithetical (Richson, para. 6): directly opposed (adjective)

obligation (Richson, para. 8): something that must be done because it is right (noun)

gripe (Overton, para. 2): complaint (noun)

predict (Overton, para. 3): to foretell (verb)

motivations (Overton, para. 7): incentives (noun)

empathy (Overton, para. 7): identification with the feelings and thoughts of another (noun)

initiate (Overton, para. 7): to begin (verb)

Brianne Richson and Jon Overton were students at the University of Iowa at the time these selections were written.

Brianne Richson

Colleges Should Adopt Trigger Warnings

[*The Daily Iowan*, University of Iowa, May 6, 2014]

We all have that one memory we'd prefer people not bring up because we want to block it from our consciousness forever. Hopefully, such memories become more vague as we grow further removed from them with time, but what about a memory that has legitimately traumatized a person? A memory that has even made its holder a victim of post-traumatic stress disorder (PTSD)? 1

Students at colleges across the country are taking a term originating from the world of blogs, "trigger warning," and calling for its direct use on class syllabi, to alert them to potential adverse reactions to sensitive academic material. This might include anything from sexual assault — a prominent issue on college campuses — to eating disorders, violent graphic content, or topics of race. The list goes on. 2

One might consider such measures dramatic and symptomatic of what I have often heard my father refer to as the "every kid gets a trophy" generation: a generation full of coddling and cushioning when things go wrong. It isn't fair, however, to compare modern parents' affinity for sheltering their children from failure with the generation's demand to be protected from reliving that which was traumatic. 3

Is it too much to ask that a rape survivor be forewarned when a professor is about to cover material on the topic or to ask that a person who was confronted with a racial slur and beaten up be allowed to leave the lecture hall before course material sends her or him into a tizzy of hypervigilance, a hallmark characteristic of PTSD? 4

A great difficulty of PTSD is that it can surface at any given time following a traumatic event — in weeks or years. It is one thing to be aware of what sensory elements could trigger an episode for you, but it is another to have the ability to actively avoid these potentially toxic situations. 5

University of California–Santa Barbara has passed a resolution that professors should indicate in syllabi when emotionally or physically stressful material would be presented in class, prompting a *Los Angeles Times* editorial to stamp the measure as "antithetical to college life." The same editorial suggests that trigger warnings are a cop-out for students 6 not wishing to engage with a diverse set of subject material or to face traditionally uncomfortable issues head-on.

Victims of PTSD do not have more to learn about the academic   7
subject matter that is traumatic for them; they have lived it. Not everyone has the luxury of dealing with issues

> Victims of PTSD do not have more to learn about the academic subject matter that is traumatic for them; they have lived it.

upfront and immediately after a trauma. And no one has the right to force you to do so. In Ohio, Oberlin College has gone so far as to suggest that trigger material should not even be included in a course if it is not clear how the students might learn from the material.

Such measures certainly have a poten-   8
tial to be taken too far, but our obligation to prevent a trauma survivor's class time becoming a living hell outweighs concerns about a stunted learning environment.

Jon Overton

Beware the Trigger Warning

[*The Daily Iowan*, University of Iowa, May 7, 2014]

Brianne Richson suggests that U.S. colleges and universities should   1
adopt trigger warnings on syllabi, on the grounds that people who've suffered traumatic experiences may be exposed to course material that would trigger memories of those events.

I agree that we should be considerate toward people who suffer   2
from psychological illnesses. My main gripe with trigger warnings more broadly, however, is that while they aim to be sensitive to people suffering from afflictions like post-traumatic stress disorder, they threaten to stifle some of the most important conversations and lessons in college.

Trigger warnings run into the same   3
problem as proposed hate-speech laws:

> Trigger warnings run into the same problem as proposed hate-speech laws: Where do they stop?

Where do they stop? Anything can be a trigger, from hot dogs to Nazis to Mike Tyson to the color yellow. The right smell, sound, word, or image can initiate a painful flashback for a particular person, who can't always anticipate them. The triggers don't have to be traditionally traumatic words, phrases, or concepts, so you can't easily predict what will set someone off.

And yet in Ohio, Oberlin College recently issued a policy that   4
advised instructors to "remove triggering material when it does not contribute directly to the course learning goals." This implies that professors ought to go through their syllabi line by line to consider what might trigger a traumatic memory for some students.

Students at the University of California–Santa Barbara also passed   5
a resolution encouraging faculty to include a list of potential triggers on course syllabi and not punish students for leaving early if triggering content arises. Some of the most extreme trigger warning advocates have even attacked classical literature like *Things Fall Apart* and *The Great Gatsby*.

Thanks to some highly vocal faculty at Oberlin, the attack on aca-   6
demic freedom there was shot down, but these examples illustrate perfectly what is so dangerous about trigger warnings. They threaten to transform higher education into a horrific nightmare in which political correctness on steroids allows students to avoid any information with which they disagree. One of the great things about colleges and universities is that they challenge your worldview. They force you to confront information that makes you rethink cherished beliefs. This can be distressing, but that's the point: to expose yourself to new ideas and points of view.

The motivations behind trigger warnings are undoubtedly admi-   7
rable. They reflect the pinnacle of empathy and compassion. However, it's up to the students who suffer from PTSD to tell their instructors in advance if they're concerned about a potential trigger from specific course material. As much as we'd like to help trauma victims, we can't know what's going to initiate a panic attack, and trying to prevent any and all of them endangers academic discourse.

VOCABULARY/USING A DICTIONARY

1. What part of speech is *stifle* (Overton, para. 2)? What does it mean?

2. What is the difference between the words *advise* (Overton, para. 4) and *advice*?

3. What is *vigilance*? What is *hypervigilance* (Richson, para. 4)?

RESPONDING TO WORDS IN CONTEXT

1. What is a *slur* (Richson, para. 4)? What part of speech is it?

2. Can you think of some of the *traumatic* (Overton, para. 4) issues trigger warnings might cover for students?

3. How might trigger warnings lead to "a stunted learning environment" (Richson, para. 8)?

DISCUSSING MAIN POINT AND MEANING

1. What opposition to the idea of trigger warnings does Richson consider in her essay?

2. What point of Richson's does Overton agree with?

3. Does Overton think trigger warnings have come about for worthy or unworthy reasons?

EXAMINING SENTENCES, PARAGRAPHS, AND ORGANIZATION

1. Why does Richson include a sentence with dashes in the second paragraph of this essay?

2. How does Overton indicate that his essay is a response to another's work? Is that indication necessary to the essay?

3. Do you think that Richson could go further in her conclusion? Why or why not?

THINKING CRITICALLY

1. Overton writes, "I agree that we should be considerate toward people who suffer from psychological illnesses" (para. 2). Do you think from his essay that this statement is true? Explain.

2. Do you think the generation of students considering trigger warnings for their material has grown accustomed to "coddling and cushioning" (Richson, para. 3)? How might trigger warnings be an extension of that?

3. What are some alternatives to trigger warnings for students with PTSD? Are there any alternatives or are trigger warnings the best solution for these students?

WRITING ACTIVITIES

1. Read some of the arguments for and against trigger warnings that have surfaced recently in the news. Do you find these arguments more or less compelling than Richson's? Why or why not?

2. In an exercise, respond to Overton's essay. Try to address his points one by one (paragraph by paragraph). When you have finished, try to craft your exercise into an essay that is a rough response to Overton.

3. Research the rise of interest in trigger warnings at Oberlin College. What led to the interest in having warnings there? What led to the policy that was "shot down" (Overton, para. 6)? What do you think of the debate Oberlin College is having there?

Moving from General to Specific

A common and effective way to develop an essay is to move from a general point to a specific instance. A writer may open an essay by claiming that ever since its beginnings the English language has undergone incessant change: The original Old English of the Anglo-Saxons is unreadable today. That could prepare the way for the following paragraph to show specifically how the new social media — text-messaging, tweeting, etc. — are also changing the English language and that such changes are natural and inevitable.

Notice how University of Iowa student Brianne Richson, who makes a case for including trigger warnings in academic syllabi, begins with a firm, strong argument about PTSD and then moves into a paragraph giving specific instances of students who might be affected by triggering material. She not only supports her argument with concrete examples but also brings it to life startlingly in this paragraph, which forces us to confront particular instances that may challenge the notions of victims we brought to her argument.

1
Strong examples make the best possible case.

2
A technical term shows depth of understanding.

Is it too much to ask that a rape survivor be forewarned when a professor is about to cover material on the topic or to ask that (1) <u>a person who was confronted with a racial slur and beaten up</u> be allowed to leave the lecture hall before course material sends her or him into a tizzy of (2) <u>hypervigilance</u>, a hallmark characteristic of PTSD?

Lenore Skenazy

How Helicoptered Kids Grow Up to Become Hypersensitive College Students

[*Reason*, August 17, 2015]

BEFORE YOU READ
Does super-safe equal super-sensitive on our college campuses? Are we feeding student anxieties at the expense of encouraging confidence and resiliency?

WORDS TO LEARN
perturb (para. 1): disturb (verb)
unendurable (para. 11): unbearable (adjective)

resiliency (para. 13): ability to return to original form (noun)

T his is the article everyone's talking about: "The Coddling of the American Mind," by Greg Lukianoff and Jonathan Haidt, on the cover of this month's *Atlantic*. It discusses the idea taking root on college campuses that students cannot be exposed to ideas, words, or phrases that perturb them.   1

That's why schools are embracing "trigger warnings," which are placed at the top of readings that might trigger flashbacks to some unpleasant episode in a student's life. Some Harvard University law students, for instance, balk at the idea that they would have to learn about rape law — hearing about that crime might re-traumatize anyone who had lived through it.   2

The article also discusses "microaggressions" — remarks made, even innocently, that are received as blows by the person being addressed. For instance, asking Asian or Hispanic students where they were born *could* come across as a hint that the speaker does not consider the other student totally American. That's the "aggression."   3

The entire article is so brilliant, I am ashamed of my simplistic reduction of it, but I want to get to the Free-Range meat of the matter: Why are college students being treated as so supremely fragile that they can't   4

Lenore Skenazy is an author, blogger, columnist, and reality show host. She founded the parenting movement Free-Range Kids, based on the concept of raising children with the freedom to function independently.

read a disturbing book, and must be constantly on the lookout for any remarks or attitudes that could somehow be labeled aggressive?

Because that's how we have been taught to raise our children these 5 past 20 or 30 years: thin-skinned, super-sensitive, and primed to turn to the authorities — parents, teachers, and now deans — any time they feel the slightest bit uncomfortable or aggrieved.

After all, this is the generation we raised 6 with "baby knee pads" to make crawling less painful, and helmets to protect them while toddling. Somehow, we became utterly convinced that our kids bruise so easily and permanently that special precautions must be taken — precautions that were never necessary until this moment in history. That message grew up into trigger warnings: *Watch out, kids! You are too easily hurt.*

> Somehow, we became utterly convinced that our kids bruise so easily and permanently that special precautions must be taken.

This is also the generation that grew 7 up getting trophies for 8th place. My son got one, on a league with nine teams. With that trophy came the same message: Kids, you are too fragile to handle the micro-misery of losing.

And this is also the generation of students who grew up surrounded 8 by posters at school exhorting them to be on the lookout for bullying. When bullying is the thing you look for, bullying is what you see. What starts as hyper-alertness to bullying in third grade ends as hypersensitivity to microaggressions on college campuses.

Are we doing our kids any favors? Lukianoff and Haidt say no: 9

What are the effects of this new protectiveness *on the students themselves*? Does it benefit the people it is supposed to help? What exactly are students learning when they spend four years or more in a community that polices unintentional slights, places warning labels on works of classic literature, and in many other ways conveys the sense that words can be forms of violence that require strict control by campus authorities?

Students are learning that they are as helpless and easily hurt as 10 infants. This, of course, is not helping them at all — not in terms of their education, and not in terms of their psychological health. The authors quote a survey of the American College Health Association (not included in the excerpt reprinted above) that found 54 percent of college students surveyed said they had felt "overwhelming anxiety" in the past 12 months, up from 49 percent just five years before.

Naturally, you are going to feel anxious if you've been told from 11
infancy that basic locomotion is dangerous, losing is unendurable, classmates are out to get you, and you are not equipped to stand up for yourself.

And it's not that I blame us parents! I blame a society that keeps tell- 12
ing us, through products and programs and even laws, that our kids are in
constant danger, so we must make things safer, safer, safer. For God's sake,
I got a press release last week from the Environmental Working Group
asking restaurants to pledge to give kids only "asbestos-free" crayons —
as if the tiny exposure to the tiny amount of asbestos in a crayon while
waiting for chicken fingers is going to scar their lungs for a lifetime. Our
society sees every "micro" as "macro."

Free-Range Kids has always championed our children's resiliency. 13
Not that we endorse danger or callousness or cruelty (who would?), but
that we believe our kids can roll with some punches — even touch an off-
brand crayon — and live to see another, non-paranoid day.

In our understandable but misdirected desire to keep our kids super- 14
safe, we have succeeded in making them super-sensitive instead. Happy
is the child, 8 or 18, who is not constantly afraid and aggrieved.

VOCABULARY/USING A DICTIONARY

1. What sort of action is *balk* (para. 2)?

2. What does it mean if someone is *primed* (para. 5) for something? In what
   other context might *primed* be used?

3. What does it mean for an action to be *directed*? What does *misdirected*
   (para. 14) mean?

RESPONDING TO WORDS IN CONTEXT

1. Skenazy speaks of the possibility of students' feeling "uncomfortable or
   aggrieved" (para. 5). Then she states that it is better not to be "afraid and
   aggrieved" (para. 14). What do you think *aggrieved* means in this context?

2. When Skenazy speaks of "basic *locomotion*" (para. 11), what is she referring to?

3. When you read the phrase "not that we endorse danger or *callousness* or
   cruelty" (para. 13), how would you define *callousness*?

DISCUSSING MAIN POINT AND MEANING

1. What, according to Skenazy, do young adults now do that they were taught
   to do as children?

2. What do "baby knee pads" (para. 6) and helmets teach children? How do
   they begin to see themselves?

3. Who does Skenazy blame for the current climate on college campuses?

EXAMINING SENTENCES, PARAGRAPHS, AND ORGANIZATION

1. How does Skenazy use "The Coddling of the American Mind" by Lukianoff and Haidt in her essay?

2. What do you notice about Skenazy's writing style? Is there anything that she does consistently in her paragraphs and sentence structures?

3. Skenazy uses a few expressions in her writing: "When bullying is the thing you look for, bullying is what you see" (para. 8). "Our society sees every 'micro' as 'macro'" (para. 12). "In our understandable but misdirected desire to keep our kids super-safe, we have succeeded in making them super-sensitive instead" (para. 14). Are these effective or ineffective statements to use in an essay?

THINKING CRITICALLY

1. How is this essay a response to "The Coddling of the American Mind" (p. 86)? How does it further the argument presented there?

2. Skenazy suggests that "asking Asian or Hispanic students where they were born *could* come across as a hint that the speaker does not consider the other student totally American" (para. 3). What are other reasons for asking that question?

3. The title of this essay is "How Helicoptered Kids Grow Up to Become Hypersensitive College Students." Do you think Skenazy effectively explains this process? Why or why not?

WRITING ACTIVITIES

1. What do you know about the idea behind Free-Range Kids, which is referenced at times in this article? Write what you know about it, or write what you think the concept behind it might be. Think about how the methodology might differ from the parenting (and young adulthood) that Skenazy describes.

2. Describe your own upbringing. Do you think you were brought up like the anxious, overprotected kids Skenazy speaks about, or do you think you were brought up to be confident and resilient? Provide examples from your childhood that support your answer.

3. Skenazy chooses a passage from Lukianoff and Haidt's essay and quotes it at length, in answer to the question "Are we doing our kids any favors?" Rewrite that question at the top of a page, and find a passage from Lukianoff and Haidt (p. 86) or from Skenazy that you feel answers this question. Then respond to the question and the passage in your own words.

Spotlight on Data and Research

Jacob Poushter
40% of Millennials OK with Limiting Speech Offensive to Minorities
[Pew Research Center, November 20, 2015]

One reason for the trend of "trigger warnings" and other forms of censorship on college campuses throughout the nation may be found in a recent poll conducted by the prestigious Pew Research Center. Younger people, the survey found, are more likely to favor restrictions on speech offensive to minorities than do older generations. For example, 40 percent of Millennials (defined as people between eighteen and thirty-four) believe that government should prevent such offensive speech, whereas only 24 percent of Baby Boomers (defined as those between fifty-one and sixty-nine) share that belief. Conducted globally, the poll also shows that European nations want the government to prevent offensive speech much more than Americans do.

American Millennials are far more likely than older generations to say   1
the government should be able to prevent people from saying offensive statements about minority groups, according to a new analysis of Pew Research Center survey data on free speech and media across the globe. We asked whether people believe that citizens should be able to make public statements that are offensive to minority groups, or whether the government should be able to prevent people from saying these things. Four-in-ten Millennials say the government should be able to prevent people publicly making statements that are offensive to minority groups, while 58% said such speech is OK.

Even though a larger share of Millennials favor allowing offensive   2
speech against minorities, the 40% who oppose it is striking given that only around a quarter of Gen Xers (27%) and Boomers (24%) and roughly one-in-ten Silents (12%) say the government should be able to prevent such speech.

Compared with people we surveyed in dozens of nations, Americans   3
as a whole are less likely to favor the government being able to prevent speech of any kind. The debate over what kind of speech should be tolerated in public has become a major story around the globe in recent weeks — from racial issues on many U.S. college campuses to questions about speech laws in Europe in the wake of concerns about refugees from the Middle East and the terrorist attacks in Paris. Overall, our global survey found that a majority of Americans say that people *should* be able to say offensive things about minority groups publicly. Two-thirds of Americans say this, compared with a median of 35% among the 38 nations we polled.

In the U.S., our findings also show a racial divide on this question, 4 with non-whites more likely (38%) to support government prevention of such speech than non-Hispanic whites (23%). Nearly twice as many Democrats say the government should be able to stop speech against minorities (35%) compared with Republicans (18%). Independents, as is often the case, find themselves in the middle. One-third of all women say the government should be able to curtail speech that is offensive to minorities vs. 23% of men who say the same.

Furthermore, Americans who have a high school degree or less 5 are more likely than those with at least a college degree to say that speech offensive to minority groups should be able to be restricted (a 9-percentage-point difference).

In Europe, where long-simmering racial tensions are of a different 6 nature, compounded by the recent flow of migrants from North Africa and the Middle East, people are more willing than Americans to accept government controls on speech against minorities. A median of 49% across the six EU nations surveyed say this compared with 28% of Americans.

Among Europeans, there is a wide range of opinion on whether 7 the government can prevent statements that are offensive to minorities. Seven-in-ten Germans say this should be the case (where there are clear laws against hate speech), as do 62% of Italians and half of Poles. The French are divided, with 48% saying that the government should have the ability to prevent speech that is offensive to minority groups, while 51% say people should be able to say these things publicly. In contrast, the balance of opinion in the UK and Spain is to allow people to say statements that might offend minorities.

In contrast with American Millennials, those ages 18 to 34 in 8 Germany and Spain are more likely to say people should be able to say things offensive to minorities compared with those ages 35 and older. On the other hand, in the UK, the younger generation follows the lead of American Millennials by being less open to this form of freedom of speech and more willing to allow government restrictions. There are no significant age differences in France, Italy and Poland on this question.

DRAWING CONCLUSIONS

1. The survey data from the United States show that the older people are, the less they want the government to prevent speech offensive to minorities. What reasons do you think might explain this?

2. In analyzing the data, why do you think American women and Democrats are more likely to want government prevention than men and Republicans are?

3. When it comes to the government prevention of offensive speech, why do you think Europeans are more in favor of it than Americans?

Wendy Kaminer

A Civic Duty to Annoy

Although many Americans say they applaud diversity (see Chapter 6), they also often prefer to be among people who think and feel the same way they do. Given the choice, most people would rather be around those who agree with them politically, culturally, and socially. Yet, in the following short essay that appeared in the Atlantic *in September 1997, the best-selling social critic Wendy Kaminer argues that a healthy civic life demands a great deal of disagreement, and that people should be much less sensitive about expressions that may offend them. Resisting the complaints of her privileged students about being "marginalized" or "oppressed," she maintains that "sometimes nurturing students means challenging their complaints instead of satisfying their demands for sympathy."*

An attorney, author, and social critic, Wendy Kaminer has won many awards and has served as president of the National Coalition against Censorship. Her numerous articles and reviews have appeared in such publications as the New York Times, *the* New Republic, *and the* Nation. *She is the author most recently of* Worst Instincts: Cowardice, Conformity, and the ACLU *(2009).*

What is there about being in a room filled with people who agree   1
with me that makes me want to change my mind? Maybe it's the self-congratulatory air of consensus among people who consider themselves and one another right-thinking. Maybe it's the consistency of belief that devolves into mere conformity. Maybe it's just that I can no longer bear to hear the word "empower."

At self-consciously feminist gatherings I feel at home in the worst   2
way. I feel the way I do at family dinners, when I want to put my feet up on the table and say something to provoke old Uncle George. To get George going, I defend affirmative action or the capital-gains tax. To irritate my more orthodox feminist colleagues, I disavow any personal guilt about being born white and middle-class. I scoff every time I hear a Harvard student complain that she's oppressed.

I'm not alone in my irreverence, but feminist pieties combined with   3
feminine courtesy keep most of us in line. Radcliffe College,[1] where I
am based, is devoted to nurturing female undergraduates. We're supposed to nod sympathetically, in solidarity, when a student speaks of
feeling silenced or invisible because she is female, of color, or both.
We're not supposed to point out that Harvard students are among the
most privileged people in the universe, regardless of race or sex.

I don't mean to scoff at the discrimination that a young woman of   4
any color may have experienced or is likely to experience someday. I do
want to remind her that as a student at Harvard/Radcliffe or any other
elite university she enjoys many more advantages than a working-class
white male attending a community college. And the kind of discrimination that students are apt to encounter at Harvard — relatively subtle
and occasional — is not "oppression." It does not systematically deprive
people of basic civil rights and liberties and is not generally sanctioned
by the administration.

Besides, everyone is bound to feel silenced, invisible, or unappreci-   5
ated at least once in a while. Imagine how a white male middle manager
feels when he's about to be downsized. Like laments about dysfunctional
families, complaints about oppression lose their power when proffered so
promiscuously. Melodramatic complaints about oppression at Harvard
are in part developmental: students in their late teens and early twen-
ties are apt to place themselves at the center of the universe. But their
extreme sensitivity reflects frequently criticized cultural trends as well.
An obsession with identity and self-esteem has encouraged students to
assume that every insult or slight is motivated by racist, sexist, or hetero-
sexist bias and gravely threatens their well-being. What's lost is a sense of
perspective. If attending Harvard is oppression, what was slavery?

Sometimes nurturing students means challenging their complaints   6
instead of satisfying their demands for sympathy. I've heard female students declare that any male classmate who makes derogatory remarks
about women online or over the telephone is guilty of sexual harassment
and should be punished. What are we teaching them if we agree? That
they aren't strong enough to withstand a few puerile sexist jokes that
may not even be directed at them? That their male classmates don't have

---

[1] Founded in 1879 in Cambridge, Radcliffe served as the women's college of the
then all-male Harvard University. It didn't fully merge with Harvard until 1999,
two years after Kaminer's essay.

the right to make statements that some women deem offensive? There would be no feminist movement if women never dared to give offense. When nurturing devolves into pandering, feminism gives way to 7 femininity. Recently a small group of female students called for disciplinary proceedings against males wearing "pornographic" T-shirts in a dining hall. They found it difficult to eat lunch in the presence of such unwholesome, sexist images. Should we encourage these young women to believe that they're fragile creatures, with particularly delicate digestive systems? Should we offer them official protection from T-shirts? Or should we point out that a group of pro-choice students might someday wear shirts emblazoned with words or images that pro-life students find deeply disturbing? Should we teach them that the art of giving and taking offense is an art of citizenship in a free society?

That is not a feminine art. Radcliffe, for example, is an unfailingly 8 polite institution. Criticism and dissatisfaction are apt to be expressed in a feminine mode, covertly or indirectly. It's particularly hard for many of us not to react with great solicitude to a student who declares herself marginalized, demeaned, or oppressed, even if we harbor doubts about her claim. If she seeks virtue in oppression, as so many do, we seek it in maternalism.

We tend to forget that criticism sometimes expresses greater respect 9 than praise. It is surely more of an honor than flattery. You challenge a student because you consider her capable of learning. You question her premises because you think she's game enough to re-examine them. You do need to take the measure of her self-confidence, and your own. Teaching — or nurturing — requires that you gain students' trust and then risk having them not like you.

Sometimes withholding sympathy feels mean, insensitive, and 10 uncaring; you acquire all the adjectives that aren't supposed to attach to women. You take on the stereotypically masculine vices at a time when the feminine virtue of niceness is being revived: Rosie O'Donnell[2] is the model talk-show host, civility the reigning civic virtue, and communitarianism the paradigmatic political theory. Communities are exalted, as if the typical community were composed solely of people who shared and cared about one another and never engaged in conflict.

In fact communities are built on compromise, and compromise pre- 11 supposes disagreement. Tolerance presupposes the existence of people and ideas you don't like. It prevails upon you to forswear censoring others

---

[2] Comedian and LGBT activist Rosie O'Donnell (b. 1962) hosted a popular television show from 1996 to 2002.

but not yourself. One test of tolerance is provocation. When you sit down to dinner with your disagreeable relations, or comrades who bask in their rectitude and compassion, you have a civic duty to annoy them.

BACKGROUND AND CONTEXT

1. According to Kaminer's title, it is our "civic duty to annoy." Explain what you think she means. What examples from her essay support your opinion?

2. How would you describe Kaminer's general attitude toward the way people think? What do you make of her opening sentence? How does it help characterize her as an author? What tends to annoy her about conversations she reports in her second paragraph?

STRATEGY, STRUCTURE, AND STYLE

1. Do you agree with Kaminer's statement that "teaching — or nurturing — requires that you gain students' trust and then risk having them not like you" (para. 9)? Have you ever had an experience with a teacher who behaved this way? If so, what did it mean to you?

2. What do you make of the phrase "If she seeks virtue in oppression . . ." (para. 8)? What can make oppression virtuous? Examine the entire sentence: Who is "she" and who is "we"?

COMPARISONS AND CONNECTIONS

1. Kaminer seems to believe that our society has gone too far to protect people from criticism and disappointment in college and social life. Do you agree with her? The essay was published back in 1997 — do you think her point is still relevant? Give a few examples of why or why not.

2. Have you ever exercised your "civic duty to annoy" as Kaminer did when "to irritate . . . [her] more orthodox feminist colleagues," she would "disavow any personal guilt about being born white and middle-class" and "to provoke old Uncle George," she would "defend affirmative action or the capital-gains tax" (para. 2)? If so, write a short essay describing a time you've exercised this duty. Or if not, explain what held you back.

Discussing the Unit

SUGGESTED TOPIC FOR DISCUSSION

While it is constitutionally protected, our right to free speech does not mean we can say anything we want whenever or wherever we want. Should speech be entirely free on a college campus? Do we invite free speech into universities, or do we protect the student body from certain ideas?

PREPARING FOR CLASS DISCUSSION

1. Today's campuses are divided over trigger warnings and what constitutes a microaggression. When might trigger warnings be called for? Is everyone subject to microaggressions, or do they tend to target people historically affected by aggressions large and small?

2. Does your campus tolerate free speech and a free exchange of ideas, whether those ideas are popular or potentially harmful? Have there been times when free speech has been limited or when students have been shielded from certain ideas or messages on your campus? How are these questions raised and these moments discussed in the essays in this chapter?

FROM DISCUSSION TO WRITING

1. Does this chapter provide clues about how past generations might have responded to similar words and situations? Do you think we are less interested today in protecting free speech on campus?

2. Do the writers who favor the use of trigger warnings in this chapter rely on the same arguments? Whether or not you agree with the use of trigger warnings, is there anything that any writer or writers say on this topic that strikes you as particularly persuasive?

TOPICS FOR CROSS-CULTURAL DISCUSSION

1. "Intolerance Doesn't Belong on Campus" (p. 84), "The Coddling of the American Mind" (p. 86), and "How Helicoptered Kids Grow Up to Become Hypersensitive College Students" (p. 102) state that shielding students from certain ideas does them a disservice. Can you make a case against that idea by comparing it with an argument from another essay in this chapter? Do gender and race play a part in that argument? Are gender and race important considerations? Why or why not?

2. Today's professors must navigate the increasingly murky waters of when to give trigger warnings to students and about what materials. Look closely at the student debate in this chapter (p. 96). Where do the debating authors show sensitivity or insensitivity to students suffering from psychological difficulties? Using the debate and at least one other reading in this chapter, make a case that colleges should or should not make accommodations for students suffering from conditions including post-traumatic stress disorder by using trigger warnings.

U.S. History: How Do We Remember Our Past?

The last chapter looked at the state of free speech on America's campuses. And just as students and instructors grapple with the ways they communicate in an ever more diverse setting, another problem hovers over the conversation—the campuses themselves. Many of America's universities were built at a time when racism, sexism, and other forms of discrimination were the default in American life. The names enshrined on college walls and the people celebrated with statues on college greens sometimes carry a dark legacy from a less inclusive past. Universities, like all institutions, want to pay homage to the men and women who built and nurtured them, but this puts students, especially minority students, in a difficult position: Should they blithely accept in their midst monuments and dedications to people who might have denied them their education? Or should they object to things that are largely symbolic, an effort other students sometimes see as petulant and pointless?

Recent years have seen several high-profile flare-ups at American schools over their physical and historical legacies. Many schools, under pressure from students and faculty, renamed buildings and institutions originally named after people who had supported slavery and white supremacy in the past. Amherst College officially shelved its mascot, Lord Jeffery Amherst, an eighteenth-century governor who promoted genocide of

Native Americans. Harvard stopped calling faculty leaders of its residential houses "masters." Although it insisted the word had nothing to do with slavery in its context, the university acknowledged it was troubling to many students. Other efforts have failed to bring about change. Students and faculty at the University of Virginia, founded in 1819 by Thomas Jefferson, America's third president, have called for images of and references to the founder, who owned slaves, to be scrubbed. Members of the communities of the University of Missouri and the College of William and Mary, which also have Jefferson statues, joined the call. So far, those efforts have foundered; Jefferson's image as an intellectual leader seems, for the moment, to trump the more troubling elements of his legacy on campus.

In this chapter, we'll examine how the call for a reevaluation of our public history has played out in the country as a whole. In the chapter's "In Brief," cartoonist Bill Bramhall imagines an extreme example of historical cleansing; notice that the cartoon indicates that "student activists" are responsible, even though its setting is far from campus.

In the real world, perhaps no symbol has stirred up more debate than the Confederate battle flag, which some southerners revere as a token of their heritage. After a white supremacist who flew the flag on his social media pages killed nine people in a historically black Charleston church, South Carolina took the controversial flag down from its statehouse grounds. The debate over the flag's meaning — oppression versus pride — has been raging for years, but a *New York Times* opinion piece by Brent Staples takes a hard line in reminding us of the flag's history as "a rallying symbol embraced by racists, night riders and white supremacy groups dating back to the 19th century."

Historian and journalist Ernest B. Furgurson may not disagree with that history, but he urges us to seek balance and caution in our consideration of historical symbols. "Before we send out the wrecking ball," he says in his own essay on Confederate monuments, "let's do nuance: Where do we start, and where do we stop?" Furgurson urges liberals to apply their very own principles — inclusivity, thoughtfulness, and understanding — to the symbols they would tear down.

Confederate symbols appear largely in one region of the country. What about our shared national legacy? Michael I. Niman takes on one of the most visible national heroes, Christopher Columbus. Niman rebukes the argument of Furgurson and others that we should keep statues up so that we can consider the figures they represent, warts and all. In "As Confederate Flags Fall, Columbus Statues Stand Tall," he argues that these statues are inextricably linked to continued American passivity to racism and other forms of oppression. Niman insists that the image of Columbus as a great explorer distracts us from the fact that his "most significant contribution to history was as the father of the transatlantic slave trade, who presided over a brutal reign of murder and rape shortly after arriving in the new world."

The desire to shake up our images of the past doesn't stop with statuary, though; it can extend into everyday objects, even into our wallets. All seven paper denominations of U.S. currency in circulation feature important figures from American history — and, as of April 2016, all of them were men. (A few women, including Susan B. Anthony, appear on coins.) But in April 2016, the Treasury Department, honoring the request of many women's groups, decided it should boot Andrew Jackson from the front of the twenty-dollar bill and feature Harriet Tubman. In its response to this opinion, "Tubman on the Twenty," the editorial staff of the conservative *National Review* — though approving of the Tubman decision — argues a larger historical point and concludes that "this whole episode has been a product less of considered opinions than of ideological whims."

This chapter's "Spotlight on Data and Research" turns from national concerns over our shared history to a very local one. The town of Whitesboro, New York, population about 3,700, struggled early in 2016 with its town seal, which seems to depict an act of violence against a Native American. Historians argued that, with the proper context, the seal told a story of racial unity, and the town voted to keep it. In the end, though, even the appearance of offense was enough to force Whitesboro to backtrack and ditch the image. A *New York Times* summary of the incident depicts residents' struggle: They " 'wanted to preserve history' while also ensuring that the village was 'seen as the inclusive place that it is.' " Does context matter when history looks ugly at first sight?

And if seals and statues do come down, what should replace them? University of Texas student Adam Hamze writes that our duty is not just to dismantle embarrassing or offensive historical markers, but to substitute better, more diverse ones. "There is only one statue on campus dedicated to a black Texan," Hamze writes, "although there have been countless contributions to the state by black individuals, many of whom have been underappreciated." He makes a case for a new statue to replace one of a Confederate leader, but provokes questions about how our colleges, our communities, and even our country ought to remember our past.

Finally, we return to the beginning of European America, with an up-close look at the legacy of Christopher Columbus. This chapter's "America Then" features Michele de Cuneo, a friend of Columbus who accompanied him on his second voyage and tells a story sometimes at odds with the heroism suggested by statues and monuments all over America. How can we tell history in a way that's fair not just to men like Columbus but to everyone in the story? Should we try to understand historical figures in their context? Or should we strive to cleanse ourselves of the horrors of the past by putting them, and their perpetrators, behind us?

Bill Bramhall

Mt. Rushmore: Student Activists Demanded Their Removal

[*New York Daily News*, November 23, 2015]

*M*ount Rushmore, a massive statue in the Black Hills of South Dakota where the faces of four American presidents seem to spring out of the natural world, is one of the country's most famous and enduring national monuments. In this cartoon, Bill Bramhall imagines its somewhat grotesque removal as a reflection on the "cleansing" of history by taking down statues and names some people find offensive. A park ranger tells some clearly disappointed tourists that the four faces — all of older white men who have been in charge of the country — have been toppled, because "student activists demanded their removal."

Bill Bramhall © New York Daily News, L.P. Used with permission.

POINTS TO CONSIDER

1. Why does the park ranger refer to "student activists"? Mount Rushmore is not on a college campus, and university movements to remove markers

of the past considered offensive include both students and faculty. How does limiting the complainants to students subtly discredit the movement Bramhall is imagining? How does the word *demanded* further argue against the students' point of view?

2. The means of dismantling Mount Rushmore that the cartoon imagines — blowing up the presidents' heads — is especially violent. What does this achieve for the cartoonist and his point of view?

3. Why does Bramhall use Mount Rushmore as his extreme example? Why does removing the massive granite memorial seem so obviously unreasonable? Do you agree with Bramhall that removing the heads would be unreasonable? What arguments might there be for "their removal"?

Brent Staples

Confederate Memorials as Instruments of Racial Terror

[*The New York Times*, July 24, 2015]

BEFORE YOU READ
Who should have a say in which memorials get placed in public places to honor our nation's history? Why are more people weighing in on this issue now than ever before?

WORDS TO LEARN
barbaric (para. 1): very rude or offensive (adjective)

unleashed (para. 2): caused something (powerful) to happen suddenly (verb)

reign (para. 2): period of time during which sovereign power is exercised (noun)

enlightened (para. 6): informed (adjective)

reactionary (para. 6): having to do with extreme conservatism or right-wing political leanings (adjective)

expunged (para. 8): erased (verb)

antipathy (para. 10): strong feeling of dislike (noun)

subjugation (para. 11): enslavement (noun)

valorized (para. 12): validated (verb)

Brent Staples is an author and a journalist for the New York Times. *His work focuses on politics and cultural issues, and he has published two books:* Parallel Time: Growing Up in Black and White *(1995) and* An American Love Story *(1999).*

T he Confederate-flag-waving[1] white supremacist charged with 1
murdering nine African-Americans in a Charleston, S.C., church
in June [2015] demolished the fiction that the flag was an innoc-
uous symbol of "Southern pride." This barbaric act made it impossible
for politicians to hide from the fact that the Confederate banner has been
a rallying symbol embraced by racists, night riders and white supremacy
groups dating back to the 19th century.

This long-denied truth applies as well to Confederate memorials 2
that occupy public space all over the South. Most were erected in the
late 19th and early 20th centuries, when the Southern states were eagerly
dismantling the rights and liberties that African-Americans had enjoyed
just after the Civil War, during Reconstruction.[2] These states unleashed
a racialized reign of terror and shored up white supremacy by rewriting
their Constitutions to disqualify African-Americans from full citizenship.

As nonpersons in the eyes of the state, black people had no standing 3
to challenge the rush of Civil War nostalgia that led the South to stock its
parks and public squares with symbols that celebrated the Confederate
cause of slavery and instilled racial fear. Only in recent decades have
black elected officials and some whites started to push back against the
Confederate narrative of Southern civic life.

In the wake of the Charleston massacre, for example, the parks and 4
recreation board of Birmingham, Ala., voted to explore a proposal that
would remove a 52-foot Confederate memorial from the entrance of a
prominent park and place it with a Confederate heritage group.

Not all monuments warrant that kind of challenge. But those hon- 5
oring the Confederate general Nathan Bedford Forrest deserve the backlash they have generated. Forrest presided over the 1864 massacre of
Union soldiers, many of them black, at Fort Pillow in Tennessee. He was
also a prominent slave trader and served as the first grand wizard of the
Ku Klux Klan.[3]

Apologists argue that his involvement with the Klan was unimpor- 6
tant because he later adopted more enlightened views. But as the Forrest

---

[1] Confederate (para. 1): The eleven states that seceded from the Union from
1861 to 1865 and formed the Confederacy: Virginia, North Carolina, South
Carolina, Georgia, Mississippi, Alabama, Florida, Louisiana, Texas, Arkansas,
and Tennessee

[2] Reconstruction (para. 2): The period following the Civil War in which the
government set the terms for the Southern states' reentry into the Union

[3] Ku Klux Klan (para. 5): An organization designed to terrorize African
Americans and other groups with violence in order to promote white supremacy and white nationalism

biographer Jack Hurst writes, by lending his name to the K.K.K. even temporarily, the general accelerated its development. "As the Klan's first national leader," Mr. Hurst writes, "he became the Lost Cause's avenging angel, galvanizing a loose collection of boyish secret social clubs into a reactionary instrument of terror still feared today."

Protests erupted in Selma, Ala., in 2000 when a bust of Forrest was   7
unveiled on the grounds of a museum. (One critic likened it to erecting a statue of Hitler in a Jewish neighborhood.) The sculpture was subsequently moved to a cemetery.

> One critic likened it to erecting a statue of Hitler in a Jewish neighborhood.

Two years ago, the Memphis City Coun-   8
cil expunged Confederate names from three parks, one of them named in honor of Forrest. The Council argued that the names were inappropriate for a majority-black city and inconsistent with the cosmopolitan image that Memphis wished to cultivate. The Ku Klux Klan marched in protest.

The Council went further this month, when it voted to begin the   9
process of removing the towering statue of Forrest from what is now known as Health Sciences Park. The plan also calls for removing the remains of Forrest and his wife, which were moved from their original graves and transferred to the park in 1905.

Memphis leaders are not alone in their antipathy toward Forrest.   10
Just days after the Charleston killings in June, Bill Haslam, Tennessee's Republican governor, said he supported removing a bust of Forrest from the state Capitol, adding that the general was not someone he would choose to honor.

Critics predictably condemn these efforts as bad-faith attempts to   11
rewrite history. But what's happening is that communities that were once bound and gagged on this issue are now free to contest a version of history that was created to reinforce racial subjugation.

They are reflecting on how to honor history — including the ne-   12
glected history of African-Americans — and rightly deciding that some figures who were enshrined as heroes in the past do not deserve to be valorized in public places.

VOCABULARY/USING A DICTIONARY

1. When something is *demolished* (para. 1), what happens to it?

2. What prefix and word make up the word *dismantling* (para. 2)? How do you define it?

3. If the Confederate flag is a *rallying* (para. 1) symbol, what does it do?

RESPONDING TO WORDS IN CONTEXT

1. What does *shored* (para. 2) mean in this context? What part of speech is it here?

2. If Memphis wants to present a *cosmopolitan* (para. 8) image, what image is it trying to project?

3. What part of speech is *contest* (para. 11) in this essay? What other parts of speech can this word be?

DISCUSSING MAIN POINT AND MEANING

1. What recent event has called into question the Confederate flag as merely a symbol of "Southern pride" (para. 1)?

2. Does Brent Staples think all Confederate memorials should be removed? Which ones does he think should be removed? Which ones does he think should stay?

3. Why do some people object to the statue of Nathan Bedford Forrest? Why would some choose to erect such a memorial?

EXAMINING SENTENCES, PARAGRAPHS, AND ORGANIZATION

1. How much attention does Staples devote to Nathan Bedford Forrest's memorialization? Are Staples's remarks about the honoring of this particular general important to his argument? Why or why not?

2. In his opening paragraph, Staples asserts that the Confederate flag has finally been exposed as a racist symbol. He begins the second paragraph by writing, "This long-denied truth applies as well to Confederate memorials that occupy public space all over the South." What do you think of Staples's transition from one idea to the next? Are his transitions effective and well connected?

3. Characterize the way in which Staples presents his material. Would you describe his approach as personal, historical, or analytical, or would you use some other term? Explain.

THINKING CRITICALLY

1. Do you think that the current debate over Confederate war memorials indicates that communities are "reflecting on how to honor history" (para. 12)? Explain.

2. When people are deciding whether or not to honor a particular public figure, do they consider some offenses to be worse than others? Who should decide where to draw the line?

3. Do you believe that efforts to remove some Confederate memorials are "bad-faith attempts to rewrite history" (para. 11)? How does Staples explain what's happening?

WRITING ACTIVITIES

1. How often do you look at war memorials and notice whether they honor a particular ideology? Can you think of war memorials that would not offend the opposing side in the war? Are any inclusive? Consider a memorial that someone—it can be you, if applicable—finds offensive, or consider one that you believe helps a diverse group of people honor their history.

2. When recounting how the Forrest statue was received in Selma, Alabama, Staples notes that "one critic likened it to erecting a statue of Hitler in a Jewish neighborhood" (para. 7). Consider this comparison and write a brief essay that explains how the erection of the Forrest statue in Selma is analogous to erecting a statue of Hitler in a Jewish neighborhood, conducting research as needed.

3. In small groups, brainstorm figures who are neglected in history but who might deserve to have statues or memorials erected. Once you have at least a page of little-recognized, but important, historical figures, report back to the class and compare your findings.

Ernest B. Furgurson

The End of History?

[*The American Scholar*, Autumn 2015]

BEFORE YOU READ

Where do you stand in the debate over war memorials, particularly Civil War memorials? How do you think history should be honored?

WORDS TO LEARN

nuance (para. 2): a subtle difference (noun)

obelisk (para. 3): a tall, four-sided stone column that tapers at the top (noun)

rearguard (para. 7): part of a military formation that protects the back of the troops (often during retreat) (noun)

Ernest B. Furgurson is a former correspondent and columnist for the Baltimore Sun. *A historian and biographer, Furgurson has written a number of books, including* Chancellorsville 1863 *(1993),* Ashes of Glory *(1997),* Not War but Murder *(2001), and* Freedom Rising *(2005).*

vigorous (para. 7): strong or active (adjective)

eloquently (para. 10): fluently or expressively (adverb)

egregious (para. 11): glaring or flagrant (adjective)

conspicuously (para. 11): noticeably (adverb)

With the lowering of the Confederate battle flag in South Carolina and elsewhere, some diehards still insist that the banner had nothing to do with race, that it was just a symbol of their Southern heritage. Other Americans long offended by the Confederate monuments that stand all across Dixie are urging that those memorials come down along with the flag. Still others clarify the matter in three words: black lives matter, spray-painted on monuments north and south. Somewhere amid all this, I am trying to place myself.   1

So far, the debate lacks nuance. It seems simple: the Confederate States of America existed to preserve slavery, so anything honoring its memory should be erased from modern America. But before we send out the wrecking ball, let's do nuance: Where do we start, and where do we stop?   2

> So far, the debate lacks nuance.

What about statues that were cast to mourn for the dead, erected not by the Ku Klux Klan or its descendants, but by grieving widows? Should those in graveyards be allowed to stand? What about the memorial in Green Hill Cemetery in my hometown, Danville, Virginia? It's a tall obelisk erected in 1878 by the Ladies Memorial Association, standing in what is today a mostly black neighborhood. It's a monument to the dead, but it's by no means neutral. It features bas-reliefs of Robert E. Lee and Stonewall Jackson, and says,   3

> Patriots! Know that these fell in the effort to establish just government and perpetuate Constitutional Liberty. Who thus die, will live in lofty example.

If it should go, what about the simple government-issued headstone nearby, which identifies my Civil War great-grandfather as "1st Sgt Co I 53rd Va Infantry," and thousands of others like it?

What about Monument Avenue in Richmond, with its grand likenesses of Lee, Jackson, Jefferson Davis, J. E. B. Stuart, Matthew Fontaine Maury? Might we differentiate between fiery politicians such as Davis, who wasn't even a Virginian, and the generals they dragged into war? If the generals should go, then what about the privates who marched because their neighbors did, defending slavery even though they never   4 owned a slave? What about the statues of Confederate soldiers standing before hundreds of county courthouses? Most face north defiantly, muskets at the ready. But others, like the one facing south in the center of Alexandria, Virginia, are unarmed, hats off, heads bowed, clearly mourning fallen comrades. Shall we appoint committees to decide what each sculptor was thinking? You're right: this could get silly.

But suppose we did decide to tear those down — what about all   5
the other reminders of our shameful past? Mount Vernon, Monticello, Montpelier, and the other homes of our slave-owning presidents? What about the statues of Confederate soldiers on every Civil War battlefield site?

To take down every offensive monument in the South willy-nilly   6
reminds me of the wholesale de-Stalinization campaign that I witnessed in the old Soviet Union, and the destruction of ancient monuments by ISIS and Taliban fanatics today. Totalitarian states may decree that the painful past never happened, but any such official effort in our country, even one executed selectively, would be tragic.

Saying all this, and considering my ancestors, I might be shrugged   7
off as just another rearguard Rebel. I qualify four times over for membership in the Sons of Confederate Veterans, vigorous defenders of their heritage and its symbols. Because I'd written Civil War history, I was invited about 20 years ago to speak to the SCV camp in Alexandria. In my talk, I recalled my great-grandfather who died of smallpox in the Yankee prison at Fort Delaware, and the three others who were wounded later in the war. The Sons were impressed. And then I told them that the Confederate battle flag was a provocation that should be retired to the museum. I haven't been invited back.

The punch line of that talk was a pale version of everything I've said   8
and written about race and racism since I did my first column for the late, lamented *Danville Commercial Appeal* at the age of 18. Yet, because I remain concerned that I might be misunderstood when I suggest going slow in the current debate, I've let others say what I've been thinking.

Mayor Stephanie Rawlings-Blake of Baltimore, with hard-earned   9
experience trying to cool public anger, has wisely punted these matters by naming a committee to dig into the issue and stir public dialogue. Roger Davidson Jr., a professor at Baltimore's Coppin State University — who, like the mayor, is African American — thinks that demolishing the monuments would be "horrible" because they can be teaching tools about a chapter still misunderstood by too many people.

New York Times editorialist Brent Staples [see previous selection on   10
p. 118], who has written eloquently about growing up black, strongly supports removing statues of villains like Confederate general Nathan Bedford

Forrest, who was a postwar organizer of the Klan. Such efforts are not "bad-faith attempts to rewrite history," he says, but reflections on "how to honor history . . . and rightly deciding that some figures who were enshrined as heroes in the past do not deserve to be valorized in public places."

Interesting that Staples says "some figures," which may suggest just 11 the most egregious offenders, or just Confederates. But neither he nor the mayor nor the professor nor I want to start bulldozing without serious "reflections on how to honor history." For me, that should mean enshrining other heroes at least as conspicuously as the ones who now stir such passions.

Imagine Martin Luther King Jr. standing tall in the capital of every 12 state in the old Confederacy, indeed the whole Union . . . Move Arthur Ashe's token memorial off Monument Avenue and put a grander one on the broad Boulevard nearby, renaming it Ashe Boulevard. Along it, raise Powhatan Beaty, Decatur Dorsey, and Edward Ratcliff, who fled slavery in Virginia to join the U.S. Colored Troops and won the Medal of Honor fighting for freedom . . . Erect Thurgood Marshall, Sojourner Truth, Frederick Douglass, Medgar Evers, Crispus Attucks, A. Philip Randolph, Dred Scott, Rosa Parks, Harriet Tubman . . . The list stretches from 1619 into tomorrow.

If we're going to honor our history, let us honor all of it. 13

VOCABULARY/USING A DICTIONARY

1. What is a *widow* (para. 3)?

2. How would you describe something that happens *willy-nilly* (para. 6)?

3. What is the definition of *totalitarian* (para. 6)? What part of speech is it?

RESPONDING TO WORDS IN CONTEXT

1. If the soldiers depicted are mourning their *comrades* (para. 4), whom are they mourning?

2. If a matter is *punted* (para. 9), what does that mean? When is the word *punted* likely to be used?

3. What is the meaning of *provocation* (para. 7)? From what language does it derive?

DISCUSSING MAIN POINT AND MEANING

1. What two main questions does Furgurson believe are important to ask before we decide how to rethink our memorials?

2. Does Furgurson suggest we should remove all offensive memorials? Why or why not?

3. How does Furgurson think history should be honored?

EXAMINING SENTENCES, PARAGRAPHS, AND ORGANIZATION

1. What do you notice about Furgurson's conclusion? Why do you think he ends his essay the way he does?

2. In his opening paragraph, Furgurson outlines different positions taken on war memorials and the idea of reconsidering their place in our public spaces. He states, "Somewhere amid all this, I am trying to place myself" (para. 1). Does he explore these positions thoroughly in his body paragraphs?

3. It is fine for a writer to take different positions into account in an essay — often it makes an essay stronger — but many essays present one particular position, known as the thesis. In Furgurson's essay, which sentence do you think is closest to his thesis?

THINKING CRITICALLY

1. Why does Furgurson hesitate to get rid of Confederate memorials?

2. Is it surprising that Furgurson moves from a discussion of removing Confederate monuments to a discussion of getting rid of Mount Vernon, Monticello, and Montpelier? Why or why not?

3. Based on the arguments Furgurson presents, do you think Mayor Rawlings-Blake will find any consensus by forming "a committee to dig into the issue and stir public dialogue" (para. 9)? Explain.

WRITING ACTIVITIES

1. Copy the names of the other heroes Furgurson suggests. If you don't recognize a name, do a quick online search to familiarize yourself. Choose one name and make a case in writing for why that person's contributions were valuable to society and why a statue or memorial should be erected in his or her honor. Describe the sort of memorial you envision and where it would be placed.

2. Looking at the names you copied out for question 1, think about another person *not already on the list* whom the public might want to see honored with a memorial. Would that person's name fit in this particular list? Why or why not? Whether the name belongs in this list or not, write a portrait of the individual you have chosen and explain why that person's contributions were valuable to society. Discuss the reasons for a memorial in small groups, as if you and your classmates were members of a committee choosing to honor one individual. In discussion, determine if any of your reasons for wanting to memorialize someone are the same as those of the other group members.

3. Create an outline of the main points Furgurson uses in his essay. What is this essay about? What conclusion does Furgurson reach at the end? Furgurson states in the beginning: "Somewhere amid all this, I am trying to place myself" (para. 1). Construct an *if . . . then* statement that reflects Furgurson's position at the end of the essay.

Michael I. Niman

As Confederate Flags Fall, Columbus Statues Stand Tall

[*The Public*, October 12, 2015]

BEFORE YOU READ

Many people in the United States identify the Confederate flag as a racist symbol and question its presence in public places. Do you believe statues of Christopher Columbus should be subject to the same deliberation? What do you know about Columbus? How has he been presented to you as a historical figure?

WORDS TO LEARN

treasonous (para. 1): traitorous (adjective)

resurgence (para. 1): growth or increase (noun)

desegregation (para. 1): the process of ending a law or practice that kept people separate (noun)

subjugation (para. 1): enslavement (noun)

genocidal (para. 2): having to do with the extermination of a group that shares a common identity (adjective)

moniker (para. 2): name (noun)

boycott (para. 2): protest (by refusing to buy or participate in something) (noun)

vandalism (para. 4): the act of deliberately destroying property (noun)

snitch (para. 4): to inform on someone (verb)

recap (para. 6): to give a concise summary (verb)

meticulous (para. 6): careful and exact (adjective)

Michael I. Niman is a professor of journalism and critical media studies at Buffalo State College whose work has appeared in Truthout, The Humanist, Artvoice, AlterNet, *and* ColdType, *among many other publications. He is the author of* People of the Rainbow: A Nomadic Utopia *(2nd ed., 2011).*

commodity (para. 7): something bought and sold (noun)

subsequent (para. 7): happening after something else (adjective)

graphically (para. 8): clearly (adverb)

forte (para. 9): one's strong point (noun)

persistence (para. 10): perseverance (adjective)

infrastructure (para. 15): underlying framework (noun)

municipal (para. 16): relating to local government (adjective)

contentious (para. 16): quarrelsome (adjective)

South Carolina removed the Confederate battle flag from its state-house grounds this summer. Walmart removed it from its stores. Virginia is removing it from vanity license plates. Ridding popular culture of this racist symbol is long overdue, considering the stars and bars first rose to support a treasonous rebellion in support of state-supported white supremacy, manifested in the most grotesque fashion as legally sanctioned enslavement, wanton murder, and rape of black Americans. The flag later had a resurgence beginning in the 1940s, with white supremacists raising it in opposition to civil rights and desegregation. It's not the Southern heritage of lemonade and hospitality that Confederate symbol represents, but this darker heritage of white privilege and the horrific subjugation of blacks — and no number of *Dukes of Hazzard*[1] reruns can erase that. 1

Also this year, the Lancaster, New York, school board voted unanimously to change the racist name of their high school sports teams. The original name began its life in the 19th century, referring to the dried scalp-skins of Native Americans which could be exchanged for cash by bounty hunters during a genocidal period of American history. Supporters of the racist name protested and, in a last-ditch effort to keep their town in the middle 1800s, imported a rather random Native American from South Dakota and a Cuban Indian impersonator from Connecticut to testify that they were okay with the racist moniker. The school board, however, feeling the tidal pull of the 21st century — and, probably more importantly, confronting a growing boycott of their teams by other schools — ditched the name. 2

It seemed like we were finally confronting the enduring symbols of our racist past, albeit with tiny baby steps. 3

---

[1] *The Dukes of Hazzard* (para. 1): A long-running TV show that aired in 1979 about two country boys who were outlaws. Their getaway car, known as the General Lee, had a large Confederate flag on its hood.

PECCA VESTRA EXPONUNTUR

Sometime over the Labor Day weekend, someone, or some group of   4
people, painted a rather accurate history lesson on the City of Buffalo's
Christopher Columbus statue, located in Columbus Park on the city's
Lower West Side, adjacent to a neighborhood that hosts one of New York
State's largest urban Native American communities. Three local TV news
crews covered the story on September 7 (Time Warner Cable News)
and 8 (WIVB and WGRZ), all contextualizing the incident as vandalism
and asking viewers to snitch out the writers to police, with two reports
broadcasting a tip line number.

The writers painted the word "rape" across the front of the statue's base,   5
"slaver" on one side, "genocide" on another. Most interestingly, they wrote
the Latin phrase *"pecca vestra exponuntur,"* which translates to "your sins are
exposed," across the back of the base. All three television crews chose to
ignore this last message; one (WIVB) also ignored "slaver," while another
(TWC) misstated it as "slave," which would reverse the meaning. None of
the reporters expressed any understanding of the context of the story —
why, in the run-up to Columbus Day, these messages appeared, or why
other writers have been painting similar messages on this statue for decades.

To quickly recap the history behind the Columbus myth: The char-   6
acter of Christopher Columbus, "the great discoverer," was created in
1828 by the American writer, Washington Irving, as a piece of historical fiction based on the life of Cristóbal Colón. Colón, along with other
members of the "voyages of discovery," kept logs and took meticulous
notes in journals, leaving a strong record of evidence describing events
from multiple perspectives. These logs and journals exist to this day in
the Spanish archives and paint a pretty damning picture of Colón. Far
from being the fabled explorer who argued to an unbelieving world that
the earth was round, Colón actually lived out his life arguing that it was
pear-shaped even though the concept of a round earth was well accepted
by 1492. His most significant contribution to history was as the father of
the transatlantic slave trade, who presided over a brutal reign of murder
and rape shortly after arriving in the new world.

When he did not find gold in the Caribbean, Colón looked for an   7
alternative commodity to satisfy his investors and win funding for subsequent voyages. That commodity turned out to be his hosts, the Taino
people. Colón, impressed by their friendliness, generosity, and peaceful
nature, wrote in his journal that "They are the best people in the world
and above all the gentlest." What this meant, he wrote, was that "with 50
men they could all be subjected and made to do all that one might wish."
The Taino, he explained, were "fit to be ordered about, to sow, and do
everything else that may be needed."

Colón captured up what he described as "seven head of women,   8
young ones and adults, and three small children" to bring back to Spain
as cargo, along with exotic birds and fruits. This act by Colón, who
claimed previous experience as a slave trader in Africa, laid the precedent
and foundation for one of the darkest chapters in world history — the
transatlantic slave trade, which, after most of the indigenous population
in the Caribbean was worked to death or killed by genocide and disease,
thrived bringing captured Africans to the Americas. The journals from
Colón's voyages graphically document acts of rape and depraved brutal-
ity, beyond the pale even for 15th-century Europe. There is no place in
any American city for a statue of this man, much less a holiday in his
honor.

The TWC reporter sought his explanation for the Columbus statue   9
"vandalism" from a confused passerby, who explained to viewers that
the writers must be "ignorant people with small minds" who "do stupid
things," which, he added, "doesn't make any sense." Seeking out folks for
comment based solely on the fact that they are clueless on the subject
matter seems to be a forte of Buffalo television news reporters.

The fact that news producers chose to broadcast this embarrassing   10
idiocy speaks volumes not only about the crisis of journalism but about
the epidemic of ignorance regarding issues of racism. One of the most
noticeable aspects of white privilege is the privilege to remain ignorant
of, or just not give a damn about, the persistence of racism. TWC's interview subject concluded that "The statue isn't bothering anybody and has
been there for years." The ignorance exemplified by this reporting clues
us in to why it's still there. . . .

There are Columbus statues and place names around the United   11
States; only George Washington has more cities, roads, parks, etc. named
after him. As more people continue to become historically literate about
the Colón legacy, the continued existence of these tributes has become
more controversial and offensive to larger segments of the population.

In Buffalo, TWC interviewed Niagara District Councilman David   12
Rivera on camera about the writing on the Columbus statue. Rivera
promised, "We're going to be looking at what we can do to find the folks"
who did the writing. The TWC reporter also claimed in their report that
"with Columbus Day approaching next month, Rivera says the statue's
historical value should still be respected." In an interview for this column, Rivera denies this interpretation of what he said, which doesn't
appear on-camera on TWC's televised report. Instead he explained that
he is fully aware of the history surrounding Colón and is sympathetic to
complaints about the statue and the name of the park.

BRING IT ON

Rivera went on to explain how the Buffalo City Council voted unani-   13
mously in June of this year to change the name of an island in the Niagara
River from Squaw Island to Unity Island after Seneca Nation leaders
complained about the racist and misogynist name — a name that dates
back more than three centuries. Rivera's complaint about the painting
of the Columbus statue, he reiterated, is against the method of protest,
which he considers damaging public property, rather than the sentiment
of the protest or the accuracy of the message. Yes, "Columbus" was a
rapist and slaver, but the statue honoring his legacy is protected public
property. Rivera suggests that activists protest legally and petition the
city government with any demands or complaints regarding the statue.

Buffalo's Columbus statue, like others around the country, is liter-   14
ally anchored by a deep foundation. Once erected, it's hard to muster the
funding and political capital to tear such things down, no matter what
they represent and whom they offend. Rivera uses the Unity Island case,
however, to argue that city government is open to responding to protests
and petitions. What they would be willing to do, however, would likely
depend on the strength of the protests and political threats generated by
such protests. Anything is possible. The Unity Island name change came
after more than three centuries. In historical terms, the Columbus statue,
despite being anchored in stone, is just an adolescent, dating back only
63 years.

> Given our nation's
> history, many
> cities are saddled
> with such racist
> infrastructure.

Given our nation's history, many cities   15
are saddled with such racist infrastructure.
As the political class in the country becomes
more diverse, there increase the demands to
end the whitewashing of American history
and challenge the mythology that distorts
the teaching of history. How municipali-
ties deal with this infrastructure is reveal-
ing. Government officials in Alabama still refuse to change the name
of the Edmund Pettus Bridge, for example, despite the fact that the
high-visibility bridge, scene to historic 1965 police attacks on civil rights
protesters, is named after a grand dragon of the Ku Klux Klan.

PLYMOUTH ROCKS

By contrast, the town of Plymouth, Massachusetts, erected a monument   16
near their historic rock, honoring the National Day of Mourning, which is
a Native American alternative to Thanksgiving. Cast in bronze, the monument explains why many Native Americans don't celebrate the arrival

of the Pilgrims, referencing how, to Native Americans, Thanksgiving "is a reminder of the genocide of millions of their people, the theft of their lands, and the relentless assault on their culture." The Plymouth monument goes on to explain that the National Day of Mourning honors "Native ancestors and the struggles of Native peoples to survive today . . . as well as a protest of the racism and oppression which Native Americans continue to experience." In a similar vein, Neto Hatinakwe Onkwehonwe, a Native American arts and cultural organization, erected a monument in Buffalo at a public park at the mouth of Lake Erie. The Neto monument offers an alternative to an older municipal monument emblazoned with a historically contentious narrative about warlike Indians. Five years ago, however, the City of Buffalo hired a Missouri restoration firm to renew its Columbus statue.

In an era when Confederate flags and racist team names are regularly   17 being challenged around the country; when the narratives on other historical monuments meet empirical challenges cast in bronze and stone; and decades after Eastern Europeans demonstrated how statues, in their case hundreds of statues of Lenin, can be torn down, our Columbus statues continue to stand tall as enduring symbols of racism beyond the reach of change.

VOCABULARY/USING A DICTIONARY

1. What does it mean to be in *opposition* (para. 1) to something or someone?

2. What does an *impersonator* (para. 2) do?

3. What sort of word is *albeit* (para. 3)?

RESPONDING TO WORDS IN CONTEXT

1. If a school board voted *unanimously* (para. 2) to change the name of its high school team, what percentage of members voted in favor of changing the name?

2. What is a *last-ditch* (para. 2) effort?

3. What is a *fabled* (para. 6) explorer?

DISCUSSING MAIN POINT AND MEANING

1. What two events give Niman hope that we are confronting our past and dealing with symbols of past racism?

2. Does Niman understand and accept the journalists' confusion about and reaction to what happened to the Columbus statue? How do you know?

3. Does this essay "challenge the mythology" (para. 15) of what we're taught about our history? Where does it do that?

EXAMINING SENTENCES, PARAGRAPHS, AND ORGANIZATION

1. The essay's subjects are grouped in several distinct parts. What are they?

2. The title is "As Confederate Flags Fall, Columbus Statues Stand Tall." Is this title misleading? Why or why not?

3. What is the effect of including Christopher Columbus's own words in the essay?

THINKING CRITICALLY

1. The Buffalo news channels seem conflicted about what to make of it, but why do you think the messages "*pecca vestra exponuntur*," "rape," "slaver," and "genocide" were painted on a Christopher Columbus statue?

2. What is the biggest revelation about Christopher Columbus, "fabled explorer" (para. 6), in this essay?

3. What is the National Day of Mourning? Why was a monument erected near Plymouth Rock to honor the National Day of Mourning?

WRITING ACTIVITIES

1. Write an outline for an essay describing the vandalism of the Christopher Columbus statue. Given the information that you know, what do you want to be sure to include in your essay? What questions do you want to try to answer in your essay? Take some notes on what you know about Columbus, as well as notes that attempt to place the vandalism story in historical context.

2. Niman refers to the "whitewashing of American history" in paragraph 15. What does this mean? Think of the history you know. Is it "whitewashed"? Write down a few examples of history that you learned about from a common source like schools, books, or television. Discuss the examples you've chosen. Explain why you think the history you learned is, or is not, whitewashed.

3. In a freewriting exercise, consider the phrase *pecca vestra exponuntur*. Write down some questions as prompts before you begin. For instance, why would someone choose to write a message in Latin? What is the weight of each word ("your sins are exposed")? What does this phrase have to do with Columbus? Why would someone write on his statue?

National Review Editorial Board

Tubman on the Twenty

[*National Review*, April 21, 2016]

BEFORE YOU READ
Should substitutions be made to replace the original faces on paper money?
Why are these changes being proposed?

WORDS TO LEARN

faction (para. 1): a group within a larger group (noun)

chaperone (para. 2): an older person who accompanies or helps a younger person (noun)

staunch (para. 2): steadfast (adjective)

outweigh (para. 3): to exceed (verb)

facilitate (para. 4): to assist (verb)

episode (para. 5): incident (noun)

whims (para. 5): odd or sudden desires (noun)

fortuitous (para. 5): lucky (adjective)

array (para. 5): arrangement (noun)

accommodate (para. 5): to oblige (verb)

suffrage (para. 6): the right to vote (noun)

prompt (para. 7): to encourage an action (verb)

aesthetic (para. 7): relating to ideas of beauty (adjective)

contretemps (para. 7): unfortunate or embarrassing event (noun)

extent (para. 7): degree (noun)

progressive (para. 7): favoring progress and reform (adjective)

Last year, a faction of the feminist Left discovered that it was being oppressed by the absence of a woman on at least one piece of America's paper currency. After much baying from activists, Treasury Secretary Jack Lew has struck upon a reasonable compromise. Lew announced on Wednesday that the place of Alexander Hamilton, currently experiencing a historical renascence, on the $10 bill is safe. Instead, Harriet Tubman, the great abolitionist, will replace Andrew Jackson on the front of the $20 bill, and the seventh president will be moved to the back.

Tubman is an admirable choice. Not only was she a courageous chaperone along the Underground Railroad, responsible for escorting more than 300 slaves to freedom; she was also a scout and spy for the Union Army, the first woman in American history to lead a military raid (against Combahee Ferry, in South Carolina, where she helped liberate

1

2

The National Review *is a conservative weekly journal founded in 1955.*

more than 700 slaves), a Republican, a devout Christian, and a staunch defender of the right to bear arms.

Andrew Jackson, for his part, was a giant of American history, and   3
the animating spirit of the Democratic party. But moods change, and in the current public consciousness, Jackson's considerable flaws have come to outweigh his also considerable merits. If there is a reason to remove Jackson from the currency, perhaps it should simply be that he hated paper money.

Meanwhile, Lew's compromise leaves Alexander Hamilton on the   4
$10 bill. And as long as great Americans adorn our currency, it would be difficult to think of a person more deserving than Hamilton, who not only was one of the original American rags-to-riches stories but was also, as the first secretary of the Treasury, responsible for establishing the national financial structure that facilitated the greatest engine of prosperity in human history: the American economy. If Hamilton does not deserve a place on our money, who does?

Unfortunately, though, this whole episode has been a product less   5
of considered opinions than of ideological whims. Hamilton became a target not out of any principled opposition, but because feminists decided that it was time for our currency to boast "a woman," and the
$10 bill was next due to be redesigned, in 2019.

| The notes and coins of our currency are not national monuments. |

(Incidentally, Hamilton also was saved by timing: the fortuitous opening of a hit Broadway musical about his life.) The notes and coins of our currency are not national monuments — they are periodically redesigned to reflect shifts in national values, and the American public clearly wants currency that showcases a more diverse array of Americans who have contributed to the ongoing work of winning liberty and justice for all — but decisions about who adorns our currency shouldn't be made to accommodate momentary fancies.

Resisting that temptation will be harder, given the slate of changes   6
the Treasury Department is planning beyond the $20 bill. According to Lew, the $10 bill will be redesigned to display on its back, instead of the Treasury building, portraits of leaders of the women's-suffrage movement. And the back of the $5 bill will be refashioned to include images of Martin Luther King Jr., Eleanor Roosevelt, and opera singer-cum-civil-rights activist Marian Anderson.

Each of those persons made valuable contributions to the American   7
way of life. But printing a *Who's Who*[1] volume on the currency is sure to

---

[1] *Who's Who* (para. 7): A directory, published annually, of notable people

prompt calls to include a representative from this cause and that one. After all, why not Cesar Chavez? Why not Harvey Milk? And it prompts straightforward aesthetic concerns: Who wants a dollar bill that looks like a photo album? This contretemps highlights, once again, the extent to which the histories of particular groups and interests are now so often preferred to a larger, unifying American history. The current administration may have satisfied progressive demands momentarily. But we'll be fighting this battle again, soon enough. You can put money on it.

VOCABULARY/USING A DICTIONARY

1. What did the *abolitionists* (para. 1) do?

2. The word *animating* (para. 3) is related to what word? What part of speech is *animating* here?

3. What does a period of *prosperity* (para. 4) look like?

RESPONDING TO WORDS IN CONTEXT

1. What is a *renascence* (para. 1)? Is it different from a *renaissance*?

2. In paragraphs 4 and 5, the authors choose the word *adorn* when speaking of the placement of people on U.S. currency. Is this word appropriate? Why is this word used?

3. The authors use the word *compromise* (para. 4) when speaking of the decision to leave Hamilton on the ten-dollar bill and replace Jackson with Tubman on the twenty. How is this move a *compromise*?

DISCUSSING MAIN POINT AND MEANING

1. According to this essay, why is Tubman a good choice to be on paper money?

2. Why has Hamilton been spared his place on the ten-dollar bill?

3. What does the *National Review* mean when it speaks of the pitfalls of running "a *Who's Who* volume on the currency" (para. 7)?

EXAMINING SENTENCES, PARAGRAPHS, AND ORGANIZATION

1. The authors write, "After much baying from activists, Treasury Secretary Jack Lew has struck upon a reasonable compromise" (para. 1). What tone is set in the language of that sentence?

2. Who is the focus of this essay: Hamilton, Tubman, or Jackson? How do you know?

3. In the concluding paragraph, what problems or issues do the authors identify about the changes being made to America's currency? Is the conclusion an effective spot to raise these issues? Why or why not?

THINKING CRITICALLY

1. Do you think about who is on our paper currency? Does it matter to you whether or not Jackson remains, or Tubman replaces him?

2. What considerations must be made before taking someone off currency and adding someone new? Do you think there are other considerations not taken into account in this essay?

3. What did you know about Andrew Jackson before you read this essay? Did this editorial add to your knowledge? If so, in what way?

WRITING ACTIVITIES

1. Consider another face found on paper currency or coins. Write a brief description of the person pictured and answer the following questions:

   • What is this person best known for?

   • Is there anything about this person that makes you question his or her place on money?

   • Is currency an appropriate place to memorialize this person? Why or why not?

2. Write your own essay in support of keeping Jackson or Hamilton on paper money, or in favor of replacing one of them with Tubman. Persuade the reader of your choice without discussing the attributes of other potential candidates.

3. In an informal writing exercise, consider the changing face of American history. Who has received the most attention in various time periods and why? This is not a formal essay, so the conversation can look at one time period or many different ones, changing focus when needed in the manner of freewriting. But retain the other formal conventions of complete sentences and paragraphs.

Spotlight on Data and Research

Marc Santora

Whitesboro, N.Y., in Reversal, Will Change a Logo Called Racist

[*The New York Times*, January 22, 2016]

The tiny town of Whitesboro, New York, provides a microcosm of the problem of historical memory in an age of diversity. The town's seal looks horrifically racist at first sight, though local historians claim the image is actually one that promotes cross-cultural understanding, with the right historical context. This story is by Marc Santora, a reporter at the New York Times, who has reported on a wide range of political topics, including the invasion of Iraq, statehouse politics, and homeland security.

The former village seal of Whitesboro, New York, as seen on a welcome sign

Observer-Dispatch via AP Images

The official seal of the Village of Whitesboro in central New York, de- 1
picting a wrestling match between the community's founding father
and the local American Indian chief, has survived decades of debate
and discussion.

The emblem seems to show a white man throttling a Native Ameri- 2
can as he falls to the ground in agony. Local leaders have defended the

seal, pointing to its historical accuracy, even as criticism and derision mounted.

But no matter how much fuss the seal caused, it endured. As 3 recently as two weeks ago, residents cast 157 of 212 votes in favor of letting the image represent the Oneida County village, which has a population of roughly 3,700.

But what it could not survive, it seems, is widespread attention 4 online.

On Friday, the village said that it would work with the Oneida 5 Indian Nation to discuss the creation of a new emblem.

"In speaking with a lot of the residents that voted to keep the seal, 6 I think they were surprised at the negative attention that Whitesboro was receiving as a result of the vote," Mayor Patrick O'Connor said in a statement.

Mr. O'Connor said residents "wanted to preserve history" while 7 also ensuring that the village was "seen as the inclusive place that it is."

The story of the seal dates back to 1784, when a man named Hugh 8 White moved to Sedauquate, now Whitesboro, which was home to the Oneida Indians.

According to the official village history, in the spirit of fostering 9 good relations between the Indians and the new settlers, Mr. White challenged the local chief to a wrestling match.

The seal depicting that event first came under fire in 1977 when 10 a notice was filed with the Village Board saying the seal depicted a "white man choking an Indian" and was demeaning and degrading. The emblem was altered, ever so slightly, to make it clear that Mr. White's hands were on the chief's shoulders, not around his neck. But for many, the new seal was no better than the old one.

And after the nonbinding vote to keep the seal on Jan. 11 was 11 reported, the negative reaction and mockery was fast and furious, including a widely shared segment on *The Daily Show* on Comedy Central.

Mr. O'Connor said descendants of the White family even reached 12 out to his office to let the village know that while they appreciated the attempt to remain faithful to the historical story, they were open to changing the image.

Ray Halbritter, the Oneida Indian Nation representative and chief 13 executive officer, said he welcomed the decision.

"As we've always said, we are happy to work with anyone who 14 wants to make sure the symbols they are promoting are honoring and respecting all people," he said. "We applaud the village leaders' willingness to evaluate their own symbols and how to make sure they accurately reflect their community's core values."

continued

DRAWING CONCLUSIONS

1. What did you think when you first saw the seal? Did reading the story behind it change your view?

2. What arguments do you imagine the people who voted to preserve the seal made? What arguments do you imagine those who voted against it made?

3. To what extent should context be considered in keeping or ditching historical tokens that seem dated or offensive? Imagine a situation in which you would vote to keep a town seal some found problematic and one in which you would vote to get rid of it. Where would you draw the line?

Adam Hamze (student essay)

Removal of the Jefferson Davis Statue Falls Short

[*The Daily Texan*, University of Texas, August 20, 2015]

BEFORE YOU READ

Adam Hamze suggests that a statue of Heman Marion Sweatt be erected to honor the first black student at the University of Texas. Do you think this is an appropriate replacement? Do you understand Hamze's impulse to fill Jefferson Davis's space with the lesser-known Sweatt?

WORDS TO LEARN

grueling (para. 4): very difficult or taxing (adjective)

viable (para. 4): able to succeed (adjective)

O n August 13, [University of Texas] President Gregory Fenves announced his decision to relocate the statue of Jefferson Davis, President of the Confederacy, from the UT Main Mall to the Dolph Briscoe Center for American History. Additionally, Fenves announced he will relocate the statue of Woodrow Wilson, which sits

1

Adam Hamze is a student at the University of Texas.

adjacent to the Davis statue, for the sake of "symmetry." If Fenves is to show his dedication to equality and diversity to the black student population, he must make plans to erect a new statue in Davis's place — not only of someone who is a crucial part of Texan and University history, but of someone who is black as well.

The demonstrations against the statue's presence on campus, which include vandalism of the statue, public forums discussing its future and the appointment of a University task force to deliberate possible solutions, were not the first of their kind. Black students have been expressing their grievances against the multiple Confederate monuments across campus since at least the '60s. The charges against the statues cited they create a hostile environment, represent the legacy of racism rather than the legacy of black resistance and provide black students with a constant reminder of the hateful history of Texas and the Confederacy. 2

Fenves's decision is a compromise at best. While the remaining Confederate monuments do represent aspects of Texan history, they also represent white supremacy's role in institutionalized oppression, past and present. There is only one statue on campus dedicated to a black Texan, although there have been countless contributions to the state by black individuals, many of whom have been underappreciated. One of the most notable, courageous and relevant individuals, not only to Texas and UT, but to public education across the nation, is Heman Marion Sweatt — the first black student at UT. 3

Sweatt endured a grueling and emotionally tolling legal battle with the University after being denied admission solely due to his blackness. His victory paved the way for reform of the racist educational system plaguing the country, although it is often overshadowed by the significantly more discussed *Brown v. Board of Education*, which took place four years later. Sweatt's significance to the University is undeniable, but his legacy is not prioritized. There is a building named after the UT President that originally denied Sweatt's admission because he was black. There is little to no established recognition devoted to Sweatt. Fenves has the power and ability to highlight Sweatt's contributions to the state and the nation. If he is concerned about "symmetry," erecting a statue of Sweatt is a viable solution that can be a small step to further establishing trust between the black UT community and the administration. 4

> His victory paved the way for reform of the racist educational system plaguing the country.

VOCABULARY/USING A DICTIONARY

1. What is the origin of the word *grievance* (para. 2)?
2. If something is not *prioritized* (para. 4), how important is it? What do we mean when we say something is a *priority*?
3. What is the root word of *undeniable* (para. 4)? What does *undeniable* mean?

RESPONDING TO WORDS IN CONTEXT

1. Why do you think the word *symmetry* (para. 1) is in quotation marks? What does *symmetry* mean?
2. What does Hamze mean when he writes that black individuals have been *underappreciated* (para. 3) by the University of Texas?
3. Hamze sees Fenves's decision to remove the Davis statue as a *compromise* (para. 3). What is the *compromise* being made?

DISCUSSING MAIN POINT AND MEANING

1. Why did Fenves remove the statue of Jefferson Davis?
2. Why is this removal an important step, according to Hamze, but not enough?
3. What does Hamze think needs to be done next in order to acknowledge and honor diversity on the campus?

EXAMINING SENTENCES, PARAGRAPHS, AND ORGANIZATION

1. Why might Hamze have included the date, August 13, in his opening paragraph? Why is it important? What does it add to his essay?
2. The title of this essay is "Removal of the Jefferson Davis Statue Falls Short." Why do you think there isn't more discussion of Jefferson Davis himself? What, or who, is the focus of Hamze's essay?
3. How does Hamze bring the piece back to Fenves in his conclusion? How does this return to Fenves provide a certain "symmetry" to the article?

THINKING CRITICALLY

1. Why would a student publish an op-ed piece such as this? What reactions might a student writer hope for from his or her fellow students?
2. Does the presence of statues like the one of Davis support a legacy of racism on campus? Why or why not?
3. Why is Jefferson Davis honored with a statue on a college campus? Would Heman Marion Sweatt be a better candidate to honor on the University of Texas campus? Why or why not?

WRITING ACTIVITIES

1. Write your own op-ed in defense of Hamze's argument for a statue of Sweatt, or in opposition to it. If you oppose his choice, make your case for another individual to honor in Jefferson Davis's place. Make your op-ed similar in length and format to Hamze's, and comment in support of Sweatt or your other choice at the end.

2. Hamze acknowledges that "the remaining Confederate monuments do represent aspects of Texan history" (para. 3). What aspects of Texas history do they represent? Write down your answers to this question. If you don't know what historical aspects they represent, write a list of five to ten questions whose answers would help clarify Hamze's meaning. After you write, research online to check your knowledge or to answer your own questions.

3. Hamze explains that few people know about Sweatt, but that his legal struggle was similar to and overshadowed by the struggle highlighted in the landmark Supreme Court case *Brown v. Board of Education*. Research the two cases online if necessary, and write down key differences you can identify between them. In a brief essay, discuss the two cases, pointing out their similarities and differences.

LOOKING CLOSELY

Effective Persuasion: Recommending a Course of Action

A primary purpose of a persuasive essay is to change someone's attitude or opinion, usually on a matter of public policy. On Election Day, for example, a newspaper editorial will encourage its readers to vote for a particular candidate; in the same paper, a film review may discourage moviegoers from attending a certain film the critic finds pointless, trivial, and profoundly dumb. An opinion column may try to dissuade parents from buying their children fast food. All of these examples call for someone to *do* something, to take some course of action.

In "Removal of the Jefferson Davis Statue Falls Short," University of Texas student Adam Hamze specifically calls upon the university's president to replace the removed statue of Jefferson Davis, the leader of the Confederacy during the Civil War, with a statue that would commemorate one of the university's outstanding black graduates.

1
Offers reasons for a statue of Sweatt

(1) <u>Sweatt endured a grueling and emotionally tolling legal battle with the University after being denied admission solely due to his blackness.</u> His victory paved the way for reform of the racist educational system plaguing the country, although it is often overshadowed by the significantly more discussed *Brown v. Board of Education,* which took place four years later. Sweatt's significance to the University is undeniable, but his legacy is not prioritized. There is a building named after the UT President that originally denied Sweatt's admission because he was black. There is little to no established recognition devoted to Sweatt.

2
Proposes a call to action

(2) <u>Fenves has the power and ability to highlight Sweatt's contributions to the state and the nation. If he is concerned about "symmetry," erecting a statue of Sweatt is a viable solution that can be a small step to further establishing trust between the black UT community and the administration.</u>

Michele de Cuneo

Violence in the Virgin Islands

*Less than a year after Christopher Columbus made his famed discovery of
the New World on October 12, 1492, he set out on a second voyage that he
hoped would prove more commercially successful for Spain than the first.
Columbus, of course, did not "discover" new lands; the native peoples he
found on his voyages already had. But Columbus was the first European to
discover that the world was larger than geographers imagined and that it
contained lands that no one previously knew existed. The Vikings had landed
at Newfoundland in the year 1000, but that expedition had no impact on
future exploration, and it is very possible that mariners and fishermen had
frequently made unrecorded landings in North America for quite some time
before Columbus. But although he never knew exactly what he had found, it
was Columbus's voyages that led to the exploration and eventual coloniza-
tion of North and South America.*

*On the second voyage Columbus encountered Puerto Rico, parts of
Cuba, Jamaica, the Virgin Islands, and the Lesser Antilles. To his great
disappointment, once again he found no gold or silver and no wealthy cities with which to establish a lucrative trade. No official log or journal of
that voyage remains, but we have a vivid and at times lurid account of that
second expedition. Though he sailed for Spain, Columbus was an Italian
and on his second trip he brought with him a friend from the Genoa region,
Michele de Cuneo. A few years after he returned to Italy, de Cuneo wrote
a long report to another friend describing the details of the second voyage.
Written in Italian in 1495, the original report has disappeared, but a copy
made in 1511 was made public in 1885. The translation of the portion
below is provided by Elissa Weaver of the University of Chicago.*

*Note: In de Cuneo's original report, he refers to the indigenous people as
Camballi, which can be translated as "Caribs" or "Cannibals." It is generally
believed that the word* cannibal *came about as a linguistic corruption of* Carib.

On the island of Santa Maria la Gallante we got water and wood. The   1
island is uninhabited even though it's full of trees and plains. We set sail
from there that day and arrived at a large island inhabited by Caribs,

who fled immediately to the mountains when they saw us. We landed on this island and stayed about six days since eleven of our men, who had banded together in order to steal, went five or six miles into the deserted area by such a route that when they wanted to return, they were unable to find their way, even though they were all sailors and could follow the sun, which they couldn't see well for the thick and full woods. When the admiral[1] saw that these men had not returned and were nowhere to be found, he sent two hundred men divided into four squadrons with trumpets, horns, and lanterns but even they were unable to find the lost men, and there was a time when we were more worried about the two hundred men than the others before them. But, as it pleased God, the two hundred returned with great difficulty and greater hunger; we judged that the eleven had been eaten by the Caribs as they are wont to do. However, after five or six days, the eleven men, as it pleased God, when there remained little hope of ever finding them, built a fire on a cape; seeing the fire, we judged it to be them and we sent a boat and in that way recovered them. Had it not been that an old woman showed them the way back with gestures, they'd have been done for since we had planned to set sail on the following day.

On that island we took twelve very beautiful and fat females about fifteen or sixteen years old and two boys of the same age whose genital member had been cut off down to their belly; and we judged that this had been done to keep them from mixing with their women or at least to fatten them and then eat them. These boys and girls had been picked by the Caribs for us to send to Spain to the king as an exhibit. The admiral named this island Santa Maria di Guadalupe.   2

We set sail from this island of Santa Maria di Guadalupe, the   3 Island of Caribs, on November tenth and on the fourteenth we reached another beautiful and fertile island of Caribs and came to a very beautiful port. When the Caribs caught sight of us they fled, as the others had, to the mountains and abandoned their houses where we went and took what we liked. In these few days we found many islands where we didn't disembark, but others where we did — for the night. When we didn't leave the ship we kept it tied, and this we did so we wouldn't travel on and out of fear of running aground. Because these islands were closely adjoining, the admiral called them the Eleven Thousand Virgins, and the previous one, Santa Croce.[2]

---

[1] Admiral (para. 1): Columbus
[2] Santa Croce (para. 3): Now St. Croix

We had anchored and gone ashore one day when we saw, coming from a cape, a canoe — that is, a boat, for so it is called in their speech — and it was beating oars, as though it were a well-armed brigantine.[3] On it there were three or four male Caribs with two female Caribs and two captured Indian slaves — so the Caribs call their other neighbors from those other islands; they had also just cut off their genital member down to their belly and so they were still sick. Since we had the captain's boat ashore with us, when we saw this canoe we quickly jumped into the boat and gave chase to the canoe. As we approached it, the Caribs shot hard at us with their bows, and if we had not had our Pavian shields[4] we would have been half destroyed. I must also tell you that a companion who had a shield in his hand got hit by an arrow, which went through the shield and into his chest three inches, causing him to die within a few days. We captured this canoe with all the men. One Carib was wounded by a lance-blow and thinking him dead we left him in the sea. Suddenly we saw him begin to swim away; therefore we caught him and with a long hook we pulled him aboard where we cut off his head with an axe. We sent the other Caribs together with the two slaves to Spain.

4

BACKGROUND AND CONTEXT

1. Although he isn't described directly, what image of Columbus do you come away with? What sort of leader does he appear to be in the context of de Cuneo's report?

2. It is often said that we must take historical contexts into account when judging the behavior of people in the distant past. For example, at the time de Cuneo was writing, democratic governments did not exist and slavery was not universally condemned. Do you believe this justifies or mitigates the conduct of de Cuneo and Columbus's crew?

STRATEGY, STRUCTURE, AND STYLE

1. De Cuneo's report was composed not as an "official" account of the expedition but as a letter to a friend. What elements of his account strike you as "unofficial"? That is, what details do you think might not have found their way into an official report to the authorities who sponsored the trip?

2. How do you react to the ugly events de Cuneo depicts? To start, does de Cuneo himself appear to recognize his and the crew's villainy and violence? How do you think he wanted his friend, the intended reader of his letter, to react?

---

[3] This incident took place at the current site of Salt River, St. Croix.

[4] Pavian shields (para. 4): Large shields made in Pavia, Italy

COMPARISONS AND CONNECTIONS

1. How does reading de Cuneo's account of Columbus's second voyage affect the way you think about Columbus himself? Do you think that those who want to diminish Columbus's accomplishments and see him not as a hero but as a villain (see Michael I. Niman's essay on p. 127) are justified? What connections do you see between de Cuneo's report and the anti-Columbus movement that Niman describes?

2. If you think that the anti-Columbus attitudes reported by Niman have merit, would you advocate removing Columbus monuments and his name from the public record? Would you urge legislators and appropriate organizations to change the name of the District of Columbia; Columbia, South Carolina; Columbus, Ohio; the Columbia River; and Columbia University and Columbus Circle in New York City, along with countless other similar place names across the nation? Explain why or why not.

Discussing the Unit

SUGGESTED TOPIC FOR DISCUSSION

There is an old saying that history is written by the victors. However, the authors in this chapter suggest new approaches that provide new windows of perspective on historical events. Is history fixed and one-sided? How can we promote a broader, more inclusive understanding of our past?

PREPARING FOR CLASS DISCUSSION

1. When you see historical monuments, do you ever identify with what is presented there? Do you ever feel that your history is not represented or that something, or someone, is missing?

2. Who are your historical heroes? Where do you find them represented or memorialized? Do you think more should be done to promote their presence in our national consciousness, whether they are a currently established or an emerging historical figure?

FROM DISCUSSION TO WRITING

1. What associations do you have of Christopher Columbus and the "discovery" of America? Do your associations match or conflict with what is presented in Michael I. Niman's "As Confederate Flags Fall, Columbus Statues Stand Tall" (p. 127) or Michele de Cuneo's "Violence in the Virgin Islands" (p. 145)? Write a reflective essay that explores your personal associations with Columbus and their intersection with or divergence from what you read in these essays.

2. Keeping in mind the essays by Brent Staples, Michael I. Niman, Marc Santora, and the *National Review*'s editors, as well as the cartoon by Bill Bramhall, ask yourself whether or not more changes should be made to whom we honor in history. Explain your answer in a brief essay that responds directly to the ideas in at least two of the essays mentioned.

TOPICS FOR CROSS-CULTURAL DISCUSSION

1. Many of the essays in this chapter confront the preservation or removal of historical monuments dedicated to figures or events from the Civil War era. These essays clearly pinpoint both regional and racial differences in how history is remembered. Using examples from an essay concerned with a different moment in American history, discuss the role of gender and/or race in the argument to preserve or dismantle certain ideas about the historical experience.

2. What is the effect when one particular group has control over how history is perceived? What changes when it does not? Discuss these questions, using any two essays from this chapter to support your answers.

A College Education: How Valuable Is It?

For many years, a college education has been seen as a path to personal, intellectual, and financial success. However, in times of economic instability, the financial benefits of a college degree usually receive the most attention. According to a recent report from the Georgetown University Center on Education and the Workplace, full-time workers holding a bachelor's degree make, on average, 74 percent more over the course of their careers than workers who have obtained a high school diploma only. But with tuition costs and student-loan debts soaring, more and more people are questioning the value of a college education. Given its high cost, is it really the best choice for everyone? And do students, parents, and educational institutions need to focus more on majors that will provide the most financial bang for the tuition buck? Or is emphasizing the economic benefits of college selling short the other, less quantifiable advantages it offers students — for example, the potential to be better, and happier, citizens and thinkers?

This chapter's "In Brief" takes a quick look at one of the noneconomic advantages of attending college. Going to college, regardless of how it pays off financially, can make enormous differences in our social life and the way we see ourselves. This perspective is followed up by a tougher view of higher education. In "Why College Is Necessary but Gets You Nowhere," former secretary of labor and prominent economist Robert Reich makes a strong case for the importance of a college education, but his essay comes with a warning: "Though college costs are rising, the financial return to a college degree compared to not having one is rising even faster." For Reich that is the good news. But he doesn't flinch from the bad news: "A college degree no longer guarantees a *good* job. The main reason it pays better than the job of someone without a degree is the latter's wages are dropping." Reich admits that some college graduates today are finding only dead-end jobs and diminished prospects.

Like many commentators on education, Reich acknowledges the noneconomic advantages of college. "Don't get me wrong," he writes. "I don't believe the main reason to go to college — or to choose one career over another — should be to make lots of money." That viewpoint is the main contention of well-known columnist Suzanne Fields in "There's More to Learning Than a Job Search." As Fields sees it, the concern that college costs so much has led students and parents to feel more strongly that it should then pay off, thus placing a premium on the vocational value of certain courses that can result in higher-paying careers. "Graduates in science, technology, engineering, and mathematics, known as the STEM courses, think their training aimed them in the right direction for jobs," Fields argues, but then adds that "only 1 in 5 recent STEM graduates get those jobs." She points out the "unhappy corollary of this narrowing focus": "Fewer students study literature or other subjects of the liberal arts that would enrich their lives and broaden their intellectual perspectives with insights that enhance critical thinking."

If the rising costs of a college education are currently placing more emphasis on courses that will lead more readily to a job — and these would be the STEM courses Fields lists above — then one consequence of this vocational trend is that female graduates may not be as eligible as males for the nation's best-paying careers. In "83 Seconds: How Fast-Paced Standardized Testing Has Created a New Glass Ceiling," prominent economic journalist Andrew Hacker points out how and why girls and women are disadvantaged by the many standardized tests used to measure and identify mathematical and scientific talent. In showing how the timed and quantitative tests favor males, he cites a researcher from the University of California,

Berkeley, who notes succinctly that in mathematics especially, "females turn out to be better course takers," whereas "males turn out to be better test takers."

So, is college worth the cost? A well-publicized Gallup-Purdue Index (summarized in this chapter's "Spotlight on Data and Research" feature) polled 30,000 college alumni and found that only half "strongly agreed that their higher education was worth the cost." Recent graduates were even less likely to agree and, not surprisingly, the more student debt recent alumni had acquired, the less worthwhile they considered their educational expenses to have been. Basically, the poll discovered that many students today are not satisfied customers.

A STEM degree is usually a BS, and a liberal arts degree a BA. In "The Problem with Choosing between BS and BA," University of Oregon student Desiree Bergstrom points out that "whichever one of these you choose as a freshman follows you all the way through your time at school." Acknowledging the importance of both concentrations, she wonders why "students need to choose in the first place."

Attracting applicants has long been a goal of educational institutions, as a 1989 advertisement for New York's Adelphi University clearly indicates. Notice how this nearly thirty-year-old ad seems to straddle two worlds: one quaintly old-fashioned and the other pointing to some of the difficult issues raised in this chapter.

Piyush Mangukiya

Is College Worth the Cost? Absolutely

[*Huffington Post*, December 2, 2015]

As you will see throughout this chapter, the cost of obtaining a college education has been increasingly questioned at a time of economic uncertainty and unprecedented rise in student debt. Most arguments made in favor of higher education focus on the better employment opportunities and higher lifetime income of college graduates. But not all arguments in support of college take an economic perspective. Below, media marketing strategist Piyush Mangukiya briefly suggests one reason to attend college: It will improve our social and emotional lives.

College is more than classes, papers, and exams. It is also a meaningful 1
social experience, where people develop friendships and long-term relationships. People who don't attend college miss out on several important experiences that, like income potential, have lifelong implications.

College offers young people the opportunity to live, work, and socialize 2
within a contained society made up almost exclusively of people their age.
They share experiences and develop close personal relationships. Almost
30% of Americans report meeting their future spouses in college. Not all of
these marriages began with college relationships, but they did find a spark
in a friendship developed on campus. Even though the cliché of the "high
school sweethearts" is still well known, in fact, only 15% of Americans
marry someone with whom they had a relationship in high school.

Finding a spouse is not the only social/emotional benefit of a college 3
education. College-educated Americans, according to several studies:

- Are more self-confident in social situations
- Are more effective communicators
- Have more friends
- Suffer less frequently from anxiety
- Have higher self-esteem
- Are more likely to believe they have control over their own lives

POINTS TO CONSIDER

1. Do you think going to college can enhance a person's social life? Don't
   people who haven't attended college still retain friendships and family ties?

Do you agree that those who don't attend college "miss out on" some of life's important experiences?

2. In your opinion, is the fact that you have a close to 30 percent chance of meeting your marriage partner on campus a good reason to attend college? Why do you think the article emphasizes this statistic?

3. Of all the reasons offered to show that college can enhance one's social life, which one do you find most compelling? Why?

Robert Reich

Why College Is Necessary but Gets You Nowhere

[*RobertReich.org*, November 24, 2014]

BEFORE YOU READ
Based on the title of this selection, do you think Robert Reich believes it's important to go to college? In his essay, Reich asserts that it is important "to know the economics" involved in getting a college education. Do you agree?

WORDS TO LEARN
qualification (para. 2): modification; restriction (noun)
overqualified (para. 9): having more education or training than needed (adjective)

outsource (para. 15): to contract out (verb)
prerequisite (para. 22): something required beforehand (noun)
enable (para. 23): to make able (verb)

T his is the time of year when high school seniors apply to college, and when I get lots of mail about whether college is worth the cost.

1

Robert Reich is a professor of public policy at the University of California, Berkeley, and a senior fellow at the Blum Center for Developing Economies. He has written fourteen books, served as secretary of labor for the Clinton administration, and worked as a contributing editor for the New York Times, New Republic, *the* Harvard Business Review, *the* American Prospect, *the* Atlantic, *and the* Wall Street Journal.

The answer is unequivocally yes, but with one big qualification. I'll   2
come to the qualification in a moment but first the financial case for why
it's worth going to college.

Put simply, people with college degrees continue to earn far more   3
than people without them. And that college "premium" keeps rising.

Last year, Americans with four-year college degrees earned on aver-   4
age 98 percent more per hour than people without college degrees.

In the early 1980s, graduates earned 64 percent more.   5

So even though college costs are rising, the financial return to a col-   6
lege degree compared to not having one is rising even faster.

But here's the qualification, and it's a big one.   7

A college degree no longer guarantees a *good* job. The main reason it   8
pays better than the job of someone without a degree is the latter's wages
are dropping.

In fact, it's likely that new college graduates will spend some years in   9
jobs for which they're overqualified.

According to the Federal Reserve Bank of New York, 46 percent of   10
recent college graduates are now working in jobs that don't require college degrees. (The same is true for more than a third of college graduates
overall.)

Their employers still choose college grads over non-college grads on   11
the assumption that more education is better than less.

As a result, non-grads are being pushed into ever more menial work, if   12
they can get work at all. Which is a major reason why their pay is dropping.

What's going on? For years we've been told globalization and tech-   13
nological advances increase the demand for well-educated workers.
(Confession: I was one of the ones making this argument.)

This was correct until around 2000. But since then two things have   14
reversed the trend.

First, millions of people in developing nations are now far better   15
educated, and the Internet has given them an easy way to sell their skills
in advanced economies like the United States. Hence, more and more
complex work is being outsourced to them.

Second, advanced software is taking over many tasks that had been   16
done by well-educated professionals — including data analysis, accounting, legal and engineering work, even some medical diagnoses.

As a result, the demand for well-educated workers in the United   17
States seems to have peaked around 2000 and fallen since. But the supply of well-educated workers has continued to grow.

What happens when demand drops and supply increases? You   18
guessed it. This is why the incomes of young people who graduated college after 2000 have barely risen.

Those just within the top 10 percent of college graduate earnings have seen their incomes increase by only 4.4 percent since 2000. 19

When it comes to beginning their careers, it's even worse. The starting wages of college graduates have actually dropped since 2000. The starting wage of women grads has dropped 8.1 percent, and for men, 6.7 percent. 20

> The starting wages of college graduates have actually dropped since 2000.

I hear it all the time from my former students. The *New York Times* calls them "Generation Limbo" — well-educated young adults "whose careers are stuck in neutral, coping with dead-end jobs and listless prospects." A record number are living at home. 21

The deeper problem is this. While a college education is now a prerequisite for joining the middle class, the middle class is in lousy shape. Its share of the total economic pie continues to shrink, while the share going to the very top continues to grow. 22

Given all this, a college degree is worth the cost because it at least enables a young person to tread water. Without the degree, young people can easily drown. 23

Some young college graduates will make it into the top 1 percent. But that route is narrower than ever. The on-ramp often requires the right connections (especially parents well inside the top 1 percent). 24

And the off-ramps basically go in only three directions: Wall Street, corporate consulting, and Silicon Valley. 25

Don't get me wrong. I don't believe the main reason to go to college — or to choose one career over another — should be to make lots of money. 26

Hopefully, a college education gives young people tools for leading full and purposeful lives, and having meaningful careers. 27

Even if they don't change the world for the better, I want my students to be responsible and engaged citizens. 28

But when considering a college education in a perilous economy like this, it's also important to know the economics. 29

VOCABULARY/USING A DICTIONARY

1. What's the difference between something answered *equivocally* and *unequivocally* (para. 2)?

2. What is the opposite of *latter* (para. 8)?

3. What is an *assumption* (para. 11)? What other word embedded within it might lead you to your definition?

RESPONDING TO WORDS IN CONTEXT

1. Do you think *menial* (para. 12) work is desirable based on what you read in Reich's piece?

2. What sort of prospects do you face if they are *listless* (para. 21)? How can you tell based on the rest of the quotation in which the word appears?

3. What is the root of the word *perilous* (para. 29)? Does the word within *perilous* shed light on what kind of economy the reader is facing?

DISCUSSING MAIN POINT AND MEANING

1. Why, according to Reich, is it important for people to go to college?

2. How has the job market changed for college graduates in recent years?

3. What has happened to the middle class, according to Reich? How does the U.S. class system look at this time?

EXAMINING SENTENCES, PARAGRAPHS, AND ORGANIZATION

1. Reich uses an analogy in paragraph 23. Can you identify it? How does that analogy convey the meaning he wants to get across? How would you rewrite those two sentences to express Reich's point?

2. Who is the audience for this essay? How do you know?

3. Is there a benefit to using brief, one- to two-sentence paragraphs in this essay? Why or why not?

THINKING CRITICALLY

1. If the main reason to go to college isn't to make a lot of money, why do you think Reich wrote this article?

2. Why might being overqualified for a job be a problem?

3. What kinds of jobs will you be qualified to do when you graduate? Are you concerned about the statistics Reich cites? Why or why not?

WRITING ACTIVITIES

1. Do you think it is important to pursue a college education? Do you think it's important for the reasons Reich is stressing in his essay, or for different reasons? Write a response to "Why College Is Necessary but Gets You Nowhere" that takes Reich's arguments into account and includes some of your own reasons for whether or not you believe that it is necessary to go to college.

2. Besides jobs and earnings, what other factors could Reich have considered? What other reasons are there for going to college? In a freewriting exercise, consider other reasons — beyond the financial picture Reich discusses here — for going to college.

3. Write a personal response to the term "Generation Limbo" (para. 21). How do you react to that term? Do you think it applies to recent or soon-to-be college graduates? Consider the points Reich enumerates from the *New York Times*: "Young adults '[have] careers . . . stuck in neutral [and are] coping with dead-end jobs and listless prospects.' A record number are living at home." In your opinion, is this an accurate picture? Does it concern you? Why or why not?

Suzanne Fields

There's More to Learning Than a Job Search

[*The Washington Times*, September 9, 2015]

BEFORE YOU READ

What should the main focus of today's college education be? As you read, ask yourself whether you agree that the focus Suzanne Fields identifies is the ultimate goal for a college graduate.

WORDS TO LEARN

ebb (para. 1): a flowing backward or decline (noun)

dominate (para. 2): to rule over (verb)

amorphous (para. 5): formless (adjective)

grievously (para. 5): extremely badly; atrociously (adverb)

corollary (para. 7): an immediate consequence or conclusion (noun)

enrich (para. 7): to add greater significance to (verb)

tenured (para. 7): holding a permanent position in the university (adjective)

consensus (para. 7): general agreement (noun)

altar (para. 9): an elevated structure for religious rites (noun)

aspiration (para. 9): ambition (noun)

I n autumn a young man's fancy (and a young woman's, too) turns to thoughts of school. Even the melancholy chirping of the crickets becomes a sad song of the ebb of summer. Flip-flops and summer tees, like Cinderella's glass slippers and silk gowns, are replaced by

1

Suzanne Fields is an author and a widely syndicated columnist for the Washington Times. *In addition to writing, she has appeared on CNN and on* Nightline, *Larry King Live,* Oprah, The Today Show, *and* Good Morning America, *among other programs.*

"appropriate" dress, and book bags bulge with pencils and notebooks (paper and electronic). If a girl loses her flip-flops now, there's no young man on the beach to search for the foot to fit. Those days have passed.

The approach of autumn ushers in anxiety in the faculty lounge, too, as debates rage over the best way to prepare the rising classes to fit into the complex world. Economic issues dominate the discussion. Once upon a time the emphasis was on preparation to learn how to think critically, how to ask the right questions. A "well-rounded" man or woman got that way through study of the liberal arts. Now the point of an education, though more expensive than ever, has little to do with critical thinking or an acquired appreciation of history, culture and government. 2

"No idea has had more influence on education policy than the notion that colleges teach their students specific, marketable skills, which they can use to get a good job," writes John Cassidy in *The New Yorker*, examining the current college "calculus," or strategy, of higher education. A college education now offers better job prospects to make it a good investment for future earnings, but a college education was once understood to include a broad education in the liberal arts and sciences. Employers would be assured that the prospective employee had achieved a certain level of "cognitive competence." 3

But not today. Vocational majors have narrowed traditional college requirements in many ways. Vocational courses at some colleges, for example, limit access to knowledge by emphasizing "practical approaches" to information. At Kansas State, for example, bakery science and management as an undergraduate major might lead to better "bread," as in a better raisin and nut loaf (or perhaps, metaphorically, as in "earning the bread"). But is that what should be acquired in a university degree? No doubt Oklahoma State's degree in fire protection and safety engineering and technology suggests skill in acquiring valuable tips for making society safer, but should the university be the place to collect such tips? 4

A popular major is that amorphous umbrella called "communications," but one new study finds that few "communications" graduates are happy with their first jobs. "They show up on their first day," an editor in D.C. tells me, "and are grievously wounded when they aren't assigned to cover the White House." Since the recession, of course, increasing numbers of graduates find their degrees entitle them to no job at all. In 2007, only 5.5 percent of college graduates joined the jobless, and today that number is almost 9 percent. 5

Graduates in science, technology, engineering, and mathematics, known as the STEM courses, think their training aimed them in the right direction for jobs, but only 1 in 5 recent STEM graduates get those jobs. 6

An unhappy corollary of this narrowing focus is that fewer students 7
study literature or other subjects of the liberal arts that would enrich
their lives and broaden their intellectual perspectives with insights that
enhance critical thinking. Part of this is due to cost-benefit analysis (even
if it's not thought of that way), and part due
to the way literature is taught. Tenured and
untouchable professors reinforce groupthink by teaching literature through a narrow, politically correct focus rather than
search for great books to introduce diverse
points of view. A great novel engaging on
moral issues with a diversity of voices provides a context very different from consensus, one that opens minds. That's missing
from many campuses.

> A great novel
> engaging on
> moral issues with a
> diversity of voices
> provides a context
> very different from
> consensus, one
> that opens minds.

In a previous century I once taught English literature to a scatter- 8
ing of engineering students in a sophomore survey course at Catholic
University of America. I tried to impress upon them that this was the
last time they would be exposed to great literature within an academic
environment, so make it count. My best students worked their way from
Chaucer to T.S. Eliot, finding reflection and depth of insight in writers
now often dismissed as politically incorrect dead white men.

I don't know how those engineers fared in the economy, but when 9
they wanted to think about the ways of the world, they could enjoy "The
Wife of Bath's Tale" without worrying about feminism, or read T.S. Eliot
to grasp the critical meaning of "The Hollow Men" as a perspective of
another time and place that says something clear and right today, too.
Literary empathy broadens moral viewpoints and engages the reader
more deeply in his own time. It's a waste to sacrifice that kind of learning
on the altar of vocational aspiration.

VOCABULARY/USING A DICTIONARY

1. How would you describe *melancholy* (para. 1)?

2. From what language does the word *emphasis* (para. 2) derive?

3. What is the opposite of *groupthink* (para. 7)?

RESPONDING TO WORDS IN CONTEXT

1. What part of speech is *usher* (para. 2) in this context? What does it mean?

2. What is "an *acquired* appreciation of history, culture and government" (para. 2)? What might its opposite be?

3. What do you think "cognitive competence" (para. 3) means?

DISCUSSING MAIN POINT AND MEANING

1. How have the goals of education changed, according to Fields?

2. What do many communications majors expect when they graduate? Why are they disappointed?

3. What did Fields introduce her students to in the past in order to better prepare them for working in the world? How would her choices be perceived today?

EXAMINING SENTENCES, PARAGRAPHS, AND ORGANIZATION

1. Fields's introduction is different from the other paragraphs in her essay. What is different about it? Is it a strong opening? Why or why not?

2. Consider how Fields weaves quotations throughout her essay. How do these quotations strengthen her argument and support her essay's organization?

3. Paragraph 6 is the shortest paragraph in the essay. Is it necessary? Is its brevity effective?

THINKING CRITICALLY

1. Do you think most students today go to college with the job market as their primary concern? Why or why not? Would you say that the situation for students on your campus is typical or atypical of the environment throughout the country? Are vocational courses and their limited focus an important aspect of education?

2. Do you understand why Fields's choices for her English literature students were relevant to their lives? Do you think literature courses are as important as Fields argues they are?

3. Should teachers worry that students either (1) aren't learning enough marketable skills, or (2) aren't receiving a broad education that encourages them to think? Do you see instructors placing more emphasis on one or another of these methods in your own classes?

WRITING ACTIVITIES

1. Write a brief essay in response to Fields's essay that explores these questions: Is it more important to learn to think critically or to acquire specific marketable skills? Is balance between the two possible? Bring in examples from your own education as you respond.

2. Read through your college catalogue. Create two lists of courses — those that fall under "vocational" and those you think would teach critical thinking and fall under the heading "liberal arts." If you are unsure of where a course falls, put it in a third "unknown" category. In small groups, discuss your lists

and try to move as many "unknown" courses into "vocational" or "liberal arts." As a class, consider whether your school places more emphasis on vocational or liberal arts classes, or if it strikes a balance between them.

3. The title of this essay is "There's More to Learning Than a Job Search." Are its intended readers students or educators? Why do you think so? In writing, analyze who the intended audience is, with an eye on Fields's language, writing style, and choice of examples.

Andrew Hacker

83 Seconds: How Fast-Paced Standardized Testing Has Created a New Glass Ceiling

[*The Nation*, March 21, 2016]

BEFORE YOU READ

Do you have more difficulty taking a class in school or taking a standardized test in the same subject? Have you ever considered why there might be a difference in how you perform in one situation or another?

WORDS TO LEARN

sentient (para. 3): conscious (adjective)

disgorge (para. 3): to discharge forcefully (verb)

tout (para. 3): to describe proudly (verb)

intimate (para. 3): to suggest (verb)

conscientious (para. 5): meticulous (adjective)

venerable (para. 7): worthy of reverence (adjective)

brazen (para. 7): shameless (adjective)

vie (para. 8): to compete (verb)

purport (para. 8): to claim (verb)

steadfastly (para. 8): unwaveringly (adverb)

surmise (para. 9): to guess (verb)

discernibly (para. 9): recognizably (adverb)

penultimate (para. 10): next to the last (adjective)

Andrew Hacker is a professor emeritus in the department of political science at Queens College in New York City. He has written a number of books, including Higher Education? How Colleges Are Wasting Our Money and Failing Our Kids — and What We Can Do about It *(2010) and* The Math Myth, and Other STEM Delusions *(2016).*

androgynous (para. 10): having both masculine and feminine character- istics (adjective)

decisively (para. 11): indisputably; definitely (adverb)

torque (para. 12): having to do with torsion or force (noun)

delude (para. 12): to deceive (verb)

patent (para. 13): evident; obvious (adjective)

premise (para. 13): assumption (noun)

nascent (para. 14): beginning to develop (adjective)

imperium (para. 14): empire (noun)

blatantly (para. 14): undeniably (adverb)

surpass (para. 14): to excel (verb)

Hardly a week goes by without a panel, conference, or sympo- 1
sium on luring women into STEM (science, technology, engineering, and mathematics) careers. Even the president has
joined in: "We've got half the population that is way underrepresented
in those fields." He has his numbers right. Women currently receive less
than a fifth of all bachelor's degrees in physics, computer science, and
engineering. In the last national count, only 8,851 women had majored
in mathematics and statistics.

We've heard most of the reasons, not least hostility in laborato- 2
ries. But a more central cause became apparent as I began researching
the teaching and testing of mathematics. Standardized testing in math,
where women do significantly worse than men, is setting women back
before they even begin college. Since mathematics is the first hurdle for
STEM fields, women are unlikely to sign on if they've already been told
that they don't measure up. We know that the problem is the test. It's
not the students, because girls and women are getting better grades than
boys and men in high-school and college mathematics courses. Without changing our methods for measuring ability, we stand little chance
of changing the gender imbalance among our scientists and engineers.

The importance we assign to standardized tests is eclipsing that of 3
assessments by sentient teachers. Each year, more weight is given to
scores disgorged by the ACT and the SAT, backstopped by the GRE,
MCAT, and LSAT, not to mention standardized Common Core tests,
which are given over to firms like Pearson and McGraw-Hill. Computer-
awarded scores are touted as objective, whereas grades bestowed by
teachers are seen as subjective, if not tainted by biases. (An ACT study
intimated that the principal victims of prejudice were boys.)

On last year's SAT, boys averaged 527 in the mathematics section 4
against 496 for girls — a far wider gulf than elsewhere in the test. The
ACT's gap is smaller, largely because its test is closer to what schools
actually teach, but boys are still visibly ahead. In fact, a more reliable

gauge is performance in high school before they take tests and in college courses afterward. I did some calculations to see what would happen if the SAT's mathematics scores reflected classroom grades. If that were the case, girls would not only erase their current 31-point deficit, but would move 32 points ahead of their male classmates. With the ACT, they would gain 28 points and also pass the boys. (I've converted ACT scores here to the SAT range.)

Since we know that girls and women are just as intelligent and adapt- 5
able as boys and men, why aren't they faring equally well with an instru-ment that has been in place for over half a century? I turned to Marcia Linn at the University of California, Berkeley, who has studied grades and scores for over 20 years, especially gender differences in mathemat-ics. "Females turn out to be better course takers," she has concluded; "males turn out to be better test takers." She notes that boys are more apt to take physics and computer science, which sharpen quantitative and spatial skills. And more college-aspiring girls come from lower-income homes with fewer resources for tutoring. But what ultimately separates the scores, Linn says, is the "tendency of girls to be more conscientious than boys."

Diligence pays off in complex class assignments, which results in 6
higher grades. But pausing to ponder can spell death in multiple-choice testing, since speed is crucial for a high score. The ACT's 60 mathematics problems must be assessed and answered in 60 minutes, although a more generous SAT, set to start this spring, allots 83 seconds. Given the ticking clock, the tests openly advise swift skimming and blind guessing. Hence this advice from Axiom Learning, a coaching company: "It's Not What You Know, It's How Fast You Can Show It."

I next conferred with Jonathan Chiu, who oversees Princeton Re- 7
view's tutorial services. He began by saying that he warns girls not to double-check their answers, because that wastes crucial seconds. Girls tend to "overanalyze" the options, he added, while boys cotton to the idea that there is "only one right answer." The ACT and the SAT con-cede that it's not possible to truly solve all of their problems in the allot-ted time. So along with speed, there's what some coaches call "stabbing," which can yield precious points. Suppose you know the bell is about to ring, and you have 10 items still to go. Chiu recommends that you not even read them, but simply stab a bubble for each one. He says that girls are more apt to feel it's not honest to fill in answers if you haven't done the questions. A venerable College Board study found they were 12 times more likely to leave the bubbles blank because they weren't sure. Chiu notes that too many girls enter the tests feeling their knowledge is being weighed, while boys perceive them as contests to be gamed.

The keys to a successful score are an impulsive pace, brazen confidence, and a cynical view of the entire enterprise.

> The keys to a successful score are an impulsive pace, brazen confidence, and a cynical view of the entire enterprise.

Let us consider one outcome of these tests. 8 Each year, the National Merit Scholarship Corporation induces some 1.6 million high-school juniors to vie for its 7,400 awards. It purports to be a national talent search, funded by companies like McDonald's, Boeing, and Lorillard Tobacco, eager to show a social commitment. While NMS releases reams of data, it steadfastly refuses to provide gender breakdowns, either for its initial pool of entrants or the final winners. When I asked for a few figures, an NMS spokesperson replied that the company didn't keep them because gender "is not used in the selection process."

So I did some digging of my own. NMS awards are based almost 9 entirely on the PSAT, an abridged version of the SAT. In recent years, girls have comprised 53 percent of those taking this test. (NMS never mentions this figure.) The PSAT does release its ranges of scores, where its three parts — reading, writing, and mathematics — get equal weight. In fact, the genders are just a point or so apart in reading and writing. But the difference in mathematics is striking, with twice as many boys landing in the top tier. This edge boosts them overall, and it seems valid to surmise that discernibly more boys will be getting NMS scholarships. (In fact, if we had reading and writing results that mirrored classroom accomplishment, girls' scores would be substantially higher than the boys'.)

NMS also declines to print a list of its ultimate winners. However, 10 it does release the names of each state's "semifinalists," the penultimate draw. I chose Ohio as a sample state and examined its 626 names to identify them by gender. (Some of the names were androgynous or unfamiliar to me, so I split them evenly.) I found that girls comprised 47 percent of Ohio's NMS semifinalists. Here, too, it was the standardized mathematics scores that brought girls, who started as 53 percent of the entrants, down to 47 percent of the NMS awardees. Here, the PSAT's gender bias results in more boys than girls receiving national recognition, not to mention money for college.

Consider another outcome of biased testing: More men than women 11 are admitted to top-tier schools, even though 57 percent of the bachelor's degrees awarded nationwide go to women. At Stanford and Yale, for example, less than half of their undergraduates are women. Here's the reason: These elite colleges demand that most of the students they admit have SAT scores of at least 700 (or above 33 on the ACT) on both the reading and, more decisively, the mathematics segment. What Yale, Stanford, and others know is that women make up only 38 percent of the SAT's 700-plus mathematics pool and 34 percent of the ACT's 33-plus circle. As a result, more men are routinely deemed to have the dossier these colleges seek. Might these colleges be worried about their public image if women began to outnumber men on their campuses, producing a large gender imbalance?

So what's to be done? Machine-graded testing is so entrenched that about all we get is tinkering. (SAT items now have four choices instead of five.) In the past, questions involving the torque of racing cars were deemed sexually biased. It's hard to find anything slanted quite so obviously today. If more mathematics problems can be attuned to today's girls and women, there should be efforts to include them. But we shouldn't delude ourselves that female-friendly wording will turn the tide.   12

The generally accepted antidote follows Henry Higgins's plea (here faintly amended) in *My Fair Lady*: "Why Can't Women Be More Like Men?" This is a patent premise in coaching courses. Kaplan has even produced a special "Study Guide for Girls." Essentially, they're told to forget what got them A's in their mathematics classes and urged instead to deliberate less on questions, answer even if they don't know, and tackle the test as a game to be outwitted.   13

Is that what we want? If anything, I would have supposed we want to encourage young people — nascent adults — to be thoughtful. And that entails taking your time, not taking shortcuts. But the real charge against our testing imperium is how it blatantly slights the talents of half our society, just when girls and women are revealing abilities that match or surpass those of boys and men. That they are denied their share of seats at selective schools and colleges, and of corporate-sponsored scholarships, should be broadly known and reproached. Setting 83 seconds for advanced algebra problems as the key to attending Yale is to sustain yet another ceiling for women.   14

VOCABULARY/USING A DICTIONARY

1. What part of speech is *diligence* (para. 6)? How would you define it?
2. What is the difference between the word *advise* (para. 6) and the word *advice* (para. 6)?
3. How do you feel about the world if you are *cynical* (para. 7)?

RESPONDING TO WORDS IN CONTEXT

1. What part of speech is *gauge* (para. 4)?
2. What is a *dossier* (para. 11)?
3. What part of speech is *cotton* (para. 7)? What does it mean in this context?

DISCUSSING MAIN POINT AND MEANING

1. What must change if we are going to fix the gender imbalance in the fields of science and engineering?

2. While women statistically don't do as well on standardized tests in STEM subjects, what does Hacker discover about their grades in these courses in school?

3. According to Hacker, what is the trick to scoring well on SAT and ACT tests?

EXAMINING SENTENCES, PARAGRAPHS, AND ORGANIZATION

1. What does the introduction suggest the relationship between women and STEM careers is? How is this in contrast to the rest of the essay?

2. How does Hacker strategically use questions throughout the essay? Are they effective?

3. From what point of view does Hacker write his essay? In this essay, what is the effect of point of view on the reader?

THINKING CRITICALLY

1. Is there value to a high-stakes test that encourages speed and blind guessing over reasoned thought? Why or why not? Should standardized tests be as important as they are?

2. Do you believe the scores prove that girls tend to be more conscientious than boys? Why do critics of the tests believe this?

3. Is it important to be a fast standardized test taker *and* be thoughtful when applying for higher education programs in STEM fields, or is possessing one of these qualities sufficient? Explain.

WRITING ACTIVITIES

1. In a brief response, consider the idea of a glass ceiling. What does this phrase mean? How has it been used to talk about women and their potential? How is the situation with standardized testing a glass ceiling? What can be done to break through it?

2. Write about your personal experience with standardized testing in a reflective essay. How do you study for a test, standardized or otherwise? Do you consider yourself a good standardized test taker? What factors — timing pressures, unfamiliar material, or answer limitations, for example — do you find to be hindrances when you take a test? What strategies have you used to become a better test taker? Have you ever needed coaching to improve your score?

3. Hacker mentions the demand for high scores at some elite colleges, which then only admit a small fraction of women in their STEM programs. Should colleges put as much weight on standardized tests as they do? Cite Hacker or another source of your choice to support your position.

Spotlight on Data and Research

Goldie Blumenstyk

Just Half of Graduates Strongly Agree Their College Education Was Worth the Cost

[*The Chronicle of Higher Education*, September 29, 2015]

How do college graduates feel about the cost of their educations? Do they think their degree was worth the expense? Do they regret the expenditure? The following report that appeared in the Chronicle of Higher Education *summarizes a poll conducted by a leading research institution that surveyed 30,000 alumni about whether they thought college was worth the cost. Only half agreed that it was. The results appeared disturbing to one of the head researchers in charge of education at Gallup, who is quoted in the article. "If we don't figure out how to improve that value proposition," he says, "the great tidal wave of demand for higher education in the U.S. could easily come crashing down on us." Dissatisfaction with college costs, the survey also indicates, is felt more strongly by recent graduates carrying heavy student debt.*

Only half of 30,000 college alumni polled for the Gallup-Purdue Index 1
strongly agreed that their higher education was worth the cost, according to the results of the second annual national survey, being published on Tuesday.

Among recent graduates, the proportion who were unequivocally 2
positive was even lower: only 38 percent of those graduating from 2006 through 2015.

The overall results did not differ widely depending on the kind 3
of institution attended — except when it came to alumni of for-profit colleges. Only 26 percent of those alumni strongly agreed that their postsecondary education was worth the cost. And 13 percent strongly disagreed that it was worth it, a proportion that was notably higher than the national average of 4 percent.

Perhaps not surprisingly, younger alumni carrying student-loan 4
debt were more negative than those without debt. Among those with debt, only one in three strongly agreed that their college education was worth the cost.

The 2015 findings highlight a continuing challenge for colleges, 5
said Brandon Busteed, Gallup's executive director for education and workforce development. "If we don't figure out how to improve that value proposition," he said in an interview, "the great tidal wave of demand for higher education in the U.S. could easily come crashing down on us."

continued

For the 2015 poll, Gallup interviewed a nationally representative 6
sample of more than 30,000 college alumni.

Debt concerns are affecting more than alumni's attitudes about their 7
undergraduate experience. Nearly half of recent graduates with student-
loan debt said they had delayed postgraduate education because of it.
Their levels of debt mattered too: 40 percent of those with student debt
below $25,000 said they had delayed going back to school, but for those
with debt in excess of that amount, the proportion was 56 percent.

Student debt also had other effects. Of recent alumni with more 8
than $25,000 in student debt, 43 percent said it had caused them to
delay buying a home, 40 percent said it had delayed their purchase of
a car, 27 percent said it had delayed their moving out of their parents'
home, 25 percent said it had delayed their starting their own business,
19 percent said it had delayed their getting married, and 26 percent said
it had delayed their having children.

The 2015 poll builds on the findings of last year's survey, which 9
sought to identify educational practices that correlate with graduates'
later satisfaction with their careers and overall level of well-being. The
new poll found that alumni were more likely to believe their education
was worth the cost if they had taken part in experiences like an internship relevant to their studies or a long-term project.

DRAWING CONCLUSIONS

1. Of what significance is it that alumni of for-profit colleges were least
   likely to agree that their costs were worth it? What explanation can
   you offer as to why this may be the case?

2. From this brief summary, what appears to be the chief reason that
   recent alumni feel their education was not worth the cost?

3. The poll summarized above resembles in many ways "customer
   satisfaction surveys" taken by businesses. Note that Brandon
   Busteed's quote supports this comparison. Do you think students
   are "customers" and an education is a "product"? Discuss the
   implications of this model in assessing the "value" of a college
   education.

Desiree Bergstrom (student essay)

The Problem with Choosing between BS and BA

[*Daily Emerald*, University of Oregon, April 4, 2016]

BEFORE YOU READ

What subjects should students be encouraged to take to complete a well-rounded education? Is it important for students to take a foreign language and math, no matter what degree they are studying for?

WORDS TO LEARN

prerequisite (para. 3): a class required before taking another (noun)

applicable (para. 8): relevant (adjective)

As college students, we make decisions every day, like whether or not we can spare the time for one more episode of our favorite Netflix show before we write our nine-page paper, or if $5 is better spent on gas than a Starbucks drink. However, it's not very often that one small decision can shape your college experience as a whole. 1

Deciding between pursuing a bachelor of science or a bachelor of arts is one of the few exceptions. Whichever one of these you choose as a freshman follows you all the way through your time at school. While it seems simple enough, considering that the only difference is one requires a foreign language and the other requires math, the real question is why do students need to choose in the first place? 2

College is not only about learning your field of study and gaining detailed knowledge in that area, but also about making sure you have a basic knowledge in many areas, which is why everyone has to take prerequisites. 3

Whether or not students are required to take language or math classes is based on what type of degree they are pursuing. Writing, however, is required across the board. Furthermore, according to the University of Oregon Admissions website, transfer students are required to meet foreign language, math and writing requirements, while many other students go through their time at school never having taken a math or language course. 4

Desiree Bergstrom is a student at the University of Oregon.

Every degree should require students to learn some level of math   5
and some amount of a foreign language. The basics of a language should
be taught with the idea that if you are in a pinch, you could break a
language barrier enough to get directions or report an emergency. On
the other side of things, math is comparable to foreign language in the
sense that no matter what profession you are going into, it will pop up
eventually.

Kylie Davis, a communications disorders and sciences major, said,   6
"An art major doesn't need to know calculus." While she may be right
about calculus, that doesn't mean basic college math wouldn't help. Art
students at some point could need to know how to calculate profits and
losses while marketing their pieces.

> It's about learning
> to be a well-
> rounded student
> ready for anything
> in the workforce.

Some would make an argument that   7
college students learned enough math or
language in high school to get them by, but
this isn't simply about getting by. It's about
learning to be a well-rounded student ready
for anything in the workforce.

Art major Leisa Boles said, "If math is   8
required, students should be required to
understand basic math that would help further knowledge in things like
taxes, paying bills and understanding the fundamentals of math used in
everyday life." Essentially, Boles is describing a basic level of math, taught
in all bachelor degrees, in which students would actually learn applicable math as opposed to calculus, unless of course they are getting their
degrees in a math-related field.

Boles went on to discuss foreign language. "Learning a language pre-   9
pares one to learn more than communication," Boles said. "It improves
one's understanding of how others communicate, as well as the understanding of other cultures." Understanding other cultures is an important
part of being a student because we are surrounded by so many different
cultures while we are here at school, and will be as we enter our preferred
career paths as well.

While one could argue that, no matter what path you decide to take,   10
you can still take math and/or language classes, it can be difficult for students to take these classes if they are not required for their major because
of a lack of time. Most college students want to get their degree done and
over with as fast as possible so as not to pay more than they have to in
tuition costs.

This decision between a BA and a BS bears more weight than you   11
might think and it is necessary to treat it seriously, just as it is worth considering revising the way these degrees are structured in the first place.

Let's not make these decisions the same way we decide to watch another Netflix episode, but think about them from a long-term view and make sure we are making the best decision possible.

VOCABULARY/USING A DICTIONARY

1. What is a *pinch*? What is meant by the phrase *in a pinch* (para. 5)?

2. What is the difference between *eventually* (para. 5) and *essentially* (para. 8)?

3. Name an antonym for *well-rounded* (para. 7).

RESPONDING TO WORDS IN CONTEXT

1. If students are *pursuing* (para. 4) a degree, what are they doing?

2. What kind of math is *calculus* (para. 6)? How is it different from the math Bergstrom says is necessary?

3. What is an example of a *field of study* (para. 3)?

DISCUSSING MAIN POINT AND MEANING

1. How does the decision about which degree to pursue differ from most decisions students make?

2. What is Bergstrom's position on taking classes in math and a foreign language in college?

3. Why, according to Bergstrom's essay, is taking a foreign language important to all students?

EXAMINING SENTENCES, PARAGRAPHS, AND ORGANIZATION

1. Reread Bergstrom's first paragraph. She might have written, "As college students, we make decisions every day. However, it's not very often that one small decision can shape your college experience as a whole." What does she add to her first sentence? How does that addition influence what the reader takes away from her first paragraph?

2. Does Bergstrom sufficiently explain the differences between the bachelor of science and the bachelor of arts degrees? Why or why not? If you were to add information, where would you place it?

3. Where does Bergstrom show adeptness with symmetry in her organizing of information and writing? Point out specific examples.

THINKING CRITICALLY

1. The author states that while learning math or languages is dependent on whatever degree is being pursued, "writing . . . is required across the board" (para. 4). Why might this be so?

2. Is it difficult — or will it be difficult — to fit classes that are not specific to your major into your schedule? Why or why not?

3. Would you like to revise the way your current degree is structured? Explain. What is working in the current structure, or how would you revise it?

WRITING ACTIVITIES

1. Bergstrom quotes Kylie Davis, who offers a counterargument to Bergstrom's position: "An art major doesn't need to know calculus" (para. 6). Create your own sentence based on your proposed major (or a major you are considering) and fill in the unnecessary subject matter: "A _____ major doesn't need to know _____." Then, in a paragraph, write a rebuttal to that statement.

2. Write a list of all the classes you will need to take in order to fulfill the requirements of your particular major. How full is your list? Are there other classes you wish you could take outside your field of study? Do you agree with Bergstrom's statement that taking a variety of courses in college is "about learning to be a well-rounded student ready for anything in the workforce" (para. 7)? Write a response to that statement, and incorporate your answers to the preceding questions.

3. Bergstrom writes, "Every degree should require students to learn some level of math and some amount of a foreign language" (para. 5). Write a brief essay in which you agree or disagree with this statement. Incorporate examples from your own experience and considerations for your future career.

LOOKING CLOSELY

Posing a Question

Effective essays often pose a question and then attempt to answer it. An essayist might ask what can be done about a certain problem: How can we make police forces more responsible to a community? Or what can human populations do to improve the environment? Or do women college athletes receive poorer playing fields than college men? The questions are often asked outright and the reader thus knows what the writer's topic will be.

That is exactly the case in Desiree Bergstrom's "The Problem with Choosing between BS and BA." After introducing a few trivial choices that college students often make, she launches into the serious choice that is the topic of her essay. Note that she states her question clearly and directly, so there is little doubt about the essay's main topic.

1
Opens with small decisions

(1) <u>As college students, we make decisions every day,</u> <u>like whether or not we can spare the time for one more</u> <u>episode of our favorite Netflix show before we write our</u> <u>nine-page paper, or if $5 is better spent on gas than a Star-</u> <u>bucks drink.</u> However, it's not very often that one small decision can shape your college experience as a whole.

2
Brings in the big decision

(2) <u>Deciding between pursuing a bachelor of science</u> <u>or a bachelor of arts is one of the few exceptions. Which-</u> <u>ever one of these you choose as a freshman follows you</u> <u>all the way through your time at school.</u> While it seems simple enough, considering that the only difference is one requires a foreign language and the other requires math,

3
Establishes her topic with a key question

(3) <u>the real question is why do students need to choose in</u> <u>the first place?</u>

Advertisement: "There Are Three Things Everyone Should Read before Entering College . . ."

In an attempt to attract students, educational institutions have been advertising since the nineteenth century. And anyone who watches college sports on television today is aware of how often schools run commercials promoting their campuses, special programs, illustrious history, prominent faculty, outstanding alumni, and — most importantly — student satisfaction. In 1989, Adelphi University ran advertisements like the following one to stimulate applications. The ad, which reads like a mini-essay in itself, captures a world that seems at once old-fashioned and forward-looking as it tries to persuade potential students that philosophy and the liberal arts are wholly relevant to whatever career one wants to pursue. (For more on how to read an advertisement, see p. 40 in the Introduction.)

THERE ARE THREE THINGS EVERYONE SHOULD READ BEFORE ENTERING COLLEGE:

PLATO'S REPUBLIC, THE COMPLETE WORKS OF ARISTOTLE, AND THIS AD.

Not so fast.

If you think you can get away with ignoring the first two works and get right into this ad, stop. Rip this page out and stick it in your sock drawer.

Don't read this ad until you've first savoured Plato. And discovered Aristotle, if not the complete works at least the incomplete collection, maybe the *Ethics* or the *Politics*.

Then you'll be able to deal with the Madison Avenue manipulators who market universities the same way they market sausages or deodorant soap.

Your mind will then be keen enough to dismiss the vapid slogans that university marketers conjure up to attract you, the consumers, who enter the education marketplace each spring. Slogans also designed to soothe parents whose checks enter the universities' treasuries each autumn.

(Used to be a school's slogan would be a nice Latin phrase such as *lux et veritas* or *semper paratus* or *ut omnes te cognoscant*. Now we get corporate gobbledygook like: People making successful people ever more successful, successfully).

If you're heading for business school, for example, you'll not only note the obvious: how many successful graduates in all fields that Adelphi can point to. You'll also investigate what you can learn at Adelphi besides LIFO, FIFO, and the other Principles of Accounting. What is it that a liberal arts environment imparts that a trade school can't?

(continued)

The same is true of the psychology student or the communications major. Or the pre-law and pre-med students who are, after all, students of the Arts and Sciences, respectively.

When you visit our school, ask to see a dean, even the President. (The President of Adelphi still teaches his philosophy class every Thursday at 5:10 PM. If you drop in with an inquiring mind, he'll welcome you, albeit argumentatively).

The premise of Adelphi is that all students (whether of nursing, psychology, business, the humanities, the physical sciences, education, the fine arts) deserve the opportunity to enrich themselves by exposure to ideas.

Now: will your day-to-day involvement in those ideas make you a better investment banker? Or social worker? Or lawyer? Or high school teacher? Or nurse? Or statesman? Or accountant? Or psychologist? Or doctor? Does a liberal education make a difference in one's ability to make a living in 20th Century America, not to mention 21st Century America?

Yes. And we believe a profound difference. It has done that for 2500 years in every corner of the world. It will be no less efficacious today in the Western Hemisphere, in the United States, on Long Island 45 minutes from Manhattan and a five-block stroll from the Nassau Boulevard station of the Long Island Railroad.

Now that you've removed this ad from your sock drawer, there are three more things to do before entering college. One, give us a call. Two, read our publications and look at our video. And three, visit our campus and say hello.

ADELPHI UNIVERSITY

Garden City, New York 11530. (516) 663-1100.
For application materials and a video, write or call.

BACKGROUND AND CONTEXT

1. Madison Avenue in New York City has long been the home of American advertising, and the location has become synonymous with advertising (e.g., *Mad Men*). Why does the ad introduce "Madison Avenue manipulators"? What do you think the point is about marketing "sausages or deodorant soap"? Why are you supposed to think this ad is different from what the "manipulators" do?

2. How do you think you, as reader of the ad, are supposed to feel about "the education marketplace"? Why doesn't the ad say you'll be entering "colleges" or "universities" here instead? Why does it use the word *consumers*? What does the term *marketplace* suggest?

STRATEGY, STRUCTURE, AND STYLE

1. How do you immediately respond to the ad's headline? Do you think anyone would stop reading the ad, turn to the formidable works of Greek philosophy it recommends, then return to the ad? What is the point of the headline?

2. Why doesn't the ad define what the Latin expressions mean in the sixth paragraph? Or explain *LIFO* and *FIFO* in the next paragraph? What is the purpose of leaving these expressions unexplained?

COMPARISONS AND CONNECTIONS

1. Note the ad's illustration. Why do you think the ad never refers to it? What purpose do you think it serves? What does the image suggest? What era does it seem to come from? How does it reinforce the ad's message about the way the ad is composed?

2. How do you think the ad, though it appeared nearly thirty years ago, addresses the issues introduced in this chapter? What educational issues still pertain? What parts of the ad seem no longer applicable to the present? Can you identify any elements in the ad that you do not think would appear if it were written today?

Discussing the Unit

SUGGESTED TOPIC FOR DISCUSSION

Value can be related to monetary worth, or it could be related to where something falls in our personal — and less tangible — estimation. The authors in this chapter debate the value of an education, both monetary and personal. After reading these essays, consider what a college education offers and whether or not it is worth the cost.

PREPARING FOR CLASS DISCUSSION

1. How much are you willing to pay for a college education? Are you willing to go into debt? What factors must you consider before you apply to college and before you decide how much debt you are willing to face after graduation?

2. Why go to college? Do you find any of the arguments in this chapter, either for or against a college education, convincing? Which argument makes the most sense to you?

FROM DISCUSSION TO WRITING

1. Do you think money is a deciding factor when choosing to go or not to go to college? Are you more influenced by the money you must pay to go or the potential to make money once you graduate? Consider the sway of money on this particular decision, and explain how you see money as a force that compels you to or propels you away from the idea of college. Use examples from the essays to illustrate your point.

2. What are some of the reasons people go to college? Are your reasons more in line with Robert Reich's arguments (p. 155) or with Suzanne Fields's (p. 159)? Did testing play a role in what you decided to study, as Andrew Hacker suggests in his essay (p. 163)? In an essay, explain your answers.

TOPICS FOR CROSS-CULTURAL DISCUSSION

1. What do you think your generation expects from college, in terms of achieving satisfaction with the experience? Consider the points made in Piyush Mangukiya's "Is College Worth the Cost? Absolutely" (p. 154), and contrast these with the points made in Goldie Blumenstyk's "Just Half of Graduates Strongly Agree Their College Education Was Worth the Cost" (p. 169).

2. Do you think standardized testing is unfair to women? Respond to this question using Andrew Hacker's essay (p. 163) as a reference; also bring in Suzanne Fields's perspective on education (p. 159). Comment on how education may be changing from the encouragement of critical thinking to an expectation of specialized, black-or-white answers.

5

Race: Does It Still Matter?

For as long as America has existed, race has been one of its most challenging issues. In the era of the first mixed-race president, some observers say we can finally shelve it — they claim we're living in a "postracial" America, in which systematic oppression of certain ethnic groups by others is no longer a serious problem, in which Martin Luther King Jr.'s dream of a society that judges its individuals "not by the color of their skin but by the content of their character" has come true.

Not everyone agrees with this vision of progress. Some cultural critics argue that racial injustice still plagues American society, and in particular that African Americans and other minorities are the persistent victims — sometimes unknowingly — of "institutional racism," persecution that's not direct (like segregation) but systemic. Such systemic racism is the pointed subject of this chapter's "In Brief" selection, a prose poem by the prominent poet Claudia Rankine that uses a single compressed incident to show how racial prejudice can insinuate itself into the ordinary moments of everyday life.

In a less compressed form, Robin DiAngelo, author of *What Does It Mean to Be White?*, offers a systematic account of how and why even well-intentioned white people — those who do not believe they hold racist views — are clueless when it comes to detecting their own privileges and entitlements, which they too often take for granted. In "White America's Racial Illiteracy: Why Our National Conversation Is Poisoned from the Start," she argues that "white people have extremely low thresholds for enduring any discomfort associated with challenges to our racial worldviews." She then clearly enumerates all the challenges to a dominant white perspective.

One of the major movements of recent years, one that still powerfully affects all Americans, is the Black Lives Matter movement, which began as large demonstrations against recent well-publicized killings by police officers of mostly young unarmed black citizens in cities like Atlanta, Ferguson, Cleveland, Baltimore, and Chicago. In an essay that disrupted the Wesleyan University campus, a sophomore questioned the legitimacy of Black Lives Matter. In "Why Black Lives Matter Isn't What You Think," Bryan Stascavage, though he doesn't question claims of racism, asks, "Is the movement itself actually achieving anything positive? Does it have the potential for positive change?" Looking at other campuses across the country, Dawn Lundy Martin, a poet and professor, sees an apparently serene "ivy-encrusted" world in which African American students confront enormous pressures that transform leisure into labor. In "Weary Oracle," she explains the "labor of having to name racism when it is already nakedly visible; the labor of being perpetually suspect, never afforded the possibility of neutral innocence; . . . the very special labor of pretending (because you are tired) that everything is fine."

Psychologists and sociologists have for decades attempted to study racism by means of experiments designed to measure instinctive reactions. This chapter's "Spotlight on Data and Research" examines a very recent psychological study conducted at the University of Iowa. Written by journalist Tom Jacobs, "Racism in the Kindergarten Classroom" shows that whites in an experimental situation instantly reacted to images of black male faces "in ways that indicated a heightened level of perceived threat." Surprisingly, these negative reactions extended even to the facial images of five-year-old African American children.

No discussion of race in America can be complete without references to the legacy of slavery. Although abolished by Lincoln with the Emancipation Proclamation that took effect in the midst of the Civil War on January 1, 1863, slavery has had an enduring impact on American society. The horrific daily facts of slavery and its human abuses were commonly witnessed by millions of earlier Americans, and they were felt especially by those living in the volatile years leading up to the Civil War. One of America's most influential anti-slavery advocates was himself a former slave who taught himself to read and write and eventually escaped to New York City. Frederick Douglass became perhaps the nation's most prominent orator of his time, and this chapter's "America Then" features the most famous portion of his most famous speech, called "What to a Slave, Is the Fourth of July?" Hardly a rhetorical question, it was one Douglass was fully prepared to answer: To the slave it was "a day that reveals to him, more than all other days in the year, the gross injustice and cruelty to which he is the constant victim."

Claudia Rankine

You and your partner go to see the film *The House We Live In . . .*

A New York Times *best seller and the winner of numerous poetry awards, Claudia Rankine's 2014 book* Citizen: An American Lyric *is a meticulous exploration in poetry and prose of what it means to be black in a supposedly postracial society. With a keen eye and ear, along with a remarkable sensitivity to nuance, Rankine dramatizes throughout the book the unsettling and often hidden ways — such as those seen in the following passage — that racism emerges in everyday life even among people who abhor racism.*

You and your partner go to see the film *The House We Live In.* You ask a friend to pick up your child from school. On your way home your phone rings. Your neighbor tells you he is standing at his window watching a menacing black guy casing both your homes. The guy is walking back and forth talking to himself and seems disturbed.   1

You tell your neighbor that your friend, whom he has met, is babysitting. He says, no, it's not him. He's met your friend and this isn't that nice young man. Anyway, he wants you to know, he's called the police.   2

Your partner calls your friend and asks him if there's a guy walking back and forth in front of your home. Your friend says that if anyone were outside he would see him because he is standing outside. You hear the sirens through the speakerphone.   3

Your friend is speaking to your neighbor when you arrive home. The four police cars are gone. Your neighbor has apologized to your friend and is now apologizing to you. Feeling somewhat responsible for the actions of your neighbor, you clumsily tell your friend that the next time he wants to talk on the phone he should just go in the backyard. He looks at you a long minute before saying he can speak on the phone wherever he wants. Yes, of course, you say. Yes, of course.   4

POINTS TO CONSIDER

1. In your own words, describe exactly what has happened in Rankine's account. What mistake was made? How do you interpret the mistake?

2. How does Rankine herself compound the mistake? Why do you think she uses the word *clumsily* to describe what she tells her friend in the last paragraph?

3. What is the effect of Rankine's final words? Why does she repeat them? What does the repetition suggest about the entire incident?

Robin DiAngelo

White America's Racial Illiteracy: Why Our National Conversation Is Poisoned from the Start

[*The Good Men Project*, April 9, 2015]

BEFORE YOU READ

Do you think of yourself as living in an inherently racist society? What aspects of daily life might we take into consideration when we define the word *racist*?

WORDS TO LEARN

mainstream (para. 1): belonging to the prevailing or dominant current or group (adjective)

hierarchies (para. 3): ranking systems (noun)

adaptive (para. 4): having capacity to change (adjective)

insulate (para. 6): to keep separate (verb)

benign (para. 6): not harmful (adjective)

solidarity (para. 7): unity (noun)

centrality (para. 7): the state of being in the center (noun)

equilibrium (para. 8): balance (noun)

platitudes (para. 10): statements expressing ideas that are not new (noun)

binary (para. 14): based on two things (noun)

penalization (para. 16): punishment (noun)

antidote (para. 21): something that corrects or fixes a problem (noun)

certitude (para. 25): freedom from doubt (noun)

Robin DiAngelo was a professor of multicultural education at Westfield State University and now serves as a lecturer at the University of Washington. For over two decades she has been a trainer and consultant on racial and social justice issues.

I am white. I have spent years studying what it means to be white   1
in a society that proclaims race meaningless, yet is deeply divided
by race. This is what I have learned: Any white person living in the
United States will develop opinions about race simply by swimming in
the water of our culture. But mainstream sources — schools, textbooks,
media — don't provide us with the multiple perspectives we need.

Yes, we will develop strong emotionally laden opinions, but they   2
will not be informed opinions. Our socialization renders us racially
illiterate. When you add a lack of humility to that illiteracy (because we
don't know what we don't know), you get the breakdown we so often
see when trying to engage white people in meaningful conversations
about race.

Mainstream dictionary definitions reduce racism to individual racial   3
prejudice and the intentional actions that result. The people that commit
these intentional acts are deemed bad, and those that don't are good. If
we are against racism and unaware of committing racist acts, we can't be
racist; racism and being a good person have become mutually exclusive.
But this definition does little to explain how racial hierarchies are consistently reproduced.

Social scientists understand racism as a multidimensional and   4
highly adaptive *system* — a system that ensures an unequal distribution
of resources between racial groups. Because whites built and dominate
all significant institutions (often at the expense of and on the uncompensated labor of other groups), their interests are embedded in the foundation of U.S. society.

While individual whites may be against racism, they still benefit   5
from the distribution of resources controlled by their group. Yes, an
individual person of color can sit at the tables of power, but the overwhelming majority of decision-makers will be white. Yes, white people
can have problems and face barriers, but systematic racism won't be one
of them. This distinction — between individual prejudice and a system
of unequal institutionalized racial power — is fundamental. One cannot
understand how racism functions in the U.S. today if one ignores group
power relations.

This systemic and institutional control allows those of us who are   6
white in North America to live in a social environment that protects and
insulates us from race-based stress. We have organized society to repro-
duce and reinforce our racial interests and perspectives. Further, we are
centered in all matters deemed normal, universal, benign, neutral, and
good. Thus, we move through a wholly racialized world with an unracial-
ized identity (e.g., white people can represent all of humanity, people of
color can only represent their racial selves).

Challenges to this identity become highly stressful and even intoler- 7
able. The following are examples of the kinds of challenges that trigger
racial stress for white people:

- Suggesting that a white person's viewpoint comes from a
  racialized frame of reference (challenge to objectivity);
- People of color talking directly about their own racial
  perspectives (challenge to white taboos on talking openly
  about race);
- People of color choosing not to protect the racial feelings
  of white people in regards to race (challenge to white racial
  expectations and need/entitlement to racial comfort);
- People of color not being willing to tell their stories or answer
  questions about their racial experiences (challenge to the
  expectation that people of color will serve us);
- A fellow white not providing agreement with one's racial
  perspective (challenge to white solidarity);
- Receiving feedback that one's behavior had a racist impact
  (challenge to white racial innocence);
- Suggesting that group membership is significant (challenge to
  individualism);
- An acknowledgment that access is unequal between racial
  groups (challenge to meritocracy);
- Being presented with a person of color in a position of leadership (challenge to white authority);
- Being presented with information about other racial groups
  through, for example, movies in which people of color drive the
  action but are not in stereotypical roles, or multicultural education (challenge to white centrality).

Not often encountering these challenges, we withdraw, defend, cry, 8
argue, minimize, ignore, and in other ways push back to regain our racial
position and equilibrium. I term that push back *white fragility*.

This concept came out of my ongoing experience leading discus- 9
sions on race, racism, white privilege, and white supremacy with primarily white audiences. It became clear over time that white people have
extremely low thresholds for enduring any discomfort associated with
challenges to our racial worldviews.

We can manage the first round of challenge by ending the discus- 10
sion through platitudes — usually something that starts with "People
just need to," or "Race doesn't really have any meaning to me," or
"Everybody's racist." Scratch any further on that surface, however, and
we fall apart.

Socialized into a deeply internalized sense of superiority and enti-   11
tlement that we are either not consciously aware of or can never admit
to ourselves, we become highly fragile in conversations about race. We
experience a challenge to our racial worldview as a challenge to our very
identities as good, moral people. It also challenges our sense of rightful
place in the hierarchy. Thus, we perceive any attempt to connect us to the
system of racism as a very unsettling and unfair moral offense.

The following patterns make it difficult for white people to under-   12
stand racism as a *system* and lead to the dynamics of white fragility. While
they do not apply to every white person, they are well-documented overall:

Segregation. Most whites live, grow, play, learn, love, work, and die   13
primarily in social and geographic racial segregation. Yet, our society
does not teach us to see this as a loss. Pause for a moment and consider the
magnitude of this message: We lose nothing of value by having no cross-
racial relationships. In fact, the whiter our schools and neighborhoods
are, the more likely they are to be seen as "good." The implicit message is
that there is no inherent value in the presence or perspectives of people
of color. This is an example of the relentless messages of white superiority
that circulate all around us, shaping our identities and worldviews.

The good/bad binary. The most effective adaptation of racism   14
over time is the idea that racism is conscious bias held by mean people.
If we are not aware of having negative thoughts about people of color,
don't tell racist jokes, are nice people, and
even have friends of color, then we cannot
be racist. Thus, a person is either racist or
not racist; if a person is racist, that person
is bad; if a person is not racist, that person
is good. Although racism does of course
occur in individual acts, these acts are part
of a larger system that we all participate in.
The focus on individual incidences pre-
vents the analysis that is necessary in order to challenge this larger system. The good/bad binary is the fundamental misunderstanding driving
white defensiveness about being connected to racism. We simply do not
understand how socialization and implicit bias work.

> We find intolerable
> any suggestion
> that our behavior
> or perspectives
> are typical of our
> group as a whole.

Individualism. Whites are taught to see themselves as individu-   15
als, rather than as part of a racial group. Individualism enables us to
deny that racism is structured into the fabric of society. This erases
our history and hides the way in which wealth has accumulated over
generations and benefits us, *as a group*, today. It also allows us to distance ourselves from the history and actions of our group. Thus, we
get very irate when we are "accused" of racism, because as individuals,

we are "different" from other white people and expect to be seen as such; we find intolerable any suggestion that our behavior or perspectives are typical of our group as a whole.

Entitlement to racial comfort. In the dominant position, whites 16 are almost always racially comfortable and thus have developed unchallenged expectations to remain so. We have not had to build tolerance for racial discomfort and thus when racial discomfort arises, whites typically respond as if something is "wrong," and blame the person or event that triggered the discomfort (usually a person of color). This blame results in a socially sanctioned array of responses toward the perceived source of the discomfort, including: penalization; retaliation; isolation; and refusal to continue engagement. Since racism is necessarily uncomfortable in that it is oppressive, white insistence on racial comfort guarantees racism will not be faced except in the most superficial of ways.

Racial arrogance. Most whites have a very limited understanding 17 of racism because we have not been trained to think in complex ways about it and because it benefits white dominance not to do so. Yet, we have no compunction about debating the knowledge of people who have thought complexly about race. Whites generally feel free to dismiss these informed perspectives rather than have the humility to acknowledge that they are unfamiliar, reflect on them further, or seek more information.

Racial belonging. White people enjoy a deeply internalized, largely 18 unconscious sense of racial belonging in U.S. society. In virtually any situation or image deemed valuable in dominant society, whites belong. The interruption of racial belonging is rare and thus destabilizing and frightening to whites and usually avoided.

Psychic freedom. Because race is constructed as residing in people 19 of color, whites don't bear the social burden of race. We move easily through our society without a sense of ourselves as racialized. Race is for people of color to think about — it is what happens to "them" — they can bring it up if it is an issue for them (although if they do, we can dismiss it as a personal problem, the race card, or the reason for their problems). This allows whites much more psychological energy to devote to other issues and prevents us from developing the stamina to sustain attention on an issue as charged and uncomfortable as race.

Constant messages that we are more valuable. Living in a white 20 dominant context, we receive constant messages that we are better and more important than people of color. For example: our centrality in history textbooks, historical representations, and perspectives; our centrality in media and advertising; our teachers, role models, heroes, and heroines; everyday discourse on "good" neighborhoods and schools and who is in them; popular TV shows centered around friendship circles that are all white; religious iconography that depicts God, Adam and Eve, and other key figures as white. While one may explicitly reject the notion that one is inherently better than another, one cannot avoid internalizing the message of white superiority, as it is ubiquitous in mainstream culture.

These privileges and the white fragility that results prevent us from 21 listening to or comprehending the perspectives of people of color and bridging cross-racial divides. The antidote to white fragility is ongoing and lifelong, and includes sustained engagement, humility, and education. We can begin by:

- Being willing to tolerate the discomfort associated with an honest appraisal and discussion of our internalized superiority and racial privilege.
- Challenging our own racial reality by acknowledging ourselves as racial beings with a particular and limited perspective on race.
- Attempting to understand the racial realities of people of color through authentic interaction rather than through the media or unequal relationships.
- Taking action to address our own racism, the racism of other whites, and the racism embedded in our institutions — e.g., get educated and act.

"Getting it" when it comes to race and racism challenges our very 22 identities as good white people. It's an ongoing and often painful process of seeking to uncover our socialization at its very roots. It asks us to rebuild this identity in new and often uncomfortable ways. But I can testify that it is also the most exciting, powerful, intellectually stimulating, and emotionally fulfilling journey I have ever undertaken. It has impacted every aspect of my life — personal and professional.

I have a much deeper and more complex understanding of how soci- 23 ety works. I can challenge much more racism in my daily life, and I have developed cherished and fulfilling cross-racial friendships I did not have before.

I do not expect racism to end in my lifetime, and I know that I con- 24 tinue to have problematic racist patterns and perspectives. Yet, I am also confident that I do less harm to people of color than I used to. This is not a minor point of growth, for it impacts my lived experience and that of the people of color who interact with me. If you are white I urge you to take the first step — let go of your racial certitude and reach for humility.

VOCABULARY/USING A DICTIONARY

1. What do you think *socialization* (para. 2) means?
2. What is an *uncompensated* (para. 4) worker paid?
3. What is a *meritocracy* (para. 7)?

RESPONDING TO WORDS IN CONTEXT

1. What is the difference between *everyday* (para. 20) and *every day*?
2. What does DiAngelo mean when she says that "racism and being a good person have become *mutually exclusive*" (para. 3)?
3. DiAngelo talks about "religious *iconography* that depicts God, Adam and Eve, and other key figures as white" (para. 20). What do you think *iconography* means?

DISCUSSING MAIN POINT AND MEANING

1. When the word *racism* is used, what does it usually mean? How are we beginning to rethink what it means to be a racist person?
2. What are some of the factors that lead to what DiAngelo terms "white fragility" (para. 8)?
3. What are some of the dynamics of white fragility, as outlined by DiAngelo?

EXAMINING SENTENCES, PARAGRAPHS, AND ORGANIZATION

1. What information does DiAngelo establish in her introductory paragraph? Why do you think she starts with this information?
2. DiAngelo uses bullet points and subheadings at different points in her essay. Why does she do this? Are they effective?
3. You may have heard that it is effective to start an essay with a definition. DiAngelo's essay tries to redefine *racism*, and she includes a dictionary definition in paragraph 3. What would be the effect of starting her essay with that paragraph? Why do you think she chose to begin the essay as she did?

THINKING CRITICALLY

1. Do you understand DiAngelo's reaction against the mainstream definition and mainstream understanding of racism and what it means to be racist? Does her definition place more emphasis on the individual or society — or both?
2. If you are white, do you think it is important to understand what DiAngelo calls "a deeply internalized sense of superiority and entitlement" (para. 11)?

If you do not identify as white, do you perceive this sense in whites as "white fragility" (para. 8)? Why or why not?

3. We do not necessarily think of ourselves as living in a segregated society (segregation was abolished in the United States in 1964). However, DiAngelo includes segregation as one of the things whites do when they feel unsettled by the challenges of confronting a racialized world. Do you see segregation in your world? Does it match what DiAngelo identifies as segregation (para. 13)?

WRITING ACTIVITIES

1. Choose one of the "dynamics of white fragility" (para. 12) that DiAngelo identifies in her essay. Write an analysis of how you see this dynamic working on your own college campus or in your community. You can write about it generally, or you can provide very specific examples and/or narrative.

2. DiAngelo says she doesn't expect racism to end in her lifetime, and she suggests that combating white fragility is "ongoing and lifelong, and includes sustained engagement, humility, and education" (para. 21). Do you agree that racism is unlikely to end in the near future (or hasn't ended yet)? Do you think her solution to racism is the right one? Take some notes about what you think on these matters and write some responses to DiAngelo's points; then argue your position in a short essay.

3. Create a list of acts of racism, both those perpetrated by an individual and those perpetrated by a society. After you have generated a list of possible acts (these can be acts you've read about in the news, acts you've heard about anecdotally, things you've perceived to be racist in daily interactions, or events that you've studied in school), label them as either "individual" or "society." Decide, after considering how you've labeled them, whether most racist acts occur on an individual level or are part of a greater system of societal racism, as DiAngelo suggests.

Bryan Stascavage (student essay)

Why Black Lives Matter Isn't What You Think

[*The Wesleyan Argus*, Wesleyan University, September 14, 2015]

BEFORE YOU READ

What do you know about the Black Lives Matter movement and what it stands for? How do you see its principles and contributions at work in the world around you?

WORDS TO LEARN

plausible (para. 14): believable (adjective)

vilification (para. 18): abuse (noun)

denigration (para. 18): defamation (noun)

vocally (para. 23): with voice; audibly (adverb)

A 20-year-old man walks into a church and massacres nine people, claiming that he was afraid that America was being taken over by black Americans, citing American race relations as evidence. About a month later, a man wears a GoPro, tapes himself walking up to a local reporter and a cameraman, and shoots them both on camera, proclaiming racial injustice in this country as his motive.   1

Police officers are looking over their shoulders as several cops have been targeted and gunned down. The week before classes started, seven officers were killed in the line of duty; a few were execution-style targeted killings.   2

An officer I talked to put it succinctly: "If they want to come after me, fine. Just come at me head-on. Don't shoot me in the back of my head. I'd rather go down with a fighting chance."   3

Is this an atmosphere created by the police officers and racist elements in society itself? Many, including individuals in the Black Lives Matter movement, believe so.   4

Or is it because of Black Lives Matter? Many believe that as well, including a police chief who made his remarks after one of his officers   5

Bryan Stascavage is a government major at Wesleyan University and a staff writer for the Opinion section of the Wesleyan Argus.

was shot and killed — he claimed that Black Lives Matter was responsible for the officer's death. Some want Black Lives Matter labeled as a hate group.

I talked to a Black Lives Matter supporter, Michael Smith '18, who recoiled when I told him I was wondering if the movement was legitimate. This is not questioning their claims of racism among the police, or in society itself. Rather, is the movement itself actually achieving anything positive? Does it have the potential for positive change?   6

There is evidence to support both views. Police forces around the country are making more of an effort to be more transparent, have undergone investigations to root out racist officers and policies, and have forced the conversation to the front pages after being buried on the back pages for far too long.   7

On the other hand, following the Baltimore riots [protests following the death of Freddie Gray in April 2015], the city saw a big spike in murders. Good officers, like the one I talked to, go to work every day even more worried that they won't come home. The officer's comments reminded me of what soldiers used to say after being hit with IEDs in Iraq. Police forces with a wartime-like mentality are never a good thing.   8

Smith countered with, "You can't judge an entire movement off the actions of a few extremists."   9

I responded with, "Isn't that what the movement is doing with the police? Judging an entire profession off the actions of a few members?"   10

Hence, my concerns that the movement is not legitimate, or at the very least, hypocritical.   11

It is apparent that the man who shot the reporter and her cameraman isn't a representation of Black Lives Matter. The question is whether or not the movement is setting the conditions for the more extreme or mentally disturbed individuals to commit atrocities.   12

Smith explained further. "Yes, but the police have an established system of reporting the bad officers. BLM is decentralized, they aren't as organized. You can't hold the more moderate elements responsible for what a crazy person does in their name."   13

Perhaps. But that doesn't explain Black Lives Matter rallies, cheering after an officer is killed, chanting that they want more pigs to fry like bacon. That wasn't one or two people. The movement also doesn't want to be associated with looters and rioters, calling them opportunistic. But it is plausible that Black Lives Matter has created the conditions for these individuals to exploit for their own personal gain.   14

I warned in an article last semester that a movement that does not combat its own extremists will quickly run into trouble. The reasons why are now self-evident. If Black Lives Matter is going to be the one   15 responsible for generating these conversations, then a significant portion of that conversation needs to be about peace. They need to stand with police units that lose a member, decrying it with as much passion as they do when a police officer kills an unarmed civilian.

> There is a reason why so many have shown up at protests across the country: There is clearly something wrong.

Smith does have a point, though. An organization cannot be labeled based on a small percentage of its membership. There is a reason why so many have shown up at protests across the country: There is clearly something wrong, and wrong enough to motivate them to exit their homes and express their frustration publicly. That is no small effort. The system is clearly failing many, and unfortunately they feel like they will only be listened to if their protests reach the front pages of the news. And so far, they are correct. 16

But this principle needs to be applied universally. I know many of us here at Wesleyan realize that most police officers are good people simply doing a service for their community, and that there are only a few bad apples. But those chanting to fry the pigs seem to have missed this message. 17

It boils down to this for me: If vilification and denigration of the police force continue to be a significant portion of Black Lives Matter's message, then I will not support the movement, I cannot support the movement. And many Americans feel the same. I should repeat, I do support many of the efforts by the more moderate activists. 18

It is advice that I need to take myself. After the Supreme Court ruling that legalized gay marriage nationwide, a few liberals gloated in a conservative political forum that I like to read. They were surprised by the reaction: Every conservative who responded was happy with the ruling. 19

I realize that moderate conservatives need to speak up more as well. If we had, gay marriage might have been legalized years ago. Instead, I got the feeling that a lot of moderate conservatives were afraid of speaking up about the issue and being labeled as a RINO (Republican In Name Only). 20

I also understand the frustration of moderate Black Lives Matter members, like the one I talked to, about being stereotyped based on a few radical and vocal members. 21

Kim Davis, the misguided Kentucky clerk who is refusing to hand out marriage licenses [she defied a U.S. court order in August 2015] is a perfect example of this. As a conservative, I am infuriated to see one clerk in one city out of the thousands in conservative states making headlines, 22 when the rest are handing out licenses with no issue. One clerk is making headlines and is being held up as evidence that conservatives hate homosexuality. Kim Davis generated a couple of hundred supporters, a very small showing.

Yet I am not innocent when it comes to Kim Davis. I could have   23
gone down to the courthouse and joined the counterprotest, holding up a sign that says "conservatives for gay marriage rights," and made a statement that Kim Davis is not representative of the mainstream conservative views. I don't blame those who can't support conservatives for not being more vocally pro–gay rights, though many liberal politicians were also silent on the issue during the 1990s and 2000s.

Returning to Black Lives Matter, the country is nervously waiting   24
to see what happens next — the next unarmed civilian to be killed, the next officer to be killed, the next radical racist to take their views to the next level.

At some point Black Lives Matter is going to be confronted with an   25
uncomfortable question, if they haven't already begun asking it: Is this all worth it? Is it worth another riot that destroys a downtown district? Another death, another massacre? At what point will Black Lives Matter go back to the drawing table and rethink how they are approaching the problem?

VOCABULARY/USING A DICTIONARY

1. What does *IED* (para. 8) stand for?
2. How would you define *atrocities* (para. 12)?
3. What Latin words make up the word *opportunistic* (para. 14)? What part of speech is *opportunistic*?

RESPONDING TO WORDS IN CONTEXT

1. When Stascavage says that after the Baltimore riots there was a *big spike* (para. 8) in murders, what does he mean?
2. If Black Lives Matter is *decentralized* (para. 13), how is it organized?
3. What part of speech is *exploit* (para. 14) in this context? What does it mean?

DISCUSSING MAIN POINT AND MEANING

1. What are the forces at work in this country that have helped create the wartime-like mentality that Stascavage points out is becoming more and more frequent in police officers?
2. Who does Stascavage suggest might be responsible for recent racial violence and unrest in the United States?
3. What does Stascavage think he should have done when Kim Davis refused to hand out marriage licenses to gay couples? Why?

EXAMINING SENTENCES, PARAGRAPHS, AND ORGANIZATION

1. Are you surprised by the quotation Stascavage includes in paragraph 3? Do the preceding paragraphs prepare you for this quotation?

2. How do you respond to Stascavage's topic shifts between paragraphs 18 and 19 and back again between 23 and 24? Do you feel enough connection has been established between these topics?

3. Do you think Stascavage's introduction is effective? Is his thesis clear? Why or why not?

THINKING CRITICALLY

1. How does Stascavage identify himself politically? Does his identification matter?

2. Stascavage states that Black Lives Matter supporter Michael Smith "recoiled" (para. 6) when asked if the movement is legitimate. Why do you think Smith had this reaction?

3. At various times, Stascavage tries to present a balanced viewpoint, as if he's considering both sides of the story. Can you find passages that indicate this attempt to find balance? Do you think he has made up his mind about how he perceives Black Lives Matter?

WRITING ACTIVITIES

1. Three words: *Black Lives Matter*. Consider what each word means. In a free-writing exercise, write as many associations as you can for each word separately. Then try another freewriting based on the entire phrase. What sort of images, emotions, and ideas emerge when you write about the phrase without stopping? In small groups, share your freewritings and compare, without judgment, what these words bring up for different people.

2. Smith's quote, "You can't judge an entire movement off the actions of a few extremists" (para. 9), might be echoed by a variety of people on a variety of topics. Consider issues such as gun control, abortion rights, and political extremism. Do you think Smith has a point, or do you agree with Stascavage that any group with certain beliefs has a responsibility to be aware of and vocal about extremists in its midst?

3. Since the deaths of Michael Brown, Freddie Gray, Tamir Rice, and others, much has been made about racism in the police force, spurring much of the Black Lives Matter movement. How do you view police in your community? Do you agree with Stascavage, who says many police are currently trau-matized by how they're perceived (and hated) and most are "good people simply doing a service for their community" (para. 17)? Explain your point of view. Do you think race plays a role in how you view law enforcement? Consider this possibility, as well, as you respond.

Conceding an Opposing View's Good Points

In any argument or debate, it is rare that one side is 100 percent right and the other side 100 percent wrong. Therefore, when writing opinion essays it is often a good idea to notice and acknowledge points made by the opposing side that you agree with. This is called conceding a point. Such a concession clearly indicates that you recognize the opposing side's full position and are willing to admit that it has some things right. Making concessions shows that a writer is being reasonable and is not simply intent on demonizing the opposition as being entirely in the wrong.

Note how Wesleyan University student Bryan Stascavage, in a controversial essay on the Black Lives Matter movement, concedes a very significant point — that the movement is clearly reacting to something that is wrong. Responding to a fellow student he has interviewed who supports the Black Lives Matter movement, Stascavage acknowledges that the student "does have a point" and goes on to explain in what ways the movement is "correct."

1 *Concedes that supporters of BLM have a point*	(1) <u>Smith does have a point, though.</u> An organization cannot be labeled based on a small percentage of its membership. There is a reason why so many have shown up at protests across the country: There is clearly something wrong, and wrong enough to motivate them to exit their homes and express their frustration publicly. That is no small effort. (2) <u>The system is clearly failing many, and unfortunately they feel like they will only be listened to if their protests reach the front pages of the news. And so far, they are correct.</u>
2 *Points out BLM's methods of protest are correct*	

STUDENT WRITER AT WORK
Bryan Stascavage

R.A. What inspired you to write this essay? And publish it?

B.S. I was looking at the news surrounding the Black Lives Matter movement in summer 2014. I noticed a disturbing pattern: Black Lives Matter was receiving media attention for the more violent aspects of the movement, and as a former intelligence analyst, I've seen this pattern before. A movement starts to gain momentum, which attracts radicals to the ranks. Those radicals start acting in the name of the movement, which starts sapping away popular support. Ultimately, the movement is forced to a decision point — do we go down a more radical path, or do we try to moderate and distance ourselves from our more radical factions? Those that choose the former rarely do well; those that choose the latter usually achieve a much higher level of success. And I wanted to share this thought process with the school.

R.A. What response have you received to this piece? Has the feedback you have received affected your views on the topic you wrote about?

B.S. I received a lot of negative feedback, very little of which was constructive criticism. Instead of attacking the points that I made, a portion of the student body instead tried to silence me and defunded the *Argus*, the student newspaper. This then caught the attention of the national media, which caused the conversation to move away from Black Lives Matter and toward a debate over free speech. Is dissenting opinion intrinsically valuable?

R.A. Have you written on this topic since? Have you read or seen other work on the topic that has interested you?

B.S. There was an article in the *Atlantic*, written by a self-described Black Lives Matter supporter who criticized some of my points, but also criticized the movement for its reaction and tendency to try and push the more radical aspects of the movement under the carpet. That was the kind of response and discussion that I was hoping for.

R.A. Are you pursuing a career in which writing will be a component?

B.S. Yes, I am interested in a career as a political pundit or journalist. I only found this path after the controversy over my article. Before that, I viewed writing as more of a hobby that will suit me well in another career field. Sometimes you never know where inspiration or clarity will come from.

R.A. What advice do you have for other student writers?

B.S. Dig, dig, dig. Keep thinking that everything you are being told is a lie until you are satisfied otherwise. Even a pure news article contains bias, omitted information, and other manipulations. Textbooks contain bias, magazines contain bias. The truth exists out there, but you will never find it by reading just one book, or one article, or one magazine. Have a viewpoint, then challenge it. I'll write an article, and then pretend what I just wrote is totally false and write a counterarticle.

Dawn Lundy Martin
Weary Oracle

[*Harper's Magazine*, March 2016]

BEFORE YOU READ
Why do you think people process race trauma so differently? Do you understand why race is an important (or hot-button) topic on campuses today?

WORDS TO LEARN

derogatory (para. 1): disparaging (adjective)

disparage (para. 1): to belittle (verb)

reducible (para. 2): able to be reduced (adjective)

redress (para. 3): compensation (noun)

stoicism (para. 3): conduct that represses emotion and shows little concern for pleasure or pain (noun)

incorporate (para. 4): to introduce or include (verb)

serenity (para. 5): sereneness (noun)

manicured (para. 5): well trimmed and cared for (adjective)

perpetually (para. 5): continuously (adverb)

intimately (para. 5): personally (adverb)

My mother, who was born more than eighty years ago, deep in the   1
Jim Crow[1] South, insists that she has never experienced a single
moment of racism. I have never heard her say a derogatory word about white people as a race or use the word "white" as an insult. When she calls people "black," she does not do so affectionately, to suggest kinship, community, or belonging. And she gets visibly annoyed when black people organize around black*ness*, as though claiming the category that is also used to disparage them were a criminal act. Why excite the ghost?

---

[1] Jim Crow (para. 1): Jim Crow laws enforced racial segregation from Reconstruction until 1965.

Poet and activist Dawn Lundy Martin is currently an associate professor in the University of Pittsburgh's English department. Her most recent collection of poetry, Good Stock, was published in 2016.

Why call its hideous name? Yet when I ask her whether she remembers black people getting lynched, she says, "Yeah, they did sometimes."

That is what race trauma looks like — although it is not reducible to that. 2

At Claremont McKenna College, a young woman's voice cracks 3 as she speaks into a megaphone handed to her by protesters who seek redress for the racial slights that they believe have been encouraged by the culture of the campus. Instead of talking about her own experiences of racism, the woman testifies to the more generalized experiences of others. She weeps; her whole body vibrates. Against my mother's stoicism, the weeping almost reads as performance. It has the texture of a sleeve pulled up to reveal a sore and disgust the viewer. *Put it away.*

But the pitch of the reactions on campuses is not a display of "excessive vulnerability" resulting in "self-diminishment," as some critics of 4 student tactics claim. Something is pressing on these students, making them burst at the seams, and it's not imaginary. They are like oracles whose bodies bear the collective weight of what others do not — or will not — see: the lynchings my mother cannot incorporate into her worldview, the black boy the police shot down in the street just yesterday. They feel all of it when, for example, a white person mistakes them for another brown person who looks nothing like them.

> Something is pressing on these students, making them burst at the seams, and it's not imaginary.

It is not unreasonable for college students to desire to be carefully 5 held by the universities that courted them. In fact, universities and colleges imply a promise, in their mottoes of "Light and Truth," in their ivy-encrusted buildings, in the serenity around their lakes and on their manicured greens, and especially in their invitations for students to engage in the leisure of intellectual work. That's one place where I think students of color hurt: right where leisurely study becomes labor. As a professor who has spent more than half my life on college campuses, I know this labor intimately — the labor of having to name racism when it is already nakedly visible; the labor of being perpetually suspect, never afforded the possibility of neutral innocence; the labor of negotiating others' racially offensive speech; or the very special labor of pretending (because you are tired) that everything is fine. Instead of being protected by the institution that you see your white counterparts inhabiting so casually, you find the institution protected from you. That it is guarded by historical figures such as Woodrow Wilson, a KKK sympathizer whose name is emblazoned on a campus building, is not lost on you. Still, folks want to know, why are you so enraged, what is causing your pain, why do you act so insane?

VOCABULARY/USING A DICTIONARY

1. What is another word for *lynch* (para. 1)?

2. When might you have heard the word *oracle* (para. 4) before? In what context?

3. What word embedded in the word *collective* (para. 4) gives you a clue to its meaning?

RESPONDING TO WORDS IN CONTEXT

1. What does Martin mean by the phrase *race trauma* (para. 2)?

2. What is the opposite of a *generalized* experience (para. 3)?

3. When Martin writes that Woodrow Wilson's name is *emblazoned* (para. 5) on a school building, what is she suggesting about its presence?

DISCUSSING MAIN POINT AND MEANING

1. Has Martin's mother ever experienced racism? How do you know?

2. What is Martin referring to when she writes about a sore revealed to "disgust the viewer" (para. 3)? What is the sore?

3. At college, what work are students of color engaged in that white students don't have to do?

EXAMINING SENTENCES, PARAGRAPHS, AND ORGANIZATION

1. Martin brings the example of her mother into the first paragraph. How does her example connect to what the essay is about? Do you think the essay is more or less effective with that example in the introduction?

2. Look at Martin's use of the words *labor* and *leisure* in paragraph 5. How does she create the contrast between them? What activities does she connect with those two words? Does she see college as a place of "labor" or "leisure"?

3. Does the essay feel finished? Why or why not?

THINKING CRITICALLY

1. Why do you think Martin's mother denies experiences of racism? Why might her responses be considered an expression of race trauma?

2. Is campus the place for expressing one's feelings about race trauma? Why or why not?

3. Do you think people experience and express experiences of racism differently? Do you think the differences between Martin's experiences and responses and those of her mother are due to a generational difference or something else? What else might cause these kinds of differences?

WRITING ACTIVITIES

1. Martin ends her essay with a question. Imagine if Martin had more to say in this fairly short essay. Outline where the essay might go from here.

2. In writing, respond to Martin's statement, "It is not unreasonable for college students to desire to be carefully held by the universities that courted them" (para. 5). Do you think this statement is true? In what ways, or under what circumstances, should students be "carefully held"?

3. Martin gives examples of "race trauma" that college students are responding to, acting as "oracles" for others. Write down some of the examples she offers in this essay, and then try to come up with some others, based on personal experience or generalized experience. Look around your campus and ask yourself if there is anything else that might be added to Martin's essay. Consider current events as you write.

Spotlight on Data and Research

Tom Jacobs

Racism in the Kindergarten Classroom
[*Pacific Standard*, February 2, 2016]

A senior staff writer for Pacific Standard *and a longtime journalist, Tom Jacobs is an expert at making scholarly research and academic studies more accessible to the average reader. In a recent item for the magazine, he summarized a study from the* RAND Journal of Economics *showing that when collectible baseball cards were auctioned on eBay, cards shown held by black hands fetched less money (approximately 20 percent less) than those held by white hands. There was no other determining factor than skin color to cause this result.*

In the following report, Jacobs summarizes another racial study, this one conducted by University of Iowa researchers who found that white college students shown images of black male faces experienced a "heightened level of perceived threat," even when those faces were of five-year-olds.

If the current election cycle hasn't convinced you that racism has yet to be eradicated, consider this: The mere image of a black man is enough to stimulate an automatic threat response in whites. Research has found faces of African American males are more likely to be perceived as angry, and can trigger neural activity associated with rapid detection of danger. While even preteens can stimulate this reaction (which helps explain the tragic shooting of a 12-year-old holding a pellet gun in Cleveland

continued

two years ago), it presumably doesn't apply to very young black boys. It's hard to believe they are perceived as dangerous as they emerge from the womb.

So when do they start coming across as threatening? Newly pub- 2
lished research provides a depressing answer: by the time they enter kindergarten.

In a series of studies, a University of Iowa research team led by 3
Andrew Todd finds images of the faces of five-year-old black boys are sufficient to trigger whites into heightened-threat mode. "Implicit biases commonly observed for black men appear to generalize even to young black boys," the researchers write in the journal *Psychological Science*.

The first of their experiments featured 63 college undergraduates, 4
who "completed a categorization task in which two images flashed on the monitor in quick succession. Participants were instructed to ignore the first time, which was always a face; it merely signaled that the second image was about to appear. Their task was to quickly and accurately categorize the second image (the target object) as a gun or a toy, by pressing one of two response keys." In fact, the faces — all of five-year-old boys with neutral facial expressions — were a key component of the experiment. Six of them featured black children, and six white. Researchers wanted to know whether the race of the child would affect the speed and accuracy of the white participants' responses.

It did. "Participants identified guns more quickly after black-child 5
primes than after white-child primes," the researchers report, "whereas they identified toys more quickly after the white-child primes than after black-child primes."

Subsequent experiments found black five-year-old faces produced 6
just as strong an effect as photographs of adult black males. This held true when white participants were labeling images as guns or tools, and when they were shown a list of words (including "criminal" and "peaceful") and asked to categorize each as "safe" or "threatening."

In that last experiment, participants misidentified safe words as 7
threatening more often after seeing a black face, and misidentified threatening words as safe more often after seeing a white one — child or adult.

"These racial biases were driven entirely by differences in auto- 8
matic processing," Todd and his colleagues write. In other words, no conscious thought was involved; whites simply saw a black male face and reacted in ways that indicated a heightened level of perceived threat.

Even when the face was that of a five-year-old. 9

DRAWING CONCLUSIONS

1. What in your opinion were the researchers trying to find out? Why, for example, were images of African American children introduced into the experiment?

2. Does it make any difference to you that the experimenters focused only on white college students? What results might you expect if the college students represented a more diverse group? Do you think results would be different if some of the college students were themselves black?

3. Of what significance is it that, as the researchers explain, the "racial biases were driven entirely by differences in automatic processing," or, as Jacobs puts it, "no conscious thought was involved" (para. 8)? Why would the researchers design the experiment with this concern in mind?

Frederick Douglass

From "What to a Slave, Is the Fourth of July?"

One of America's greatest public figures, Frederick Douglass (1817–1895), was born into slavery in Maryland and worked as a field hand and servant until he managed to escape to New York City in 1838 at the age of twenty-one. Self-educated (he taught himself to read and write) and fiercely determined, Douglass transformed himself into one of the nation's most formidable intellectuals and writers of his time. He served in a number of government positions, published his own periodicals, and was known as an outstanding orator and eloquent civil rights advocate. His life and career became a model for such powerful African American leaders as W. E. B. Du Bois and Martin Luther King Jr. Besides a large number of famous speeches (such as his 1852 Fourth of July oration), Douglass is also the author of the enduring American memoir, The Life and Times of Frederick Douglass, *which first appeared in 1881.*

Douglass delivered his best-known speech on July 5, 1852, in Rochester, New York, where he was invited to help celebrate the nation's seventy-sixth birthday. The speech is very long and for those interested the full text can easily be found online. Early in the speech, Douglass makes his position clear when he famously says: "This Fourth of July is yours, not mine. You may rejoice, I must mourn." It must be remembered that the address was delivered in an era when slavery not only was still widely practiced in America but also had many defenders. Although abolitionism — the movement to abolish slavery — was gaining ground in northern states, the Civil War and Lincoln's Emancipation Proclamation were years away. In the following excerpt, which demonstrates the intricate art of persuasion, Douglass passionately argues not about the evils of slavery but about why arguments to abolish it are needed at all.

Fellow-citizens; above your national, tumultuous joy, I hear the mournful wail of millions! whose chains, heavy and grievous yesterday, are, today, rendered more intolerable by the jubilee shouts that reach them. If I do forget, if I do not faithfully remember those bleeding

1

children of sorrow this day, "may my right hand forget her cunning, and may my tongue cleave to the roof of my mouth!"[1] To forget them, to pass lightly over their wrongs, and to chime in with the popular theme, would be treason most scandalous and shocking, and would make me a reproach before God and the world. My subject, then, fellow-citizens, is AMERICAN SLAVERY. I shall see, this day, and its popular characteristics, from the slave's point of view. Standing, there, identified with the American bondman, making his wrongs mine, I do not hesitate to declare, with all my soul, that the character and conduct of this nation never looked blacker to me than on this 4th of July! Whether we turn to the declarations of the past, or to the professions of the present, the conduct of the nation seems equally hideous and revolting. America is false to the past, false to the present, and solemnly binds herself to be false to the future. Standing with God and the crushed and bleeding slave on this occasion, I will, in the name of humanity which is outraged, in the name of liberty which is fettered, in the name of the constitution and the Bible, which are disregarded and trampled upon, dare to call in question and to denounce, with all the emphasis I can command, everything that serves to perpetuate slavery — the great sin and shame of America! "I will not equivocate; I will not excuse;"[2] I will use the severest language I can command; and yet not one word shall escape me that any man, whose judgment is not blinded by prejudice, or who is not at heart a slaveholder, shall not confess to be right and just.

But I fancy I hear some one of my audience say, it is just in this circumstance that you and your brother abolitionists fail to make a favorable impression on the public mind. Would you argue more, and denounce less, would you persuade more, and rebuke less, your cause would be much more likely to succeed. But, I submit, where all is plain there is nothing to be argued. What point in the anti-slavery creed would you have me argue? On what branch of the subject do the people of this country need light? Must I undertake to prove that the slave is a man? That point is conceded already. Nobody doubts it. The slaveholders themselves acknowledge it in the enactment of laws for their government. They acknowledge it when they punish disobedience

2

---

[1] Biblical quotation, from Psalm 137

[2] Douglass quotes noted abolitionist William Lloyd Garrison (1805–1879).

on the part of the slave. There are seventy-two crimes in the State of Virginia, which, if committed by a black man, (no matter how ignorant he be), subject him to the punishment of death; while only two of the same crimes will subject a white man to the like punishment. What is this but the acknowledgment that the slave is a moral, intellectual and responsible being? The manhood of the slave is conceded. It is admitted in the fact that Southern statute books are covered with enactments forbidding, under severe fines and penalties, the teaching of the slave to read or to write. When you can point to any such laws, in reference to the beasts of the field, then I may consent to argue the manhood of the slave. When the dogs in your streets, when the fowls of the air, when the cattle on your hills, when the fish of the sea, and the reptiles that crawl, shall be unable to distinguish the slave from a brute, *then* will I argue with you that the slave is a man!

For the present, it is enough to affirm the equal manhood of the   3
Negro race. Is it not astonishing that, while we are ploughing, planting and reaping, using all kinds of mechanical tools, erecting houses, constructing bridges, building ships, working in metals of brass, iron, copper, silver and gold; that, while we are reading, writing and cyphering, acting as clerks, merchants and secretaries, having among us lawyers, doctors, ministers, poets, authors, editors, orators and teachers; that, while we are engaged in all manner of enterprises common to other men, digging gold in California, capturing the whale in the Pacific, feeding sheep and cattle on the hill-side, living, moving, acting, thinking, planning, living in families as husbands, wives and children, and, above all, confessing and worshipping the Christian's God, and looking hopefully for life and immortality beyond the grave, we are called upon to prove that we are men!

Would you have me argue that man is entitled to liberty? that he is   4
the rightful owner of his own body? You have already declared it. Must I argue the wrongfulness of slavery? Is that a question for Republicans?[3] Is it to be settled by the rules of logic and argumentation, as a matter beset with great difficulty, involving a doubtful application of the principle of justice, hard to be understood? How should I look to-day, in the presence of Americans, dividing, and subdividing a discourse, to show that men have a natural right to freedom? speaking of it relatively,

---

[3] He means citizens of a republic, not the political party that Lincoln belonged to.

and positively, negatively, and affirmatively. To do so, would be to make myself ridiculous, and to offer an insult to your understanding. — There is not a man beneath the canopy of heaven that does not know that slavery is wrong *for him*.

What, am I to argue that it is wrong to make men brutes, to rob   5 them of their liberty, to work them without wages, to keep them ignorant of their relations to their fellow men, to beat them with sticks, to flay their flesh with the lash, to load their limbs with irons, to hunt them with dogs, to sell them at auction, to sunder their families, to knock out their teeth, to burn their flesh, to starve them into obedience and submission to their masters? Must I argue that a system thus marked with blood, and stained with pollution, is *wrong*? No! I will not. I have better employments for my time and strength than such arguments would imply. What, then, remains to be argued? Is it that slavery is not divine; that God did not establish it; that our doctors of divinity are mistaken? There is blasphemy in the thought. That which is inhuman, cannot be divine! Who can reason on such a proposition? They that can, may; I cannot. The time for such argument is passed.

At a time like this, scorching irony, not convincing argument, is   6 needed. O! had I the ability, and could I reach the nation's ear, I would, today, pour out a fiery stream of biting ridicule, blasting reproach, withering sarcasm, and stern rebuke. For it is not light that is needed, but fire; it is not the gentle shower, but thunder. We need the storm, the whirlwind, and the earthquake. The feeling of the nation must be quickened; the conscience of the nation must be roused; the propriety of the nation must be startled; the hypocrisy of the nation must be exposed; and its crimes against God and man must be proclaimed and denounced.

What, to the American slave, is your Fourth of July? I answer: a   7 day that reveals to him, more than all other days in the year, the gross injustice and cruelty to which he is the constant victim. To him, your celebration is a sham; your boasted liberty, an unholy license; your national greatness, swelling vanity; your sounds of rejoicing are empty and heartless; your denunciations of tyrants, brass fronted impudence; your shouts of liberty and equality, hollow mockery; your prayers and hymns, your sermons and thanksgivings, with all your religious parade, and solemnity, are, to him, mere bombast, fraud, deception, impiety, and hypocrisy — a thin veil to cover up crimes which would disgrace a nation of savages. There is not a nation on the earth guilty of practices, more shocking and bloody, than are the people of the United States, at this very hour.

Go where you may, search where you will, roam through all the   8
monarchies and despotisms of the old world, travel through South
America, search out every abuse, and when you have found the last, lay
your facts by the side of the everyday practices of this nation, and you
will say with me, that, for revolting barbarity and shameless hypocrisy,
America reigns without a rival.

BACKGROUND AND CONTEXT

1. Although Douglass realizes his audience is gathered to celebrate
   Independence Day, why do you think he brings up the unpleasant subject
   of slavery? How is slavery related to the festive occasion?

2. Who are the "millions" Douglass refers to in the opening line of this portion
   of his speech? What is their relation to his audience and how is it expressed
   in sound?

STRATEGY, STRUCTURE, AND STYLE

1. In paragraph 2, note Douglass's question about argument: "What point in
   the anti-slavery creed would you have me argue?" How does he use the
   claim that there is nothing to argue about as a way to help him organize his
   argument?

2. Douglass writes, "Must I undertake to prove that the slave is a man? That
   point is conceded already. Nobody doubts it. The slaveholders themselves
   acknowledge it in the enactment of laws for their government" (para. 2).
   What does he mean? How does the slaveholder's enactment of laws
   "acknowledge" that slaves are human beings?

COMPARISONS AND CONNECTIONS

1. A decade after Douglass delivered his address, Abraham Lincoln would issue
   the Emancipation Proclamation that legally ended the institution of slavery.
   How does that historical fact affect your response to the Fourth of July oration?
   Would Douglass's speech still be relevant after Lincoln's act? In a short essay,
   discuss how relevant you think Douglass's address is today. Does it possess
   only historical interest to twenty-first-century readers or do parts still resonate?

2. Read Douglass's address in the context of the other selections in this unit.
   In a short essay, describe how you think Douglass might respond to current
   thinking on the topic of race. How do you think Douglass, as an ardent abolitionist who advocated for the elimination of slavery, would perceive race
   relations today?

Discussing the Unit

SUGGESTED TOPIC FOR DISCUSSION

Americans would like to think that the United States is no longer a racist society, all these years after the end of slavery and the introduction of the civil rights movement. However, racism lingers in the nation's historical consciousness. How do the writers in this chapter approach the subject of race in America? What do they tell us about the history of blacks and whites, our perception of race, and the continued experience of racism in this country?

PREPARING FOR CLASS DISCUSSION

1. Do you think of yourself as prejudiced? Do you identify as a particular race? How does your experience of race influence your thinking about yourself and others? Have you witnessed racially motivated actions or speech that made you pause and think more deeply about the racism that continues to exist in this country?

2. When you consider race or learn more about the experience of race and racism in this country, do you respond more to poetry, narrative, argument, or straight data? All these forms are offered in this chapter. Why do you think you respond more to one form of writing over another? What do you find particularly persuasive about one form or other?

FROM DISCUSSION TO WRITING

1. Does our racial identity affect how we understand and relate to our fellow human beings? Is our reaction specific to the race with which we identify? Using three essays — Robin DiAngelo's "White America's Racial Illiteracy" (p. 185), Bryan Stascavage's "Why Black Lives Matter Isn't What You Think" (p. 193), and Dawn Lundy Martin's "Weary Oracle" (p. 200) — write about how different races respond to each other. Where do those responses come from? How might they be explained?

2. What do you know about the Black Lives Matter movement? Do you think it is a positive or negative movement? Why do you think there has been backlash against Black Lives Matter? Write an essay about your response to the Black Lives Matter movement, but add to your own understanding by drawing material from at least three essays from this chapter.

TOPICS FOR CROSS-CULTURAL DISCUSSION

1. What was America like at the time Frederick Douglass was speaking and writing? What is America like in the time Claudia Rankine is writing? What situations and actions were perceived as racist in Douglass's time? How have those situations and actions changed or not changed in Rankine's time?

Compare these two writers in a brief essay, and bring in examples from Rankine's and Douglass's selections (pp. 184 and 206) as you write.

2. Consider Douglass's statements about how blacks are perceived in "What to a Slave, Is the Fourth of July?" (p. 206). How does his essay from 1852 connect with ideas presented in Tom Jacobs's article "Racism in the Kindergarten Classroom" (p. 203)? Explain what these writings tell us about racial bias, then and now.

6

Diversity and Identity: How Well Is American Immigration Working?

For centuries, Americans have referred to their country — most often but not always proudly — as a "melting pot," a place where people of all backgrounds, colors, and creeds come to live and work together freely and harmoniously. Today, there is often heated debate about the extent to which immigrant groups should assimilate or retain their distinctive ethnic or racial differences. Is diversity still a relevant category of discourse? Or should Americans be focusing on what brings us together more than on what separates us?

This chapter examines the voices of immigrants and minorities in America and begins with an "In Brief" examination of two important categories, as two CNN reporters — Michael Martinez and Miguel Marquez — set out the differences between "immigrant" and "refugee." The distinction is significant because it can determine whether someone can be deported from the United States or be granted asylum.

Current debates over immigration have focused on a number of issues, among them whether the United States needs better security over the length of the Mexican border, whether people in the country without proper documentation (some estimates run to twelve million) should be subject to mass deportation, and whether amnesty should be granted to many undocumented workers and their families. The range of topics under dispute would require an entire book to cover fairly. Here we look at one key issue that for centuries has been taken for granted but was recently raised amidst much controversy during the Republican debates in 2015. Should the Fourteenth Amendment to the Constitution, which grants automatic citizenship to any person born in the United States, regardless of the legal status of the parents, be repealed or revised? In "Birthright Citizenship Is the Good Kind of American Exceptionalism," historian Eric Foner discusses the origins of the "birthright" principle (unique in much of the world) and explains why it "remains an eloquent statement of what our country is or would like to be."

Aside from its economic and legal defenses, immigration is often promoted culturally and intellectually because it helps increase diversity, a contemporary public value that — according to some critics — often goes unquestioned in our quest to achieve multiculturalist ideals. Yet one educator asks: "How much immigration diversity is too much?" In "Come See What Mass Immigration Looks Like in My School," Nashville, Tennessee, teacher Wendy Wilson discusses the educational and socialization problems she finds in unrestricted immigration. Although she confronts these problems firsthand on a daily basis, she wonders if someone like her can question diversity "anymore without the risk of getting called a xenophobe."

Our next contributor to the chapter was recently a college student who, though a United States citizen born to Brazilians in California, lived an immigrant life that even included learning English as a second language. In Tadeu Velloso's essay "Brown," written while he was a student at the University of Portland, we see how difficult it can be, even for those born here, to form a stable American identity. As he writes, "There are weird transition phases that the children of immigrants go through, most notably the declaration of our United States American identity over our other identities. We become cultural straddlers."

Is there really such a thing as an "American"? Since earliest colonial times, people have been trying to define the essential characteristics of the American identity. This chapter concludes with two such efforts, one based on a recent research survey and the other written by a classic eighteenth-century essayist who wrote one of the earliest interpretations of what makes an American. In the "Spotlight on Data and Research" feature, "What Makes an American?," Matthew Bulger reports on a 2015 survey that surprisingly found that many Americans considered a belief in God, along with speaking English and native birth, to be essential components of an American identity. Writing in 1782, the French American J. Hector St. Jean de Crèvecoeur made an attempt to formulate a definition of the American. In doing so, as we can see in the chapter's "America Then" feature, he came up with the famous concept of the "melting pot." "Here," Crèvecoeur forecasted, "individuals of all nations are melted into a new race of men, whose labors and posterity will one day cause great changes in the world."

Michael Martinez and Miguel Marquez

What's the Difference between Immigrant and Refugee?

[*CNN Report*, July 16, 2014]

*N*ews stories, whether in print or on video, often need background information so readers and viewers can better understand what's being
reported. "What's the Difference between Immigrant and Refugee?"
by Michael Martinez and Miguel Marquez offers a succinct explanation of
a major news event that occurred in the summer of 2014 as a massive wave
of Central Americans crossed the U.S. border. As the news item points out,
it made an enormous difference whether the people fleeing Central America
would be considered immigrants or refugees.

The Central Americans crossing the U.S. border in massive waves have   1
been described as immigrants or refugees.

The distinction is significant and could determine whether the mi-   2
grants are subject to deportation to their home country or eligible to
remain in the United States under asylum.

WHAT IS AN IMMIGRANT?

An immigrant is someone who chooses to resettle to another country.   3

The United States has a legal process for that immigrant to seek legal   4
residency and eventually citizenship.

Many immigrants, however, don't have such legal status and are thus   5
undocumented. As such, they are subject to "removal" or deportation
from the United States.

There are 11 million undocumented immigrants in the United   6
States—a problem that has led Democrats and Republicans alike to
declare the U.S. immigration system as "broken." Congress has been
deadlocked for years on how to reform immigration laws.

"Migrants, especially economic migrants, choose to move in order   7
to improve the future prospects of themselves and their families," the
U.N. High Commissioner for Refugees says. "Refugees have to move if
they are to save their lives or preserve their freedom."

WHAT IS A REFUGEE?

A refugee is someone who has been forced to flee his or her home country. 8

As such, refugees can apply for asylum in the United States, a process that could take years. 9

Getting refugee status isn't easy. 10

The applicants have to prove that if they return to their home country, they'll be injured because of their race, religion, nationality, membership in a particular social group or their political opinion. 11

"Refugees are generally people outside of their country who are unable or unwilling to return home because they fear serious harm," the U.S. Citizenship and Immigration Services says. 12

The Central Americans overwhelming the U.S.-Mexican border are Hondurans, Guatemalans and Salvadorans. Many are fleeing drug- and gang-fueled violence back home. 13

Is the violence — any kind — grounds for a refugee claim? Not necessarily. 14

The violence has to be targeted to a person specifically, and that's where things get complicated. Every case is different, and because of a law signed by President George W. Bush in 2008, children fall into a special class. 15

The William Wilberforce Trafficking Victims Protection Action Act, named after a 19th-century British abolitionist, is designed to crack down on the global child slave trade. The U.S. law ensured that children who came to the country got a full immigration hearing instead of being turned away or sent back. The hearing would determine whether the children had a valid claim for asylum. 16

The law is now cited as one cause behind a projected 90,000 children from Central America and Mexico who will cross the U.S. border alone or with other children this year, a huge increase over the 39,000 that the Border Patrol detained last year. 17

Asylum is a protection available to people who are already in the United States or are seeking admission at the U.S. border. 18

POINTS TO CONSIDER

1. How does the news item link itself directly to a specific incident? How does it also convey information that can be applied to all sorts of similar incidents?

2. According to the item, why is it difficult in general to obtain refugee status? What are the difficulties in this particular instance?

3. Why does the presence of so many children also complicate the issue of immigration versus asylum?

Eric Foner

Birthright Citizenship Is the Good Kind of American Exceptionalism

[*The Nation*, August 27, 2015]

BEFORE YOU READ

Why is birthright citizenship part of our Constitution? Do you think anyone born here should be considered an American citizen?

WORDS TO LEARN

principle (para. 1): a basic truth or rule (noun)

ratification (para. 1): confirmation (noun)

exceptionalism (para. 2): uniqueness (noun)

delineate (para. 3): to indicate or portray (verb)

naturalization (para. 4): the act of becoming a citizen (noun)

associate (para. 5): to be connected with others (verb)

repudiation (para. 6): rejection (noun)

undifferentiated (para. 6): not showing difference (adjective)

jurisdiction (para. 7): area where particular laws are used (noun)

minuscule (para. 7): very small (adjective)

invalidate (para. 8): to discredit (verb)

specter (para. 8): apparition (noun)

polygamists (para. 9): people who have more than one wife at a time (noun)

subsequent (para. 9): happening later (adjective)

titanic (para. 10): having great power (adjective)

B irthright citizenship — the principle that any person born in the United States is automatically a citizen — has been embedded in the Constitution since the ratification of the 14th Amendment[1] in 1868. This summer, it has suddenly emerged as a major issue in the Republican presidential campaign. Following the lead of Donald Trump,   1

Eric Foner is an American historian who has been a faculty member of Columbia University's history department since 1982. His writing interests include, among other topics, American political history and post–Civil War Reconstruction, and in 2011 he won the Pulitzer Prize for History.

candidates like Rick Santorum, Bobby Jindal, Ted Cruz, and Rand Paul have called for the repeal or reinterpretation of the amendment, to prevent children born to undocumented immigrants from being recognized as American citizens.

The situation abounds in ironies. Now a Republican target, the 14th   2 Amendment was for many decades considered a crowning achievement of what once called itself the party of Lincoln. Today, moreover, birthright citizenship stands as an example of the much-abused idea of American exceptionalism, which Republicans have berated President Obama for supposedly not embracing. Many things claimed as uniquely American — a devotion to individual freedom, for example, or social opportunity — exist in other countries. But birthright citizenship does make the United States (along with Canada) unique in the developed world. No European nation recognizes the principle. Yet, oddly, those most insistent on proclaiming their belief in American exceptionalism seem keenest on abolishing it.

Why is birthright citizenship part of our Constitution? Until   3 after the Civil War, there existed no commonly agreed-upon definition of American citizenship or the rights that it entailed. The original Constitution mentioned citizens but did not delineate who they were. The individual states determined the boundaries and rights of citizenship.

The Constitution does, however, empower Congress to create a   4 system of naturalization, and a law of 1790 offered the first legislative definition of American nationality. Although the new nation proclaimed itself, in the words of Thomas Paine, an "asylum for mankind," that law restricted the process of becoming a citizen from abroad to any "free white person." Thus, at the outset, ideas of American citizenship were closely linked to race.

Slaves, of course, were not part of the body politic. But in 1860, there   5 were half a million free blacks in the United States, nearly all of them born in this country. For decades, their citizenship had been hotly contested. Finally, in the *Dred Scott*[2] decision of 1857, the Supreme Court

---

[1] 14th Amendment (para. 1): Amendment to the Constitution that grants birthright citizenship. The amendment was passed as part of Reconstruction after the Civil War and granted citizenship to former slaves.

[2] *Dred Scott* (para. 5): The *Dred Scott* decision refers to a Supreme Court case that resulted in the decision that African Americans, slave or free, were not citizens. Dred Scott was a slave taken by his masters to free states, where he tried to sue for his freedom.

declared that no black person could be a citizen. The framers of the Constitution, Chief Justice Roger Taney insisted, regarded blacks, free and slave, as "beings of an inferior order, and altogether unfit to associate with the white race . . . and so far inferior, that they had no rights which the white man was bound to respect." (This statement, the Radical Republican leader Thaddeus Stevens later remarked, "damned [Taney] to everlasting fame; and, I fear, to everlasting fire.")

The destruction of slavery in the Civil War, coupled with the service   6
of 200,000 black men in the Union Army and Navy, put the question of black citizenship on the national agenda. The era of Reconstruction produced the first formal delineation of American citizenship, a vast expansion of citizens' rights, and a repudiation of the idea that these rights attached to persons in their capacity as members of certain ethnic or racial groups, rather than as part of an undifferentiated American people. Birthright citizenship is one expression of the commitment to equality and the expansion of national consciousness that marked Reconstruction.

In June 1866, Congress approved and sent to the states the 14th   7
Amendment, whose opening section declares that "all persons born or naturalized in the United States, and subject to the jurisdiction thereof, are citizens of the United States and of the state wherein they reside." What persons are not subject to national jurisdiction? The debates in Congress in 1866 make clear that the language was meant to exclude Native Americans, still considered members of their tribal sovereignties. Two minuscule other groups were mentioned: children born in the United States to the wives of foreign diplomats, and those fathered by members of occupying armies (fortunately, the latter case hasn't arisen since the amendment's ratification).

While the immediate purpose of this part of the 14th Amendment   8
was to invalidate the *Dred Scott* decision, the language says nothing about race — it was meant to establish a principle applicable to all. Opponents raised the specter of Chinese citizenship, or citizenship for "gypsies"; one senator said that he'd heard more about gypsies during the debate than in his entire previous life. Lyman Trumbull, chairman of the Senate Judiciary Committee, made it crystal clear that "all persons" meant what it said: Children born to Chinese, gypsies, or anybody else one could think of would be citizens.

What about the children of "illegal aliens" today? No such group   9
existed in 1866; at the time, just about anyone who wished to enter the United States was free to do so. Only later did the law single out certain groups for exclusion: prostitutes, polygamists, lunatics, anarchists, and, starting in 1882, the entire population of China. In fact, the closest

analogy to today's debate concerns children born to the 50,000 or so Chinese in the United States in 1866, all of whose parents were ineligible for citizenship. The authors of the amendment, and subsequent decisions by the Supreme Court, made it clear that these children must be considered American citizens. The legal status of the parents does not determine the rights of the child; anyone born here can be a good American. These are the principles the Republicans now seek to overturn.

> The authors of the amendment, and subsequent decisions by the Supreme Court, made it clear that these children must be considered American citizens.

The 14th Amendment, as Republican editor George Curtis wrote, was part of a process that changed the U.S. government from one "for white men" to one "for mankind." Birthright citizenship is one legacy of the titanic struggle of the Reconstruction era to create a genuine democracy grounded in the principle of equality. It remains an eloquent statement of what our country is or would like to be. We should think long and hard before abandoning it.

10

VOCABULARY/USING A DICTIONARY

1. What does it mean to *berate* (para. 2) someone?

2. If a person is *keenest* (para. 2) to do something, how eager is that person?

3. What part of speech is *empower* (para. 4)? What does it mean?

RESPONDING TO WORDS IN CONTEXT

1. What is a *body politic* (para. 5)?

2. If Americans have a *devotion* (para. 2) to individual freedom, how do they feel about it?

3. If there is a "*legislative* definition of American nationality" (para. 4), who provided it?

DISCUSSING MAIN POINT AND MEANING

1. Is Foner trying to persuade us of anything? If so, what does he want to persuade us of?

2. What does Foner find ironic about the position of many of the most recent Republican candidates?

3. Does legal status of the parents matter in deciding the baby's nationality when he or she is born in the United States?

EXAMINING SENTENCES, PARAGRAPHS, AND ORGANIZATION

1. Describe the construction of Foner's first sentence. Why do you think he begins with this sentence?

2. Explain how Foner transitions between the ideas in paragraphs 2, 3, and 4. Are his transitions effective?

3. Which particular paragraph does the conclusion reflect back upon with the statement "Birthright citizenship is one legacy of the titanic struggle of the Reconstruction era to create a genuine democracy grounded in the principle of equality" (para. 10)?

THINKING CRITICALLY

1. Why would birthright citizenship have been of particular importance to slaves?

2. Why do some recent Republican presidential candidates want to repeal or reinterpret the Fourteenth Amendment? Who don't they want to provide the benefit of birthright citizenship to?

3. What is meant by "American exceptionalism"? Why does Foner say it is a "much-abused idea" (para. 2)?

WRITING ACTIVITIES

1. Do you think birthright citizenship is a good or bad policy for the United States to have in place? Using Foner's argument as a starting point, explain your own view on birthright citizenship. You can explore both sides of the story (explaining why it is both good and bad) if you wish, but you need to bring in solid examples and evidence to support what you say.

2. What do you think about the desire to overturn or rewrite an amendment to the Constitution? Some people feel that amendments are inviolable (consider how staunchly some people defend the Second Amendment). But there is at least one amendment that was passed and then repealed — the Eighteenth Amendment. Discuss your feelings about amendments to the Constitution: what they represent, when they should be questioned, how important they are to the country. Include in your response a consideration of what it might mean to repeal the Fourteenth Amendment.

3. In two or three paragraphs, summarize Eric Foner's essay. Remember that a summary does not need to include *all* points made in an essay — only the main points.

Wendy Wilson

Come See What Mass Immigration Looks Like in My School

[*The Federalist*, March, 21, 2016]

BEFORE YOU READ

As you read, ask yourself what sorts of resources are needed to support children in the school systems the author describes. Are these students' needs being adequately met?

WORDS TO LEARN

monolingual (para. 1): using only one language (adjective)

advocates (para. 2): people who act in support or defense of someone or something (noun)

unassailable (para. 5): indisputable (adjective)

demographic (para. 7): relating to the statistics of populations and their characteristics (adjective)

manipulation (para. 8): the handling and changing of something (noun)

intervention (para. 9): the act of interceding (noun)

tedious (para. 9): tiresome (adjective)

compensate (para. 13): to offset (verb)

seamlessly (para. 17): smoothly (adverb)

prioritize (para. 21): to give special attention to (verb)

I live in Nashville, Tennessee, a city that prides itself on welcoming a growing immigrant population. For civic leaders, it has become a badge of honor. School officials boast of the number of native languages represented in local schools, seemingly pleased to be part of a new era that leaves behind the boring monolingual days of the past.   1

Like immigration advocates across the country, many in town echo the refrain that we'll become a greater nation as we become even more diverse, with only the fearful posing a threat to progress.   2

I don't consider myself a person paralyzed by fear. As someone who has taught English language learners in public schools for more than 10 years, I enjoy working with those from other countries. It can be exciting and rewarding. I've learned a lot from my students. Even when the challenges become exhausting, at least I can say there is rarely a dull day.   3

A former newspaper reporter, Wendy Wilson currently teaches high school ESL and Spanish in Nashville and is a freelance writer. She holds a master's degree in intercultural studies.

But over the past few years, I've found myself asking this: How much   4
immigration diversity is too much? Is it even possible to ask this question
anymore without the risk of getting called a xenophobe?

FROM A BIRD'S EYE VIEW, IT LOOKS GREAT

In a recent article for *The Atlantic*, David Frum writes that in elite circles,   5
the large-scale influx of low-skill immigrants in recent decades is considered an unassailable good. "Even as immigration becomes ever-more
controversial with the larger American public, within the policy elite it
preserves an unquestioned status as something utterly beyond discussion," he laments.

I teach for Metro Nashville Public Schools at a high school with hun-   6
dreds of English learners. As in other cities across the nation, the immigrant population in Nashville has boomed in recent years. We have a mix
of refugees and legal and illegal immigrants. Around 30 percent of the
total student population has a first language other than English, with as
many as 120 languages represented. More than 14 percent need English
language (ELL) services, a number that reflects national trends for urban
areas. Nationally, the percentage of ELL students grew in all but 11 states
between 2002–03 and 2012–13.

The national media often portray growing immigration rates in pos-   7
itive terms, presenting immigration as exactly what's needed to give the
United States an economic and demographic boost. A series that ran in
USA Today in 2014 is one such example. Rosy predictions in such stories are rarely seriously challenged on any front, including in relation to
education. Scant attention is paid to the enormity of the day-to-day challenges in schools with high immigrant populations.

One problem is that school officials make things look better on   8
paper than they are in reality. Immigrant students pass classes and graduate at surprising rates given their continual low skills, and districts like
Nashville still find a way to tout overall progress. A local Nashville TV
station has been investigating the manipulation of grades and testing
data across the district, and one story in their series focused on English
learners.

IT IS REALLY HARD TO LEARN A NEW LANGUAGE

School districts nationwide are pouring millions of dollars into helping   9
students learn English. But there is no magic bullet to make this happen
faster, no matter how hard educators search for just the right intervention. Learning another language is slow and tedious, even for students
who are bright and motivated, even for students with bright and capable

teachers and good instructional materials. Researchers say it takes students five to seven years, sometimes more, to attain the English proficiency necessary to do the academic work of grade-level peers.

As those students are catching up, more newcomers are coming in   10
the door, making the achievement gap between mainstream students and English learners a permanent fixture. But that doesn't stop high-ranking education and government leaders from wanting it all — a welcome mat rolled out for immigrants who require numerous supports, *and* high graduation rates and test scores. Principals and teachers get smashed between a rock and a hard place. Don't lower your standards, but make sure that 15-year-old who just arrived from Honduras speaking no English graduates.

My school is in an immigrant neighborhood, so our percentage of   11
ELL students is above the district average. Around a quarter of students at my school are English learners, and numerous others who had ELL services at some time in the past still struggle. At nearby middle and elementary schools, 30 to 65 percent of students are English learners. My school has many immigrants from Latin America as well as refugees from Burma, Nepal, Iraq, and parts of Africa. Some students arrive with limited schooling in their native language. For those arriving in their middle or high school years, the challenges are particularly steep.

THE EDUCATION GAP IS HUGE

Last year, I had a newcomer from Somalia who on the first day of class   12
wrote her name across the word bank near the top of a worksheet instead of on the line at the top right-hand corner. Another student, a boy from Central America, had left school to work in the fields after second grade and now found staying alert during the school day a nearly intolerable experience.

In addition to a language barrier, students like these face other enor-   13
mous obstacles. At first, they have special schedules that shield them from traditional core classes. But a year or two after arriving, in addition to special language classes, they're expected to engage with the standard curriculum in science, history, and other subjects. Teachers are to make this happen using "differentiation strategies" that are somehow supposed to compensate for a language barrier, cultural differences, and years of inconsistent prior schooling.

Even after students are well on their way toward English fluency, the   14
gaps remain significant, slowing down comprehension of basic material that struggling native speakers can grasp much more readily. I recently was teaching the idiom "It's nuts" to a group of seniors, but they drew

a blank on the concrete definition of nuts, so I had to show a visual of peanuts, almonds, and cashews to remind them.

School officials want students at this level to be analyzing complex   15
ideas and producing sophisticated written work. But my students are still developing their vocabulary and need continual refreshers. Many still struggle to write a coherent paragraph. Even if they have good ideas in their heads, it's hard to get them on paper. So while education officials dream of the ways my students will show multiple layers of understanding, I worry about what will happen if someone asks them if they're allergic to nuts.

SUCCESS STORIES ARE EXCEPTIONS

Before teaching in Nashville, I taught for a neighboring suburban district   16
with far fewer immigrants. Even so, the numbers were growing there, too, as they are in suburbs, towns, and rural areas across the country. In this suburban district, there were fewer refugees and more students with a stronger education background in their own language. But some of the frustrations were the same.

I taught history classes for ELL students in addition to language   17
classes. I adapted content to the language level of my students, but they still had to take district benchmark assessments, with the expectation that my differentiation strategies would seamlessly pave the way for their success. Not surprisingly (to me anyway), my students were unable to answer detailed questions about the Protestant Reformation, given that some of them needed basic instruction about Christianity. Likewise, they had a hard time answering questions about the world wars, because I had to spend class time teaching words like *soldier, tank,* and *submarine.*

Despite the challenges, there are immigrant students making re-   18
markable progress. President Obama and immigration advocates love to publicly hold these children up as examples, with the implication that the system is working just fine. But the reality is that many are average in their efforts, and like other kids, are easily distracted by cell phones, video games, and the opposite sex.

> Despite the challenges, there are immigrant students making remarkable progress.

Then there are those who don't seem to   19
care, are rude to their teachers, and get suspended for fighting and drugs. I have had the joy of having highly motivated, high-achieving students in my classroom over the years, and their hard work and maturity really are an inspiration. Unfortunately, they are exceptions.

WE'RE NOT RACISTS FOR CONSIDERING THESE FACTORS

One shouldn't have to fear being tarnished as anti-immigrant for con- 20
cerns about the strain on public schools. American families shouldn't be
made to feel like they're ignorant if they wonder about the quality of a
neighborhood school that has gone global, serving numerous students
with language barriers and low skills. And educators, social workers, and
others shouldn't have to fear being presumed heartless for thinking, like
me, that our immigration system has spiraled out of control.

In his article in *The Atlantic*, Frum makes the point that while immi- 21
grants benefit from coming to the United States, we don't stop to consider enough whether America is benefitting. He writes, "Nobody is
making conscious decisions about who is wanted and who is not, about
how much immigration to accept and what kind to prioritize — not even
for the portion of U.S. migration conducted according to law, much less
for the larger portion that is not."

Regrettably, such advice is likely to be ignored by the elites Frum 22
addresses, those who habitually fail to draw lines and don't even see the
value in doing so. Frum suggests those elites could find themselves out
of a job as pressure builds for new immigration policies. But that remains
to be seen.

VOCABULARY/USING A DICTIONARY

1. What does *xenophobe* (para. 4) mean? From what language does it derive?
2. If something is *scant* (para. 7), is much of it available?
3. What part of speech is *tout* (para. 8)? What does it mean?

RESPONDING TO WORDS IN CONTEXT

1. What part of speech is the word *native* (para. 1) here? What other part of
   speech could it be? What does it mean in this context?
2. What is an *influx* (para. 5) of immigrants?
3. What does Wilson mean when she says her students are struggling to write
   a *coherent* (para. 15) paragraph? What is the opposite of *coherent*?

DISCUSSING MAIN POINT AND MEANING

1. What are some of the obstacles children of recent immigrants face in their
   schools and education?
2. What is the main difficulty immigrant students face, according to
   Wilson?
3. When Wilson adapted her course content in her history classes, what was
   the result when students had to take benchmark assessments?

EXAMINING SENTENCES, PARAGRAPHS, AND ORGANIZATION

1. In one sentence, Wilson writes, "One shouldn't have to fear being *tarnished* as anti-immigrant for concerns about the strain on public schools" (para. 20). Is she using the word *tarnished* literally? What does she mean?

2. What techniques does Wilson use to organize her material? Are her techniques helpful? Explain.

3. Do you think a paragraph offering suggestions about what to do about the problem of immigration would strengthen or weaken the last section ("We're Not Racists for Considering These Factors"), which is only a few paragraphs long? Would it add or detract from what's being said there?

THINKING CRITICALLY

1. Do you think immigration should be limited? Explain your answer.

2. Why is immigration often praised as a benefit to the schools?

3. Does Wilson's position as a teacher of a large immigrant population make her an authority on the subject she is writing about? Why or why not?

WRITING ACTIVITIES

1. Do you wish you knew more about how to solve the issues Wilson raises about immigration and its effects on the schools? What sorts of questions would you like to have answered?

2. In a brief essay, without stating a particular position, consider the question of whether or not people who think immigration should be more controlled are being racist. It can be a casual discussion of why someone might deem Wilson's concerns about immigration and its effects on her school system racist.

3. Spend some time thinking about what it must be like to take classes in a language in which you are not fluent. List some of the subjects you have taken in school and analyze some of the difficulties a nonfluent speaker might have. Try to write down a handful of subjects that differ from each other and explore the obstacles the non-English speaker might encounter in each.

Tadeu Velloso (student essay)

Brown

[*Portland Magazine*, University of Portland, Summer 2014]

BEFORE YOU READ

Are race relations in America particularly problematic for the children of immigrants? What challenges do they face in terms of determining their own identities or understanding the perceptions of others?

WORDS TO LEARN

avid (para. 1): ardent; enthusiastic (adjective)

declaration (para. 6): announcement; formal statement (noun)

implications (para. 7): suggestions; associations (noun)

advocacy (para. 9): active pleading for something (noun)

predominantly (para. 10): preeminently (adverb)

rehabilitation (para. 11): restoration (noun)

incarcerated (para. 11): imprisoned (adjective)

collaboratively (para. 12): cooperatively (adverb)

extant (para. 12): in existence (adjective)

Growing up I always dealt with the question *What are you?* From my earliest years I knew this was a loaded question — people weren't asking if I was an avid reader, an adventurer, a jokester; they wanted to know who I was racially, so that they could classify me and figure out how to interact with me. 1

I am American, the son of Brazilian immigrants. I grew up first in California, where I was constantly mixing with immigrants from El Salvador, Mexico, and Guatemala. When I was four, we moved to Brazil. I returned to the States at age seven. By the time I returned to the States I didn't speak any English, so from second grade I was *foreign* and *international* and an *English as a second language student*, even though I was, as I tried to say, a United States American, when people asked me *What are you?* 2

Tadeu Velloso is a 2014 graduate of the University of Portland and currently attends the University of Washington School of Law.

But my answer wasn't good enough. No one believed it. My skin   3
color and my accent didn't add up to United States American in their
minds.

"I'm Brazilian," I'd try. But that didn't work either — I had adopted   4
too many attributes of the "white" culture, whatever that is, to claim
Latino identity.

I began to notice how differently people looked at me if I was with   5
my Latino friends' families or black families as opposed to with a white
family. Curious eyes were trying to figure out what the relation was
between white family and brown boy.

There are weird transition phases that the children of immigrants   6
go through, most notably the declaration of our United States American
identity over our other identities. We become cultural straddlers. I felt
that I had to choose one. In a culture that shames immigrants on a daily
basis, I tried my hardest to claim my United States American identity,
and rid myself of my Latino identity.

This grew complicated once I began to learn about the civil rights   7
movement. Seeing the images of segregated places made me think, *if I
was alive during this time would I have been considered black or white?* I
began to realize the implications that claiming blackness or brownness
historically had on people in the United States; at the same time I grew
increasingly fascinated by the possibilities of a world where race could be
embraced *positively.*

In California, however, where I spent the next ten years of my child-   8
hood, there are clear and definite divisions among whites and people of
color. In my schools, immigrants and the children of immigrants were
often assumed to be gangbangers and troublemakers. Though I was neither, I was aware from an early age that
people I was growing up with were seen
as threats and probable criminals simply
because of their color or ancestry. At age 14,
I took part in my first public protest against
those divisions — an immigrant rights
march. A group of us kids left school and
marched around our town. This was a monumental moment for me. It was the first time
that I embraced the fact that my mom was an

> A group of us kids
> left school and
> marched around
> our town. This was
> a monumental
> moment for me.

immigrant, that my mom had an accent, that my mom was a part of a rich
culture, and that all those things were a part of me as well. For the first time
in my life, I was proud of being Latino; I was proud of being brown.

That realization has shaped my life since then. I have been dedicated   9
to advocacy and social justice awareness since that moment. I worked

with migrant workers, people experiencing homelessness, low-income families. I always approached it from the perspective that I was engaging with a community, and separated myself from any ideology that I was somehow capable of saving anyone.

When I came to the university, a traditionally white space, in   10
Portland, a predominantly white space, I began to engage with social justice in an academic way also, particularly modern race relations and the reflections of modern race relations through music like hip-hop. But after going on the Moreau Center's[1] civil rights immersion through the South, I really struggled with everything I had witnessed, and felt that I needed to find something to *do* to make a change.

For me it became criminal justice reform, the rehabilitation of   11
formerly incarcerated people, and the push for systemic racial equity. One of the most obvious and ignored forms of institutional racism is the criminal justice system. Low-income communities and communities of color are disproportionately affected by incarceration and its consequences — which include, if prisoners are even freed, inability to find employment, inability to qualify for assistance with housing and food and student loans, and inability to vote.

I have tried to figure out tangible ways to get people talking about   12
these issues, while also directly helping people affected by incarceration; and so came the idea of a "transparent" clothing company — one that told the stories and struggles of people in prison making the clothes, while also helping those same incarcerated people learn job skills, work collaboratively and productively, and get a rare chance to be proud of their work. After a while I discovered an extant company called Stripes. I connected with them about my vision for a brand of clothing that would empower incarcerated people while also telling their story to the wider world, and we went into business together. I'll be working with Stripes after I graduate, working to introduce this new business model to the market, and looking for more ways to help create a world where race isn't ignored but celebrated in honest and productive ways. It's been a racially brutal world for a long time; it doesn't have to stay that way.

VOCABULARY/USING A DICTIONARY

1. What part of speech is *formerly* (para. 11)? What does it mean?

2. What is a synonym for *transparent* (para. 12)?

3. What does *systemic* (para. 11) mean?

---

[1] Moreau Center (para. 10): A division of the University of Portland that offers service opportunities to students as well as justice and leadership learning

RESPONDING TO WORDS IN CONTEXT

1. What is meant by *Latino* (para. 5)?

2. How would you define *cultural straddlers* (para. 6)?

3. What do *migrant workers* (para. 9) do?

DISCUSSING MAIN POINT AND MEANING

1. Why is Velloso asked "What are you?"

2. What sort of assumptions are made about the essayist because he is part of a community of immigrants and children of immigrants?

3. What activity does Velloso engage in that he describes as monumental in changing how he views himself?

EXAMINING SENTENCES, PARAGRAPHS, AND ORGANIZATION

1. Why is the first paragraph important to the essay?

2. Why is the essay called "Brown"?

3. Why does Velloso repeat "*What are you?*" in paragraphs 1 and 2?

THINKING CRITICALLY

1. Why do you think Velloso took an interest in social justice in college?

2. What attributes mark the essayist as an immigrant? What attributes mark the essayist as an American?

3. What is eye-opening about the immigrants rights march? What does it teach Velloso about himself?

WRITING ACTIVITIES

1. Consider the question "What are you?" How would you answer this question? What aspects of yourself do you highlight when answering this question? Try answering it in a freewriting exercise in which you write for ten to fifteen minutes without stopping. When you've finished, try to craft a personal narrative about *what* (not *who*) you are that mines your freewriting for material.

2. What assumptions do we make about what it means to be an American? Using Velloso's narrative as research, write a brief essay about who Americans are and how presuppositions can be misleading.

3. In small groups, discuss the ending of Velloso's essay. In a collaborative effort, write an essay that considers Velloso's interest in incarceration as a form of institutional racism and how he chooses to combat that form by creating a " 'transparent' clothing company" (para. 12). Do you and other

members of the group think this is an effective way to bring attention to incarceration and racism? How does this bring the issue to light? Does it help those institutionalized? Does it help the rest of the world think about prisoners differently?

Describing a Defining Moment

In personal essays, writers often turn to moments in their lives that had a major impact on their perspectives, choices, and careers. Years ago, students were often given writing assignments that asked them to describe a "turning point" in their lives. Sometimes, especially in literature, such moments are called "epiphanies," referring to a life-altering "sudden realization."

In his personal essay "Brown," University of Portland student Tadeu Velloso memorably describes such "a monumental moment." Note that he first establishes a context by observing that the children of immigrants, like him, are often stereotyped as "probable criminals." Then he introduces a specific moment that altered his life — an immigrant rights march that he joined as a means to protest against the "divisions" he had become conscious of. At fourteen, he realized that he was proud of both his origins and the color of his skin. His essay then goes on to show how this sudden realization has ultimately "shaped" his life since then.

1
Sets the context for his defining moment

2
Introduces the specific event that led to it

3
Clearly describes the defining moment

(1) In my schools, immigrants and the children of immigrants were often assumed to be gangbangers and troublemakers. Though I was neither, I was aware from an early age that people I was growing up with were seen as threats and probable criminals simply because of their color or ancestry. (2) At age 14, I took part in my first public protest against those divisions — an immigrant rights march. A group of us kids left school and marched around our town. (3) This was a monumental moment for me. It was the first time that I embraced the fact that my mom was an immigrant, that my mom had an accent, that my mom was a part of a rich culture, and that all those things were a part of me as well. For the first time in my life, I was proud of being Latino; I was proud of being brown.

STUDENT WRITER AT WORK
Tadeu Velloso

© Carly Romeo

R.A. What inspired you to write this essay? And publish it?

T.V. I wrote the essay before graduating from the University of Portland. During my time as a student, there were several incidents of explicit and implicit racism. However, the institution wasn't doing anything to address or teach its students about racism. I was approached to write this piece about my work with a company (with which I am no longer affiliated). I believe that incarcerated people deserve a second chance, and I believe that my conviction about this second chance stems from my experience as a person of color. As a student of color, I felt as if I wasn't often afforded the benefit of the doubt; that I had to go above and beyond to prove my credibility. Given that people of color are disproportionately represented in the criminal justice system and face serious collateral consequences upon their release, it is important for me to be an advocate to ensure that everyone, regardless of their mistakes, can live a meaningful life.

At the University of Portland, people weren't talking about race. But by ignoring race, I (as a student of color) felt like the institution was ignoring me. Our identities shape who we are and how we see the world, so dismissing those experiences is a complete disservice to your students.

R.A. Do you generally show your writing to friends before submitting it? Do you collaborate with others or bounce your ideas off them? To what extent did discussion with others help you develop your point of view on the topic you wrote about?

T.V. When it's something so personal, I usually won't show it to friends. When writing about my own experience, I make sure to reflect on the message. What point am I trying to make? What stories will illustrate my point? I want my work to be fueled by passion, but I also understand that I need to lead the reader throughout the piece.

R.A. What advice do you have for other student writers?

T.V. Don't be scared. Sometimes you need to write about things that are unpopular, but your writing often needs to exist in the world. I had a lot of great supporters and mentors at the University of Portland, but I wanted them to know that I am proud of being a person of color.

Spotlight on Data and Research

Matthew Bulger
What Makes an American?
[*The Humanist*, July 2, 2015]

One of the common functions of journalism is to describe and interpret the results of scientific polls and research reports. In "What Makes an American?," a columnist for the Humanist *magazine, Matthew Bulger, interprets a recent survey taken by the Public Religion Research Institute. Founded in 2009, this organization describes itself as "a nonprofit, nonpartisan organization dedicated to research at the intersection of religion, values, and public life." Its "mission is to help journalists, opinion leaders, scholars, clergy, and the general public better understand debates on public policy issues and the role of religion and values in American public life by conducting high quality public opinion surveys and qualitative research." The* Humanist *magazine is a publication of the American Humanist Association, which was founded in 1941 and is located in Washington, D.C. According to its Web site, "The American Humanist Association advocates progressive values and equality for humanists, atheists, freethinkers, and the non-religious." The association's motto is "Good without a God."*

As the Fourth of July rapidly approaches, red, white, and blue banners (as well as hundreds of tacky Independence Day–themed advertisements for bars and nightclubs) seem to be everywhere in our nation's capital. While patriotic fireworks and large quantities of alcohol tend to mark the way we celebrate our country's independence on this special day, discussions regarding patriotism and the American identity reveal disagreement on just what and who we're celebrating. 1

Coming from conservative Texas, I've heard more than my fair share of xenophobic remarks regarding immigrants and other communities that weren't seen as authentically "American." But what exactly do Americans think constitutes being American? 2

According to a recent Public Religion Research Institute survey, several factors contribute to making a person seem distinctly American. By far the most important factor according to the study is the ability to speak English, with 89 percent of participants saying this was necessary for a person to be considered truly American. This is a bit strange, considering that our country does not maintain English as our official language and because we have more Spanish speakers than any country in the world excluding Mexico (but including Spain). 3

Another strange finding was that 58 percent of respondents said being born in the United States is a requirement to be considered a real 4

continued

American. Sadly, this means that only 42 percent of people recognize and respect our country's proud history as a nation of immigrants.

But strangest of all was the survey's finding on the relationship 5 between religious belief and American identity. Sixty-nine percent of those surveyed said that a belief in God is required to be a true American, while 53 percent believe only Christians can be true Americans.

There are a few ways to look at these numbers. On a positive 6 note, 31 percent of Americans don't make a connection between religious beliefs and American identity, which is a higher number than the roughly 23 percent of Americans who are religiously unaffiliated. That means there are a significant number of Americans who maintain a belief in a god or gods, but who don't see their religion, or any religion for that matter, as a prerequisite for being considered an American. And while nearly 71 percent of Americans identify as Christian, only half of those surveyed think that being specifically Christian is a fundamental part of being an American.

Still, these numbers do seem to show that for a significant amount 7 of Americans, religious beliefs, and a specific type of religious belief at that, are required for an individual to be considered an American. By doing so, many of those surveyed alienated Jews, Muslims, Hindus, and Buddhists, as well as humanists and atheists, from a community that is ostensibly open to all regardless of religious beliefs.

Our nation has a proud history of religious diversity, but this sur- 8 vey shows that many Americans are either unaware of that history or are opposed to the values that made this country what it is today. As the growth of the nonreligious continues, it's unlikely that religion will continue to remain so intertwined with American identity. But until that day arrives, it's crucially important that attempts to wed patriotism with religious belief and with perceptions of national identity be exposed both as theocratically intolerant and historically inaccurate.

DRAWING CONCLUSIONS

1. Given the goal of the *Humanist* magazine, as described in the lead-in to the selection, why do you think it took an interest in this particular survey?

2. Why do you think Bulger links his report to the Fourth of July holiday? From the tone of the opening paragraph, what attitude do you detect on the part of the author?

3. What does the author find most distressing about the result of the survey? Do you agree with him? Do you think the poll numbers that show a link between "religious belief and American identity" (para. 5) are a cause for concern? Why or why not?

Negin Farsad and Dean Obeidallah

The Muslims Are Coming!

[Vaguely Qualified Productions, April 28, 2015]

This poster is one of a series of ads that appeared in numerous New York City subway stations in the spring of 2016. The posters were designed to promote *The Muslims Are Coming!*, an award-winning documentary covering a national tour of Muslim American comedians. At first, New York City refused to allow the ads to be posted, but eventually the comedians won their case. Do you think the strategy behind the posters is correct—that we can fight negative stereotypes with humor?

J. Hector St. Jean de Crèvecoeur

The Melting Pot

[*Letters from an American Farmer*, 1782]

"What then is the American, this new man?" With that question, a French-born aristocrat who had made New York State his home launched one of the first inquiries into the puzzling nature of the American identity. In 1782, J. Hector St. Jean de Crèvecoeur (1735–1813) published a book of a dozen epistolary essays called Letters from an American Farmer *that made him an instant literary success. The most important of the letters is the third, "What Is an American?" The short excerpt below (the original essay is quite long) is often reprinted and remains one of the most famous passages of early American literature.*

What attachment can a poor European emigrant have for a country   1
where he had nothing? The knowledge of the language, the love of a
few kindred as poor as himself, were the only cords that tied him; his
country is now that which gives him land, bread, protection, and consequence: *Ubi panis ibi patria* [Where there is bread, there is my country],
is the motto of all emigrants. What then is the American, this new man?
He is either a European, or the descendant of a European, hence that
strange mixture of blood, which you will find in no other country. I
could point out to you a family whose grandfather was an Englishman,
whose wife was Dutch, whose son married a Frenchwoman, and whose
present four sons have now four wives of different nations. *He* is an
American, who leaving behind him all his ancient prejudices and manners, receives new ones from the new mode of life he has embraced, the
new government he obeys, and the new rank he holds. He becomes an
American by being received in the broad lap of our great *alma mater.*
Here individuals of all nations are melted into a new race of men, whose
labors and posterity will one day cause great changes in the world.
Americans are the Western pilgrims, who are carrying along with them
that great mass of arts, sciences, vigor, and industry which began long
since in the East; they will finish the great circle. The Americans were

once scattered all over Europe; here they are incorporated into one of the finest systems of population which has ever appeared, and which will hereafter become distinct by the power of the different climates they inhabit. The American ought therefore to love this country much better than that wherein either he or his forefathers were born. Here the rewards of his industry follow with equal steps the progress of his labor; his labor is founded on the basis of nature, *self-interest*; can it want a stronger allurement? Wives and children, who before in vain demanded of him a morsel of bread, now, fat and frolicsome, gladly help their father to clear those fields whence exuberant crops are to arise to feed and to clothe them all; without any part being claimed, either by a despotic prince, a rich abbot, or a mighty lord. Here religion demands but little of him; a small voluntary salary to the minister, and gratitude to God; can he refuse these? The American is a new man, who acts upon new principles; he must therefore entertain new ideas and form new opinions. From involuntary idleness, servile dependence, penury, and useless labor he has passed to toils of a very different nature, rewarded by ample subsistence — this is an American.

BACKGROUND AND CONTEXT

1. Early in the passage, Crèvecoeur cites a famous Latin saying that is translated as "Where there is bread, there is my country." How do you interpret this saying? Why does Crèvecoeur suggest it is the "motto" of all immigrants?

2. Crèvecoeur uses another Latin expression, *alma mater*. This is commonly used to signify the college or university one graduates from, but in Latin it literally means "bounteous mother." What does it mean in the context in which Crèvecoeur uses it?

STRATEGY, STRUCTURE, AND STYLE

1. Note that Crèvecoeur does not use the expression "melting pot." How does he describe the process of immigrants all becoming a "new race of men"? What other image does he use to suggest a blending together?

2. For Crèvecoeur, what are some of the advantages America has over Europe? How does he describe the old world?

COMPARISONS AND CONNECTIONS

1. What economic background does Crèvecoeur assume the immigrant comes from? How is this background suggested in his descriptions of the "American"? How does Crèvecoeur picture the occupation of the new

American? How do you interpret the phrase "ample subsistence" at the conclusion? What sort of life do these words suggest to you?

2. Note how gender-specific Crèvecoeur's writing is throughout: "What then is the American, this new *man*?" Do you think that defining the American as "he" is a result of an older literary style that regularly used the male pronoun grammatically to suggest both sexes, or do you think Crèvecoeur actually considers the American as male? What in the passage causes you to think one way or the other? For example, how are women mentioned?

Discussing the Unit

SUGGESTED TOPIC FOR DISCUSSION

America is supposedly the land of the immigrant, but there are wide differences in perceptions across the country about immigrants. Immigrants do not always feel immediately welcome in American society. There are so many types of immigrants (legal, illegal, the refugee) and they come from countries all over the globe. While reading these essays, try to identify reasons people might come to America to make a new life, and decide whether or not Americans and American culture respond to them appropriately.

PREPARING FOR CLASS DISCUSSION

1. If you are an American who isn't strictly Native American, at some point there is immigration in your family history. Which members of your family were immigrants? How long ago did they emigrate from their home country? Why did they immigrate? Do you think your immigrant relatives or ancestors had regrets?

2. Who do you think of when you think of American immigrants? What do they look like? What language do they speak? How does this compare to your concept of yourself as an American? Do you think of America as the great melting pot, or are there divisions between groups of people (immigrant versus citizen, for example) that are too great to mend?

FROM DISCUSSION TO WRITING

1. Do you think most people, immigrant and life-long citizen, in the United States identify themselves and one another as Americans? What does this mean? Based on what you've read, how do we form our identity? Is it different for the immigrant as opposed to the citizen? What are some of the differences?

2. How well is American immigration working? What does this question mean to you? Write your response to this question, citing at least three essays from the chapter that support your position.

TOPICS FOR CROSS-CULTURAL DISCUSSION

1. Ask the question that Matthew Bulger (p. 235) asked: What makes an American? Compare your answer to the answer offered by J. Hector St. John de Crèvecoeur (p. 238). Has the answer changed between 1782 and today? How has it changed, and how has it not?

2. How many of our reactions to immigrants and immigration are based on race? Why do you think so? Write a brief essay that explores this question, and as you write, bring in at least two essays from this chapter that support your argument.

7

Guns: Can the Second Amendment Survive?

To the perpetual confusion of this country, its founders wrote in the Second Amendment to the Constitution that "a well regulated Militia, being necessary to the security of a free State, the right of the people to keep and bear Arms, shall not be infringed." The precise meaning of this right, and whether it still applies to modern society, has been the subject of heated debate. In particular, tragic public events like the 2015 shootings in San Bernardino, California, and the 2016 massacre in Orlando, Florida, have raised the question of whether public safety trumps an antiquated liberty to own guns.

Our chapter opens with a brief poem that summarizes the conflict between public safety and the "open carry" laws a number of states are putting into place. Jane Vincent Taylor's poem "New Law Makes Local Poet Nervous" tells a subtle story of fear and surprise in consequence of an Oklahoma law allowing private citizens to carry unconcealed guns.

Advocates of gun control — government efforts to ban or restrict private ownership of guns — often respond to terrible mass shootings by declaring that tighter control of firearms might have averted the many tragedies. Supporters of tighter regulations would specifically restrict the purchase of certain types of weapons they deem more suitable for combat than for hunting or private safety. Immediately after the slaughter in San Bernardino, the *New York Times* ran an editorial saying, "It is a moral outrage and a national disgrace that civilians can legally purchase weapons designed specifically to kill people with brutal speed and efficiency." To underscore the urgency of this issue, the paper ran the editorial on the front page; it was the first time an editorial appeared on page one since 1920.

Although some pro-gun activists see a problem with the government's banning any type of weapon (once one type is restricted, they argue, others will follow), many of them are more interested in the security that guns allow law-abiding people than they are in the type of weapon. In "My Gun Was 100 Yards Away, Completely Useless," gun-rights advocate Suzanna Hupp offers an unforgettable example that shows how a weapon might come in handy during a crisis and help protect innocent lives. She tells the story about a horrendous mass shooting in Killeen, Texas, that she witnessed in 1991 in which twenty-three people were murdered, including her parents. Even though it was illegal at the time to carry a gun, she often did carry a revolver in her purse—except on this day. "Having a gun is never a guarantee," she says. "But it changes the odds. It just changes the odds."

But others don't see similar odds. Responding to the numerous campus shootings in recent years and various calls to allow students and faculty to carry weapons for self-protection, John A. Fry, the president of Philadelphia's Drexel University, stressed the dangers of such a policy. In "Allowing Guns Won't Make Campuses Safer," Fry wonders if "someone with a gun" at the Oregon community college where nine students were killed and nine wounded in October 2015 "could have intervened in the recent massacre." He concludes that "the odds are very small that another person with a gun would have been in a position to stop it." "The best answer to the shootings," he believes, "is fewer guns, not more." California State University, Sacramento, student Brittney Christ expressed her opinions on the subject just months before the Oregon school shootings that Fry refers to, but in "We Should Be Allowed to Protect Ourselves," she offers an opposing view. She argues that "allowing guns on campuses will not only make students feel more secure, but hopefully eliminate a potential school shooting that ends up in the death of innocent people."

This chapter's "Spotlight on Data and Research" features a prominent southwestern essayist and columnist, David A. Fryxell, who cites statistics from various sources to bolster his argument that the nation needs a reasonable debate on the topic of gun control. In his aptly titled "Shooting from the Lip," he writes, "If you come away from this column thinking I'm advocating gun control, you're missing the point." He emphasizes, "I'm advocating a gun conversation."

The amendment that started the gun control debate in America remains, itself, a matter of debate. What does the Constitution mean by "a well regulated Militia" or "keep and bear Arms"? In this chapter's "America Then," literary critic Paul Fussell examines the question with detailed attention to language. He concludes that while the authors of the Second Amendment might not have approved of banning guns, they weren't setting out a provision for complete freedom, either; they intended government to control the use of deadly weapons to keep it orderly. "If interstate bus fares can be regulated," Fussell says, "it is hard to see why the Militia can't be, especially since the Constitution says it must be." As you read through this chapter, keep in mind this essential tension between freedom and public safety — a common theme in our public affairs.

Jane Vincent Taylor

New Law Makes Local Poet Nervous

[*This Land*, February 1, 2013]

O n November 1, 2012, Oklahoma passed an "open carry" law allowing people to carry guns in public. According to the online journal ThinkProgress, "Oklahoma's new 'open carry' law allows individuals with permits to openly carry guns in public and into many types of businesses including restaurants, grocery stores and banks, unless they post a sign prohibiting guns."

Writing in the Oklahoma literary journal This Land, poet Jane Vincent Taylor describes one of the effects the new law had on her while visiting a local coffee shop. Jane Vincent Taylor's work has appeared in This Land, Nimrod, and Still Point Quarterly, among other periodicals. Her most recent book of poetry is Pencil Light (2015). She teaches creative writing at Ghost Ranch, a retreat and education center in New Mexico.

Do you think her first reaction of fear was justified? What do you think is her personal response to the new law?

O thers have book fests, opera
and garden expos.
We have gun shows. Ammo.
Freedom
and now more freedom: open carry.

Like an old decoy I sit in my local coffee shop.
Post-holiday parents, toddlers in tow, order the special —
peppermint pancakes, dollar-size.

Megan fills the ketchup bottles.
Poinsettias wrinkle and curl. The radio plays Reba.
In walks a vested cowboy sporting a leather holster.

I react the way a gun insists: with fear. But nearer now,
I see his fancy shoulder bag
holds only oxygen,

precious sips of life — protection,
safety — openly carried, so we can all
breathe a little easier.

POINTS TO CONSIDER

1. Whom do you think Taylor refers to in the first word — who are the "Others"? And whom would "We" refer to in the third line?

2. How does the common expression "breathe a little easier" take on additional significance in the context of the poem?

3. Consider the words *protection* and *safety*. What sense do they have here? How do they refer to a larger argument about guns? How would you explain the poet's position on the topic?

The New York Times Editorial Board

End the Gun Epidemic in America

[*The New York Times*, December 5, 2015]

BEFORE YOU READ

Are we encouraging an epidemic of gun violence in this country by not working harder to control gun ownership and use? Have recent events shown that the Second Amendment must be reconsidered?

WORDS TO LEARN

premium (para. 2): value (noun)
unfettered (para. 2): freed from restraints (adjective)
disgrace (para. 3): shame (noun)

abet (para. 5): to encourage or support (verb)
drastically (para. 5): extremely; extensively (adverb)

A ll decent people feel sorrow and righteous fury about the lat-   1
est slaughter of innocents, in California. Law enforcement and
intelligence agencies are searching for motivations, including the
vital question of how the murderers might have been connected to international terrorism. That is right and proper.

But motives do not matter to the dead in California, nor did they   2
in Colorado, Oregon, South Carolina, Virginia, Connecticut and far
too many other places. The attention and anger of Americans should
also be directed at the elected leaders whose job is to keep us safe but
who place a higher premium on the money and political power of an
industry dedicated to profiting from the unfettered spread of ever more
powerful firearms.

It is a moral outrage and a national disgrace that civilians can legally   3
purchase weapons designed specifically to kill people with brutal speed
and efficiency. These are weapons of war, barely modified and deliberately marketed as tools of macho vigilantism and even insurrection.
America's elected leaders offer prayers for gun victims and then, callously
and without fear of consequence, reject the most basic restrictions on
weapons of mass killing, as they did on Thursday. They distract us with

---

arguments about the word *terrorism*. Let's be clear: These spree killings are all, in their own ways, acts of terrorism.

Opponents of gun control are saying, as they do after every killing,   4 that no law can unfailingly forestall a specific criminal. That is true. They are talking, many with sincerity, about the constitutional challenges to effective gun regulation. Those challenges exist. They point out that determined killers obtained weapons illegally in places like France, England and Norway that have strict gun laws. Yes, they did.

> These spree killings are all, in their own ways, acts of terrorism.

But at least those countries are trying. The United States is not.   5 Worse, politicians abet would-be killers by creating gun markets for them, and voters allow those politicians to keep their jobs. It is past time to stop talking about halting the spread of firearms, and instead to reduce their number drastically — eliminating some large categories of weapons and ammunition.

It is not necessary to debate the peculiar wording of the Second   6 Amendment. No right is unlimited and immune from reasonable regulation.

Certain kinds of weapons, like the slightly modified combat rifles   7 used in California, and certain kinds of ammunition, must be outlawed for civilian ownership. It is possible to define those guns in a clear and effective way and, yes, it would require Americans who own those kinds of weapons to give them up for the good of their fellow citizens.

What better time than during a presidential election to show, at long   8 last, that our nation has retained its sense of decency?

VOCABULARY/USING A DICTIONARY

1. If something has been *modified* (para. 3), what has happened to it?

2. Where does the word *macho* (para. 3) come from?

3. What part of speech is *callously* (para. 3)?

RESPONDING TO WORDS IN CONTEXT

1. What is a *vigilante*? If you can define *vigilante*, can you guess the meaning of *vigilantism* (para. 3)?

2. Have you ever heard of a shopping spree? What is it? If you can define *shopping spree*, what might a *spree killing* (para. 3) be?

3. What does *immunity* mean? In what context is the term usually used? What do the writers mean when they say, "No right is unlimited and *immune* from reasonable regulation" (para. 6)?

DISCUSSING MAIN POINT AND MEANING

1. What has spurred the *New York Times* staff to write this editorial?

2. What argument do opponents of gun control make against changing the current laws about guns?

3. What change does the editorial board of the *New York Times* hope to see happen?

EXAMINING SENTENCES, PARAGRAPHS, AND ORGANIZATION

1. The editorial begins, "All decent people feel sorry and righteous fury about the latest slaughter of innocents, in California" (para. 1). What do you notice about the diction in the first sentence? How is the reader being influenced by the language used here?

2. What do you notice about sentence structures and the organization of the argument in paragraph 4?

3. How would you describe the organization of this essay? If you put it in outline form, how might it look?

THINKING CRITICALLY

1. Why did the editorial board decide to write this editorial in December 2015? Why was it important to voice these concerns before a presidential election?

2. Do opponents of gun control have valid points in their argument? Where does the editorial board differ from its opponents?

3. Do you agree that slightly modified combat rifles are not necessary for civilians to own? Why or why not?

WRITING ACTIVITIES

1. The editorial "End the Gun Epidemic in America" was the first front-page editorial published in the *New York Times* since 1920. In your own words, write about the arguments over gun control in this country, explain why it has become such an important issue, and explain how and why the issue is getting significant media attention. Is there a gun epidemic? If so, what does that mean to you?

2. Write a paragraph in which you make an argument on a subject of your choice. Then, in another paragraph, offer a clear counterargument (one that you can articulate in writing). Once you have written both of these, structure a paragraph that imitates paragraph 4 in this editorial — use your counterargument and give credit where credit is due: What points does your opponent make that are valid?

3. Choose one sentence that you agree or disagree with in this editorial and offer a brief written response. As you write, bring in your own examples to support your position.

Suzanna Hupp, as told to Dave Mann

My Gun Was 100 Yards Away, Completely Useless

[*Texas Monthly*, April 2016]

BEFORE YOU READ

Do you think experiencing gun-related violence on a large or small scale would make you more or less in favor of gun laws? Do you think having the right to carry a gun makes you safer?

WORDS TO LEARN

vividly (para. 1): distinctly (adverb)

testify (para. 9): to bear witness under oath (verb)

absence (para. 10): a period of being away (noun)

onerous (para. 12): oppressive (adjective)

guarantee (para. 14): a promise or assurance (noun)

I did not grow up in a house with guns. When I was eighteen and moved out on my own, a friend of mine gave me a handgun and taught me how to use it. Fast-forwarding a bit, I went and became a chiropractor, and shortly after that, in my first year out of school, one of my patients was an assistant DA in Harris County. I was living just outside Houston, in Pasadena. He used to come in on a regular basis and would ask me about my gun. And I would tell him, "You know, I don't carry it with me all the time, because, of course, that's illegal." I remember vividly him saying, "You need to carry it. You're a single woman in a big city. You need to carry it."   1

I did begin to carry it. At that time, it was illegal in the state of Texas. But I bought a purse that was specially made for concealed carry.[1] Didn't carry it all the time, but I carried it much of the time.   2

---

[1] concealed carry (para. 2): The practice of carrying a gun, hidden, on one's person in public

---

Suzanna Hupp survived the 1991 Luby's shooting and became an important advocate of gun rights, voicing support for an individual's right to carry a concealed weapon. She served as a Republican member of the Texas House of Representatives from 1997 to 2007.

In 1991 I was with my parents at a local Luby's cafeteria in Killeen.   3
We were eating lunch with a friend of mine who was also the manager
of the restaurant. We'd finished eating when a madman drove his truck
through the window and very methodically began executing people with
a handgun. And it took a good 45 seconds, which is an eternity, to realize
that that's what he was there to do. At that time, the mass shootings that
we see frequently now were not occurring. So it wasn't the first thing that
came to your mind.

My purse was on the floor next to me. I actually reached for it. I used   4
to carry that gun in my purse, but I'd taken it out about three months earlier, leaving it in my car, because I was concerned about losing my license
to practice as a chiropractor. I was afraid that if I got caught, I'd go to jail.
So my gun was a hundred yards away, completely useless.

Could I have hit the guy? He was fifteen feet from me. He was up.   5
Everybody in the restaurant was down. I've hit much smaller targets at
much greater distances. Was I completely prepared to do it? Absolutely.
Could my gun have jammed? It's a revolver, so it's possible, but is it likely?
Could I have missed? Yeah, it's possible. But the one thing nobody can
argue with is that it would have changed the odds.

Twenty-three people were killed, including my parents.   · 6

I'm telling you, we were like fish in a barrel. Sitting there waiting   7
for it to be your turn is not a fun place to be. Anyone who thinks differently, I try to put them in that same situation in their mind, only instead
of having their parents with them, having their kids with them. And as
that madman is leveling his weapon at your two-year-old's forehead,
even if you've chosen not to have a gun,
don't you hope the guy behind you has
one and knows how to use it? To me, it's
cut-and-dried.

> I made it crystal
> clear that I was mad
> at the Legislature,
> because they had
> legislated me out
> of the right to pro-
> tect myself and my
> family.

I decided to talk to the media, and I   8
made it crystal clear that I was mad at the
Legislature, because they had legislated me
out of the right to protect myself and my
family. Even now I get angry thinking about
it. That's always been my dominant emotion. I get — not sad — I get angry.

I've been on every slime-bag talk show you can imagine — and some   9
of them twice. I would always wash my hands well after I finished, but I
think I'm glad I did them. I testified in a couple dozen states and hopefully helped to change a vote or two.

People would ask me to run for the Legislature, but I held off for a   10
long time, because I couldn't afford it. As you well know, the Legislature

here doesn't pay. So eventually when we felt like we could afford to have an absence from my clinic, I ran and was fortunate enough to be elected.

It was a great experience. If money were no object, I would run for 11 office again in a heartbeat [Hupp left the Legislature in 2007]. It was really a wonderful experience overall, though Lord knows there were moments when a stiff drink was called for.

Huge strides for gun rights have been made not only in Texas but 12 across the U.S. When I first started doing this, there were only a handful of states that had any kind of concealed carry at all. Now I think all states do. Some of the laws are still a bit onerous.

One of my bugaboos is gun laws. Anytime we list a place where you 13 can't carry guns, to me, that's like a shopping list for a madman. If I'm a crazy guy who wants to rack up a high body count, I'm not going to go to an NRA convention. I'm not going to go to the gun show or places where there are thousands of guns in the hands of law-abiding citizens. I'm going to go where somebody has said that guns aren't allowed. If you think about nearly every one of these mass shootings, they have occurred at places where guns weren't allowed. That's frustrating to me, particularly when you talk about schools. Where do these madmen go? They go to schools and slaughter people.

I don't have any love for guns, one way or the other. I don't care 14 about them. They're just a tool. Having a gun is never a guarantee either. But it changes the odds. It just changes the odds.

VOCABULARY/USING A DICTIONARY

1. Hupp identifies herself as a *chiropractor* (para. 1). Do you know what that is?

2. What word, included in *methodically* (para. 3), gives you a clue to its definition?

3. Where does the word *bugaboo* (para. 13) come from? What does it mean?

RESPONDING TO WORDS IN CONTEXT

1. When Hupp says that forty-five seconds was an *eternity* (para. 3), what do you think she means? How is *eternity* defined?

2. The essay is titled "My Gun Was 100 Yards Away, Completely Useless." Based on Hupp's argument, what do you think an *advocate* is?

3. What does the phrase *cut-and-dried* mean (para. 7)? What does Hupp mean when she uses that phrase in this context?

DISCUSSING MAIN POINT AND MEANING

1. What event led Hupp to become a gun-rights advocate?

2. What does Hupp identify as her primary emotional reaction to the events that happened to her? Why is that her main emotion?

3. What is Hupp's main objection to laws that restrict gun ownership and the ability to carry guns?

EXAMINING SENTENCES, PARAGRAPHS, AND ORGANIZATION

1. The style of this essay is more informal than that of many of the other essays in this book, presumably because this essay was written from a conversation ("as told to Dave Mann"). Can you find examples of where the writing seems more informal than what you would find in most essays?

2. There is an editorial insertion in paragraph 11: "[Hupp left the Legislature in 2007]." Do you think this insertion is necessary? Why might it have been included?

3. Hupp's concluding paragraph is brief. What makes it an effective conclusion?

THINKING CRITICALLY

1. Was Hupp a gun-rights supporter before the shooting at Luby's in Killeen? Why do you think she was, or wasn't?

2. Do you think Hupp's argument in favor of carrying a gun is convincing? Explain your answer.

3. If Hupp had been able to reach her gun, do you think that would have made a difference?

WRITING ACTIVITIES

1. Find a controversial topic that interests you (one that is somewhat visible in the media — abortion rights, raising the minimum wage, illegal immigration, gun control, climate change, etc.), and write a short narrative essay that argues in favor of or against a position on that topic. Write from your own experience and authority, instead of bringing in statistics (unless they are statistics that draw from your experience — for example, Hupp says in paragraph 6, "Twenty-three people were killed, including my parents").

2. In small groups, consider the effect of introductions, using Hupp's essay as a model. Have one member read Hupp's essay out loud, beginning with the current introduction. Have another member read the essay, beginning with paragraph 3 and ending with the current conclusion. Have another begin at paragraph 10, read to the end, pick up at the beginning, and read paragraph 9 as the conclusion. Groups can discuss the effect of starting with different information and the reader responses.

3. Write a letter to Hupp in order to gather research on the question of gun control. Whether you support gun rights or feel there should be more restrictions, your letter should explain your beliefs about gun control.

Articulate your position while responding to Hupp's personal position. You may ask questions about her stance or how her life has continued to be affected — about her private life or her work in the legislature. You may propose alternative scenarios in which tight gun laws exist or concealed carry is permitted and ask her opinion on them.

John A. Fry

Allowing Guns Won't Make Campuses Safer

[*The Philadelphia Inquirer*, October 19, 2015]

BEFORE YOU READ

What can we do to make campuses safer from the gun violence we see happening across the country? What are some of the suggestions raised in this essay and elsewhere on how to make colleges safer?

WORDS TO LEARN

volatile (para. 7): explosive (adjective)

exacerbate (para. 7): to aggravate (verb)

preposterous (para. 10): absurd (adjective)

mayhem (para. 11): random violence; disorder (noun)

prominent (para. 13): standing out (adjective)

Just eight days after a gunman massacred nine people at a community college in Oregon, two more students were killed in separate shootings on college campuses in Texas and Florida.   1

In many parts of the country, the shootings prompted a call to arm students and faculty.   2

Only in America do we respond to shootings with the need for more guns. Arming college campuses will do little to reduce mass attacks, and will likely lead to more shooting deaths.   3

There are already 300 million civilian firearms in the United States. That's more than one for every adult. At what point do Americans say enough is enough?   4

It didn't happen last year after a student killed six and injured 13 near the University of California, Santa Barbara. It didn't happen in 2013   5

John A. Fry is the president of Drexel University in Philadelphia, Pennsylvania.

after a 23-year-old shot his father and brother before killing three others at Santa Monica College. It didn't happen in 2012 when a 43-year-old former student shot and killed seven people and injured three others at Oikos University in Oakland, Calif. And it obviously didn't happen after a senior killed 32 people at Virginia Tech University in 2007 — the largest campus massacre ever.

> It defies logic to think that allowing students, faculty, and administrators to carry guns will somehow make college campuses safer.

It defies logic to think that allowing stu-   6
dents, faculty, and administrators to carry guns will somehow make college campuses safer. Indeed, experts from the Harvard School of Public Health found that wherever there are more guns, there are more murders.

Many college campuses are already   7
confronting thorny issues of how best to combat suicide, sexual assault, and binge drinking. Introducing more guns into that volatile mix will only exacerbate the problems.

Yet, in the past few years, campus-carry bills have been introduced   8
in almost half the states. Thankfully, most of the measures have failed.

But starting in August, students and faculty members at universities   9
in Texas will be allowed to carry handguns into classrooms, dormitories, and other campus buildings.

Supporters claim the so-called concealed-carry law will make cam-   10
puses safer by allowing gun owners to defend themselves, and possibly save lives, should a mass shooting occur. Some have even made the preposterous claim that legalizing guns on college campuses will help women defend themselves from sexual assault.

The reality is that allowing more guns will lead to more fear and   11
mayhem, while having a chilling effect on campus life. Will students be willing to engage in thoughtful debate if they know a fellow classmate has a gun in his backpack? Will professors meet with struggling students to discuss their grades if the person is armed?

If anything, allowing guns on college campuses will likely lead to   12
more accidental shootings and suicides. Just imagine all the things that could go wrong with gun-carrying students at a fraternity party or concert.

There's a reason why the U.S. military bars most troops from carry-   13
ing weapons on their bases outside of combat zones. In fact, one of the most prominent opponents of the campus-carry bill is a former commander of the U.S. Special Operations forces who directed the raid that killed Osama bin Laden.

Adm. William McRaven is now the chancellor at the University of 14
Texas and a gun owner. Yet, he opposed allowing guns on college campuses in Texas.

"I feel the presence of concealed weapons will make a campus less 15
safe," McRaven wrote in a letter to the Texas legislature.

In all, eight states allow the carrying of concealed weapons on public 16
college campuses. Nineteen states ban concealed weapons on campus,
and 23 others leave the decision to the individual colleges or state board
of regents.

Oregon is one of the states that allows guns on college campuses, 17
though not in classrooms. Perhaps someone with a gun could have intervened in the recent massacre. But the odds are very small that another
person with a gun would have been in a position to stop it.

The best answer to the shootings is fewer guns, not more. Witness 18
how strict gun laws in other developed countries have resulted in fewer
deaths by firearms.

Short of that, the best way to reduce campus shootings is to increase 19
efforts to identify and treat disturbed students, while preventing them
from buying guns. A well-trained, well-equipped campus police force is
also critical to campus safety.

Other sensible steps include universal background checks, tighter 20
regulation of gun dealers, safe storage requirements, and prohibiting gun
ownership for anyone convicted of domestic violence or assault.

There are many steps that can be taken to make college campuses 21
safe. But allowing more guns on campus is not one of them.

VOCABULARY/USING A DICTIONARY

1. What is a *thorn*? What is a *thorny* (para. 7) situation or problem?
2. Who might a state board of *regents* (para. 16) be?
3. What is the opposite of *reduce* (para. 19)?

RESPONDING TO WORDS IN CONTEXT

1. What part of speech is *massacred* (para. 1)?
2. How is the word *bars* (para. 13) used in this essay?
3. When Fry speaks of *disturbed students* (para. 19), what kind of students do
   you think he means?

DISCUSSING MAIN POINT AND MEANING

1. What is the United States' usual response to shootings around the country,
   according to Fry?

2. What is Fry's response to the impulse to arm people on college campuses?

3. Does the military encourage carrying weapons outside of combat zones? Why or why not?

EXAMINING SENTENCES, PARAGRAPHS, AND ORGANIZATION

1. How does Fry begin his essay? Is his introduction effective? What would you think if he started instead with paragraph 4?

2. Do you think Fry spends enough time suggesting the alternative to guns on campus? Why or why not?

3. Fry includes the sentence "Thankfully, most of the measures have failed" in paragraph 8. He is commenting on the introduction of campus-carry bills in various states. Can you tell Fry's position on campus carry based on the wording of his sentence?

THINKING CRITICALLY

1. Does it surprise you that campus-carry bills are being introduced? What, if anything, surprises you? If you aren't surprised by this, explain why not.

2. What will be the effect of arming students and faculty on college campuses? Why do you think this is so?

3. What are some of the ways Fry suggests helping students (besides giving them guns)? What do you think of Fry's call to help students? Would it reduce gun violence on campuses?

WRITING ACTIVITIES

1. Write a short piece that expresses your feelings and beliefs about guns on campus. Once you have written it, try to rewrite it imitating Fry's style — short paragraphs, one or two sentences long (you may need to cut and/or rearrange your draft to do this effectively). Then write it again with longer, denser paragraphs (again, you may need to write more or cut portions that don't carry as much weight). In small groups, discuss which version you prefer and why.

2. Outline Fry's essay. Your outline should have anywhere from five to twenty points that cover the ideas in Fry's paragraphs, and you should use only words and phrases (rather than complete sentences) to indicate what each part is about.

3. Analyze Fry's concerns about what carrying guns on campus will do. Do you think his concerns are valid? Which of his concerns are convincing, and which are less convincing? Why?

Brittney Christ (student essay)

We Should Be Allowed to Protect Ourselves

[*The State Hornet*, California State University, Sacramento, June 25, 2015]

BEFORE YOU READ

What do you know about campus-carry bills that have been passed in states like Texas? Would allowing people on campus to carry guns make you feel more or less secure when you are there?

WORDS TO LEARN

infamous (para. 1): known for evil
    deeds (adjective)
hype (para. 5): publicity used to
    promote something (noun)

potential (para. 6): possible
    (adjective)

Guns on college campuses in particular have become a hot topic   1
in the last few years because of infamous shootings such as
Columbine High School in '99 and Virginia Tech in '07. These
massacres have sparked debate over gun control laws as well as gun violence involving youth.

Texas lawmakers have passed a campus-carry bill that could come   2
into action in August 2016 for universities and August 2017 for community colleges. Those in support of this bill, such as women who have
been assaulted on campus or students who just feel unsafe and want the
right to protect themselves against another Virginia Tech incident, claim
this new law will give gun owners the security to know that they have the
right to defend themselves in overtly dangerous situations.

According to the University of Iowa, 53 percent of students think   3
guns should not be allowed, and would be upset if they were legal to
have on campus. In addition, many professors are worried about frenzied
students coming into their offices and threatening the professors over
bad grades. However, surely there will be rules to allow these guns to be
carried onto campus.

Brittney Christ served as the State Hornet's *opinion editor and graduated from
California State University, Sacramento, in 2015 with a degree in English.*

The popular phrase that comes to mind is, "Guns don't kill people,   4 people kill people." There have been many hilarious memes about gun control. One in particular that has gotten people talking is the picture of the newspaper clipping of the man who says that he left his gun on the porch all day and it never shot anyone.

> The popular phrase that comes to mind is, "Guns don't kill people, people kill people."

The man behind the photo, Donald   5 Martin, said, "Can you imagine how surprised I was, with all of the hype about how dangerous guns are and how they kill people? . . . Either the killing is by people misusing guns or I'm in the possession of the laziest gun in the world. So now I'm off to check my spoons, because I heard they make people fat."

Allowing guns on campuses will not only make students feel more   6 secure, but hopefully eliminate a potential school shooting that ends up in the death of innocent people. Of course, every school within the eight states (Texas, Colorado, Idaho, Kansas, Mississippi, Oregon, Utah and Wisconsin) allowing this bill will have strict rules about gun usage and will have training courses in addition to those required to own a gun in the first place. Furthermore, gun registration will probably be required as well. So why is everyone worrying so much?

Let's promote self-defense and stop shaming those who want to   7 exercise their Second Amendment rights.

VOCABULARY/USING A DICTIONARY

1. What is an example of an *overtly* (para. 2) dangerous situation? What is the opposite of *overt* or *overtly*?

2. What is a *meme* (para. 4)?

3. What part of speech is *eliminate* (para. 6)? What does it mean?

RESPONDING TO WORDS IN CONTEXT

1. What is Christ describing when she speaks of *frenzied* (para. 3) students?

2. Donald Martin says that maybe he's "*in the possession of* the laziest gun in the world" (para. 5). What does the phrase *in the possession of* mean?

3. In her last sentence, Christ says, "Let's . . . stop *shaming* those who want to exercise their Second Amendment rights" (para. 7). What does she mean? How might people who want to exercise their Second Amendment rights be *shamed* in the conversation about gun control?

DISCUSSING MAIN POINT AND MEANING

1. Why does Christ think it is OK for guns to be carried on campus, despite various objections to that possibility?

2. What do the statistics Christ cites suggest about how many people view campus carry?

3. How will guns keep schools safer, according to Christ?

EXAMINING SENTENCES, PARAGRAPHS, AND ORGANIZATION

1. In paragraph 3, Christ looks at some data from the University of Iowa. She ends the paragraph with her response to this data. How does she indicate the introduction of a different point of view?

2. Does the mid-essay anecdote about the meme support Christ's position or further her argument about campus carry? Explain your answer.

3. Do you think Christ's one-sentence conclusion is sufficient as an ending to the essay? Why or why not?

THINKING CRITICALLY

1. How have incidents like Columbine and Virginia Tech influenced ideas about gun control laws and violence?

2. Does the meme Christ includes work in favor of campus carry? Why or why not?

3. Does Christ explain how allowing guns on campus will make students feel more secure? What about the claim that it will "hopefully eliminate a potential school shooting that ends up in the death of innocent people" (para. 6)? Are you convinced by her essay?

WRITING ACTIVITIES

1. How do you feel about campus-carry bills that allow students, faculty, and staff to have guns on campus? What potential drawbacks to allowing campus carry can you think of? What sort of rules would you put in place to make you feel safer (whether you are for or against campus carry)?

2. Come up with your own gun control meme. What would it look like? What would the text be? What is the message you are trying to convey?

3. How do you understand the wording of the Second Amendment? Is it literal and inviolable? How do you interpret what it says? Answer these questions in one to three short paragraphs.

Effective Openings: Establishing a Clear Context for an Argument

When writing an essay that advances an opinion about a current issue, one of the best approaches a writer can take is to summarize the general context or situation that gave rise to the issue. This approach is effectively demonstrated in Brittney Christ's "We Should Be Allowed to Protect Ourselves." Note how her opening paragraph sets out in a clear and direct fashion the situation that has prompted her essay — the debate about whether students should be permitted to carry guns on campus for self-protection. She not only establishes her main topic in her first sentence but efficiently provides a reason for why it is a "hot topic." Her opening paragraph takes us directly into the debate, and she will express her opinions on the issue in the body of her paper.

1
Establishes her topic

2
Shows specific examples that fueled the debate

(1) <u>Guns on college campuses in particular have become a hot topic in the last few years</u> (2) <u>because of infamous shootings such as Columbine High School in '99 and Virginia Tech in '07.</u> These massacres have sparked debate over gun control laws as well as gun violence involving youth.

STUDENT WRITER AT WORK
Brittney Christ

R.A. What inspired you to write this essay? And publish it?

B.C. Campus shootings were the hot topic to talk about and I wanted to share my take on it, especially since it is not a common opinion to have. It was also one of my first pieces as an editor on the paper, so I got to really express my thoughts without too much censoring.

R.A. What was your main purpose in writing this piece?

B.C. Campus shootings were extremely prevalent during this time, and a campus-carry law was passed by Texas lawmakers, which in turn sparked a debate in many classrooms.

R.A. Are your opinions unusual or fairly mainstream, given the general climate of discourse on campus?

B.C. My views were widely out of place for the environment. Most people I came into contact with wanted more gun control, and fewer guns in America in general.

R.A. What topics most interest you as a writer?

B.C. I am very passionate about social issues such as feminism, gay pride, and the environment. Issues such as fracking, abortion, and equal rights are the types of topics I love to dig into.

R.A. Are you pursuing a career in which writing will be a component?

B.C. Yes, in every job I take I make sure that writing is a component. I plan to one day become a best-selling fiction author!

R.A. What advice do you have for other student writers?

B.C. You need to write from the heart and make it authentic. You should pick something you are passionate about. You need to find your niche and stick with it. Trust me, someone out there in the world is writing about whatever it is that you have set your heart on.

Spotlight on Data and Research

David A. Fryxell

Shooting from the Lip

[*Desert Exposure*, October 2014]

To be persuasive, many arguments require some use of research and statistics to support their point (see "How to Support Opinions" on p. 15). As the following selection shows, this is true even of brief arguments. The columnist David A. Fryxell doesn't have much space, yet he finds a way to cite several sources of data and research in an attempt to show that, in his view, the National Rifle Association (NRA) shuts down honest debate by taking more extreme positions than do gun control advocates. Hoping to encourage more open conversation on the topic, Fryxell suggests that "responsible gun owners — who, after all, know guns best — could contribute the most to a search for solutions that would ratchet down the carnage while preserving what's most important to them." He believes these voices are not being heard.

The reaction of gun advocates to the recent tragedy at a shooting range   1
near Las Vegas was sadly typical of the tunnel vision that characterizes
what passes for debate on America's firearms fixation. A nine-year-old
girl accidentally shot and killed an instructor at Bullets and Burgers when
she lost control of an Uzi. The incident might lead reasonable people to
question the wisdom of a nine-year-old wielding an automatic weapon
capable of firing 600 rounds a minute, or at least to wonder if such enter-
tainments need stricter age or size restrictions. But the National Rifle
Association responded instead to the death of a fellow gun enthusiast
by tweeting a list of ways kids can "have fun at the shooting range" with
colorful, kid-oriented targets. That Twitter entry was quickly deleted,
belatedly showing more respect than "Joe the Plumber" (Samuel Joseph
Wurzelbacher) did earlier this year in commenting on an interview with
the father of one of the six victims in the UC–Santa Barbara shooting:
"Your dead kids don't trump my Constitutional rights."

That such a crude thought should even enter the vacant space of   2
Joe the Plumber's head, much less be given utterance, betrays how
remote we remain from sensible solutions to gun violence. Even
the U.S. Supreme Court has joined in gun advocates' collective amnesia
about the first clause of the much-cited Second Amendment: "A well regulated Militia, being necessary to the security of a free state. . . ." Surely
the Founding Fathers never envisioned that mentally ill individuals like
the UC–Santa Barbara shooter should have access to semiautomatic
handguns, or that nine-year-olds would have fun with Uzis. Neither
shooter seems a promising candidate for militia membership.

To be clear, despite the NRA's fearmongering to fire up its mem-   3
bership and fundraising, no one in a position of authority — from

President Obama on down — has seriously proposed taking away the guns of mentally competent, law-abiding citizens. (No need, folks, for those bumper stickers about your "cold, dead hands.") Notwithstanding the run on ammunition at gun stores ever since Obama's election, even the most draconian proposals to restrict firearms would amount to little more than minor inconvenience for gun enthusiasts — a little paperwork, maybe reloading more often with smaller clips. Even in the wildest fantasies of would-be gun regulators, guns would remain less tightly governed than automobiles.

"Slippery slope" warnings about Uncle Sam seizing guns simply 4 distract from serious conversations about dealing with America's gun violence. Instead of dire pronouncements unmoored to reality, the NRA should offer sensible proposals that gun owners could live with. But the extremism on these complicated questions is entirely one-sided. You might not agree with the ideas of ex–New York City Mayor Michael Bloomberg or the Brady Campaign to Prevent Gun Violence, but such gun control advocates are much closer to a middle ground than the NRA's leadership. (The extreme gun control equivalent of the NRA position would be something along the lines of "confiscate all guns and melt them down." Neither Bloomberg nor the Brady group says anything remotely like that.)

Many grassroots NRA members, we're sure, would be much more 5 open to dialog. For most of its history, in fact, the NRA supported reasonable gun control measures; as recently as 1968, it did not oppose the landmark Gun Control Act. Ironically, responsible gun owners — who, after all, know guns best — could contribute the most to a search for solutions that would ratchet down the carnage while preserving what's most important to them.

And, yes, there is carnage and there is a uniquely American 6 problem — despite the NRA leadership's insistence that "guns don't kill people, people kill people." The NRA has even sought to block the Centers for Disease Control and Prevention from gathering data about gun violence. But that hasn't kept some researchers from showing that, indeed, guns do kill people and they do so disproportionately in the United States.

A 2013 study found that the U.S. has 88 guns per 100 people and 7 10 gun-related deaths per 100,000 population — the most on both counts of 28 developed countries. Japan has both the fewest guns (0.6 per 100 people) and gun-related deaths (0.06 per 100,000). (Those who blame violent video games rather than guns for Americans' violent habits might note that Japan spends 25% more per capita on video games than the U.S.)

You might have heard, however, that England and Wales — with 8 strict gun control laws — have triple the rate of violent crime as the U.S. Those who cite that statistic fail to add that "violent crime" statistics

continued

in the U.S. and Britain, perversely, don't count homicides, which are a separate category. The per capita homicide rate in gun-toting America is quadruple that of England and Wales: 14,022 homicides in 2011 (11,101 committed with firearms) versus 622 in England and Wales (equivalent to 3,421 when adjusted for population).

But surely owning a firearm keeps you safer, doesn't it? A study   9 released early this year reported that Americans with access to a gun are almost twice as likely to be killed by a gun (and three times as likely to commit suicide with a gun). A gender gap in the statistics is startling: Men with firearm access were 29% more likely to die in a gun-related homicide, while women were nearly three times as likely to be victims than those in gun-free households.

In a *New York Times* column earlier this year, Nicholas Kristof 10 compared the need for informed, sensible gun reforms to the early 20th-century dilemma of automobile deaths. "If we had the same auto fatality rate today that we had in 1921, by my calculations we would have 715,000 Americans dying annually in vehicle accidents." Instead, thanks to traffic laws, driver's licenses, seatbelts, air bags, and other changes, that number is less than 34,000 (about the same as all firearm-related deaths). Motorists still enjoy their God-given right to travel — just not at 130 miles an hour, or drunk, or in unsafe vehicles.

Is it too much to ask that gun enthusiasts put forward similar com- 11 monsense approaches to reduce the toll of gun violence? (Instead, when an entrepreneur introduced a "smart gun" that only the owner could fire, the NRA condemned it and stores dropped it after anonymous death threats.) I'm sure that people who enjoy owning and using guns could come up with much better and more palatable strategies than those thrust into this debate by becoming victims of gun violence. The parents in Newtown or Santa Barbara don't know about guns, only their grief. If you come away from this column thinking I'm advocating gun control, you're missing the point. I'm advocating a gun conversation. And it's impossible to have a meaningful conversation when one side is shouting instead of talking.

DRAWING CONCLUSIONS

1. Consider Fryxell's title. What common expression is behind it? What expression do you think his twist on *shooting* refers to? Why is his title appropriate given his position?

2. What does Fryxell mean by "'slippery slope' warnings" (para. 4)? What are some ways such arguments apply to the gun debate? Do you think "slippery slope" arguments are inherently wrong? Why or why not?

3. Fryxell claims to be evenhanded. In other words, he's not advocating gun control, as he explicitly says. Do you believe him?

Paul Fussell

A Well-Regulated Militia

[*The New Republic,* June 27, 1981]

The Second Amendment to the U.S. Constitution consists of a fairly brief sentence: "A well regulated Militia, being necessary to the security of a free State, the right of the people to keep and bear Arms, shall not be infringed." For centuries, this amendment seemed straightforward and was rarely a legal issue. Yet in the politically turbulent 1960s, following the shooting deaths of President John F. Kennedy, his brother Senator Robert Kennedy, and civil rights leader Martin Luther King Jr., an anti-gun sentiment began growing. The anti-gun movement gained momentum with the attempted assassination of President Ronald Reagan in 1981, when one of the men also shot in the incident, James Brady, initiated a congressional bill that would subject gun buyers to a federal background check. Hotly contested by such pro-gun organizations as the National Rifle Association (founded in 1871 but not an influential lobbying group until 1975), the Brady Act was finally enacted in 1993. Today, with an estimated 300,000 firearm-related deaths a year — and with one highly publicized school shooting following right on the heels of another — an accurate understanding of the Second Amendment has become more important than ever: What did the framers mean by a militia and by the phrase "to keep and bear Arms," and does the Second Amendment guarantee the right of individual citizens to own weapons or only those who are part of a "militia"? Many legal scholars, historians, and journalists have covered this issue but few with the concision, wit, and irony of Paul Fussell. At a time when many believe the Second Amendment should itself be amended, given its increasingly costly consequences, Fussell argues that it should not be revised or abolished but just be taken literally and enforced.

An eighteenth-century scholar who taught for many years at Rutgers University before moving to the University of Pennsylvania, Paul Fussell wrote numerous academic studies — on such topics as poetic meter, rhetoric, and eighteenth-century literature. But after winning the National Book Award in nonfiction for The Great War and Modern Memory *in 1975 (Fussell served in the infantry in World War II), he began writing essays on a variety of topics for a general public. One of those essays, "A Well-Regulated Militia," was published in the* New Republic *in 1981.*

In the spring Washington swarms with high school graduating classes. 1
They come to the great pulsating heart of the Republic — which no
one has yet told them is Wall Street — to be impressed by the White
House and the Capitol and the monuments and the Smithsonian and
the space capsules. Given the state of public secondary education, I
doubt if many of these young people are at all interested in language
and rhetoric, and I imagine few are fascinated by such attendants of
power and pressure as verbal misrepresentation and disingenuous
quotation. But any who are can profit from a stroll past the headquar-
ters of the National Rifle Association of America, its slick marble
façade conspicuous at 1600 Rhode Island Avenue, NW.

There they would see an entrance flanked by two marble panels 2
offering language, and language more dignified and traditional than
that customarily associated with the Association's gun-freak con-
stituency, with its T-shirts reading GUNS, GUTS, AND GLORY
ARE WHAT MADE AMERICA GREAT and its belt buckles proclaiming I'LL GIVE UP MY GUN WHEN THEY PRY MY COLD
DEAD FINGERS FROM AROUND IT. The marble panel on the
right reads, "The right of the people to keep and bear arms shall not
be infringed," which sounds familiar. So familiar that the student
naturally expects the left-hand panel to honor the principle of symmetry by presenting the first half of the quotation, namely: "A well-
regulated Militia, being necessary to the security of a free state, . . ."
But looking to the left, the inquirer discovers not that clause at all but
rather this lame list of NRA functions and specializations: "Firearms
Safety Education. Marksmanship Training. Shooting for Recreation."
It's as if in presenting its well-washed, shiny public face the NRA
doesn't want to remind anyone of the crucial dependent clause of the
Second Amendment, whose latter half alone it is so fond of invok-
ing to urge its prerogatives. (Some legible belt buckles of members retreat further into a seductive vagueness, reading only, "Our
American Heritage: the Second Amendment.") We infer that for the
Association, the less emphasis on the clause about the militia, the
better. Hence its pretense on the front of its premises that the quoted
main clause is not crucially dependent on the now unadvertised
subordinate clause — indeed, it's meaningless without it.

Because flying .38- and .45-caliber bullets rank close to cancer, 3
heart disease, and AIDS as menaces to public health in this country, the firearm lobby, led by the NRA, comes under liberal attack
regularly, and with special vigor immediately after an assault on some
conspicuous person like Ronald Reagan or John Lennon. Thus the
New Republic, in April 1981, deplored the state of things but offered
as a solution only the suggestion that the whole Second Amendment
be perceived as obsolete and amended out of the Constitution. This
would leave the NRA with not a leg to stand on.

But here as elsewhere a better solution would be not to fiddle 4
with the Constitution but to take it seriously, the way we've done
with the First Amendment, say, or with the Thirteenth, the one
forbidding open and avowed slavery. And by taking the Second
Amendment seriously I mean taking it literally. We should "close
read" it and thus focus lots of attention on the grammatical reasoning of its two clauses. This might shame the NRA into pulling the
dependent clause out of the closet, displaying it on its façade, and
accepting its not entirely pleasant implications. These could be par-
ticularized in an Act of Congress providing:

(1) that the Militia shall now, after these many years, be "well-
     regulated," as the Constitution requires.
(2) that any person who has chosen to possess at home a gun of
     any kind, and who is not a member of the police or the mili-
     tary or an appropriate government agency, shall be deemed to
     have enrolled automatically in the Militia of the United States.
     Members of the Militia, who will be issued identifying badges,
     will be organized in units of battalion, company, or platoon size
     representing counties, towns, or boroughs. If they bear arms
     while not proceeding to or from scheduled exercises of the
     Militia, they will be punished "as a court martial may direct."
(3) that any gun owner who declines to join the regulated Militia
     may opt out by selling his firearms to the federal government
     for $1,000 each. He will sign an undertaking that if he ever
     again owns firearms he will be considered to have enlisted in the
     Militia.
(4) that because the Constitution specifically requires that the
     Militia shall be "well regulated," a regular training program,
     of the sort familiar to all who have belonged to military units

charged with the orderly management of small arms, shall be instituted. This will require at least eight hours of drill each Saturday at some convenient field or park, rain or shine or snow or ice. There will be weekly supervised target practice (separation from the service, publicly announced, for those who can't hit a barn door). And there will be ample practice in digging simple defense works, like foxholes and trenches, as well as necessary sanitary installations like field latrines and straddle trenches. Each summer there will be a six-week bivouac (without spouses), and this, like all the other exercises, will be under the close supervision of long-service noncommissioned officers of the United States Army and the Marine Corps. On bivouac, liquor will be forbidden under extreme penalty, but there will be an issue every Friday night of two cans of 3.2 beer, and feeding will follow traditional military lines, the cuisine consisting largely of shit-on-a-shingle, sandwiches made of bull dick (baloney) and choke-ass (cheese), beans, and fatty pork. On Sundays and holidays, powdered eggs for breakfast. Chlorinated water will often be available, in Lister Bags. Further obligatory exercises designed to toughen up the Militia will include twenty-five-mile hikes and the negotiation of obstacle courses. In addition, there will be instruction of the sort appropriate to other lightly armed, well-regulated military units: in map-reading, the erection of double-apron barbed-wire fences, and the rudiments of military courtesy and the traditions of the Militia, beginning with the Minute Men. Per diem payments will be made to those participating in these exercises.

(5) that since the purpose of the Militia is, as the Constitution says, to safeguard "the security of a free state," at times when invasion threatens (perhaps now the threat will come from Nicaragua, national security no longer being menaced by North Vietnam) all units of the Militia will be trucked to the borders for the duration of the emergency, there to remain in field conditions (here's where the practice in latrine-digging pays off) until Congress declares that the emergency has passed. Congress may also order the Militia to perform other duties consistent with its constitutional identity as a regulated volunteer force: for example, flood and emergency and disaster service (digging, sandbag filling, rescuing old people); patrolling angry or incinerated cities; or controlling crowds at large public events like patriotic parades, motor races, and professional football games.

(6) that failure to appear for these scheduled drills, practices, bivouacs, and mobilizations shall result in the Militiaperson's dismissal from the service and forfeiture of badge, pay, and firearm.

Why did the Framers of the Constitution add the word *bear* to   5
the phrase "keep and bear arms"? Because they conceived that keeping arms at home implied the public obligation to bear them in a regulated way for "the security of" not a private household but "a free state." If interstate bus fares can be regulated, it is hard to see why the Militia can't be, especially since the Constitution says it must be. The *New Republic* has recognized that "the Second Amendment to the Constitution clearly connects the right to bear arms to the eighteenth-century national need to raise a militia." But it goes on: "That need is now obsolete, and so is the amendment." And it concludes: "If the only way this country can get control of firearms is to amend the Constitution, then it's time for Congress to get the process under way."

I think not. Rather, it's time not to amend Article II of the Bill of   6
Rights (and Obligations) but to read it, publicize it, embrace it, and enforce it. That the Second Amendment stems from concerns that can be stigmatized as "eighteenth-century" cuts little ice. The First Amendment stems precisely from such concerns, and no one but yahoos wants to amend it. Also "eighteenth-century" is that lovely bit in Section 9 of Article I forbidding any "Title of Nobility" to be granted by the United States. That's why we've been spared Lord Annenberg and Sir Leonard Bernstein, Knight.[1] Thank God for the eighteenth century, I say. It understood not just what a firearm is and what a Militia is. It also understood what "well regulated" means. It knew how to compose a constitutional article and it knew how to read it. And it assumed that everyone, gun lobbyists and touring students alike, would understand and correctly quote it. Both halves of it.

---

[1] Lord Annenberg . . . Knight (para. 6): Walter H. Annenberg (1908–2002) was a controversial billionaire publisher, known both for his philanthropy and for using his publication for direct personal or political ends; Leonard H. Bernstein (1919–1990) was a massively influential composer whose many works include the score for *West Side Story.*

BACKGROUND AND CONTEXT

1. Why does Fussell mention that at the National Rifle Association's entrance, the panels cite only one part of the Second Amendment? What part is that? How does the complete sentence alter the way someone, like Fussell, may interpret the amendment?

2. Much of what Fussell writes about the duties of a "militia" can be found in the National Guard — regular training periods, disaster service, etc. But does Fussell equate the National Guard with a militia? Why would the National Guard — given Fussell's point of view — not be equivalent to the militia Fussell calls for? Describe what you think Fussell means by a "militia" and why it is central to his argument.

STRATEGY, STRUCTURE, AND STYLE

1. Although he never claims it directly, how can you tell Fussell supports gun control? Why doesn't he believe the Second Amendment should be repealed or revised? Do you think gun proponents would endorse Fussell's proposal? Why or why not? For Fussell, how would a militia work as a form of gun control?

2. Can you find any examples of humor in Fussell's proposal? Look carefully at his six suggestions on how Congress should proceed. What details do you think he means to be comic? What makes them funny?

COMPARISONS AND CONNECTIONS

1. How do you evaluate Fussell's main point: that we can understand the meaning of the Second Amendment only if we take into account both halves of the sentence? In a short essay, provide your own interpretation of the amendment: Do you think the true meaning of the amendment rests on the second part alone? Or does Fussell get it right?

2. Compare Fussell's essay to Wendy Kaminer's "A Civic Duty to Annoy" (p. 108). What do they have in common? How does each writer set forward an argument against an opposing view? How does each use humor to make a point?

Discussing the Unit

SUGGESTED TOPIC FOR DISCUSSION

Should we take the wording in the Second Amendment at face value? What would a literal interpretation look like? This chapter includes essays that present arguments made by writers both for and against gun control. Some believe that the Second Amendment provides us with the right to own — and carry — guns for our protection, at any time, in any place. Others believe that hazards are associated with citizens' owning guns and that relaxed gun laws decrease public safety. Still others question how to interpret the Second Amendment.

PREPARING FOR CLASS DISCUSSION

1. Do you believe it is inherently dangerous for a person to be able to own a gun? Why or why not? What rules, if any, do you think should be in place for purchasing, owning, and carrying a gun? Are you concerned about gun violence? Why or why not?

2. What are some of the reasons for wanting to own a gun? Does owning a gun make the owner safer or put him or her in more danger? Explain your answer.

FROM DISCUSSION TO WRITING

1. What do you think the Second Amendment means? Write a short paper in which you examine the wording of the Second Amendment and explain what right(s) you think it secures, and why. Choose two essays from this section to support your interpretation of the Second Amendment.

2. The current debate is over not only gun ownership but the right to carry a gun in public places, either as a concealed weapon or as open carry. How do the authors in this chapter debate this issue? In a comparison paper, show how two of the authors in this chapter argue for and against carrying guns in public. Which viewpoint do you agree with most, and why?

TOPICS FOR CROSS-CULTURAL DISCUSSION

1. Do any of the articles in this chapter address the question of inner-city violence in their examination of gun rights and the gun debate? If so, which ones look at this issue? Which ones seem to be blind to that particular side of the debate, and what aspect of the gun question is their focus? In a short response, address these questions using specific passages from the essays as examples.

2. How has the discussion of gun rights changed over the last thirty years? Write a brief description of what the issues were in 1981 (see Paul Fussell's essay on p. 267) and what they are now. Then try to describe what the issues might have been when the Founding Fathers drafted the Second Amendment.

8

Prisons, Police, Punishment: Is Our Criminal Justice System Broken?

According to the latest statistics, U.S. prisons and jails currently house some 2.2 to 2.3 million inmates, or approximately 1 in every 100 adults, giving us the highest incarceration rate in the developed world. How did we get to this point? And what have the consequences been for the prison population and the larger society? Is it possible to reduce both the incarceration rate and the significant proportion of released prisoners who reenter the criminal justice system?

Experts tie the growth of the prison population to a fivefold increase in the U.S. crime rate between 1960 and 1990, resulting in measures that incarcerated more offenders (some of whom might not have been imprisoned in the past) and lengthened sentences. While some argue that mass imprisonment has helped lower the crime rate, others contend that the reduction isn't as great as often claimed.

Millions of American adults experience prison life every day. We open the chapter with an account of one individual's experience in southern Arizona. In "The Storm," Elijah Paschelke describes a violent prison disruption that takes place in the midst of a monsoon and also while he is following an "aerial battle" between a huge hawk and a flock of sparrows. He realizes not only that he will never see the world the way he did before, but more importantly that he "will never *not* see it" the way he did before.

If prison writing can be a step forward for many inmates and a path to rehabilitation and improved self-esteem, prison reading may be even more important. As former prisoner Chandra Bozelko maintains (citing a Proliteracy America study) in "To Fix the U.S. Prison System, Give Every Inmate the Daily Newspaper," the "majority of U.S. inmates cannot read or read at a very low level." Believing that books can be too daunting to inexperienced readers, she argues that the advantages of newspapers "for any remedial reader are many: the journalistic approach to stories enhances comprehension, stories are varied and change daily, reading editorials and op-eds fosters critical thinking skills."

In their essays, neither Paschelke nor Bozelko mention why they wound up in prison. What are most Americans arrested for? This chapter's "Spotlight on Data and Research" presents data that reveal the top ten offenses leading to arrest. At the top of Haisam Hussein's infographic are driving under the influence, larceny and theft, and drug possession. "When it comes to prisons," he maintains, "the U.S. favors quantity over quality." But his principal causes of arrest are not the crimes that make the news and remain in the public eye. Lately, the crimes receiving the most media attention are those that inspired the Black Lives Matter movement. (For more, see Chapter 5, on race.) And these are crimes committed not by criminals but by those in charge of making the arrests. In "The Case for Compassionate Policing," a University of Virginia law professor, Josh Bowers, responds to a rash of shootings by police of unarmed African American citizens. Seeking to find a middle ground between respectful policing and maintaining public order, Bowers believes arrest should be the "last resort" of policing, not its primary purpose.

The fact that so many crimes involve drugs has led many on both sides of the political spectrum to make a distinction between violent and nonviolent offenses. In "Unlock 'Em Up?," columnist Mona Charen takes a skeptical look at proposals to end mass incarceration by releasing "nonviolent" inmates. Showing how important it is to make a distinction between state and federal prisons, she reexamines the statistics and points out that the majority of state prisoners (54 percent) are there for violent crimes.

Though she is open to suggestions about what to do with the 46 percent incarcerated for nonviolent crimes, she raises a number of issues to show how difficult it is to "grapple" with the problem.

Yet society still faces the issue of what to do with violent criminals, especially those who appear to show no regard for human life. For decades, such criminals, if found guilty, were often sentenced to death. Although the death penalty has been abolished in a number of states and is not as common as it once was, there were, nevertheless, thirteen executions in the United States between January 1 and May 1 of 2016. While many prisoners remain on death row awaiting the ultimate penalty, the nation continues to debate both the morality and effectiveness of capital punishment. In "The Death Sentence: An Inefficient Method of Punishment," Kansas State student Sonia Kumar joins the debate with her views on this controversial issue. "In my opinion," she argues, "capital punishment is an inefficient way to punish criminals because it is an outdated, ineffective, biased and expensive practice that furthers a cycle of violence."

The chapter concludes with one of America's greatest poets grappling with the same problem as Sonia Kumar, but over 150 years earlier. In an 1858 newspaper editorial, Walt Whitman weighed in on this long-debated issue. The law on capital punishment, he argues, "is in a very unsatisfactory state."

Elijah Paschelke

The Storm

[*Orion*, January/February 2015]

*I*n 1974, writer and poet Richard Shelton founded the Creative Writing Workshop at the Arizona state prison where he has been teaching continuously. In 2015, he collected a number of works by prisoners within that system and published them in the nature magazine Orion. The following short essay, Elijah Paschelke's "The Storm," was one of these works.

It's monsoon season in southern Arizona. A flash of lightning sparks in the shadowy sky. Even through the cement walls I can taste the alkaline flavor of electricity. I'm in "the hole" again, laid back on a hard mattress that smells faintly of mildew. Crackling thunder breaks what's left of the calm out there. It starts out like several power transformers blowing at once and then rolls into a terrific BOOM.

The smell of rain leaks in through poorly constructed Plexiglass seals. The sky quickly becomes a deep gray, and cool wind blows down. I cannot feel it but I can see the dust blowing across the bare exercise field. The ferocity of the lightning and thunder is apocalyptic. More thunder. Then I realize that my mind has drifted off again as it sometimes does in here. I am actually hearing gunshots and thinking it is thunder. The booming in the distance is concussion grenades exploding. Another race riot must have kicked off out on the yard.

I've been in this stinking sweatbox for seven months now, with two more to go. I will never see the world the way I did before. Or actually, I will never *not* see it the way I did before. I will never willingly miss a sunset, and I will revel in the huge white clouds, which well up this time of year on the southern horizon promising rain. I will walk in the rain and feel its cold passionate fingers on my face.

My cage is on the second floor, wedged in the corner with a view of the "dry cells" where uncooperative inmates are placed until they "act right." If there's been a riot, the dry cell I can see will soon be occupied. Watching men get dragged in there is an ugly form of entertainment for the rest of us. I always feel guilty later.

Inside the prison fence, the land is barren — just dirt and barbed wire. Even the cactus has been cleared out. Something catches my attention. I look up to see a huge Cooper's hawk with a wingspan like a B-52. It's surfing the wind, focusing on a creosote bush outside the fence.

Commotion in the dry cell draws my eyes back down. It's eight men 6 in Bureau of Prison uniforms. Each of them is wearing gloves with black fiberglass knuckle pieces for beating prisoners into "compliance." Billy clubs, SAPS,[1] and pepper spray canisters swing from utility belts as they work. The officers are struggling with a naked black man. He has a fresh shiner. The eye is swollen shut and blood pours from a gash on his forehead. The power of the emotion in his wild, fearful eyes causes me to look away.

An aerial battle pulls my attention back to the sky. A flock of seem- 7 ingly suicidal sparrows are diving at the hawk. There are ten or twelve of them. The hawk is screeching savagely at the hostile sparrows. When I look back down, the black man is being strapped to a concrete slab in the middle of the dry cell with thick canvas wrist and ankle restraints. The officers seem to be smothering the man, twisting and wrenching his limbs as they secure them one by one. They've got both arms and a leg, but the other leg kicks wildly.

In the sky the sparrows dive maniacally at the predator. The battle 8 seems one-sided, but the sparrows have numbers, speed, and agility. They are fending the giant off. In the dry cell a lieutenant in the background is filming the event. A stone-faced observer, he could just as easily be watching a Jiffy Lube oil change on his Prius. Now the officers have all the inmate's extremities pinned down. The man's chest heaves with exertion, his foaming mouth hurling insults and hollow threats.

The hawk soon tires of being swooped upon and pecked at. It 9 changes course and sails off toward the horizon. The officers are done. They stand back and admire their handiwork, patting asses and high-fiving each other on a job well done. The lieutenant gives a short sermon, then shrugs and they all head for the door, leaving the man futilely flexing and bucking against his restraints with nothing left in the room but the echoes of his screams.

In about ten years I'm due to return to the world. I pray I can leave 10 the memory of the man in the dry cell behind me, as well as the memories of all the others I have seen beaten by officers or inmates. I'm not optimistic, but I will try to keep the sparrows in mind as I go.

---

[1] SAPS (para. 6): An impact weapon similar to a blackjack

POINTS TO CONSIDER

1. Paschelke writes, "I will never see the world the way I did before. Or actually, I will never *not* see it the way I did before." What do you think he means? Try expressing his statement in other words.

2. Why would *Orion*, a magazine devoted to writing about nature, be interested in publishing this essay? What importance does the natural world possess for the writer?

3. Note how Paschelke moves back and forth between the "commotion in the dry cell" and the commotion in the sky. How are these two events linked? How do you think we as readers are meant to respond to these parallel events?

Chandra Bozelko

To Fix the U.S. Prison System, Give Every Inmate the Daily Newspaper

[*Quartz*, August 13, 2015]

BEFORE YOU READ

Do you think of reading as a way to fix the prison system? How might giving every inmate the daily newspaper make a difference?

WORDS TO LEARN

avid (para. 1): enthusiastic (adjective)
pilot (para. 6): experimental (adjective)
underwrite (para. 8): to give money as support (verb)
authorize (para. 8): to give permission (verb)

shortfall (para. 13): shortage (noun)
broadsheet (para. 14): a newspaper (noun)
intent (para. 21): having a goal or purpose (adjective)

Former inmate Chandra Bozelko served over six years at York Correctional Institution and wrote a newspaper column during her incarceration about her experience in prison. She was released in 2014 and continued writing the column as a blog, authored a book of poetry titled Up the River: An Anthology, *and is a freelance writer who focuses on prison and judicial issues.*

I was never an avid fiction reader before being incarcerated. But once   1
inside, the last page of every novel I read arrived with an emotional
thud, because I knew I would have to re-submerge myself into prison
reality.

Real life was never as good as the story I had been reading. To   2
finish a book was often so disheartening that sometimes I wondered
if I should even start another one, knowing how I would feel when I
finished.

Newspapers were different for me, at least while the prison library   3
at Connecticut's York Correctional Institute still carried them. Better
than any book, newspapers were lifesavers that pulled me closer to shore
because each new edition marked a new day, an invitation to rejoin a
world that kept moving while I was inside.

Other women would come into the library — women whom I knew   4
to be part of the 1.5 million inmates across the country who are functionally illiterate — to figure out their horoscopes in the paper, just to
confirm that something would happen that day. Even a two-sentence
horoscope reminded them that they had futures.

Reading can save an inmate. A novel is   5
a buoy in prison; it keeps you afloat because
you can enter someone else's life without
ever leaving the facility. But not everyone in

> Reading can save
> an inmate.

prison can read a whole book. Because I've
witnessed that struggle firsthand, perhaps that's why I'm one of the few
who know that reforming the U.S. corrections system means focusing
on basic adult literacy — and therefore that providing university-level
courses to inmates isn't as helpful as it sounds.

In late July, the Obama administration announced a pilot program to   6
restore Pell grants to the U.S. correctional system. Those grants — abolished for the prison population in 1993 — would now fund tuition,
books and educational expenses to inmates who want to pursue university courses while incarcerated.

Many take this as a sign of change for our broken U.S. correctional   7
system and a new approach to halting recidivism. But they seem to have
forgotten that other forms of inmate access to higher education have
already failed.

As part of the Higher Education Amendments of 1998, Penn-   8
sylvania's longest-serving senator and correctional education champion
Arlen Specter introduced "grants to States for workplace and community transition training for incarcerated individuals." These grants to
states, or "Specter funds," underwrote college classes in prisons from
1998 until 2011, when Congress refused to authorize them further.

During those 13 years when some prisoners were able to access federally funded college programming, recidivism rates remained high.

Today, considering some states' current push to reduce sentences and thin out populations in federal and state correctional facilities, it is unclear that contemporary prisoners would even spend enough time behind bars to apply to complete a college course. 9

The bigger news for criminal justice reform has actually been overlooked. It came earlier in July, when Illinois federal district court Judge Matthew Kennelly held, in the case of *Koger v. Dart*, that Cook County Jail's policy of prohibiting newspapers violated inmates' First Amendment right to read and receive news. 10

Now newspapers can come into correctional facilities. This is a huge step toward the kind of foundational education that inmates need. 11

The majority of U.S. inmates cannot read or read at a very low level, according to a 2003 study by advocacy organization Proliteracy America, and nationwide, only 9% of inmates with low literacy skills receive literacy training while incarcerated. 12

Injecting literacy into correctional facilities is hard. Many prisons lack libraries because they can't hire librarians. Ones that do have libraries can't afford to buy books. Prisoner reading programs have been shipping in books to make up for the shortfall but security concerns prevent certain books from entering: ones with spiral binding, ones about weapons, etc. 13

But all of the security concerns about newspapers were overcome in the *Koger v. Dart* decision, because there is little lethal potential in a broadsheet. The prison's claim that inmates can use newspapers to clog toilets wasn't enough to flush the Constitution. 14

Newspapers' advantages for any remedial reader are many: the journalistic approach to stories enhances comprehension, stories are varied and change daily, reading editorials and op-eds fosters critical thinking skills. 15

In the absence of sorely needed literacy training, self-appointed jailhouse lawyers and teachers instruct other inmates in almost every facility. My own privilege ended up nominating me as the jailhouse lawyer and unofficial tutor to fellow inmates at York Correctional Institute, and necessity confirmed me. 16

This is not to say that I was the only literate inmate there, but I was the literate inmate whose class and background made her feel so guilty that she felt compelled to help others. I was called upon both as the witness and the remedy to the problem of substandard literacy among incarcerated women. 17

I don't know how to teach someone to read; all I could do was explain words' meanings after students sounded them out. In my experience, 18 remedial readers are often embarrassed that they can't read better and can resent efforts to help them, so any attempt to teach them has to be short.

Starting a book with a woman who can't read well only highlights her lack of ability, because after an hour, you've only advanced two pages. But a newspaper article — when you can find one that's been discarded — she can complete. See? You did it! You finished. 19

I believe that whatever effect those millions of dollars in Pell grants to prisoners across the United States will achieve, the same could be done with simple subscriptions to *USA Today*, plus a local paper, for every inmate. Plus the right to read in their own housing units, at their own pace, with more in-prison tutors. 20

In prison, privilege always leaves you lonely. It does the same when you get out into a world intent on reform. I may be the only person in the U.S. who can tell you that Pell grants aren't a sign of social revolution. But if everyone — including inmates — has the access and ability to read a newspaper, we'll read revolution in the headlines when it comes. 21

VOCABULARY/USING A DICTIONARY
1. What is a *horoscope* (para. 4)?
2. What is the definition of *recidivism* (para. 7)?
3. Where do you usually find a *buoy* (para. 5)?

RESPONDING TO WORDS IN CONTEXT
1. What does Bozelko mean when she says finishing a book was *disheartening* (para. 2)?
2. If 1.5 million inmates are *functionally illiterate* (para. 4), what problem do they have?
3. What part of speech is *remedy* in paragraph 17?

DISCUSSING MAIN POINT AND MEANING
1. Why is reading so important in prison, according to Bozelko?
2. Why are newspapers a good choice of reading material for prisoners?
3. What happened when Bozelko tried to tutor inmates? What did her experience indicate about inmates and literacy?

EXAMINING SENTENCES, PARAGRAPHS, AND ORGANIZATION
1. In paragraph 16, Bozelko writes, "My own privilege ended up nominating me as the jailhouse lawyer and unofficial tutor to fellow inmates at York Correctional Institute, and necessity confirmed me." How is Bozelko using language in this sentence? What point is she making?

2. Look closely at the first two paragraphs. What is Bozelko's reaction to reading? What is different in the third paragraph? Describe the contrast between the first two paragraphs and the third paragraph.

3. Where in the essay does Bozelko make the case that she is an authority on the subject she's speaking about? What information is included, and how is it presented?

THINKING CRITICALLY

1. Did Bozelko's description of reading fiction in jail surprise you? Why or why not?

2. Why might newspapers have once been kept out of prisons, away from inmates? What reason did the Illinois jail give? Are there any other reasons you can think of for prohibiting them?

3. Why might Bozelko think it is important for inmates to learn to read or to have the freedom to read in prison? Do you think it's important?

WRITING ACTIVITIES

1. Take a look at a newspaper, in print or online (the front page, sports page, or any section with articles). Read one full page and take notes on what you see (subjects covered, level of language used). In writing, summarize the articles you've read. Note any words you aren't familiar with (and look them up).

2. In a brief reflective essay, discuss your response to Bozelko's experience and her call to provide inmates with newspapers. What do you think of her story? Do you think literacy is important, particularly to this segment of the population? Do you admire her work and her push for reform?

3. Think about the differences between books and newspapers. In a short writing exercise, analyze the differences between them. For points of comparison, discuss a book you've recently read and a newspaper you've looked at in the last week or so (it's fine to use the paper you read for question 1 in this section). Did you find the same differences that Bozelko noted? Did you notice any others?

Spotlight on Data and Research

Haisam Hussein

Locked Up: A Breakdown of America's Life behind Bars

[*Vice*, October 2015]

In October 2015, the popular monthly magazine Vice *devoted an entire issue to America's prison system. Along with articles and opinion, it ran a series of graphs and charts called "Locked Up: A Breakdown of America's Life behind Bars." Assembled by one of the magazine's regular contributors, Haisam Hussein, the infographics help tell the story of incarceration today. What follows is Hussein's brief introduction and one of the charts showing the top reasons for arrests.*

When it comes to prisons, the U.S. favors quantity over quality. We   1
lock up millions and then release them ill-equipped to reenter society, hampered by debt from prison fees and barred from certain forms of government assistance. Unsurprisingly, 76% are reincarcerated within five years. Those guarding the cycle of inmates don't fare well either. Correctional officers suffer alarmingly high rates of PTSD, depression, and suicide. Let's hope that the latest push for reform by politicians will finally lead to a more reasonable and effective criminal justice system.

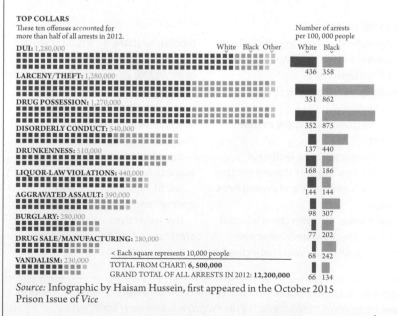

TOP COLLARS
These ten offenses accounted for more than half of all arrests in 2012.

Source: Infographic by Haisam Hussein, first appeared in the October 2015 Prison Issue of *Vice*

continued

DRAWING CONCLUSIONS

1. Do you think the chart supports Mona Charen's summary (p. 290) of violent versus nonviolent crime? Explain why or why not.

2. How many of the top arrests are related to drugs and alcohol? Do you think some of the other reasons for arrests, like burglary, might also be connected to drugs and alcohol?

3. The editors of *Vice* magazine are clearly opposed to mass incarceration and support the reform of our justice system. In what ways does the chart endorse their viewpoint? What do you think they want readers to take away from the data?

Josh Bowers

The Case for Compassionate Policing

[*University of Virginia Magazine*, Spring 2015]

BEFORE YOU READ

How do you perceive the police in your community? Does everyone respond as you do? How and why might people have different reactions?

WORDS TO LEARN

comparatively (para. 1): seeming to be something when compared with others (adverb)

candid (para. 1): honest; sincere (adjective)

cultivate (para. 1): to grow or raise (verb)

empathy (para. 1): the feeling of understanding and sharing another person's emotions and experiences (noun)

implicit (para. 2): understood without being directly stated (adjective)

trite (para. 4): not original (adjective)

touchstone (para. 4): a fundamental part or feature (noun)

counterproductive (para. 5): not helpful (adjective)

onus (para. 5): responsibility (noun)

devolve (para. 7): to decline (verb)

chaos (para. 7): a state of complete disorder (noun)

exacerbated (para. 7): to make worse (verb)

optimal (para. 7): best or most effective (adjective)

gratuitous (para. 8): unnecessary (adjective)

Josh Bowers is an associate professor of law at the University of Virginia School of Law. He serves as the codirector of the Program in Law and Public Service.

I write this on New Year's Eve, as I try to discover a silver lining to 2014's darkest clouds. In Staten Island, Ferguson and Cleveland, men and boys were killed by those obligated, first and foremost, to protect and serve. In Brooklyn, police officers were assassinated for doing their jobs. There is nothing new to violence by and against the police. But there is something comparatively new to our candid, public conversation about these events. This dialogue may lead Americans to cultivate empathy and understanding; we may come to see an old thing in a new way.

Yes, we live in a society plagued still by structural inequality and implicit bias. And yes, police officers do difficult, dangerous and critically important work. But it's off the mark even to talk of sides, as if effective policing and respect for civil rights were some zero-sum game. In fact, effective, respectful and safe policing are not mutually exclusive; they are reinforcing.

This is well known to departments that already emphasize community policing. Take the Charlottesville Police Foundation, which hosts "Teen Nights" to promote positive engagement between officers and community youth, and subsidizes housing for officers within city limits. These programs help officers and citizens see each other as neighbors, not as *others*. Neighbors may disagree, but they fight more like family members than adversaries.

It may be trite but certainly true that the touchstone is mutual respect. The situation in Ferguson was tragic enough; it was made worse when officers left Michael Brown's body to decompose for hours in the hot sun — and worse still when mourners and protesters were met by riot squads.

In this way, disrespectful policing is not just wrong; it's counterproductive. But the onus does not fall only on the police as a part of the community; it falls also on the community that is policed. Just as violence is not law enforcement, violence is also not political protest. Violence and disrespect undermine the rule of law and drown out both sides' messages.

> Just as violence is not law enforcement, violence is also not political protest.

I worked for several years as a public defender in the South Bronx. The overwhelming majority of my clients were arrested for minor public-order offenses. But the stakes of petty-crime enforcement are high. And the balance to be struck is delicate. The quality of life on city streets depends on police taking disorder seriously. At the same time, when these interactions go wrong, they may go horribly wrong. Look no further than the death of Eric Garner, who died after his forceful arrest for selling loose cigarettes without a tax stamp.

Obviously, the Garner case is exceptional, but there's always a risk   7
that an effort to preserve order may devolve into chaos. The risk is exacerbated, not diminished, by the misguided policy — dominant in some police departments — that arrest ought to be the ordinary course, not the last resort. Consider the recent "virtual work stoppage" by some New York City police officers. The city's largest police union has urged its members not to make arrests "unless absolutely necessary." Quite by accident, the union may be pushing the optimal and just policy.

In a recent article in the *Stanford Law Review*, I criticized the Supreme   8
Court for constitutionally tolerating a petty-crime arrest that even it had termed a "pointless indignity" and a "gratuitous humiliation." The Supreme Court recognized sensible policing alternatives but ultimately refused to demand them. To my thinking, the Court was much too timid.

I recognize, however, that the most likely solutions are not going to   9
come from courts, academies or legislatures. The solutions will grow out of a shift in the ways police officers see people and people see police officers. We are all human — police and civilians alike. Some of us are bad, most of us are good, and all of us are entitled to dignified treatment.

VOCABULARY/USING A DICTIONARY

1. If someone wants to *emphasize* (para. 3) something, what might he or she do?

2. What are the discrete parts of the word *decompose* (para. 4)? What does it mean?

3. If something is *diminished* (para. 7), what has happened to it?

RESPONDING TO WORDS IN CONTEXT

1. What happens in a *zero-sum game* (para. 2)?

2. When Bowers writes that respectful and safe policing are *reinforcing* (para. 2), what does he mean?

3. What might the difference be between family members and *adversaries* (para. 3)?

DISCUSSING MAIN POINT AND MEANING

1. What cases have led Bowers to write this article on compassionate policing?

2. What aspects of policing should not be mutually exclusive, according to Bowers?

3. What is Bowers's argument for why we should demand compassionate policing? What does he insist is our right when dealing with police officers?

EXAMINING SENTENCES, PARAGRAPHS, AND ORGANIZATION

1. How does Bowers introduce personal information in his essay? Does it intrude on his argument or does it enhance it?

2. At one point, as he concludes his essay, Bowers says, "The solutions will grow out of a shift in the ways police officers see people and people see police officers" (para. 9). Is this sentence too simplistic? How does it encapsulate Bowers's main point?

3. Bowers begins by placing his essay in the context of 2014. Is the focus on a particular time important? Does it carry through the whole essay?

THINKING CRITICALLY

1. How might the "Teen Nights" hosted by the Charlottesville Police Foundation be a way to create a positive and healthy relationship between teens and police officers?

2. Do you agree that the Garner case is exceptional as stated by Bowers? In what way?

3. Do you agree or disagree with Bowers's thoughts on how solutions and changes to policing will come about?

WRITING ACTIVITIES

1. Try brainstorming examples of compassionate policing. Then brainstorm examples of its opposite. Once you have plenty of ideas, create a "mind map" or other visual representation of those ideas that gathers them into different categories. In small groups, share your maps.

2. In his introduction, Bowers mentions three events in which police used lethal force against unarmed individuals — Staten Island, Ferguson, and Cleveland (he also mentions the murder of police officers in Brooklyn). Choose one of these news stories (the killing of Eric Garner, Michael Brown, or Tamir Rice) and write a brief report of the event. Write as if you are publishing in a newspaper — avoid inserting your opinion and include as many details about what happened as possible (even if that means including conflicting information). If you need to do outside research for information before you write, you are welcome to gather it.

3. This essay is called "The Case for Compassionate Policing." In a short persuasive essay, argue the case for it. You can draw from Bowers's essay for support, but come up with a few ideas on your own. You can base your arguments for such policing on what you know of incidents in which police have used excessive or lethal force, but you should also make a case for compassionate policing on a smaller scale. While the most compelling arguments are based on the deaths of people like Eric Garner, Bowers brings in a variety of arguments to support his position. Most importantly, what do you think compassionate policing looks like?

Mona Charen

Unlock 'Em Up?

[*National Review*, October 9, 2015]

BEFORE YOU READ

Is mass incarceration a problem in this country? How do we make decisions about which offense deserves a prison sentence? In what other ways might we deal with people convicted of crimes?

WORDS TO LEARN

spectrum (para. 7): a range (noun)
complacent (para. 9): untroubled (adjective)
leniency (para. 9): a state of tolerance (noun)
waning (para. 9): decreasing in strength (adjective)

epidemic (para. 9): widespread occurrence or outbreak (noun)
incapacitation (para. 9): state of being unable to function (noun)
prey (para. 10): to seize and devour a hunted animal (verb)

The Justice Department has announced that it will begin releasing 6,000 "nonviolent" inmates from federal prisons starting at the end of this month. Welcome to the era of de-incarceration. At a conference named for former New York mayor David Dinkins (who presided over the city at a time of runaway crime), Hillary Clinton decried the number of Americans behind bars and declared, "It's time to change our approach. It's time to end the era of mass incarceration." 1

In this, she is joined by Bernie Sanders and other Democrats, and also by Charles Koch, who wrote recently that "overcriminalization has led to the mass incarceration of those ensnared by our criminal-justice system, even though such imprisonment does not always enhance public safety. Indeed, more than half of federal inmates are nonviolent drug offenders." Senator Rand Paul has called mass incarceration "the new Jim Crow."[1] And Carly Fiorina suggested during the last debate that "we have 2

---

[1] Jim Crow (para. 2): Jim Crow laws enforced racial segregation in the South from Reconstruction until 1965.

Mona Charen is a conservative columnist, political analyst, and author. She has written two books: Useful Idiots: How Liberals Got It Wrong in the Cold War and Still Blame America First *(2003) and* Do-Gooders: How Liberals Hurt Those They Claim to Help (and the Rest of Us) *(2005).*

the highest incarceration rates in the world. Two-thirds of the people in our prisons are there for nonviolent offenses, mostly drug-related. It is clearly not working."

Not exactly. The U.S. does have the highest incarceration rate in the 3 world (that is, among nations that list these data honestly), but the assertion that most of the people incarcerated are there for nonviolent crimes is false. Advocates for de-incarceration often cite the number of federal prisoners who committed nonviolent drug offenses. This is highly misleading. Of the 1.6 million inmates in America, only about 200,000 are federal prisoners.

About half of federal inmates are sentenced for drug crimes, but this 4 shouldn't shock anyone. Nearly all violent crimes are state matters. It's a federal crime to transport a kidnap victim across state lines, to attempt to assassinate a federal official, and so forth. But robberies, rapes, assaults, and murder are mostly state matters. Among state inmates, only one in six is a drug offender.

Among the 50 percent of "nonviolent" federal drug offenders, it's 5 difficult to know how many were arrested for a violent crime and plea-bargained to a lesser offense. Nor do we have good data on how many were previously convicted of a violent crime. A 2004 Bureau of Justice Statistics study found that 95 percent of those who served time in state prisons for nonviolent crimes had a preceding criminal history (typically 9.3 arrests and 4.1 convictions) and 33 percent had a history of arrests for violent crime.

Among state prisoners, 54 percent are there for violent offenses. Perhaps the 46 percent who are incarcerated for nonviolent crimes should be punished some other way. But to design good policy on that, we'd have to grapple with a number of issues. What do you do with offenders who are placed on probation or parole but continue to offend? What about the "crime 6

> What do you do with offenders who are placed on probation or parole but continue to offend?

in the streets versus crime in the suites" problem? Should we sentence embezzlers, child-porn dealers, and Medicaid cheats to community service but keep armed robbers behind bars? How will that affect the perception that incarceration is the "new Jim Crow"?

Many on both sides of the political spectrum are eager to leap 7 aboard the "de-incarceration" bandwagon. It's a way to show sympathy with African Americans and (to a much lesser degree) Hispanics who are disproportionately represented among inmates.

But the primary victims of crime are also African Americans and   8
Hispanics. If "unlock 'em up" becomes the new conventional wisdom,
more innocent people will suffer and more businesses will flee.

We've become complacent about crime because the crime rate has   9
declined drastically since 1990. According to the FBI, violent crime
increased by nearly 83 percent between 1973 and 1991 — a period of
criminal-justice leniency. From 1991 to 2001, when incarceration rates
increased, violent crime declined by 33.6 percent. The decline has persisted. There are many theories about the cause of the drop in crime
(abortion, removing lead from paint, the waning of the crack epidemic,
policing strategies), and some or all of those factors may have played a
part, but the "incapacitation" argument — criminals who are behind bars
cannot be mugging people — seems awfully strong.

It would, of course, be a better world if fewer Americans were grow-   10
ing up in neighborhoods where fatherlessness, intergenerational government dependency, and poor schools contribute to high rates of crime.
But it's hard to see how releasing more criminals to prey upon those very
neighborhoods is the answer.

VOCABULARY/USING A DICTIONARY

1. What action is indicated by the verb *ensnared* (para. 2)?

2. If something happened *previously* (para. 5), when did it happen?

3. What is a *bandwagon* (para. 7)? Where did the word come from?

RESPONDING TO WORDS IN CONTEXT

1. If Hillary Clinton *decried* (para. 1) the number of people in prisons, how
   would you characterize her response?

2. What is an *advocate for de-incarceration* (para. 3)?

3. What do the words *probation* and *parole* (para. 6) mean?

DISCUSSING MAIN POINT AND MEANING

1. Who does Charen say will suffer if we start releasing many of the people currently incarcerated? Why?

2. What are some of the issues that the current state of mass incarceration has
   raised in this country?

3. What position does Charen take on mass incarceration?

EXAMINING SENTENCES, PARAGRAPHS, AND ORGANIZATION

1. Why, in the first sentence of the essay, is the word *nonviolent* in quotation
   marks? How does Charen's use of quotation marks here affect the essay?

2. Is Charen's concluding paragraph different from the preceding paragraphs? If so, what is different about it?

3. How does Charen present her argument? Do you know her position from the beginning of the essay?

THINKING CRITICALLY

1. Charen nods to her opposition when she says, "Perhaps the 46 percent who are incarcerated for nonviolent crimes should be punished some other way" (para. 6), and then she argues against this idea. What is her objection to this idea? What is your position on that 46 percent, and do you think her objections are insurmountable?

2. What decision is the policy shift Charen wants to examine? Why has that decision been made?

3. Charen states that "fatherlessness, intergenerational government dependency, and poor schools contribute to high rates of crime" (para. 10). Can you give an example of what these conditions might look like? Why might they influence crime?

WRITING ACTIVITIES

1. Can you think of counterarguments to Charen's argument ▪ (no matter what you think of the Department of Justice prisoner release)? Where would you insert them in Charen's essay? Find those spots and write a paragraph of counterargument to be inserted in each place. After writing, discuss these ideas in class.

2. What do you think of what Charen calls the " 'incapacitation' argument" (para. 9)? Write one or two paragraphs that explain the argument in your own words.

3. Do you think Charen includes enough facts in her essay to support her position? Identify any facts you find compelling and explain why you feel that way.

Sonia Kumar (student essay)

The Death Sentence: An Inefficient Method of Punishment

[*The Collegian*, Kansas State University, February 3, 2015]

BEFORE YOU READ
Why is the death penalty still being used in the United States? What are the arguments against it?

WORDS TO LEARN
dormant (para. 3): inactive; in a state of rest (adjective)
innovative (para. 4): fresh or new (adjective)
deterrent (para. 5): something that discourages (noun)

deplete (para. 14): to decrease or exhaust (verb)
credibility (para. 14): believability (noun)

Although execution as a form of punishment has existed for generations, capital punishment in the U.S. reached a peak in the 1930s, with more criminals being put to death by the government than in any other decade since. Despite many Supreme Court rulings and high-profile cases, capital punishment is still a highly debated issue, one that sheds light on how fairness and justice is upheld in the U.S. 1

In my opinion, capital punishment is an inefficient way to punish criminals because it is an outdated, ineffective, biased and expensive practice that furthers a cycle of violence. 2

OUTDATED

Capital punishment is an extremely outdated practice that has already been abolished in 18 states and the District of Columbia. Many U.S. states are coming to the realization that the death penalty is inhumane. Capital punishment is dormant in the military and in the federal system and, according to the *New York Times* article "The Slow Demise of Capital Punishment," 30 states had no executions within the past five years as of 2013. 3

Sonia Kumar is an apparel textiles and marketing major at Kansas State University, and she expects to graduate in May 2017.

For a country that prides itself on being innovative, we are one of   4
the last countries that still honors the death penalty. The U.S. is regressing with this controversial issue and should think differently. The death penalty, though still very much alive, has become less popular and is used most frequently in places such as Texas and Florida, where over half of 2013's 80 sentences occurred, according to the Death Penalty Information Center.

TAKING INNOCENT LIVES

Capital punishment is an ineffective deterrent to crime and criminals. In   5
several instances innocent people have been sent to death row. Kirk Noble Bloodsworth spent nine years in prison and two years on death row for a crime he did not commit. Bloodsworth also said Carlos DeLuna, Ruben Cantu and Cameron Todd Willingham were others put to death before their cases were fully and thoroughly closed, according to his article in *The New York Times*, "Of Course the Death Penalty Is Cruel and Unusual." All three men have since had considerable doubt cast on their convictions.

Capital punishment is ineffective because it can be erroneous and   6
biased as well. "Someone will always end up on the short end of the stick," Bloodsworth said in the article. "Most of the time, that person will be black or Latino and poor. If it can happen to me, it could happen to you."

There is an overwhelming amount   7
of evidence that minorities are facing the most disparity due to the death penalty. Several studies have indicated that minorities are more likely to be sentenced with the death penalty than other offenders, according to the *New York Times* article "Justice and Victims of Color."

> Several studies have indicated that minorities are more likely to be sentenced with the death penalty than other offenders.

If we believe that the death penalty   8
illustrates the ultimate definition of justice for victims, then we also have to accept that this form of "justice" is ineffective and biased as well.

EXPENSES

One of the more popular arguments of those in favor of the death   9
penalty is that it is cheaper to kill inmates than to sentence them to life imprisonment. However, death penalty cases are extremely costly to states and taxpayers, and in some cases are more expensive than life imprisonment. According to the *New York Times* article "The Slow Demise of Capital Punishment," these cases are also expensive due to long trials, excessive witnesses and time-consuming jury selections.

Housing prisoners on death row in Kansas costs twice as much per 10 year ($49,380) as for prisoners in the general population ($24,690). Extra security is also needed for death row inmates, according to an article in *Forbes* magazine entitled "Considering the Death Penalty: Your Tax Dollars at Work." In California, the annual cost of lifetime incarceration is a mere $11.5 million compared to the $137 million it costs to use the death penalty.

INEFFECTIVE

One may argue that this cost is justified because capital punishment 11 is a warning. It illustrates the consequences of one's horrifying actions and is used to scare people into not committing serious crimes. Millions of dollars spent as a deterrence is quite an investment. Money used to finance capital punishment could be spent on real crime deterrents such as courts, police officers, prison cells and public defenders. Regardless of the moral issue, U.S. citizens should also view the death penalty from an economic standpoint.

A CYCLE OF VIOLENCE

Capital punishment helps further a cycle of violence. Many who stand by 12 the death penalty justify "an eye for an eye." This idea only helps enforce the larger perspective that violence is justified.

Darryl Stallworth, deputy district attorney in Alameda County, 13 California, from 1992 to 2007, once fought to sentence a young man to death, but as he delved further into the case he realized that he was "witnessing a cycle of violence." The young boy had a rocky childhood in which his crime resembled the traumatic violence he had gone through as a child. Stallworth realized that he couldn't stand by the death penalty for this boy despite his crimes because it perpetuated a cycle of violence, according to the *San Jose Mercury News* article "Death Penalty Perpetuates Vicious Cycle of Violence."

Killing someone will not help bring a loved one back or make the 14 victim and the perpetrator even. Are those that have implemented capital punishment any better than the murderer? The death penalty justifies killing someone and deems that the only way to properly punish individuals is to take away their life. Capital punishment depletes the American justice system's definition of justice and takes away its credibility by perpetuating a cycle of violence that makes killing acceptable.

Abolishing the death penalty would rid the U.S. of an old-fashioned 15 and backward practice that is extremely costly, perpetuates a cycle of violence and is ineffective as a deterrent. Funds used for the death penalty could be used more effectively to reduce other crimes. We should look at this controversial issue more introspectively instead of seeing it as a matter of justice and revenge.

As Mahatma Gandhi said: "An eye for an eye only makes the whole world blind." 16

VOCABULARY/USING A DICTIONARY

1. How would you describe the movement of someone or something that is *regressing* (para. 4)?

2. What part of speech is *disparity* (para. 7)? What does it mean?

3. What is the difference between *deterrence* (para. 11) and a *deterrent* (para. 5)? How might each word be used in a sentence?

RESPONDING TO WORDS IN CONTEXT

1. How might you guess the definition of *erroneous* (para. 6), even if you don't know what it means?

2. If someone has *implemented* capital punishment (para. 14), what has he or she done?

3. What is the definition of *conviction* (para. 5) in this context? What other definition does this word have?

DISCUSSING MAIN POINT AND MEANING

1. What are the main points about capital punishment that Kumar outlines in her thesis?

2. What arguments does Kumar use to say that capital punishment is outdated?

3. How does Kumar approach the idea of prejudice and the death penalty? What does she claim is biased in the sentencing and use of the death penalty?

EXAMINING SENTENCES, PARAGRAPHS, AND ORGANIZATION

1. Is the sentence that comprises paragraph 16 a conclusion? Explain your answer.

2. Describe the organization of Kumar's essay. What techniques does she use for organizational purposes?

3. Why did Kumar separate paragraphs 1 and 2, instead of running them together?

THINKING CRITICALLY

1. Two sayings are included in this essay—"an eye for an eye" in paragraph 12 and "an eye for an eye only makes the whole world blind" in paragraph 16. How do you respond to these quotations? Does Kumar's argument make a difference in how you respond to them?

2. One of Kumar's subheadings is "Taking Innocent Lives." At first glance, one might assume that refers to the violent act that causes someone to be incarcerated and/or put on death row. What does Kumar intend that line to mean? Is her use of the phrase effective?

3. Kumar states that it costs much more to kill someone on death row than it does to keep someone in prison. Why do you think this is so? Is it worth it to execute someone if it's so expensive?

WRITING ACTIVITIES

1. Write a short essay that argues your position on a much-debated topic (capital punishment, climate change, gun control, educational reforms, etc.). After you determine your position and write a thesis statement, break your paragraphs up into subheadings that reflect the points you make in your thesis. Model your essay on Kumar's.

2. Discuss the essay you wrote for question 1 in small groups. Go over one another's subheadings. As a group, can you come up with at least two or three more possible subheadings for your essays? Consider how these additional subheadings could expand your essay. Write more and add paragraphs for the new subheadings, either in groups or individually.

3. Sometimes using a quotation in an essay is an effective way of catching the reader's attention. Kumar concludes with Gandhi's words: "An eye for an eye only makes the whole world blind." Write a short response to Kumar's essay or another essay in this book. Begin your response with a relevant quotation. In pairs, look at your responses both with and without your quotations, and determine which is the stronger version. Then share your thoughts in a larger group.

LOOKING CLOSELY

Effective Argument: Organizing Points Systematically

When writing an argument essay, especially a longer one like the preceding student essay, it is a good idea to set down your points in a systematic fashion. This not only helps you organize your thoughts, but helps your reader follow your argument more easily. A common writing practice is to declare your main point or claim near the outset and then clearly support that claim point by point. These points need not be numbered, but they should all be in a logical order, and they should all be related to your central claim or stated opinion.

In "The Death Sentence: An Inefficient Method of Punishment," Kansas State student Sonia Kumar clearly expresses her view on capital punishment: "In my opinion, capital punishment is an inefficient way to punish criminals because it is an outdated, ineffective, biased and expensive practice that furthers a cycle of violence." She outlines each of her five reasons for opposing the death penalty in a systematic way that supports her claim. Note, too, how she backs up each of her supporting points with research from authoritative sources.

1
States central opinion

(1) In my opinion, capital punishment is an inefficient way to punish criminals because it is an outdated, ineffective, biased and expensive practice that furthers a cycle of violence.

2
Is outdated

(2) Capital punishment is an extremely outdated practice . . .

3
Is ineffective as deterrence

(3) Capital punishment is an ineffective deterrent to crime and criminals.

4
Is biased

(4) Capital punishment is ineffective because it can be erroneous and biased as well.

5
Is expensive

(5) One of the more popular arguments of those in favor of the death penalty is that it is cheaper to kill inmates than to sentence them to life imprisonment.

6
Furthers violence

(6) Capital punishment helps further a cycle of violence.

STUDENT WRITER AT WORK

Sonia Kumar

R.A. What inspired you to write this essay? And publish it?

S.K. I've always felt that there is something morally wrong with the death penalty. This feeling began my senior year in high school while I was reading Truman Capote's *In Cold Blood*. It was then I realized that an eye for an eye is never justified. Additionally, capital punishment is ineffective, barbaric, and cruel. I decided to publish the essay I had written for my English class when I saw a story idea online for the opinion column about the death penalty. I realized publishing a condensed version of my essay would be a way to get people thinking about what justice should really look like, which, in my opinion, should not include the death penalty.

R.A. Who was your prime audience?

S.K. My audience was anyone who is interested in exploring the topic of the death penalty; I especially hope I was able to reach proponents of the death penalty, in order to give them a new perspective.

R.A. How long did it take for you to write this piece? Did you revise your work?

S.K. It took me about two weeks to write this paper. I revised several times along the way. I wanted to make sure my piece was clear enough so that college students from all backgrounds could understand the ineffectiveness of the death penalty.

R.A. Do you generally show your writing to friends before submitting it? Do you collaborate with others or bounce your ideas off them?

S.K. I typically do not share all my writing pieces with my friends. However, I own a fashion blog called JeMappelleChanel.com, so I usually share my blog pieces with my friends, family, and followers. When it comes to writing, in general, my ideas are always my own. I don't tend to collaborate. A close friend of mine does some editing for me and I always take her suggestions.

R.A. What do you like to read?

S.K. J. D. Salinger is my favorite author. David Levithan and Rachel Cohn's novels have fed my soul as well as *Nylon* magazine and Chuck Palahniuk novels. I read many blogs. In addition, I enjoy NPR, the *New York Times*, *The Tig*, and thredUP's blog.

R.A. What advice do you have for other student writers?

S.K. Find your voice, be authentic, and learn how to use commas.

Walt Whitman

The Death Penalty

[*Brooklyn Eagle*, January 13, 1858]

Before he became known as one of America's leading poets and literary figures, Walt Whitman (1819–1892) worked as a reporter and editor for several Brooklyn newspapers where he often contributed editorials, such as the following one on the death penalty. Later in life, Whitman strangely confessed, "I was in early life very bigoted in my anti-slavery, anti–capital punishment and so on, but I have always had a latent toleration for the people who choose a reactionary course."

Whitman, who never attended college, basically self-published his major volume of poems, Leaves of Grass, *in 1855. The book attracted little attention and sold poorly. But as he continued to revise and enlarge it over the years, his reputation grew and he eventually achieved his ambition to be the "bard of democracy." That single book became a literary bible for future generations of poets and still remains so.*

The following editorial should remind us that the debate over capital punishment has gone on for centuries. Although today many states prohibit the death penalty and others refuse to enforce it, executions are still relatively common in some parts of the country. In 2015, twenty-eight people were put to death. For those opposed to executions, that is the bad news; the good news is that it represents the lowest number since 1991.

The law, or more correctly speaking, the custom, in relation to punish- 1
ment of capital offenses, is in a very unsatisfactory state. The Southern papers are taunting New York with the charge, that while fifty or sixty murders have been committed there during the year, and only one by a negro, only one execution has taken place, and that in the case of the negro. At present there are three prisoners in New York awaiting execution. [Whitman very briefly summarizes the judicial indecisions involved in the three cases.] The law does not seem to have made up its mind about the death penalty, whether it is proper to exact it in the case of murderers or not. Hence, when a prisoner is sentenced the execution is

fixed at a ridiculously distant day, and every facility is given to romantic penny-a-liners and sympathetic old ladies to visit the cell and get up a fictitious public opinion which will justify the Executive in pardoning him. And Judges, Counsel, and everyone connected with the administration of justice, exert themselves to give the condemned every chance of evading punishment that the most hair-splitting quibbler can devise. In fact, while adhering to the death penalty, nominally, our authorities act as if they had a lurking conviction that, after all, it is very questionable whether society is justified in depriving the recreant member of life. This is not as it should be. Either society has as absolute right to hang the murderer as it has to lock up the street brawler, or the life of its worst member is sacred from its touch. If the former, let the doom and execution of the murders be certain, swift, prompt and unregretted; if the latter let the death penalty be erased from the statute book. But, above all, let there be not even the appearance of irresolution in the action of the law, or any scruple in carrying out to the letter its sternest provisions.

BACKGROUND AND CONTEXT

1. Whitman's editorial appeared a few years before the outbreak of the Civil War. Why do you think that southern papers, as Whitman notes, have been "taunting New York" with the charge that the only person to be executed over the past year in the state was African American?

2. What attitude does Whitman seem to take toward condemned prisoners? Why does he mention "sympathetic old ladies" visiting their cells, for example? What is the purpose of such visits?

STRATEGY, STRUCTURE, AND STYLE

1. What does Whitman think the authorities believe about the death penalty? What troubles him about their attitude?

2. Whitman concludes with an either-or argument. Try paraphrasing his argument in your own words. Do you think his position is reasonable?

COMPARISONS AND CONNECTIONS

1. Do you think Whitman argues for or against capital punishment in his editorial? What is it that bothers him the most about its application?

2. Do you find Whitman's editorial relevant to today's debate on the death penalty? How do you think those who strongly oppose capital punishment today would react to it? And how would those who strongly believe the practice is justified react? Which group do you think would find more support in the editorial?

Discussing the Unit

SUGGESTED TOPIC FOR DISCUSSION
How do Americans respond to the ever-rising number of people imprisoned in the United States? What punishments are justified, and is rehabilitation possible? What about the people in charge of the prisoners — are they policing well, and are they cultivating positive relationships with the community? The essays in this chapter offer many perspectives on incarceration, punishment, and life after imprisonment, if the death penalty is not imposed.

PREPARING FOR CLASS DISCUSSION
1. There are a record number of people behind bars in this country. What should we do about them? Is the answer to let some of them go free? Who should be allowed to leave prison? Should we rethink incarceration as a punishment for certain crimes? Is prison an effective tool for dealing with people who break the law?

2. What are your feelings about the death penalty? Are there situations in which you think it is the right sentence to impose? Why or why not? What are the alternatives to the death penalty?

FROM DISCUSSION TO WRITING
1. At some point our prisons will be so full that they cannot hold more inmates — something must be done to stop the overwhelming numbers of people being locked up. Describe some of the suggestions made by authors in this chapter. Which do you agree with, and why?

2. Who is the police officer, the correctional guard? What sort of portraits are you given here? In a short essay, write a sketch of the people who protect us and enforce the law. Who is in charge of the prisoner, and how humane is the system?

TOPICS FOR CROSS-CULTURAL DISCUSSION
1. Do you think opinions about the death penalty have changed over time? Based on the essays in this chapter, what evidence do you see that opinions have changed or stayed the same?

2. What do you think of Chandra Bozelko's idea for the prison system (p. 280)? Does anyone else consider the life and mind of the prisoner in this chapter? Write a response to her suggestion and show how one of the other essays complements her idea to improve the system.

9

Our Battered Economy: Is the American Dream Over?

The Great Recession that plunged American hopes and bank accounts may — fingers crossed — be over, but its effects will no doubt linger for years. Our economic self-searching, for one thing, exposed what some consider an ugly truth about America at the dawn of the twenty-first century: the enormous and growing gap between rich and poor, with 10 percent of the nation owning more than half of its wealth.

Many critics have decried the wealth gap, proposing various levers to even out the results. This chapter questions a central premise of an unequal society: Is it fair for some to have great wealth and others to have nothing, so long as hard work and skill can put the latter in the former's McMansion eventually? President Barack Obama explored this theme in a much-quoted speech he delivered on the economy in late 2013, a small portion of which can be sampled in the chapter's opening "In Brief" feature. In that speech, Obama remarks that "the combined trends of increased inequality and decreasing mobility pose a fundamental threat to the American Dream, our way of life, and what we stand for around the globe." This combination of decreasing social mobility and income inequality poses a situation that Obama calls "the defining challenge of our time."

Obama's speech, along with the Occupy Wall Street movement a few years earlier, helped push income inequality to the center of a national debate. One example of that debate took place on the Notre Dame

University campus, where students engaged in a lively discussion of the topic. When sophomore Mimi Teixeira wondered, "Is Income Inequality That Bad?" two other sophomores, Natasha Reifenberg and Patrick LeBlanc quickly responded with an answer: "Yes, Income Inequality Really Is That Bad." For Teixeira, income inequality is "not . . . the biggest issue of our time by any means," and she adds, "I would go so far as to say I don't think it's a problem at all." She then offers some reasons why the "income-inequality alarmists" get things wrong. But, in disagreement, Natasha Reifenberg and Patrick LeBlanc point to a "general lack of opportunity" that is destroying the American Dream and argue that without opportunity "the free-market system is rigged from the start."

No one doubts that economic struggles can make people anxious and miserable, but in several recent studies researchers discovered a close connection between a poor economy and the increased use of painkillers. In our "Spotlight on Data and Research," we feature a recent item from the prestigious *Harvard Business Review* by three professors, Eileen Y. Chou, Bidhan L. Parmar, and Adam D. Galinsky, who demonstrate "The Link between Income Inequality and Physical Pain." "Over numerous studies," the researchers report, "both in the lab and in the field, we have found that the experience of economic insecurity leads people to experience physical pain."

One group today that's feeling the pain is youth. Taking a global view of young people, the renowned economic journal the *Economist* considers them "an oppressed minority—albeit an unusual one—in the straight-forward sense that governments are systematically preventing them from reaching their potential." In "Young, Gifted, and Held Back," the periodical maintains that "around the world, young people gripe that it is too hard to find a job and a place to live, and that the path to adulthood has grown longer and more complicated."

Critics who would rather see the glass half full than half empty often point to the extraordinary poverty of the past in America—poverty most of us would find unimaginable. If we compare ourselves to those inhabit-ing the cities of the late nineteenth century, our economic lives may not appear so difficult. This chapter's "America Then" looks back to 1890 and the crowded, filthy, and destitute tenement houses of New York City. In the introduction to his classic text *How the Other Half Lives*, the pioneering photojournalist Jacob Riis explores the underbelly of the industrial-era city, where simply staying alive replaces upward mobility as the American Dream. Riis emphasizes the corruption and apathy that has led to the awful condition of people in the tenements: "We know now that there is no way out; that the 'system' that was the evil offspring of public neglect and private greed has come to stay, a storm-centre forever of our civilization." His is a powerful reminder that there can't be justice without all of us seeking it.

Barack Obama

The Defining Challenge of Our Time

[From a speech delivered on December 4, 2013]

*T*he concept of the American Dream goes back to colonial days, when the idea was promoted by such founders as Benjamin Franklin, who believed that anyone from any background who worked hard and lived responsibly could succeed. But the notion of the American Dream wasn't fully articulated until 1931 — at the height of the Great Depression — when historian James Truslow Adams wrote in his book The Epic of America:

> But there has been also the American dream, that dream of a land in which life should be better and richer and fuller for every man, with opportunity for each according to his ability or achievement. It is a difficult dream for the European upper classes to interpret adequately, and too many of us ourselves have grown weary and mistrustful of it. It is not a dream of motor cars and high wages merely, but a dream of social order in which each man and each woman shall be able to attain to the fullest stature of which they are innately capable, and be recognized by others for what they are, regardless of the fortuitous circumstances of birth or position.

As the forty-fourth president of the United States, Barack Obama recalled the idea of the American Dream in an emotional speech on December 4, 2013, that argued that the dream was being threatened by two forces: a growing inequality of income and a decline in social mobility. Two small portions of the long speech appear below. The first African American to serve as president, Obama was inaugurated on January 20, 2009. He was elected to the Illinois State Senate in 1996 and to the U.S. Senate in 2004. He received a BA in 1983 from Columbia University and then attended Harvard University, where he was the first African American president of the Harvard Law Review.

It's not surprising that the American people's frustrations with Washington are at an all-time high. 1

But we know that people's frustrations run deeper than these most recent political battles. Their frustration is rooted in their own daily battles — to make ends meet, to pay for college, buy a home, save for retirement. It's rooted in the nagging sense that no matter how hard they work, the deck is stacked against them. And it's rooted in the fear that their kids 2 won't be better off than they were. They may not follow the constant back-and-forth in Washington or all the policy details, but they experience in a very personal way the relentless, decades-long trend that I want to spend some time talking about today. And that is a dangerous and growing inequality and lack of upward mobility that has jeopardized middle-class America's basic bargain — that if you work hard, you have a chance to get ahead.

I believe this is the defining challenge of our time: making sure our   3
economy works for every working American. It's why I ran for President. It was at the center of last year's campaign. It drives everything I do in this office. And I know I've raised this issue before, and some will ask why I raise the issue again right now. I do it because the outcomes of the debates we're having right now — whether it's health care, or the budget, or reforming our housing and financial systems — all these things will have real, practical implications for every American. And I am convinced that the decisions we make on these issues over the next few years will determine whether or not our children will grow up in an America where opportunity is real.

Now, the premise that we're all created equal is the opening line in   4
the American story. And while we don't promise equal outcomes, we have strived to deliver equal opportunity — the idea that success doesn't depend on being born into wealth or privilege, it depends on effort and merit. And with every chapter we've added to that story, we've worked hard to put those words into practice. . . .

So let me repeat: The combined trends of increased inequality and   5
decreasing mobility pose a fundamental threat to the American Dream, our way of life, and what we stand for around the globe. And it is not simply a moral claim that I'm making here. There are practical consequences to rising inequality and reduced mobility.

For one thing, these trends are bad for our economy. One study   6
finds that growth is more fragile and recessions are more frequent in countries with greater inequality. And that makes sense. When families have less to spend, that means businesses have fewer customers, and households rack up greater mortgage and credit card debt; meanwhile, concentrated wealth at the top is less likely to result in the kind of broadly based consumer spending that drives our economy, and together with lax regulation, may contribute to risky speculative bubbles.

And rising inequality and declining mobility are also bad for our   7
families and social cohesion — not just because we tend to trust our institutions less, but studies show we actually tend to trust each other

less when there's greater inequality. And greater inequality is associated with less mobility between generations. That means it's not just temporary; the effects last. It creates a vicious cycle. For example, by the time she turns three years old, a child born into a low-income home hears 30 million fewer words than a child from a well-off family, which means by the time she starts school she's already behind, and that deficit can compound itself over time.

And finally, rising inequality and declining mobility are bad for our democracy. Ordinary folks can't write massive campaign checks or hire high-priced lobbyists and lawyers to secure policies that tilt the playing field in their favor at everyone else's expense. And so people get the bad taste that the system is rigged, and that increases cynicism and polarization, and it decreases the political participation that is a requisite part of our system of self-government.

8

POINTS TO CONSIDER

1. Why do you think Obama distinguishes between "equal outcomes" and "equal opportunity"? Why is the distinction important to him? Do you think everyone would agree with him?

2. Obama says that it is "not simply a moral claim" he's making. Why do you think he says "simply"? Do you think there is a moral claim to be made? Explain why or why not.

3. Obama mentions "ordinary folks." How do you interpret this term? In what way does this term help characterize the audience he is addressing? Are there aspects of his speech — both in vocabulary and delivery — that strike you as "ordinary"?

Mimi Teixeira

Is Income Inequality That Bad?

[*The Observer*, Notre Dame University, January 27, 2016]

Natasha Reifenberg and Patrick LeBlanc

Yes, Income Inequality Really Is That Bad

[*The Observer*, Notre Dame University, February 1, 2016]

BEFORE YOU READ

Is income inequality an important issue for politicians to debate? Why might this issue be addressed, if at all?

WORDS TO LEARN

unfettered (Teixeira, para. 3): unrestrained (adjective)

lavishly (Teixeira, para. 3): profusely
(adverb)

arbitrary (Teixeira, para. 4): done without a particular reason (adjective)

stagnant (Teixeira, para. 4): inactive
(adjective)

disparities (Teixeira, para. 5): inequalities (noun)

catastrophize (Teixeira, para. 6): to view
a situation as worse than it is (verb)

tangible (Teixeira, para. 8): capable
of being touched; having physical
existence (adjective)

alleviation (Teixeira, para. 9): the act of
lessening (noun)

redistributive (Teixeira, para. 9): supportive of or practicing income
redistribution (adjective)

contend (Reifenberg and LeBlanc,
para. 1): to assert (verb)

decry (Reifenberg and LeBlanc,
para. 2): to condemn (verb)

visceral (Reifenberg and LeBlanc,
para. 2): emotional; coming from
the inside (adjective)

deficit (Reifenberg and LeBlanc,
para. 2): lack (noun)

commodities (Reifenberg and LeBlanc,
para. 6): things that are bought and
sold (noun)

meritocracy (Reifenberg and LeBlanc,
para. 7): leadership selected on the
basis of ability (noun)

deleterious (Reifenberg and LeBlanc,
para. 7): damaging (adjective)

sacrosanct (Reifenberg and LeBlanc,
para. 8): sacred; beyond criticism
(adjective)

---

*Mimi Teixeira, Natasha Reifenberg, and Patrick LeBlanc are students at Notre Dame
University.*

Mimi Teixeira

Is Income Inequality That Bad?

[*The Observer*, Notre Dame University, January 27, 2016]

At a rally in Wisconsin in July [2015], Bernie Sanders proclaimed, 1 "The issue of wealth and income inequality, to my mind, is the great moral issue of our time. It is the greatest economic issue of our time, and it is the great political issue of our time." Based on his poll numbers and on current political discourse, many people seem to agree. Even President Obama has called income inequality "the defining challenge of our time."

However, I do not think income inequality is the biggest issue of our 2 time by any means. I would go so far as to say I don't think it's a problem at all.

Capitalism, especially unfettered capitalism, is often presented as an 3 uncontrollable monstrosity, and the numbers seem to support that. How can 1 percent of the population own almost 36 percent of the country's wealth? How is a society with both lavishly rich and ridiculously poor people fair or desirable?

There are a few preliminary problems with the arguments of income-4 inequality alarmists that I would like to point out. First, the alarmists fail to determine what level of inequality is acceptable, and without a level of comparison, today's numbers are basically arbitrary. Further, income-inequality alarmists struggle to pinpoint practical, nonpartisan implications of today's level of income inequality. Some will argue that income inequality causes economic instability and even recessions, but this is hardly a settled matter. A study by the Cato Institute, a libertarian[1] organization, points out that most statistics ignore the value of government payments to the poor and increasing workers' benefits that have kept reported salaries stagnant while increasing the real value of low- and middle-income workers' compensation.

But even if the statistics were correct, even if income inequality 5 were increasing at alarming rates, it wouldn't matter, because income-inequality statistics do not measure the general standard of living or standard of living disparities in a society. Why does it matter how much the richest person in the country has, so long as the rest of the country

---

[1] libertarian (para. 4): Subscribing to a political philosophy that promotes political freedom and the protection of private property, among other values

lives comfortably? I do not mean to say the whole country currently does live comfortably, though the standard of living in the United States is relatively high compared to the rest of the world. Instead, I mean that unless there is a direct connection between how much the rich have and the poverty level, the gap doesn't matter. If the gap does not hurt the overall economic health of the nation or speak to the level of poverty or the quality of life of the poor, to complain that some have too much is, at best, a call for a blanket redistribution of wealth for the sake of some ideological definition of "fairness" and, at worst, a natural human instinct to resent the front-runners in our economic system.

> Unless there is a direct connection between how much the rich have and the poverty level, the gap doesn't matter.

Wealth is not stagnant, and wages are not the product of a zero-sum game. There is much more in this country to go around than there was in 1920 or even 1980. Politicians who catastrophize income inequality often come up with solutions that divide the current wealth more equally, ignoring the possibility that encouraging growth instead may be the better way to help the poor and raise the real standard of living for everyone.   6

In measuring inequality, doing so in terms of the standard of living is perhaps more important than using terms of income. Dinesh D'Souza points out in his book *What's So Great About America* that standard of living inequality has shrunk over time, even as such improvements created vastly rich people. There was a time when only the rich could afford refrigerators, phones and computers. As income inequality has grown, standard of living inequality has shrunk. Today, most working Americans have the same basic appliances and necessities as the rich. With globalization and an increase in manufacturing technologies, products for Americans of all income levels are cheaper than ever, and every income bracket has seen the benefits.   7

The people we can thank for this, people like Bill Gates, Steve Jobs and Jeff Bezos, have become extremely rich, but they have made everyone better off. As income inequality grows, the tangible standard of living inequality is shrinking. People are paid the worth of what they bring into the economy, and those who make their income through honest channels contribute to the creation of wealth that works to lift up all members of our society. We should give capitalism at least part of the credit for encouraging the creation of better and cheaper technology.   8

All of this is not to say that opportunity inequality and a lack of social mobility do not matter. However, they are not necessarily connected to   9 income inequality. The alleviation of poverty and the extension of economic opportunity remain of utmost importance. However, economic growth, technological innovation and good old-fashioned capitalism over the past few hundred years have done far better than any redistributive program could. Focusing on income inequality doesn't help the poor. Honestly, I'm not sure who it does help.

You have probably guessed by now that I am a conservative. I don't 10
pretend that this article is unbiased, nor do I deny that conservatives and liberals have different ideological beliefs that cannot be compromised or reconciled.

If you find any inequality in a civilized society unfair, I won't say you 11
are objectively wrong, even though I would disagree. But I would challenge you to look at statistics and consider that their only real impact is in their shock value used for political purposes. I would challenge you to consider what you think is fair and why. I would challenge you to consider what is really best for the alleviation of poverty and growth of social mobility in the long run. And I would challenge you to consider if Bernie Sanders and all these other politicians using income inequality as their rallying cry aren't perhaps ignoring more important issues.

Natasha Reifenberg and Patrick LeBlanc

Yes, Income Inequality Really Is That Bad

[*The Observer*, Notre Dame University, February 1, 2016]

This is a response to Mimi Teixeira's viewpoint "Is Income Inequality 1
That Bad?" published January 27 [2016]. In her article, Teixeira argues that concerns surrounding income inequality are overblown and serve only as a political talking point. She contends that "even if income inequality were increasing at alarming rates, it wouldn't matter."

Income inequality *is* increasing at an alarming rate — the bonuses 2
Wall Street employees received last year alone are double the combined annual salary of 1,007,000 full-time minimum wage earners, despite a decline in profits. The 400 richest individuals in our country hold more wealth than the poorest 150 million Americans combined. In other words, the top 0.1 percent is worth more than the entire bottom

90 percent. But these statistics alone are perhaps not enough to decry income inequality — although they can arouse a visceral feeling of injustice. A depression of GDP [gross domestic product], a deficit of opportunity, and a severe decline in social mobility are, however, enough.

Teixeira claims "economic growth . . . [has done] far better than any   3
redistributive program could. Focusing on income inequality doesn't help the poor." Capitalism works because of incentives, and these incentives must naturally give rise to income inequality. Even though inequality rises, all members of society are better off.

We neither dispute the nature of this process nor seek to dissolve the   4
"uncontrollable monstrosity" of capitalism and replace it with a "redistributive program." Instead, we acknowledge the positives of capitalism as an economic system as well as the necessity of some level of income inequality. However, the potential for extreme levels of income inequality is a flaw of capitalism, which can be addressed.

The current level of income inequality is beyond what is required by   5
growth. A 2014 OECD [Organization for Economic Cooperation and Development] study found that the extreme level of income inequality in the United States has led to the loss of approximately 0.3 percentage points worth of GDP growth per year for the last twenty years. While some level of inequality is the natural result of economic growth, the current level serves only to depress economic growth by degrading educational opportunities and social mobility.

Teixeira also says, "There was a time   6
when only the rich could afford refrigera-   **Although a CEO**
tors, phones and computers. As income   **and a public**
inequality has grown, standard of living   **school teacher**
inequality has shrunk." Although we can all   **both own phones,**
appreciate the wonders of indoor plumb-   **only one of them**
ing, refrigerators, cable television — to name **can afford a col-**
a few — and how widely available these   **lege education for**
commodities now are, we cannot equate   **his or her child.**
certain material possessions with opportu-
nity. Teixeira points out that "most work-
ing Americans have the same basic appliances and necessities as the rich." Although a CEO and a public school teacher both own phones, only one of them can afford a college education for his or her child. Education is supposed to be the engine of opportunity, but studies show "increasing gaps in academic achievement and educational attainments have accompanied the growth in income inequality." When you lack the resources to invest in your children's futures or summit mountains of college loans, a refrigerator loses relevancy.

It is hard to say the United States is a meritocracy when government   7
policies, tax cuts and special interests help the rich get richer and the
poor get poorer. For example, the Federal Reserve has created "economic
distortions," according to a leading Wall Street bond expert, that result
in a transfer of wealth to those seeking short-term gains and who need it
the least. It's easy to see the world only through the lens of our own experience, but we have to realize that people face different barriers than our
own if they do not win the lottery of birth and circumstance. Without
firsthand experience of the effects of the deleterious effects of income
inequality, we should not be so quick to declare it nonproblematic.

Further, a general lack of opportunity affects the ability of the less   8
well-off to live up to their full potential. Often disadvantaged for reasons
beyond their control, they are forced to live life dreaming of what might
have been had the circumstance of their birth been different. Opportunity
lies at the crux of the American Dream — in its absence the free-market
system is rigged from the start. Not only is this fundamentally unfair,
but it violates the principles of equality of opportunity and the pursuit
of happiness we hold sacrosanct as a nation. To stand by and do nothing
while income inequality threatens these values would be irresponsible.

At some point we have to ask ourselves: Is this really the society we   9
want to live in? Teixeira says she wants to "challenge you to look at statistics and consider that their only real impact is in their shock value used
for political purposes." The "shock value" of income inequality is not so
much its usage as a political soundbite, but rather its negative impact on
everyday Americans. The entrenchment of wealth at the top, and the deficit of opportunity at the bottom — that's the real impact of economic
inequality. We challenge you not simply to discard the issue of income
inequality because it does not directly affect you, but rather to remember
Pope Francis's words: "Human rights are not only violated by terrorism,
repression or assassination, but also by unfair economic structures that
create huge inequalities."

VOCABULARY/USING A DICTIONARY

1. What is a *monstrosity* (Teixeira, para. 3)?

2. How might you guess the meaning of *crux* (Reifenberg and LeBlanc, para. 8),
   even if you didn't know the definition or the context in which it was used?

3. What part of speech is *overall* (Teixeira, para. 5)? Can you think of a synonym
   for *overall*?

RESPONDING TO WORDS IN CONTEXT

1. What do the authors mean when they use the term *redistributive* (Teixeira,
   para. 9; Reifenberg and LeBlanc, para. 3)?

2. When Reifenberg and LeBlanc speak of the *entrenchment* (para. 9) of wealth, are they describing it as a positive or negative thing?

3. Teixeira writes that "some will argue that income inequality causes economic instability and even *recessions*" (para. 4). Based on this sentence, how might you define *recession*?

DISCUSSING MAIN POINT AND MEANING

1. What point is Teixeira making about income equality? What are her feelings and beliefs about it?

2. How do Reifenberg and LeBlanc respond to Teixeira's argument?

3. How do Reifenberg and LeBlanc discuss opportunity? Does opportunity play a part in Teixeira's discussion of inequality?

EXAMINING SENTENCES, PARAGRAPHS, AND ORGANIZATION

1. Does Reifenberg and LeBlanc's essay take Teixeira's essay into account? How? Is it only a response, or are there areas that move away from Teixeira's argument?

2. Teixeira writes that "economic growth, technological innovation and good old-fashioned capitalism over the past few hundred years have done far better than any redistributive program could. Focusing on income inequality doesn't help the poor" (para. 9). Reifenberg and LeBlanc quote her words in paragraph 3. How do they change Teixeira's sentence? Do their changes, or the sentence's use out of context, affect her meaning in any way?

3. Compare Teixeira's paragraphs with Reifenberg and LeBlanc's paragraphs. Are they similar or different? How so? Describe the similarities and differences, if any, between their paragraphs.

THINKING CRITICALLY

1. What would Teixeira consider "more important [political] issues" (para. 11) than income inequality?

2. Teixeira may not believe in income inequality, but how does she feel about poverty? Does she offer any solutions to poverty?

3. What part does the American Dream (mentioned in Reifenberg and LeBlanc's essay) play in the perpetuation of income inequality?

WRITING ACTIVITIES

1. Write a response, in support of or against, Reifenberg and LeBlanc's argument. You can consider Teixeira's argument as it is presented in their essay, but do not refer to her essay otherwise.

2. On a piece of paper, copy the following sentences from paragraph 7 of Teixeira's essay: "There was a time when only the rich could afford refrigerators, phones and computers. As income inequality has grown, standard of living inequality has shrunk. Today, most working Americans have the same basic appliances and necessities as the rich." In a freewriting exercise, explore your response to these sentences. When you've finished, look back and identify the tone of your response. Circle any specific details/words that surfaced (concrete words like *refrigerators*, *phones*, and *computers*). Underline any verbs in your freewriting. In small groups, discuss what happened in this automatic writing session. How might this material be converted into a written response?

3. How much are the arguments in these two essays influenced by a party platform? Which political parties, if any, are referred to directly or indirectly in these essays? Write a short analysis of the role of party affiliation or sympathy in these two arguments about income inequality.

Using Quotations Effectively

As we have seen in the introduction to this book ("The Persuasive Writer," p. 1), opinion writing can be usefully viewed as an extension of discussion, as a way we can ourselves publicly respond to the ideas and opinions of others. Clearly, one of the most effective ways of entering into public discussion in our writing is by quoting the statements of others, usually those who represent some authority or expertise in the topic under discussion. Writers will usually employ such quotations (1) to bolster or support their own opinions, (2) to defend the opinions of others, or (3) to refute or oppose the opinions of others.

Note how in "Is Income Inequality That Bad?" Notre Dame sophomore Mimi Teixeira effectively opens her essay by citing two quotations that go to the heart of her topic. The first one is from a leading political figure and the second is from no less of an authority than the president of the United States. She cites both of these men to show that major politicians now regard income inequality as one of the most important issues facing the nation. Her two quotations make this point conclusively — they are clear, direct, and authoritative. Once she has established her point, however, she boldly declares that she does not support these authoritative statements but wholly disagrees with them. The rest of her essay will explain why she does.

1 *Opens with a key quotation*	(1) <u>At a rally in Wisconsin in July [2015], Bernie Sanders proclaimed, "The issue of wealth and income inequality, to my mind, is the great moral issue of our time. It is the greatest economic issue of our time, and it is the great political issue of our time."</u> Based on his poll num-
2 *Follows up with another to support the first*	bers and on current political discourse, many people seem to agree. (2) <u>Even President Obama has called income inequality "the defining challenge of our time."</u>
3 *Then forcefully counters by disagreeing with both*	(3) <u>However, I do not think income inequality is the biggest issue of our time by any means. I would go so far as to say I don't think it's a problem at all.</u>

Spotlight on Data and Research

Eileen Y. Chou, Bidhan L. Parmar, and Adam D. Galinsky

The Link between Income Inequality and Physical Pain

[*Harvard Business Review*, March 21, 2016]

In a series of interesting laboratory experiments and field testing, three university researchers (Eileen Y. Chou, Bidhan L. Parmar, and Adam D. Galinsky) discovered links between economic insecurity and feelings of physical pain. In one study, for example, they saw close connections to the rise in income inequality and the growing use of painkillers. In the following essay, they summarize their research and offer some practical recommendations to both government and the private sector.

The United States is in a pain crisis. The use of painkillers increased by 50% from 2006 to 2012 and one recent estimate put the cost of physical pain on the U.S. economy at $635 billion — a 1,000% increase from 20 years earlier. At the same time, a widening income gap, growing sense of financial desperation, and erosion of the middle class have elevated economic insecurity to the top of the political agenda in the United States. 1

A growing body of evidence suggests that this fiscal pain and physical pain are linked and reinforce each other. Over numerous studies, both in the lab and in the field, we have found that the experience of economic insecurity leads people to experience physical pain. Analyses of household consumption data, surveys, and controlled experiments demonstrate a causal link between economic insecurity and pain. 2

In one study, we analyzed the 2008 consumption patterns of 33,720 households across the U.S. and documented the employment 3

continued

status of heads of households. We then focused on the cumulative dollar amount each household spent on over-the-counter painkillers, while controlling for factors that might affect their consumption, such as household size, age, and use of cold and flu medicines. Compared to households in which at least one head of the household was employed, those in which both were unemployed spent 20% more on over-the-counter painkillers.

In a similar study, we informed people of their state's unemploy- 4 ment rate, asked them their employment status, and then asked them how much physical pain they were currently experiencing. Again, the person's employment status predicted the level of physical pain he or she was experiencing. In addition, simply living in a state with a high unemployment level was sufficient to induce physical pain.

These two studies confirmed the positive relationship between 5 economic insecurity and physical pain. We then turned to the laboratory to establish the causal direction.

In a series of experiments, we randomly assigned participants to 6 recall or anticipate economic insecurity; we then measured their physical pain. The results were the same: When people are in a mental state of economic insecurity, regardless of how it was induced, they experience greater physical pain.

If economic insecurity hurts, does it also decrease our tolerance 7 for pain? To find out, we first asked undergraduates to plunge their hands into ice-cold water and keep them there for as long as they could. This provided a baseline measure of pain tolerance. These undergraduate students then learned the value of their college degree for their impending job market. Half were randomly assigned to learn that their college degree would shield them from the impending economic turmoil, and the other half were told that their college degree would add little value and that they were likely to be either unemployed or underemployed.

Both groups — who would be graduating from the same univer- 8 sity — had similar pain-tolerance levels prior to the manipulation. The group facing a prospect of economic insecurity, however, reduced their pain tolerance by 25%. Expectation of economic security had no effect on pain tolerance.

Why does economic insecurity hurt? The cause is likely rooted in 9 human psychology. When people encounter economic insecurity, they typically feel a loss of control. A sense of control is one of the foundational elements of well-being. When people lose this sense of control, their body goes a bit haywire and responds to stimuli differently — displaying weakened resilience and a lower pain threshold.

We are not the first to compare the effects of economic security on 10 subjective responses. Asking poor people to think about their finances impairs their cognitive performance, while the rich show no change.

Simply holding money or having cash as a screen saver can lead people to donate less to orphanages and focus more on their goals.

Our research goes beyond the objective sense of economic insecu- 11 rity, however. We have shown that economic insecurity can elicit a pain response in individuals at any point along the spectrum of income and social economic status. From executives in the C-suite to blue-collar laborers to undergraduate students about to enter a tough job market, people's own interpretation of their economic insecurity determines how much pain they're likely to experience.

Where does that leave us? We have several suggestions. 12

First, we must acknowledge that two major social issues — economic 13 insecurity and the rise in painkiller consumption — are connected. Instead of addressing each issue separately, government agencies should coordinate their efforts. Also, the overarching goal of this shared effort must, in addition to controlling substance abuse and bridging the income gap, promote overall welfare by restoring people's sense of personal control. By targeting the underlying psychological process linking these issues, we may be able to resolve both issues simultaneously.

The same is true for the private sector. Employers bear more than 14 50% of the economic cost when their employees are in physical pain. For instance, employers shouldered more than $27 billion in 2015 for opiate misuse alone. But if organizations understand the causal link between economic insecurity and overuse of painkillers, they'll have a unique cost-saving opportunity. By creating a psychologically safer workplace and allowing employees greater control over different aspects of their job, employers will be able to more fully engage workers and boost productivity — while reducing their physical pain and the attendant costs.

These findings also suggest how healthcare practices can be im- 15 proved. It is important to recognize that a variety of factors contribute to how much pain a person experiences. Rather than focusing solely on getting the person's medical history, it is worthwhile to gauge his or her subjective sense of financial well-being and sense of control. And healthcare providers should think twice before reducing pain medications for those who are under financial duress; they may be in significantly more pain than patients who aren't worried about how they'll pay their bill.

DRAWING CONCLUSIONS

1. The authors write: "Over numerous studies, both in the lab and in the field, we have found that the experience of economic insecurity leads people to experience physical pain" (para. 2). Does the physical pain result directly from the feeling of insecurity? In other words, is the insecurity itself physically painful? Explain where the pain comes from.

continued

> **2.** Is it possible that more people are using painkillers in recent years because of intensive TV promotion, increased pharmaceutical availability, and increased healthcare coverage? How do the authors deal with rival explanations?
>
> **3.** As anyone who has complained to a doctor realizes, pain is a subjective experience and hard to quantify or articulate. How do the authors attempt to make subjective experiences scientifically objective?

The Economist

Young, Gifted, and Held Back

[*The Economist*, January 23, 2016]

BEFORE YOU READ
Do you think of today's young as an oppressed minority? How might their potential be realized?

WORDS TO LEARN

relentlessly (para. 1): incessantly (adverb)

predecessor (para. 2): one who comes before another (noun)

copious (para. 4): plentiful (adjective)

ingrained (para. 4): deep-rooted (adjective)

outpace (para. 5): to outdo or pass (verb)

subsidize (para. 7): to support financially (verb)

unprecedented (para. 7): new; not done before (adjective)

albeit (para. 9): although (conjunction)

dividend (para. 10): a benefit from an action or policy (noun)

pensioner (para. 10): person who receives a pension (noun)

stake (para. 12): an interest or share (noun)

I n the world of *The Hunger Games* youngsters are forced to fight to the death for the amusement of their white-haired rulers. Today's teen fiction is relentlessly dystopian, but the gap between fantasy and reality is often narrower than you might think. The older generation may not   1

The Economist is a weekly periodical based in London. Its mission statement is printed on each page: "First published in September 1843 to take part in 'a severe contest between intelligence, which presses forward, and an unworthy, timid ignorance obstructing our progress.'"

resort to outright murder but, as our special report this week on millennials describes, in important ways they hold their juniors down.

    Roughly a quarter of the world's people — some 1.8 billion — have turned 15 but not yet reached 30. In many ways, they are the luckiest group of young adults ever to have existed. They are richer than any previous generation, and live in a world without smallpox or Mao Zedong.[1] They are the best-educated generation ever — Haitians today spend longer in school than Italians did in 1960. Thanks to all that extra learning and to better nutrition, they are also more intelligent than their elders. If they are female or gay, they enjoy greater freedom in more countries than their predecessors would have thought possible. And they can look forward to improvements in technology that will, say, enable many of them to live well past 100. So what, exactly, are they complaining about?   2

    Plenty. Just as, for the first time in history, the world's youngsters form a common culture, so they also share the same youthful grievances. Around the world, young people gripe that it is too hard to find a job and a place to live, and that the path to adulthood has grown longer and more complicated.   3

    Many of their woes can be blamed on policies favoring the old over the young. Consider employment. In many countries, labor laws require firms to offer copious benefits and make it hard to lay workers off. That suits those with jobs, who tend to be older, but it makes firms reluctant to hire new staff. The losers are the young. In most regions they are at least twice as likely as their elders to be unemployed. The early years of any career are the worst time to be idle, because these are when the work habits of a lifetime become ingrained. Those unemployed in their 20s typically still feel the "scarring" effects of lower income, as well as unhappiness, in their 50s.   4

    Housing, too, is often rigged against the young. Homeowners dominate the bodies that decide whether new houses may be built. They often say no, so as not to spoil the view and reduce the value of their own property. Overregulation has doubled the cost of a typical home in Britain. Its effects are even worse in many of the big cities around the world where young people most want to live. Rents and home prices in such places have far outpaced incomes. The youngsters of Kuala Lumpur are known as the "homeless generation." Young American women are more likely to live with their parents or other relatives than at any time since the second world war.   5

---

[1] Mao Zedong (para. 2): The chairman of the Chinese Communist Party from 1949 to 1976. He was known as Chairman Mao.

Young people are often footloose. With the whole world to explore 6
and nothing to tie them down, they move around more often than their
elders. This makes them more productive, especially if they migrate
from a poor country to a rich one. By one estimate, global GDP would
double if people could move about freely. That is politically impossible —
indeed, the mood in rich countries is turning against immigration. But it
is striking that so many governments discourage not only cross-border
migration but also the domestic sort. China's *hukou* system treats rural folk
who move to cities as second-class citizens. India makes it hard for those
who move from one state to another to obtain public services. A UN study
found that 80% of countries had policies to reduce rural-urban migration,
although much of human progress has come from people putting down
their hoes and finding better jobs in the big smoke. All these barriers to free
movement especially harm the young, because they most want to move.

The old have always subsidized their juniors. Within families, they 7
still do. But many governments favor the old: an ever greater share of
public spending goes on pensions and health care for them. This is partly
the natural result of societies aging, but it is also because the elderly
ensure that policies work in their favor. By one calculation, the net flow
of resources (public plus private) is now from young to old in at least five
countries, including Germany and Hungary. This is unprecedented and
unjust — the old are much richer.

The young could do more to stand up for themselves. In America just 8
over a fifth of 18- to 34-year-olds turned out to vote in the latest general
election; three-fifths of over 65s did. It is the same in Indonesia and only
slightly better in Japan. It is not enough for
the young to sign online petitions. If they
want governments to listen, they should vote.

> It is not enough for the young to sign online petitions. If they want governments to listen, they should vote.

However, the old have a part to play, too. 9
The young are an oppressed minority —
albeit an unusual one — in the straightforward sense that governments are systematically preventing them from reaching their
potential.

That is a cruel waste of talent. Today's under-30s will one day domi- 10
nate the labor force. If their skills are not developed, they will be less productive than they could be. Countries such as India that are counting on
a demographic dividend from their large populations of young adults will
find that it fails to materialize. Rich, aging societies will find that, unless the
youth of today can get a foot on the career ladder, tomorrow's pensioners
will struggle. What is more, oppressing youngsters is dangerous. Countries
with lots of jobless, disaffected young men tend to be more violent and
unstable, as millions of refugees from the Middle East and Africa can attest.

The remedy is easy to prescribe — and hard to enact. Governments 11
should unleash the young by cutting the red tape that keeps them out
of jobs, and curbing the power of property-owners to stop homes from
being built. They should scrap restrictions on domestic migration and
allow more cross-border movement. They should make education a
priority.

It is a lot to expect from political leaders who often seem unequal to 12
the task of even modest reform. But every parent and grandparent has
a stake in this, too. If they put their shoulders to the wheel, who knows
what they might accomplish.

VOCABULARY/USING A DICTIONARY

1. What other words do you know that share a stem with *dominate* (para. 5)?

2. What word do you see in the word *grievance* (para. 3)? How does identifying
   that word help you determine its definition?

3. What part of speech is *prescribe* (para. 11)? What does it mean?

RESPONDING TO WORDS IN CONTEXT

1. What is *dystopian* (para. 1) fiction?

2. If young people *gripe* (para. 3) about how hard life is, what are they doing?

3. When the authors say, "Young people are often *footloose*" (para. 6), what do
   they mean?

DISCUSSING MAIN POINT AND MEANING

1. Why might some people claim that today's youth are luckier than the youth
   of previous generations?

2. What difficulties do the youth of today face?

3. What changes do the authors suggest to help today's youth?

EXAMINING SENTENCES, PARAGRAPHS, AND ORGANIZATION

1. When the authors write that today's generation of young people is excep-
   tionally lucky in some ways, they bring in three examples, two of which are
   specific references: "They are richer than any previous generation, and live
   in a world without smallpox or Mao Zedong" (para. 2). When you read this
   sentence, do these references have any resonance? Why are (or aren't) they
   effective?

2. Where in the essay do the authors switch from cataloguing the problems of
   the young to looking at possible ways to address these problems?

3. Reread the essay's final paragraph. How do you judge its tone? Does it seem
   optimistic that reform can occur?

THINKING CRITICALLY

1. Is this article more hopeful or pessimistic about the situation youth finds itself in?

2. The title is "Young, Gifted and Held Back." What talents do today's youth have that are mentioned in this article? Are there other talents you can think of that are being squandered?

3. The authors make the claim that "the young are an oppressed minority" (para. 9). Do you think this is true? Who do you think will produce the changes necessary to help the young people of today?

WRITING ACTIVITIES

1. The *Economist* writers open their essay with a comparison of the experience of youths today with the story line in *The Hunger Games*. Can you think of a TV show, movie, or book theme that is a relevant metaphor for something you see in daily life? In a brief writing exercise, compare this fictional theme to some aspect of real life (using this essay's opening as a model).

2. Look at this essay critically and make notes in the text. What are the claims, and what is the evidence to support these claims? If you find claims without sufficient evidence to back them up, where are they in the essay? Would you like more information? Once you have made your notes, write them up on a separate piece of paper.

3. In a short comparison and contrast exercise, write a little about your own experience and whether or not it matches the picture presented in this essay. Compare your experience with the experience of an older generation — or a younger one — but use personal research (interview someone you know firsthand, such as a family member, friend, employer, or coworker). Then think about how you might approach academic research to write more objectively on the subject.

Jacob Riis

From How the Other Half Lives

Toward the end of the nineteenth century, a noted reformer and one of the nation's first photojournalists, Jacob Riis, undertook a dramatic investigation of urban poverty. His book contained not only vivid verbal descriptions of New York City's worst tenement districts but also stark photography that uncovered a world that few New Yorkers liked to admit existed. The title of Riis's powerful and influential book, How the Other Half Lives, *was meant to expose the dire conditions of one half of the population to an unsuspecting other half. Curiously, today, that economic divide has changed and we now speak of a much wider division: the 1 percent versus the 99 percent. The following text is taken from the book's short introduction that explains the reasons behind the increase in poverty and crime. As you'll see, many issues have not changed in well over a hundred years, especially the lack of affordable housing.*

A Danish immigrant who came to the United States at age twenty-one, Jacob Riis (1849–1914) eventually became a reporter who focused on social issues, primarily poverty. He was also a pioneering photographer whose work would have a dramatic impact on the development of photography for the causes of social activism. Riis would go on to write other influential books, such as The Children of the Poor *(1892) and* Battle with the Slum *(1902). His 1901 autobiography,* The Making of an American, *is still a relevant and readable portrait of the immigrant experience.*

Long ago it was said that "one half of the world does not know how the other half lives."[1] That was true then. It did not know because it did not care. The half that was on top cared little for the struggles, and less for the fate of those who were underneath, so long as it was able to hold them there and keep its own seat. There came a time when the discomfort and crowding below were so great, and the consequent upheavals so violent, that it was no longer an easy thing to do, and then the upper half fell to inquiring what was the matter. Information on the subject

1

---

[1] "one . . . lives" (para. 1): The quotation is from the great English religious poet and Anglican clergyman George Herbert (1593–1633).

Jacob Riis, "Homeless Boys," New York City.
The Museum of the City of New York/Art Resource, NY

has been accumulating rapidly since, and the whole world has had its hands full answering for its old ignorance.

In New York, the youngest of the world's great cities, that time 2 came later than elsewhere, because the crowding had not been so great. There were those who believed that it would never come; but their hopes were vain. Greed and reckless selfishness wrought like results here as in the cities of older lands. "When the great riot occurred in 1863,"[2] so reads the testimony of the Secretary of the Prison Association of New York before a legislative committee appointed to investigate causes of the increase of crime in the State twenty-five years ago, "every hiding-place and nursery of crime discovered itself by imme-diate and active participation in the operations of the mob.[3] Those very

---

[2] great riot (para. 2): In July 1863, with the Civil War at its height, violent riots erupted in New York to protest a stepped-up military draft. The riots had an economic dimension, as mostly white, working-class males resented a policy that allowed richer Americans the option to avoid being drafted by paying a sub-stitute. But the violence quickly took on a racist direction as the rioters began attacking black citizens.

[3] mob (para. 2): Meaning an unruly crowd, not organized crime

places and domiciles, and all that are like them, are to-day nurseries of crime, and of the vices and disorderly courses which lead to crime. By far the largest part — eighty per cent. at least — of crimes against property and against the person are perpetrated by individuals who have either lost connection with home life, or never had any, or whose *homes had ceased to be sufficiently separate, decent, and desirable to afford what are regarded as ordinary wholesome influences of home and family.* . . . The younger criminals seem to come almost exclusively from the worst tenement house districts, that is, when traced back to the very places where they had their homes in the city here." Of one thing New York made sure at that early stage of the inquiry: the boundary line of the Other Half lies through the tenements.

It is ten years and over, now, since that line divided New York's 3 population evenly. Today three-fourths of its people live in the tenements, and the nineteenth century drift of the population to the cities is sending ever-increasing multitudes to crowd them. The fifteen thousand tenant houses that were the despair of the sanitarian in the past generation have swelled into thirty-seven thousand, and more than twelve hundred thousand persons call them home. The one way out he saw — rapid transit to the suburbs — has brought no relief. We know now that there is no way out; that the "system" that was the evil offspring of public neglect and private greed has come to stay, a storm-centre forever of our civilization. Nothing is left but to make the best of a bad bargain.

What the tenements are and how they grew to what they are, 4 we shall see hereafter [i.e., in the rest of the book]. The story is dark enough, drawn from the plain public records, to send a chill to any heart. If it shall appear that the sufferings and the sins of the "other half," and the evil they breed, are but as a just punishment upon the community that gave it no other choice, it will be because that is the truth. The boundary line lies there because, while the forces for good on one side vastly outweigh the bad — it were not well otherwise — in the tenements all the influences make for evil; because they are the hotbeds of the epidemics that carry death to rich and poor alike; the nurseries of pauperism and crime that fill our jails and police courts; that throw off a scum of forty thousand human wrecks to the island asylums and workhouses year by year; that turned out in the last eight years a round half million beggars to prey upon our charities; that maintain a standing army of ten thousand tramps with all that that implies; because, above all, they touch the family life with deadly moral contagion. This is their worst crime, inseparable from the system. That we have to own it the child of our own wrong does not excuse it, even though it gives it claim upon our utmost patience and tenderest charity.

What are you going to do about it? is the question of to-day. It 5 was asked once of our city in taunting defiance by a band of political cutthroats, the legitimate outgrowth of life on the tenement-house level.[4] Law and order found the answer then and prevailed. With our enormously swelling population held in this galling bondage, will that answer always be given? It will depend on how fully the situation that prompted the challenge is grasped. Forty per cent. of the distress among the poor, said a recent official report, is due to drunkenness. But the first legislative committee ever appointed to probe this sore went deeper down and uncovered its roots. The "conclusion forced itself upon it that certain conditions and associations of human life and habitation are the prolific parents of corresponding habits and morals," and it recommended "the prevention of drunkenness by providing for every man a clean and comfortable home." Years after, a sanitary inquiry brought to light the fact that "more than one-half of the tenements with two-thirds of their population were held by owners who made the keeping of them a business, *generally a speculation.* The owner was seeking a certain percentage on his outlay, and that percentage very rarely fell below fifteen per cent., and frequently exceeded thirty.[5]

The complaint was universal among the tenants that they were 6 entirely uncared for, and that the only answer to their requests to have the place put in order by repairs and necessary improvements was that they must pay their rent or leave. The agent's instructions were simple but emphatic: "Collect the rent in advance, or, failing, eject the occupants." Upon such a stock grew this upas-tree.[6] Small wonder the fruit is bitter. The remedy that shall be an effective answer to the coming appeal for justice must proceed from the public conscience. Neither legislation nor charity can cover the ground. The greed of capital that wrought the evil must itself undo it, as far as it can now be undone. Homes must

---

[4] political cutthroats (para. 5): A group of corrupt politicians and city bosses who controlled New York government some years earlier

[5] thirty (para. 5): [Author's note] "Forty per cent. was declared by witnesses before a Senate Committee to be a fair average interest on tenement property. Instances were given of its being one hundred per cent. and over."

[6] upas-tree (para. 5): A poisonous evergreen

be built for the working masses by those who employ their labor; but tenements must cease to be "good property" in the old, heartless sense. "Philanthropy and five per cent." is the penance exacted.

BACKGROUND AND CONTEXT

1. Why does Riis argue that awareness of "how the other half lives" came more slowly to Americans? In what ways is this important in understanding the conditions in New York City?

2. What point is Riis making by going back to the 1863 riots in New York? What relation do those riots bear to his topic? How do they help establish a context for his view of the city in 1890?

STRATEGY, STRUCTURE, AND STYLE

1. Riis writes, "The boundary line of the Other Half lies through the tenements" (para. 2). How do you interpret his words? What significance does he place on tenements throughout the essay?

2. What solutions does Riis offer for the conditions he describes? He points out toward the end that "neither legislation nor charity" can serve as a solution. How did he come to that awareness, and what does he propose as an answer?

COMPARISONS AND CONNECTIONS

1. After reading Riis's description of the conditions in New York, make a list of what he sees as the root causes of poverty and crime. In a short essay, select one of the causes and discuss how relevant you think it is today. Explain whether you think modern society has solved the urban problems Riis outlines.

2. Examine the photo that appears with the selection. Given the equipment and conditions of the time, Riis had to "stage" his pictures. In other words, he had to supply lighting and arrange his actual subjects, who were required to remain still. In a short essay, consider his photography: Do you think it supports the point he makes about poverty, or do you think the "staging" compromises the accuracy and honesty of his depiction?

Discussing the Unit

SUGGESTED TOPIC FOR DISCUSSION

Over the last decade, the American economy has faltered greatly and then struggled to right itself. Many argue that the gap between the very rich and the very poor has widened. College graduates who were once considered America's great successes, primed for the workforce, often struggle to find jobs. How would the writers in this chapter define the American Dream? Does that dream have the potential to become reality for anyone anymore?

PREPARING FOR CLASS DISCUSSION

1. How optimistic do you feel about your future? How do you think a college degree will help you in the current economy?

2. Do you think the divide between the rich and the poor is worse now than it has been in times past? What makes you think that? What can be done to address the gap between the rich and the poor? Do you think it's society's responsibility to alleviate the disparity between them?

FROM DISCUSSION TO WRITING

1. Consider the question about income inequality presented in the student debate in this chapter (p. 311). Do any of the other articles address income inequality and the points made in the student articles? Briefly discuss the student debate and one other essay that refers to the arguments the students make.

2. Using at least three of the essays in this chapter as sources, describe what income inequality looks like in this country. What composite picture emerges from the various explanations and descriptions here?

TOPICS FOR CROSS-CULTURAL DISCUSSION

1. How is the American Dream approached in the essays of this chapter? What is it? Is it still desirable or attainable? Do the essayists think the American Dream was ever something anyone could achieve?

2. What parallels can you draw between early twenty-first-century society and late nineteenth-century society from Barack Obama's speech (p. 308) and Jacob Riis's writing (p. 327)? Are there stark differences you can identify between America now and in Riis's time? If so, describe them.

10

Marriage: What Does It Mean Today?

Why do we still get married? Is the institution simply a doomed vestige of an earlier age, or does it take meaning and power from the centuries of tradition it draws on and continues? Despite the Supreme Court's ruling on gay marriage, many Americans continue to debate the consequences of same-sex marriage, and as divorce rates continue to jump to alarming levels, some critics argue for throwing out the whole notion of a legally sanctioned love relationship. Others, meanwhile, urge us to hold on tight to an important cultural construct we may be at risk of losing.

The chapter opens with an important brief statement that supports one of the most significant legal decisions of the twenty-first century: Supreme Court justice Anthony Kennedy's remarks on marriage in the 2015 landmark case *Obergefell v. Hodges*. Writing the majority opinion, Kennedy argued that the U.S. Constitution guaranteed same-sex couples the right to be married. In his conclusion, Kennedy grew nearly poetic on the subject of marriage: "No union is more profound than marriage," he wrote, "for it embodies the highest ideals of love, fidelity, devotion, sacrifice, and family. In forming a marital union, two people become something greater than once they were."

Although same-sex marriage is now legal in all states, not all states have cleared an easy path to same-sex parenting. A number of states, as reporter Suzy Khimm observes in "The New Nuclear Family: What Gay

Marriage Means for the Future of Parenthood," still retain legal obstacles to adoption or surrogacy. But Khimm points out that "there will be growing pressure — and legal challenges — to dismantle such barriers as same-sex marriage and parenthood become increasingly mainstream." She wonders, however, if same-sex marriage will lead to a revival of "old family values" or "affirm a more expansive and progressive notion of what it means to be a parent."

If Khimm's essay notes that the Supreme Court decision will make "it harder to settle on a simple definition of what makes a family," the next selection offers a firsthand description of how American family life — even in traditional opposite-sex marriage — may actually be changing. Noted columnist Susan Estrich acknowledges that with "half of all marriages ending in divorce, families are not what they used to be." In "Modern Family," she recounts an incident that shows how "divorce does not have to destroy a family."

If asked why they got married, most young couples would probably answer that it was because they "were in love." Falling in love is still perhaps the most common reason for marriage, as Mississippi State student Kyle Waltman suggests in his reflective Valentine's Day essay "Saying 'I Love You.'" Not afraid of raising some profound questions in a search for an understanding of what we mean by love, Waltman writes: "What does it mean to 'fall in love' with someone? Is it an emotion? Is it a choice? Is it both? Is loving someone a subjective or objective concept? These questions are not easily answered, yet they point to the vital importance of understanding both the love that we accept and the love that we give."

Yet, as many historians realize, love is a relatively recent reason for marriage. In the past, marriages were often entered for social, economic, or political reasons. Also, in many cultures, marriages were arranged by parents, often for purposes related to status and family connections. In "They Didn't Want an Arranged Marriage," *Washington Post* reporter Lavanya Ramanathan tells the story of a young Indian couple who enter into a personal kind of "arranged marriage" after meeting on eHarmony. In the course of her essay, Ramanathan recounts other relationships, including her own, and provides some historical background as she tries, with the help of some experts, to answer an age-old question that puts practicality ahead of passion: "Could there be some truth in our parents' insistence that romance grows over time?"

It is interesting to speculate, based on the previous selections, why the notion of marriage persists and carries such weight. Is it mainly due to tradition? Do young people marry because they see their friends marry? Is there something very basic and instinctive about marriage that makes it hard to resist? Is it a way to avoid loneliness? Is it the best way to start a family? Whatever the reasons, the most recent survey on the subject from the Pew Research Center — featured in our "Spotlight on Data and Research"— shows that young people are getting married later than at any other time in our history and that many people, especially males, are not getting married at all.

At the heart of the marriage debate, in some ways, is the value of traditional marriage itself. Long before same-sex marriage was an issue on America's radar, were marriages actually loving relationships? Or were they ways of legalizing the ownership of women by men? For a historical perspective on the question, this chapter's "America Then" presents one of the most influential voices in American radicalism, author and self-professed agitator Emma Goldman. "That marriage is a failure none but the very stupid will deny," Goldman wrote in 1910. Consider why she believed that, and whether her arguments still hold for marriages — of all new shapes, sizes, and colors — today.

Justice Anthony Kennedy

From *Obergefell v. Hodges*

O n June 26, 2015, the United States Supreme Court ruled in the land-mark case of Obergefell v. Hodges *that same-sex couples had a con-stitutional right to be married. The decision wrapped up a number of cases that had been making their way through various appeals courts for sev-eral years with varying consequences. The Supreme Court was deeply divided over the issue and the matter was settled by a five-to-four decision, with Justice Anthony Kennedy serving as the pivotal vote and writing the majority opin-ion. A brief portion of that opinion appears below.*

It is now clear that the challenged laws burden the liberty of same-sex   1
couples, and it must be further acknowledged that they abridge central precepts of equality. Here the marriage laws enforced by the respondents are in essence unequal: same-sex couples are denied all the benefits afforded to opposite-sex couples and are barred from exercising a fun-damental right. Especially against a long history of disapproval of their relationships, this denial to same-sex couples of the right to marry works a grave and continuing harm. The imposition of this disability on gays and lesbians serves to disrespect and subordinate them. And the Equal Protection Clause, like the Due Process Clause, prohibits this unjustified infringement of the fundamental right to marry. . . . These considerations lead to the conclusion that the right to marry is a fundamental right inherent in the liberty of the person, and under the Due Process and Equal Protection Clauses of the Fourteenth Amendment couples of the same sex may not be deprived of that right and that liberty. The Court now holds that same-sex couples may exercise the fundamental right to marry. No longer may this liberty be denied to them. . . .

No union is more profound than marriage, for it embodies the high-   2
est ideals of love, fidelity, devotion, sacrifice, and family. In forming a marital union, two people become something greater than once they were. As some of the petitioners in these cases demonstrate, marriage embodies a love that may endure even past death. It would misunder-stand these men and women to say they disrespect the idea of marriage. Their plea is that they do respect it, respect it so deeply that they seek to find its fulfillment for themselves. Their hope is not to be condemned to

live in loneliness, excluded from one of civilization's oldest institutions. They ask for equal dignity in the eyes of the law. The Constitution grants them that right.

POINTS TO CONSIDER

1. How does the matter of "equality" enter into the court's decision? In Justice Kennedy's opinion, what is "unequal"?

2. Explain what you think Justice Kennedy means by a "grave and continuing harm."

3. Why do you think Justice Kennedy concludes his opinion with a paragraph that celebrates marriage in general? Explain what relevance you think this has to his argument.

Suzy Khimm

The New Nuclear Family: What Gay Marriage Means for the Future of Parenthood

[*New Republic*, July 23, 2015]

BEFORE YOU READ
Has the legalization of gay marriage changed our idea of parenthood? How do newly married gay couples approach the idea of family?

WORDS TO LEARN

surrogacy (para. 3): the state of acting for another (often used when using a surrogate mother) (noun)
invasive (para. 7): intrusive (adjective)
alleviate (para. 9): to lessen (verb)
delineate (para. 10): to describe with precision (verb)
dismantle (para. 11): to take apart (verb)
nuance (para. 16): a subtle difference (noun)

asymmetry (para. 16): the quality of being unsymmetrical (noun)
artifact (para. 17): an object that reflects something about a people or a culture (noun)
constitute (para. 18): to form (verb)
foster (para. 20): to encourage (verb)
kinship (para. 21): family relationship (noun)

Suzy Khimm is a journalist based in Washington, D.C. Her work has appeared in the New Republic, *the* Washington Post, *and a number of other publications, as well as on MSNBC.*

Just days after Shawn Davis and Richard Sawyers were married in   1
September 2011, they started planning to have kids. "You started
asking fast," Davis said recently, looking over at his husband. "Was it
even on the honeymoon?"

"I think it was," Sawyers replied, recalling their time in Venice fol-   2
lowing their wedding. We were sitting on the couch of their home
in Washington, D.C.'s Brightwood neighborhood, near the border of
Maryland, which they bought last year. Their two-year-old son, Levi,
whom they adopted at birth, was napping upstairs.

The two had talked about parenthood for years before their honey-   3
moon. They had even taken a workshop for LGBT couples that laid out
the different paths to becoming same-sex parents: private adoption, public foster care adoption, surrogacy. But for Sawyers, the traditional order
of operations still mattered. "It was important to be married and to be a
family unit — I wanted that to happen first," he said.

The same was true for the Wesoleks, another couple I met on the   4
steps of the Supreme Court in June, on the day that gay marriage became
legal nationwide. "Other people do it in different orders, but for us it
was get married, buy a house, have a baby," Danielle Wesolek told me.
She and her wife, Amy Wesolek, moved to Takoma Park, Maryland,
got two Boston Terriers, and then had their daughter, Lena, who's now
18 months old.

The landmark ruling in *Obergefell v. Hodges* now paves the way for   5
other same-sex couples to follow their lead. Most states permit only married couples or unmarried individuals to adopt, and some have laws that
give married couples preference in the process. And if prospective parents want to hire a surrogate to carry their child, many states similarly
require that they be hitched.

Prior to the Supreme Court's decision, the path to parenthood for   6
gay couples was significantly more complicated. In states that prohibited
same-sex marriage, couples could pursue single-parent adoption. But
that allowed only one parent to be recognized legally, and children could
potentially be taken away from their families in the event of the illness,
death, or separation of the one legal parent. Schools, hospitals, and other
institutions could also deny nonlegal parents the ability to make decisions about their children.

This shaky legal footing forced same-sex parents to seek various   7
workarounds to protect their relationships with their children. They've
drawn up co-parenting or custody agreements and other paperwork
to build a case for their parental rights, even if they wouldn't be legally
guaranteed. In 15 states and Washington, D.C., individuals can petition
for "second-parent" adoption of children conceived through assisted

reproduction as well as adoption. The process can be costly and time-consuming — frequently involving lawyers, criminal background checks, and a home study by a social worker — which can feel particularly invasive for new mothers and fathers who already consider themselves to be the parents of their children.

Even in states that recognized same-sex marriage, couples have 8 sought additional legal protection for when they traveled to states that didn't recognize their union. When the Wesoleks went to South Carolina in May, for example, they made sure to pack the paperwork confirming Danielle's parental status, just in case. "The thing that freaked me out was that this could be all down to one person — this could be down to one judge that said, 'You know what, I'm going to take a stand,'" said Amy Wesolek, Lena's birth mother, who conceived her through a sperm donor.

> The process can be costly and time-consuming.

The Supreme Court's decision has begun to alleviate some of these 9 anxieties and lower the legal barriers to parenthood. Married same-sex couples are now allowed to adopt jointly in nearly every state, according to Emily Hecht-McGowan, director of public policy at Family Equality Council, an LGBT advocacy group. In the first ruling on the issue since *Obergefell*, a federal judge in Utah ordered that married lesbian couples who use sperm donors must be automatically recognized as legal mothers from birth, the same as with heterosexual parents.

Obergefell hasn't cleared away all of the legal obstacles to same-sex 10 parenthood. Michigan, Virginia, and North Dakota still allow child-welfare agencies to prohibit gay couples from adopting or fostering children for religious reasons. Mississippi prohibits same-sex adoption altogether. And despite the ruling in Utah, there's still no guarantee in other states that couples who use sperm donors will be automatically recognized as parents. States that allow surrogacy often lack clear laws delineating parental rights, and courts have repeatedly granted those rights to surrogate mothers over the objections of same-sex parents. Louisiana outright prohibits same-sex couples from having a child through surrogacy.

But there will be growing pressure — and legal challenges — to dis- 11 mantle such barriers as same-sex marriage and parenthood become increasingly mainstream. "One of the reasons [same-sex] couples haven't been adopting is because they didn't have confidence in the system and the legality of it," said April Dinwoodie of the Donaldson Adoption institute, a research and policy group. The Supreme Court's decision should give them more of that reassurance. Post-*Obergefell*, one of the country's biggest surrogacy agencies, is already reporting a spike in interest from newly engaged and married LGBT couples.

So will same-sex parents simply become the new beacons of old fam-   12
ily values? In his *Obergefell* decision, Supreme Court Justice Anthony Kennedy drove home the notion that marriage is essential to parenthood and childrearing. "Without the recognition, stability, and predictability marriage offers, their children suffer the stigma of knowing their families are somehow lesser," he wrote of same-sex couples.

Danielle Wesolek jokes that she feels like an "old man Republican"   13
when she talks to her younger brother, who's straight and had his first child around the same time as she did. "Don't you think you ought to be married?" she tells him. In fact, that's what pioneering gay conserva-tives had hoped for all along in their push for gay marriage. "The intent of same-sex marriage is not to establish new family structures but to reaffirm the old one," writer Jonathan Rauch said in a 2004 talk at the University of Michigan.

But the rise of LGBT families could also affirm a more expansive   14
and progressive notion of what it means to be a parent. As gay men and women come out earlier in life, fewer will have children from previous heterosexual relationships. As a matter of necessity, most gay parents have to use outside help — a donor, a surrogate, or adoption agency — to bring children into their lives. That's affirmed a model of parenting built on rela-tionships, support, and commitment, rather than biology or predeter-mined gender roles. "We will have no choice but to see the law eventually evolve with us, and we are going to see an increased, expanding definition of who makes a family and what families look like," said Hecht-McGowan.

Those differences should be recognized and respected, not simply   15
overlooked. Writer Andrew Solomon, who has a young son, recounted recently in the *New Statesman* how he and his husband are still asked "which of us is the mom," comparing his experience to a single mother being asked what it's like to be "both Mom and Dad."

"All men are created equal but not identical. New family structures   16
are different from mainstream ones," he wrote. "We are not lesser, but we are not the same, and to deny the nuance of that asymmetry is to keep us almost as ensnared as we were when our marriages and families were impossible."

The ideal of a nuclear family is itself a historical artifact that rose to   17
greatest prominence in the 1950s, when psychologists actually encour-aged couples to abandon their friendships to focus on their families, explains marriage historian Stephanie Coontz, whose work Kennedy

cited in his opinion. "In the long run, it harms your ability to call on a larger network of social support that you might need personally from the stresses of life, and that your family needs," Coontz told me. "The problem with elevating [the nuclear family] as the source of all of your strength is that it almost by definition is too small to carry all of life's burdens."

Even as people like Justice Kennedy praise the virtues of marriage   18
and a two-parent household, this traditional view of what constitutes a family is already a fiction. Only 40 percent of children now live with married heterosexual parents, and a record share of Americans have never married. "Legalizing same-sex marriage continues a trend towards more complex family relationships," said sociologist Andrew Cherlin of Johns Hopkins University. "We're becoming related to more and more people to whom we owe less and less."

Gay parenting simply adds another layer of complexity to what's   19
already a very diverse and complicated picture. In his forthcoming book, *Modern Families*, sociologist Joshua Gamson explains the many ways that assisted reproductive technology and adoption have challenged traditional notions of kinship: A lesbian couple teamed up with a gay couple to adopt two children; a woman carried a child conceived from her partner's egg and a sperm donor. He also tells his own story. His first daughter was conceived through eggs donated by one friend and carried by another. His second daughter was born through a privately hired surrogate.

Such arrangements mean that our notions of what constitutes a   20
family will continue to expand and evolve. Already, open adoptions have become increasingly popular for adoptive parents, gay and straight. When Levi's birth mother discovered she was having a boy, she personally called Davis and Sawyers to tell them. They save every text message and e-mail they receive from her to pass on one day to their son. On the bookshelf in Levi's room is a photo of the three of them in the hospital. So far, his birth mother hasn't taken up their invitation to see him, but they told her that they would always leave the door open. "It's important for him to know where he comes from, to know who his people are, to know what that foundation is," said Sawyers. "As a parent, I'm going to do everything I can to foster that relationship."

With gay marriage now legal across the country, such complexity   21
will become increasingly mainstream, making it harder to settle on a simple definition of what makes a family. "The challenges to the more conventional notions of kinship are going to come up more and more," Gamson told me. "There's just going to be more of us."

VOCABULARY/USING A DICTIONARY

1. What is the definition of *parenthood* (para. 3)?
2. What does it mean if something is *prohibited* (para. 6)?
3. Can you think of a synonym for *ensnared* (para. 16)?

RESPONDING TO WORDS IN CONTEXT

1. What might be an example of the *workarounds* Khimm mentions in paragraph 7?
2. What is the definition of *conceived* (para. 7) in this context?
3. How might same-sex parents become a *beacon* (para. 12) of old family values?

DISCUSSING MAIN POINT AND MEANING

1. What event led to the easing of difficulties for same-sex couples who want to have children? Why did it have this effect?
2. How did same-sex parents attempt to protect their rights as parents before the *Obergefell* ruling? What sort of problems might they have encountered?
3. How have reproductive technologies and adoptions changed to meet the needs of same-sex parents?

EXAMINING SENTENCES, PARAGRAPHS, AND ORGANIZATION

1. What can you tell about the couple described in paragraph 1? What do you know later that is left out of the description?
2. Summarize the meaning of the opening sentence in paragraph 18: "Even as people like Justice Kennedy praise the virtues of marriage and a two-parent household, this traditional view of what constitutes a family is already a fiction."
3. What do the quotations from and characterizations of different gay families add to the essay? How would the essay be different without this material?

THINKING CRITICALLY

1. What does the new nuclear family look like? Does it look very different from the old one?
2. What about families does change, as noted by Khimm, when the parents are gay? Is the change significant?
3. Is parenthood going to alter due to the transformation marriage is under-going?

WRITING ACTIVITIES

1. What is a family? In your own words, write a piece that reflects on what families look like and feel like. Compare and contrast different types of families — what makes them the same and what makes them different? Use as many examples of families as you can.

2. Discuss Khimm's statement that "the ideal of a nuclear family is itself a historical artifact that rose to greatest prominence in the 1950s" (para. 17). Do you think she is correct? What does this statement mean?

3. Khimm ends with the story of Davis and Sawyers and their son's open adoption. Do you think this is a healthy modern family? Why is it preferable to some other options? What issues might arise in this family that would be different from issues faced by a more "traditional" family?

Susan Estrich

Modern Family

[The Hazleton Standard-Speaker, October 1, 2015]

BEFORE YOU READ

What does the modern family look like? Do you think divorced and remarried families often can't stand each other, or do you think these days such families are able to appreciate each other?

WORDS TO LEARN

scandalous (para. 5): disgraceful; shameful (adjective)

subsequent (para. 6): coming later or after (adjective)

There is a lot going on in the world, and most of it seems frightening, depressing and utterly beyond our control. So if you have not heard, let me tell you about a really wonderful thing that happened this week, a reminder of what matters most.   1

It's the story of a wedding that took place in Ohio last weekend. The father of the bride was set to walk his daughter down the aisle. But in a surprise move, Todd Bachman, the father, stopped the procession to take the arm of his daughter's stepfather, Todd Cendrosky.   2

"For me to thank him for all the years of helping raise our daughter wouldn't be enough," said Bachman, and invited Cendrosky to join him   3

Susan Estrich is an author, lawyer, professor, and political commentator.

in walking their daughter down the aisle. There was not a dry eye in the house.

The wedding photographer, herself a stepmother, took the photo-graphs and posted them on Facebook, where they have been "Liked" by more than a million viewers. 4

With half of all marriages ending in divorce, families are not what they used to be. When I grew up, divorce was rare and often scandal-ous, particularly in states that required "grounds" for divorce. The 1970s brought a radical shift, with the sexual revolution (which I've always thought only liberated men, and put unbelievable pressure on women), and no-fault divorce (ditto) bringing divorce to almost every neighbor-hood in America, including mine. 5

Since I was all of 19 at the time, I didn't think of either of my parents' subsequent spouses as my stepmother and stepfather. That was, at least in part, because the woman my father married was a world-class jerk (the true description would not belong in a family paper) who thought she was marrying a rich guy, and was bitterly disappointed when it turned out that he wasn't. Even small gifts to his children had to be hidden in the car. 6

When it rained on the day of my college graduation (36 hours after I'd been raped) and we only got two tickets, my father didn't come, because his wife didn't want him going with my mother and without her. He kept the gift he'd bought for me in the trunk of his car, so his wife wouldn't know, and when his car was stolen, so was the gift. Three years later he died and the witch gave me back the radio I'd given my dad, but absolutely nothing of his to remember him by or to show the grandchil-dren he would never know. As for my first "stepfather" — the man my mother married on the rebound — the best thing I can say about him is that this abusive man didn't last long. When he came at my mother with a knife after she attended my father's funeral, she moved out. 7

So I'm the last person you'd expect to write an ode to stepparents. But the story of that wedding in Ohio touched my heart and reminded me that all stepparents are not alike. As an adult, I have seen many of my friends strug-gle to love and be loved by children who are not their own. Sometimes it doesn't work. But when it does, it is a blessing. 8

> Sometimes it doesn't work. But when it does, it is a blessing.

As Todd Cendrosky, the stepfather, de-scribed it to reporters, "He came and grabbed my hand, and said, 'You worked as hard as I have. You'll help us walk our daughter down the aisle.' I got weak in the knees and lost it. Nothing better in my life. The most impactful moment in my life." 9

"Our daughter." No one ever said divorce was good for children,   10
although sometimes it is the best option available. But as these two men
showed, divorce does not have to destroy a family. It takes a big man to
share his daughter's arm on that special day, and a big man to raise a step-
daughter with love and attention. Congratulations to the bride and her
fathers. God bless.

VOCABULARY/USING A DICTIONARY
1. What is an *ode* (para. 8)?
2. How do you define *believable*? What is the definition of *unbelievable* (para. 5)?
3. What is a synonym for *option* (para. 10)?

RESPONDING TO WORDS IN CONTEXT
1. What does the word *impactful* (para. 9) mean?
2. What does the phrase *radical shift* (para. 5) indicate about what was happening in the 1970s?
3. When the writer says that seeing a blended family work is a *blessing* (para. 8),
what does she mean?

DISCUSSING MAIN POINT AND MEANING
1. How does Estrich feel about her own blended families? Would you
have expected her to have a wedding like the one Bachman's daughter
experienced?
2. How is the Bachman/Cendrosky family different from the family Estrich grew
up in?
3. Why did Bachman choose to include Cendrosky in the wedding ceremony?

EXAMINING SENTENCES, PARAGRAPHS, AND ORGANIZATION
1. How does Estrich draw the reader into the essay from the first paragraph?
2. What do you make of the use of the parenthetical comment in the first
sentence of paragraph 7? Is it necessary? Why or why not?
3. How does Estrich's conclusion reflect the content of her essay?

THINKING CRITICALLY
1. When Estrich writes "families are not what they used to be" (para. 5), what
does she mean?
2. Why is Estrich writing this article? Explain your answer.
3. What does the wedding example indicate about divorce today? Do you think
this sort of experience is more common than it used to be? Why or why not?

WRITING ACTIVITIES

1. Do you think something like divorce can bring about a good effect (like the one Estrich describes)? Write about the effects divorce can have on a family, both positive and negative. Feel free to draw from Estrich's essay and make conjectures of your own.

2. Find an article that has an uplifting story or message — look in print or online magazines devoted to reporting stories that might have a meaningful or optimistic outlook (*Good* at www.good.is might be a useful online magazine to examine). Once you've found your article, in a short written response, compare it to the one by Estrich. How is the article structured? Do the two articles share a similar progression and resolution? Do you think your article is important and teaches something to its reader?

3. Estrich has pinpointed one version of the modern family. Can you think of others? Create a list of types of families that are not like the families of 1950s America. How many can you think of? What makes them different from the families of sixty years ago?

Kyle Waltman (student essay)

Saying "I Love You"

[*The Reflector*, Mississippi State University, February 11, 2016]

BEFORE YOU READ

Have you ever thought about what the words *I love you* really mean? How do you define *love*?

WORDS TO LEARN

undoubtedly (para. 1): without question (adverb)

rampant (para. 4): predominant (adjective)

assert (para. 5): to state confidently (verb)

discredit (para. 5): to give no credit to (verb)

constitute (para. 6): to compose or form (verb)

contingent (para. 6): dependent upon (adjective)

circumstance (para. 7): the conditions of a situation (noun)

Kyle Waltman is a student at Mississippi State University.

I love you." We have all said those three words with as little effort as it takes to breathe. Maybe it was to a parent before you left home to drive back to Starkville, or maybe you whispered it into the ear of someone special cuddled up on your couch. Maybe you exchanged that magical phrase this morning over a text message, or maybe it has been so long, you have forgotten what it feels like to hear someone say "I love you too." Regardless of who you said it to or how long it has been since you have said it, you have undoubtedly used the word "love" to describe an overwhelming feeling of attachment, desire, joy, and thankfulness to someone who means or meant a lot to you.

Love, of course, exists in a variety of different forms, yet I firmly believe the form of love we understand the least is the very form that our culture idolizes the most: romantic love.

What does it mean to "fall in love" with someone? Is it an emotion? Is it a choice? Is it both? Is loving someone a subjective or objective concept? These questions are not easily answered, yet they point to the vital importance of understanding both the love that we accept and the love that we give.

The Merriam-Webster dictionary defines *love* as "a feeling of strong or constant affection for a person," or "attraction that includes sexual desire." The former of these two attempts to balance only half of the love equation, and the latter is the perfect example of why our perverted concepts regarding what romantic love should look and feel like are so rampant.

If love is a "constant affection for a person," then I assert that nobody is capable of experiencing true love. Our affection for others, be it our spouses, our children, or our friends, can be described in a number of ways, but *constant* is not one of them. This is not to say that affection stops altogether, of course, but it is to acknowledge the inconsistency of human emotion. Personal intimacy brings forth a beautiful connection unlike any other, yet with this closeness comes the recognition and clarity of character flaws. As the cliché goes, nobody is perfect, and because of this, we will not wake up every single day for the rest of our lives and feel like showing unhinged love to the ones we commit ourselves to. That being said, the simple fact that our affection wavers due to circumstance does not discredit or devalue our promise to love that person with our entire body, soul, and mind.

> This is not to say that affection stops altogether, of course, but it is to acknowledge the inconsistency of human emotion.

As far as the definition regarding "sexual desire" goes, people often buy into the idea that sexual attraction and love are heavily linked. This is evident by the way teenagers and some adults treat the foundation of love as though it is little more than an emotion rooted in attraction. While some certainly cherish sexual intimacy as the ultimate physical display of love, sex, in and of itself, has absolutely nothing to do with loving someone. Having a strong physical attraction to someone while also finding that person to be nice and funny is no more a spark of true love than finding someone sexually attractive at a frat party constitutes a marriage proposal. Furthermore, if your desire to be with someone is primarily contingent on that person's physical or sexual attractiveness rather than on that person as a special, unique individual, then the foundation of your relationship was built on lust, not love.

This idea that love is centered around constant affection and sexual desire completely misses the mark. To say "I love you" is to say "I choose you today, tomorrow, and every day thereafter because you are the one that I want." To say "I love you" is to say "I see the good and the bad in you, and still, I choose you." To say "I love you" is to say "I choose to have these eyes for you and you only." Loving someone is a constant, conscious choice to show kindness, respect, loyalty, compassion, forgiveness, and appreciation for that person regardless of circumstance. The moment we begin to understand love as having a clear element of choice in its composition, we become capable of truly experiencing love with a heart of devotion and personal accountability long after the honeymoon phase has dissipated and reality has set in. 7

I know that some of you are in serious relationships, engaged, or married, while the rest of you are either going through a heartbreak, trying to stay single while you focus on your education, or waiting to feel the magic of falling in love. Perhaps, like myself, you said "I love you" to someone, yet you stopped choosing that person when the reality of the cost of love replaced the butterflies, or maybe you were on the opposite end of the pain and after your first big fight the person who said "I love you" chose to find comfort in the arms of another. Regardless of your experience with love, it is my sincerest hope that you all understand love for what it truly is, that you find it in the heart of someone who understands it too, and that you both choose to cherish the love that you share, forever and always. 8

Falling in love is certainly an emotional experience, but staying in love is a privilege of choice. Loving someone goes far beyond emotional and physical attraction and demands that a choice be made daily to guard your heart, body, and mind from the forces coaxing you to jump ship. If you are unwilling to make the daily choice to honor the promise of such a serious commitment, save someone the pain of a meaningless "I love you." 9

VOCABULARY/USING A DICTIONARY
1. What does it mean to *idolize* (para. 2) something?
2. How do you define the adjective *vital* (para. 3)?
3. If something has *dissipated* (para. 7), what happened to it?

RESPONDING TO WORDS IN CONTEXT
1. You may have an idea of what you mean when you call someone a *pervert*, but what are *"perverted* concepts" (para. 4)?
2. What is the opposite of *inconsistency* (para. 5)? What is the definition of *inconsistency* and of the word you have identified as its opposite?
3. What do you think Waltman means by *"unhinged* love" (para. 5)?

DISCUSSING MAIN POINT AND MEANING
1. What, according to Waltman, is the difference between lust and love?
2. What distinction does Waltman draw between falling in love and staying in love?
3. What is the choice that is being made in true love, according to Waltman?

EXAMINING SENTENCES, PARAGRAPHS, AND ORGANIZATION
1. What does Waltman's introduction tell us about the words "I love you"? Why do you think he starts his essay with that information?
2. How is Waltman's third paragraph different from his other paragraphs? Why do you think it is structured that way?
3. How does the dictionary definition of *love* miss the mark, according to Waltman? How many of his paragraphs are devoted to disproving Merriam-Webster's definition?

THINKING CRITICALLY
1. Waltman offers a number of different scenarios someone might find him- or herself in, but says there is one definition of *true love*. Do you think that definition applies to all of the various scenarios he describes? Explain your answer.
2. Do you think love is more of an emotion or a choice? How does Waltman define it? Which of Waltman's statements about love do you agree with, and which do you disagree with?
3. Do you understand what Waltman means by the "honeymoon phase" of a relationship (para. 7)? Why is it called that? What does that particular phase look and feel like?

WRITING ACTIVITIES

1. The final paragraph of Waltman's essay includes this sentence: "Loving someone goes far beyond emotional and physical attraction and demands that a choice be made daily to guard your heart, body, and mind from the forces coaxing you to jump ship." Take notes on Waltman's essay. How many different types of love are identified? Write down all the different forms of love you note as you read, and then try to group your list into more and more detailed categories. Does his statement about love apply to each possibility you identify? Discuss as a class.

2. How do you define "falling in love"? How do you define "staying in love"? Where are they the same, and where are they different? In a short comparison and contrast essay, compare these two states of being in love. You may bring Waltman's arguments into the discussion as well as your own.

3. Waltman claims that the type of love our culture understands the least is romantic love. What sort of ideas, feelings, and images do you associate with romantic love? Which of these are sustainable in the long term, and which are not? Write a response to Waltman that offers your understanding of romantic love and examines how our culture influences that understanding.

LOOKING CLOSELY

Editing Sexist Pronouns

Over one hundred years ago, the great British novelist W. Somerset Maugham wrote that in every love affair "there's always one who loves and one who lets himself be loved." Note that the way this is phrased (Maugham is referring here to heterosexual relationships) suggests that the one who loves must be female because the one loved is male ("himself"). Maugham did not intend this meaning — it could be either sex who loves and is loved — but the conventions of English grammar forced him into the male pronoun. Nouns like *one, someone,* or *person* are singular and require a singular pronoun. Although in conversation and informal writing many people today will avoid specificity of gender by using a plural pronoun ("there's always one who loves and one who lets *themselves* be loved"), that usage is still widely frowned upon in formal and academic writing. Many writing instructors suggest that the best way to avoid sexist pronouns and still retain proper grammatical usage is to rephrase the writing so that the nouns and pronouns remain consistent. For example, Maugham could have written that in every love affair "there are those who love and those who let themselves be loved." (For an argument defending the increasing use of *they* with a singular noun, see the "In Brief" selection in Chapter 11 on p. 371.)

In the original version of "Saying 'I Love You'" that appeared in the *Reflector*, Mississippi State's student newspaper, Kyle Waltman relied on the more informal plural pronoun to stay gender neutral. In editing his essay for this book, he revised his usage to adhere to the more formal conventions of English grammar. Below you will see the original and revised versions.

1
Uses singular nouns with plural pronouns

(1) Perhaps, like myself, you told <u>someone</u> that you loved <u>them</u>, yet you stopped choosing <u>them</u> when the reality of the cost of love replaced the butterflies, or maybe you were on the opposite end of the pain and <u>someone</u> told you <u>they</u> loved you, yet after your first big fight, <u>they</u> chose to find comfort in the arms of another.

2
Revision makes grammar more acceptable

(2) Perhaps, like myself, you said "I love you" to <u>someone,</u> yet you stopped choosing <u>that person</u> when the reality of the cost of love replaced the butterflies, or maybe you were on the opposite end of the pain and after your first big fight <u>the person</u> who said "I love you" chose to find comfort in the arms of another.

Lavanya Ramanathan

They Didn't Want an Arranged Marriage

[*The Washington Post Magazine*, February 14, 2016]

BEFORE YOU READ
Why might a couple search for common interests beyond the initial spark of passion? How might the arranged marriages of the past share similarities with online dating?

WORDS TO LEARN

voodoo (para. 1): magical rites associated with the practice of voodoo (noun)

tentatively (para. 4): hesitantly (adverb)

adamant (para. 9): unyielding (adjective)

forgo (para. 16): to give up (verb)

via (para. 16): by way of (preposition)

Lavanya Ramanathan is a features reporter for the Washington Post.

parlance (para. 20): a way of speaking (noun)

malign (para. 21): to slander or defame (verb)

amenable (para. 25): agreeable (adjective)

intrigue (para. 26): to captivate (verb)

sustain (para. 42): to keep going (verb)

pragmatic (para. 48): practical; realistic (adjective)

torrid (para. 48): passionate (adjective)

Sahil Rajan hadn't yet figured out how to upload his profile picture 1 to eHarmony, but when the site's matchmaking voodoo put forward a brown-eyed New York City beauty who also professed an interest in books, he pinged her anyway. He asked Devi Mehta what she was reading.

Although Mehta, a 31-year-old ad agency account manager, couldn't 2 see what the guy on the other end looked like, she took a chance, too. "*The Girl with the Dragon Tattoo*," she replied. And him?

Rajan, a 29-year-old software developer who lived in Jersey City, was 3 deep into *Atlas Shrugged*.

It was January 2011, and Rajan and Mehta, both Indian Americans, 4 were tentatively back on the market after recent relationships had flamed out. When they met at a restaurant, however, their differences seemed to compound.

"He's, like, 40 pounds lighter than me," Mehta recalled thinking. 5 "He's my height."

"I don't know about this Devi Mehta chick," Rajan told friends. 6

On the surface, this would not have the makings of a love story. And 7 yet, it is one.

> On the surface, this would not have the makings of a love story. And yet, it is one.

Mehta's parents had an arranged mar- 8 riage. Though Rajan's parents were in love when they wed, they had been steeped in Indian culture, which values community and family over romance.

Rajan and Mehta were adamant that 9 they didn't want arranged marriages themselves. Yet after unsuccessfully dating the American way, both decided to try splitting the difference. They would search for partners, rather than relying on anyone else to arrange a union. But they would focus on potential spouses who shared the same culture and offered the same promise of stability and commitment to family they had seen in their parents' marriages — and not worry so much about romance.

Thus, they gave each other more of a chance than they might have a 10 few years earlier. Although Rajan wasn't her type, "there's nothing wrong with this guy's character," Mehta reasoned to herself.

Almost five years later, I met the couple in Northeast Washington's 11
bustling Union Market to discuss marriage and love. Rajan, a Montgomery County native, joked that their marriage had been arranged, after all — "by an algorithm."

Mehta said that for her, the turning point came when she realized 12
that sometimes "you have to go back and listen to the people who've been married 50 years.

"Indian parents always say stuff like, 'It's not about love, it's about 13
family.' They married for family." She paused. "What is it they always say? 'The love comes later.' "

Once she shed her reservations, Mehta realized Rajan "understands 14
my family, my siblings, my world," she said. But there's more. "I feel happy and loved and fulfilled, because he makes me feel that way."

She looked over at Rajan. Bouncing on his knee in a pink fleece and 15
tiny flowered leggings was Diya, the couple's bright-eyed 7-month-old.

One Indian American couple deciding to forgo instantaneous sparks for 16
compatibility in other areas does not a trend make. But Rajan and Mehta may not be alone in forging what I call a "practical marriage" — focusing first on cultural similarities, financial goals and family, and trusting love will follow. Across the United States, thousands of Indian Americans are meeting via sites such as Shaadi.com, BharatMatrimony and the app Dil Mil, which allow them to search for such unromantic attributes such as language, education and economic status. It's unclear how many of them are children of arranged marriages and how that has shaped their views on love. But judging from a hit movie on the subject, *Meet the Patels*, there is great interest in the topic.

Actor and filmmaker Ravi Patel and his sister, Geeta Patel, cre- 17
ated the documentary, which follows Ravi's practical search for an Indian bride and his quest to understand his parents' views on love and marriage.

"In the few times I stopped to think about the future, it was a picture 18
of an Indian woman, little Indian kids," Patel told me when we met late last year during a publicity tour for the film. When, as 30 approached and he instead found himself ending a long relationship with a white girlfriend he had hidden from his parents, he decided to try to find the woman of his dreams his parents' way.

"I love being Indian. I love being American, too," he said. "I think 19
most people from our generation feel this way: Don't care that much about religion. Love culture, love the rituals that come with culture. I want to keep that going in my life, selfishly, and I want my kids to feel the same thing."

So Patel polished his résumé — called biodata in the parlance of   20
Indian arranged marriages — and set out to speed date with a series of
Indian women who had been vetted by his parents, among others.

Did he feel shame, I asked, succumbing to the system of arranged   21
unions so maligned in the West?

"It's embarrassing," he conceded. "But the same shame we're talking   22
about is the exact same shame every person I've ever met has when they
start Internet dating."

In fact, he said, Internet dating may have opened the doors to being   23
honest about the practical things we're looking for. Kids, faithfulness, a
401(k).

"The only difference with the biodata process is maybe your parents   24
are agenting the process — and maybe that's not a bad thing, to have
someone overseeing things.

"You figure out a new way to approach the dream," Patel said. "You   25
become more amenable to new ways to finding the person we love."

I first learned of Rajan and Mehta's unusual approach to marriage   26
a year ago, while hanging out with a cousin who is close to Rajan. I
was intrigued. I, too, am a child of an arranged marriage who has long
heard the parental adage that love can come later. And, after failing
more times than I care to admit at dating the American way, like Rajan,
Mehta and Patel, I've become more amenable to the idea of a new kind
of search.

This is a radical change for me: I was only 7, maybe 8, the first time   27
I insisted to my mother that I planned on falling in love and getting married. After all, my generation camped out in front of the television in the
early-morning hours to watch Diana Spencer marry her prince, and went
to the movies to see Richard Gere shower Julia Roberts in gems as if she
were Eliza Doolittle in thigh-high boots. I wanted that kind of romance,
the meet-cute, for fate to arrange my love life.

For a long time, despite my youthful protestations, my parents   28
expected my love life would go the way theirs had. My mother, Lakshmi,
met my father, Raghupathy, at her parents' house in 1973 in what was
then Madras, in southern India. He was 28 and set to leave in weeks for a
postdoctoral fellowship 8,000 miles away in Philadelphia. But first, prod-
ded by his parents, he took an overnight train to meet the 22-year-old
beanpole of a girl with a promising horoscope and a thick braid of jet-
black hair running down her back. They talked, briefly, about her cooking
skills and whether she hoped to work after marriage (her music degree,
my father says, made him worry about her job prospects).

I asked my parents, now married for more than 40 years, why they'd 29 agreed to let their parents dictate their love lives.

"It was all we knew," my mother said. She had seen so many good 30 marriages, she trusted the system would work for her.

Knowing next to nothing about each other, did they at least feel a 31 spark?

"Sometimes, the very first opinion is the girl is too big . . . or her face 32 is different, and you have disappointment," my father said.

All he will reveal about my mother is, "She was not disappointing 33 to me."

"I thought he was cute!" my mom chimed in, laughing. 34

They wed 12 days later. 35

So, could there be some truth in our parents' insistence that romance 36 grows over time? And does it mean that we, no matter our ethnicity, should focus on other, more practical matters in our search for a mate?

Indian parents aren't the only ones who believe it. Research backs 37 the theory.

Pamela Regan, a psychology professor at Cal State University in Los 38 Angeles, conducted a study that compared arranged marriages and love marriages among Americans of Indian descent. She found that 10 years into the relationships, satisfaction and passion among the couples whose marriages were arranged nearly mirrored those of the love matches.

"I love romantic love," she said. "But these things do fade. They're 39 probably not the best thing to focus on when choosing a partner."

Why, then, do Americans place so much emphasis on passion? 40

According to Ty Tashiro, a New York–based psychologist and author 41 of *The Science of Happily Ever After*, a decline in the mortality rate and the rise of Romanticism in the 1800s played roles.

With more potential mates, people began to have "the luxury to 42 choose someone based on something other than their ability to put food on the table," said Tashiro. Meanwhile, the new ideas about romantic love dovetailed with concepts of free will. It "became a moral imperative to choose somebody with whom you were passionately in love, rather than somebody who was just practical," Tashiro said. According to the romantic ideal, that passion "would sustain you for a lifetime of love."

But divorce has also risen dramatically since the late 1800s. According 43 to data from the Centers for Disease Control and Prevention, in 2014, there were 6.9 marriages for every 1,000 people and 3.2 divorces.

"The romantic ideal," Tashiro said, "hasn't worked out like we 44 thought it would."

* * *

Who is doing the better job of choosing their spouses, I want to know.   45
(Of course I do.) The people who decide based on romantic notions, or
those aiming for compatibility, if not fireworks?

Tashiro laughed when I posed this question to him.   46

"The answer is that it's the people who are able to do a little bit of   47
both," he said. Shared religious values are good indicators of stable marriages, and similar backgrounds also help, Tashiro said. "When you have
family and friends who are supportive of your relationship, there's good
data that exists that that's a protective factor for a marriage."

He added: "Although people who are pragmatic and cautious are not   48
the most thrilling partners for a torrid romance, they are exactly the kind
of person who is well-suited to sustaining a 50-year-long relationship
with the same person."

Mehta and Rajan say they hope their relationship can last that long.   49
They moved in together in Jersey City in August 2012, remodeled a
condo and married in 2014. Diya was born a year later.

When they compare their marriage to that of their friends who may   50
have had more hot-and-heavy beginnings, how do they think they're faring? I asked.

"I think we're happier than they are," Rajan said. "I do."   51

VOCABULARY/USING A DICTIONARY

1. What does it mean for people to be *compatible*? What is *compatibility*
   (para. 16)?

2. If someone is *vetted* (para. 20), what has happened to them?

3. What is an *adage* (para. 26)?

RESPONDING TO WORDS IN CONTEXT

1. What is *matchmaking* (para. 1)?

2. What part of speech is *compound* in paragraph 4?

3. What part of speech is *shed* in paragraph 14? What does it mean?

DISCUSSING MAIN POINT AND MEANING

1. When Rajan and Mehta began looking for a partner, what qualities were
   they looking for in a mate?

2. Why is so much emphasis in today's romantic relationships put on falling in
   love and passion? What was the emphasis before that time?

3. What happened in the 1800s that gave rise to the idea that passion was the
   most important factor in a relationship?

EXAMINING SENTENCES, PARAGRAPHS, AND ORGANIZATION

1. How many quotations does Ramanathan weave into this essay? What do the quotations add? (Give examples.)

2. What detail about Mehta captures Rajan's interest in the essay's first sentence? How does it begin their "romance"?

3. Does paragraph 28 mimic anything about paragraph 1 in this essay? How are the two paragraphs similar? How are they different?

THINKING CRITICALLY

1. What is dating "the American way" (para. 9)? How is the approach Rajan and Mehta have taken different?

2. Are the marriages described here the same as the couples' parents' arranged marriages?

3. What sort of things help sustain a marriage that lasts twenty, forty, or sixty years? What elements might not last?

WRITING ACTIVITIES

1. In small groups, ask one member to interview the others about dating, romance, and marriage. The group should then work together to write a short piece about these subjects that weaves in interview quotations as part of the writing. Afterward, read a few examples to the class.

2. If you were going to ask a potential mate questions that might indicate your compatibility and the chance of stability and commitment in a relationship, what would they be? Create a list of such questions, keeping in mind the different questions and considerations in Ramanathan's essay.

3. Write a short response that argues for the importance of passionate love or the importance of practical considerations (shared culture, interests, financial stability, or other factors) in a marriage. Try to stick to one argument — even if you see the benefits of the other side. Make at least three specific points that support your position.

Spotlight on Data and Research

Wendy Wang and Kim Parker
Record Share of Americans Have Never Married
[Pew Research Center, September 24, 2014]

As social values, economics, and gender patterns change, so does the institution of marriage, according to the most recent Pew Research Center's data on the subject. People, it seems, are now marrying much later than ever before in our history. In 1960, the median age for those entering a first marriage was twenty for women and twenty-three for men; today that figure is twenty-seven for women and twenty-nine for men. The survey report also "finds a public that is deeply divided over the role marriage plays in society." Along with the research data reported below, the writers offer some possible explanations for the changes.

Rising Share of Never-Married Adults, Growing Gender Gap

% of men and women ages 25 and older who have never been married

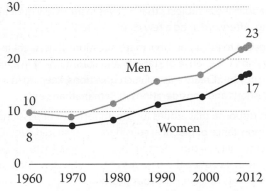

Source: Pew Research Center analysis of the 1960–2000 decennial census and 2010–2012 American Community Survey, Integrated Public Use Microdata Series (IPUMS)

PEW RESEARCH CENTER

After decades of declining marriage rates and changes in family structure, the share of American adults who have never been married is at a historic high. In 2012, one-in-five adults ages 25 and older (about 42 million people) had never been married, according to a new Pew   1

Research Center analysis of census data. In 1960, only about one-in-ten adults (9%) in that age range had never been married. Men are more likely than women to have never been married (23% vs. 17% in 2012). And this gender gap has widened since 1960, when 10% of men ages 25 and older and 8% of women of the same age had never married.

The dramatic rise in the share of never-married adults and the 2 emerging gender gap are related to a variety of factors. Adults are marrying later in life, and the shares of adults cohabiting and raising children outside of marriage have increased significantly. The median age at first marriage is now 27 for women and 29 for men, up from 20 for women and 23 for men in 1960. About a quarter (24%) of never-married young adults ages 25 to 34 are living with a partner, according to Pew Research analysis of Current Population Survey data.

In addition, shifting public attitudes, hard economic times and 3 changing demographic patterns may all be contributing to the rising share of never-married adults.

This trend cuts across all major racial and ethnic groups but has 4 been more pronounced among blacks. Fully 36% of blacks ages 25 and older had never been married in 2012, up from 9% in 1960. For whites, the share of never-married adults has doubled over that same period. In 2012, 16% of whites had never been married, compared with 8% in 1960.

Recent survey data from the Pew Research Center finds a public 5 that is deeply divided over the role marriage plays in society. Survey respondents were asked which of the following statements came closer to their own views: Society is better off if people make marriage and having children a priority, or society is just as well-off if people have priorities other than marriage and children. Some 46% of adults chose the first statement, while 50% chose the second.

Opinions on this issue differ sharply by age — with young adults 6 much more likely than older adults to say society is just as well-off if people have priorities other than marriage and children. Fully two-thirds of those ages 18 to 29 (67%) express this viewpoint, as do 53% of those ages 30 to 49. Among those ages 50 and older, most (55%) say society is better off if people make it a priority to get married and have children.

Despite these mixed views about the role of marriage in society, 7 most Americans (68%) continue to believe it is important for couples to marry if they plan to spend the rest of their lives together. Roughly half of all adults (47%) believe that this is very important, and an additional 21% consider it somewhat important.

While blacks are more likely than whites to have never been mar- 8 ried (and less likely to be currently married), a much higher share of blacks (58%) than whites (44%) say that it's very important for a couple to marry if they plan to spend their lives together.

continued

DRAWING CONCLUSIONS

1. Note that nearly a quarter of never-married young adults are living with a partner. In what ways does this information affect your interpretation of the data?

2. Of what importance is it that 50 percent of adult respondents thought that "society is just as well-off if people have priorities other than marriage and children" (para. 5)?

3. Compare the Pew Center's data to Justice Kennedy's celebration of marriage in the conclusion to his Supreme Court opinion on same-sex marriage (see p. 336). Does knowing this data have any effect on your response to his decision? Explain why or why not.

Emma Goldman

Marriage and Love

[*Anarchism and Other Essays*, 1910]

By the end of the nineteenth century and the early decades of the twentieth, the United States had entered the modern world. Industry and manufacturing transformed cities nearly overnight; inventors like Thomas Edison unprecedentedly altered the expectations of average people; newly formed advertising firms promoted the first brand-name goods with logos and created a new type of American — the consumer — and amidst these rapid changes artists, novelists, and dramatists began to challenge long-standing societal and cultural norms. One sacred institution revered by religion and society that activists and intellectuals attacked in many different ways was marriage. By the outbreak of the First World War in 1914 and the raucous era of the 1920s that F. Scott Fitzgerald named "The Jazz Age," only fairy tales would end ". . . and they lived happily ever after."

Marriage, of course, is still a respected institution, and a thriving business, if we look at the costs of a traditional wedding. Yet, despite the alarming divorce rate and the economic difficulties many couples experience today, people still debate the value of marriage and many still believe it is an institution worth saving. Over one hundred years ago, the following essay, "Marriage and Love," appeared on the same topic, yet this one (shockingly for its time) did not offer advice on how to save the institution of marriage; instead, it severely criticized marriage and suggested the lives of both women and men would be better if it were abolished. The author of the essay was political activist and anarchist Emma Goldman (1869–1940). One of the leading figures in the history of radical American politics, the Lithuanian-born Goldman came to the United States in her teens, where she soon embraced the causes of women and laborers. Goldman founded the magazine Mother Earth *in 1906 and in 1910 published her influential book,* Anarchism and Other Essays, *from which the following selection is taken. A popular lecturer on politics and literature, Goldman was imprisoned in 1917 and two years later deported to the Soviet Union.*

The popular notion about marriage and love is that they are synony- 1
mous, that they spring from the same motives, and cover the same
human needs. Like most popular notions this also rests not on actual
facts, but on superstition.

Marriage and love have nothing in common; they are as far apart 2
as the poles; are, in fact, antagonistic to each other. No doubt some
marriages have been the result of love. Not, however, because love
could assert itself only in marriage; much rather is it because few people
can completely outgrow a convention. There are today large numbers
of men and women to whom marriage is naught but a farce, but who
submit to it for the sake of public opinion. At any rate, while it is true
that some marriages are based on love, and while it is equally true that
in some cases love continues in married life, I maintain that it does so
regardless of marriage, and not because of it.

On the other hand, it is utterly false that love results from marriage. 3
On rare occasions one does hear of a miraculous case of a married
couple falling in love after marriage, but on close examination it will
be found that it is a mere adjustment to the inevitable. Certainly the
growing used to each other is far away from the spontaneity, the inten-
sity, and beauty of love, without which the intimacy of marriage must
prove degrading to both the woman and the man.

Marriage is primarily an economic arrangement, an insurance 4
pact. It differs from the ordinary life insurance agreement only in that
it is more binding, more exacting. Its returns are insignificantly small
compared with the investments. In taking out an insurance policy one
pays for it in dollars and cents, always at liberty to discontinue payments. If, however, a woman's premium is a husband, she pays for it
with her name, her privacy, her self-respect, her very life, "until death
doth part." Moreover, the marriage insurance condemns her to life-long
dependency, to parasitism, to complete uselessness, individual as well
as social. Man, too, pays his toll, but as his sphere is wider, marriage
does not limit him as much as woman. He feels his chains more in an
economic sense.

Thus Dante's motto over Inferno applies with equal force to mar- 5
riage: "Ye who enter here leave all hope behind."[1]

---

[1] Dante's motto (para. 5): Famous line from *Inferno* (Italian for "hell"), the long
poem by Dante Alighieri (1265–1321)

That marriage is a failure none but the very stupid will deny. One   6
has but to glance over the statistics of divorce to realize how bitter a
failure marriage really is. Nor will the stereotyped Philistine argument
that the laxity of divorce laws and the growing looseness of woman
account for the fact that: first, every twelfth marriage ends in divorce;
second, that since 1870 divorces have increased from 28 to 73 for
every hundred thousand population; third, that adultery, since 1867, as
ground for divorce, has increased 270.8 per cent.; fourth, that desertion
increased 369.8 per cent.

Added to these startling figures is a vast amount of material, dra-   7
matic and literary, further elucidating this subject. Robert Herrick, in
Together; Pinero, in *Mid-Channel*; Eugene Walter, in *Paid in Full*,[2] and
scores of other writers are discussing the barrenness, the monotony,
the sordidness, the inadequacy of marriage as a factor for harmony and
understanding.

The thoughtful social student will not content himself with the   8
popular superficial excuse for this phenomenon. He will have to dig
down deeper into the very life of the sexes to know why marriage proves
so disastrous.

Edward Carpenter[3] says that behind every marriage stands the   9
life-long environment of the two sexes; an environment so different
from each other that man and woman must remain strangers. Separated
by an insurmountable wall of superstition, custom, and habit, marriage
has not the potentiality of developing knowledge of, and respect for,
each other, without which every union is doomed to failure.

In our present pygmy state love is indeed a stranger to most   10
people. Misunderstood and shunned, it rarely takes root; or if it does,
it soon withers and dies. Its delicate fiber can not endure the stress and
strain of the daily grind. Its soul is too complex to adjust itself to the
slimy woof of our social fabric. It weeps and moans and suffers with
those who have need of it, yet lack the capacity to rise to love's summit.

Some day, some day men and women will rise, they will reach the   11
mountain peak, they will meet big and strong and free, ready to receive,

---

[2] Herrick, Pinero, Walter (para. 7): Popular literary figures of the day who challenged conventional morals

[3] Carpenter (para. 9): Highly influential author of many books on marriage and
human sexuality who was considered one of the earliest champions of gay rights
and lived 1844–1929

to partake, and to bask in the golden rays of love. What fancy, what imagination, what poetic genius can foresee even approximately the potentialities of such a force in the life of men and women? If the world is ever to give birth to true companionship and oneness, not marriage, but love will be the parent.

BACKGROUND AND CONTEXT

1. A popular Frank Sinatra song said that "love and marriage go together like a horse and carriage." How does Emma Goldman's opinion differ? Which does she value and why?

2. Goldman partly makes a case against marriage by citing divorce statistics. Do you think that the likelihood a marriage will end in divorce acts as a deterrent to a couple deciding to get married? Explain why or why not.

STRATEGY, STRUCTURE, AND STYLE

1. Note Goldman's analogy of a marriage to a life insurance policy. According to her, what do they have in common? What differences does she acknowledge? Evaluate her analogy. Explain whether or not you think it works as a description of marriage.

2. Consider Goldman's reference to Edward Carpenter's view of the "two sexes" (para. 9). Do you think it is applicable even today, or in your opinion do boys and girls grow up understanding each other better than they did a hundred years ago? How does Carpenter's view help support her argument?

COMPARISONS AND CONNECTIONS

1. Read Goldman's 1910 essay together with Suzy Khimm's "The New Nuclear Family" (p. 337). Based on Goldman's reasoning about marriage, what do you think her opinion would be on same-sex marriage? Or you may also want to compare Goldman's essay to Judy Brady's "I Want a Wife" (p. 390). How does Goldman's older feminist position contrast to Brady's 1970s feminism?

2. In a brief essay, compare Goldman's essay to Frederick Douglass's "What to a Slave, Is the Fourth of July?" address (p. 206). Although Goldman does not address the subject of race relations, can you find any points in common? Can you find any similar images or metaphors? Compare how each author and activist concludes his or her argument.

Discussing the Unit

SUGGESTED TOPIC FOR DISCUSSION

With the 2015 decision of the Supreme Court case *Obergefell v. Hodges*, which guarantees the right to marry for same-sex couples, the concept of marriage in the United States began to change. However, beyond this landmark decision, marriage has already been transforming from the traditional model over the last few decades. The writers in this chapter explore what marriages (and alternatives to marriage) used to look like throughout history and what they have come to look like today. What do you think is the future of marriage? Do you think today's younger generation is as interested in preserving the institution as are older generations?

PREPARING FOR CLASS DISCUSSION

1. When you imagine a marriage, what picture comes to mind? (Who is married? What do married life and families look like?) How many different configurations beyond the "traditional" marriage or family model can you think of? Do you think that a person your age thirty, fifty, or a hundred years ago would have had the same ideas about marriage and family and what it looks like?

2. Can you define *love*, as it is presented in these essays? Is it a choice or an emotion? Is it lasting, and can it endure permutations? Does it have to start off full-blown, or can it grow and deepen without a passionate beginning? Can it be as strong outside of marriage as it is within a marriage? In other words, is marriage necessary?

FROM DISCUSSION TO WRITING

1. Who do we look for, and what are we looking for, in a marriage partner? Consider the arguments made about marriage and desirable qualities in a marriage partner, and write an essay that outlines what people are looking for in these areas. What are their priorities? Do these priorities suggest a marriage will last? Why or why not? Cite at least three essays from this chapter.

2. Do you think we find a life partner through chemistry — love at first sight — or does falling in love require more thought? Write a brief persuasive essay that argues in favor of passionate love as the basis for finding a long-term partner or in favor of more rational selection. How do the writers in this chapter address this question? Make your case with their arguments in mind.

TOPICS FOR CROSS-CULTURAL DISCUSSION

1. Do Americans approach marriage differently than people in other countries do? What evidence in this chapter's essays suggests that possibility? How do Americans approach marriage, and how, if at all, is that approach changing?

2. Until *Obergefell v. Hodges*, marriage was defined as the legal union between one man and one woman. Why do you think marriage was defined in that way? What were some of the reasons marriage was important in human society? How has our perception of marriage changed over time, and what is the purpose of marriage today? Explain your answers, using examples from the essays in this chapter.

11

Gender: What Are the Issues Today?

In early 2016, the North Carolina legislature created a firestorm by passing House Bill 2, nicknamed the "bathroom bill," a law effectively banning many transgender people from using the public bathrooms of the gender with which they identify. Some conservatives applauded the law as a bulwark against what they saw as the anarchy of modern gender identity: society's increased recognition of an individual's right to determine his or her own gender, as opposed to biological sex. The logical end, they argue, is that anyone can use either bathroom according to a fluid, ever-changing self-definition, creating uncomfortable scenarios and even perhaps encouraging predators.

LGBT advocates, of course, slammed the bill as a form of backdoor discrimination against trans people, one that would further marginalize what they call one of the country's most marginalized groups. Businesses and popular musicians boycotted the state, and protesters on both sides held massive rallies. The bill and its fallout underscores a recent shift in our country's ongoing conversation about gender. Once preoccupied entirely with securing an equal place for women within society, gender studies departments in universities and gender equity movements have both shifted to promoting a more equitable overall understanding of gender, including for those who don't identify with the gender corresponding to their biological sex, or for that matter to "male" or "female" gender identities at all.

This new tension has played out even in the English language, in which some LGBT advocates suggest subtle forms of discrimination persist even as society becomes more inclusive. In 2015, the American Dialect Society voted for the singular pronoun *they*, and by extension *them* and *their* (as in "Whoever is elected president will have their work cut out for them"), as its Word of the Year. Once considered grammatically incorrect, the use of *they* to replace *he or she* when the gender of the person spoken about is uncertain has gained acceptance, especially online. This chapter's "In Brief" feature highlights the vote, in which phrases like "on fleek" and "thanks, Obama" were runners-up, and emphasizes the central role *they* now plays, particularly as "an identifier for someone who may identify as 'nonbinary' in gender terms."

This chapter's student essay, by Katie Davis of the University of Georgia, seeks to place the "bathroom bill" in a context greater than the specific state law: The bill, she writes, is "most relevant to North Carolina, but it has implications for everyone, in all states." Davis takes on the bill's proponents, arguing that the law is nothing but a blow to the liberty of trans people and that arguments about safety are wrongheaded and possibly insincere.

Naturally, big issues remain in our national conversation about women's rights in particular, issues that may extend ultimately to gender-fluid people but which, in the present, are framed by females. One issue that has persisted for over half a century is the "pay gap," the difference between women's and men's wages. Academics, politicians, and advocates often quote one of a few influential studies showing, they say, fairly conclusively that women are paid around 73 cents for every dollar a man earns. A selection by Brett Arends challenges this long-cited finding, suggesting that other factors, more subtle than gender discrimination, may be at play in the gap, most of which, he writes, "is explained by personal choices being made by millions of individual women and men." Arends believes that the jobs women choose to do, as well as their greater emphasis on childcare and family life, account for a (much smaller) wage gap that he guesses is around 5 percent.

The very question of what jobs women take, though, presents its own set of problems. Many social theorists disagree with Arends's position, claiming that behind the jobs women happen to have is merely the illusion of choice — stubborn gender roles continue to define real options. In some cases, though, feminists have been hesitant to argue for job equality, particularly where they consider the job problematic. In 1980, during the debates over the failed Equal Rights Amendment to the Constitution, many women's rights advocates balked at one particular collateral effect—eligibility for women would be automatic in the Selective Service, also known as the draft. As Christina Cauterucci writes, forty years have passed since then and it may be time to reconsider even the more unpleasant consequences of equal opportunities. Much of Cauterucci's reasoning, though, involves not women in combat positions but what the draft was originally intended to do. She writes, "If the draft is to have its desired effect—forcing decision-makers in the federal government to personally grapple with the severity of sending combat troops overseas and lessening the disproportionate consequences of war borne by poor communities and communities of color—women must be implicated by its reach."

Issues of pay and war loom large over the conversation about gender, but along with including nonwomen in the conversation, gender studies has also expanded in the last five years to discuss much more frankly the issues of "everyday feminism"—the problems of social interactions, often between men and women, that feminists claim disadvantage women and hold them down on the periphery of society. One common complaint among American women today is the tone with which they say men, both in in-person conversations and online, condescend to them with explanations of the way the world works—a phenomenon recently dubbed "mansplaining"—a runner-up, in fact, for 2013's Word of the Year from the American Dialect Society. In this chapter's "Spotlight on Data and Research," sociology professor and researcher Elizabeth Aura McClintock takes a scientific look at the issue, finding data to support the claim that large-scale condescension persists in intergender communication. She writes that the phenomenon "has caught the popular imagination because it provides a label for a common and offensive social reality: Women are often assumed to be ignorant and unintelligent, at least compared to men."

Almost all of these essays, though, whatever their positions on trans bathrooms and women's pay, essentially take for granted that men and women should be legal and social equals. In "America Then," we take a trip back to a time before that was a given. Judy Brady's essay "I Want a Wife" was practically inescapable for a student of composition when it came out in the first issue of the feminist magazine *Ms.* in 1972. "My God, who *wouldn't* want a wife?" Brady persuasively concludes after enumerating all the domestic services a dutiful wife provides. The essay almost certainly couldn't be published today, but ask yourself why not. Is its central argument still relevant? Perhaps Brady's sardonic appraisal of gender relations still applies to our modern dialogue and the goals of unity and individualism of each of its participants, however he, she, or they self-define.

American Dialect Society

The Word of the Year Is Singular *They*

[American Dialect Society, January 8, 2016]

*T*he American Dialect Society was founded in 1889. It describes itself on its Web site as "dedicated to the study of the English language in North America, and of other languages, or dialects of other languages, influencing it or influenced by it. Our members include academics and amateurs, professors and students, professionals and dilettantes, teachers and writers, undergraduates and graduates. Anyone can join the society!" Each year the society invites its members to vote on a word or phrase they consider especially significant to American culture and society. In 2014, for example, the word of the year was #blacklivesmatter. The following report announces the winner for 2015.

In its 26th annual words of the year vote, the American Dialect Society 1
voted for *they* used as a gender-neutral singular pronoun as the Word of the Year for 2015. *They* was recognized by the society for its emerging use as a pronoun to refer to a known person, often as a conscious choice by a person rejecting the traditional gender binary of *he* and *she*.

Presiding at the Jan. 8 voting session were ADS Executive Secretary 2
Allan Metcalf of MacMurray College and Ben Zimmer, chair of the New Words Committee of the American Dialect Society. Zimmer is also executive editor of Vocabulary.com and language columnist for the *Wall Street Journal*.

The use of singular *they* builds on centuries of usage, appearing in the 3
work of writers such as Chaucer, Shakespeare, and Jane Austen. In 2015, singular *they* was embraced by the *Washington Post* style guide. Bill Walsh, copy editor for the *Post*, described it as "the only sensible solution to English's lack of a gender-neutral third-person singular personal pronoun."

While editors have increasingly moved to accepting singular *they* 4
when used in a generic fashion, voters in the Word of the Year proceedings singled out its newer usage as an identifier for someone who may identify as "nonbinary" in gender terms.

"In the past year, new expressions of gender identity have generated a 5
deal of discussion, and singular *they* has become a particularly significant

element of that conversation," Zimmer said. "While many novel gender-neutral pronouns have been proposed, *they* has the advantage of already being part of the language."

Word of the Year is interpreted in its broader sense as "vocabulary item" — not just words but phrases. The words or phrases do not have to be brand-new, but they have to be newly prominent or notable in the past year.

The vote is the longest-running such vote anywhere, the only one not tied to commercial interests, and *the* word-of-the-year event up to which all others lead. It is fully informed by the members' expertise in the study of words, but it is far from a solemn occasion.

Members in the 127-year-old organization include linguists, lexicographers, etymologists, grammarians, historians, researchers, writers, editors, students, and independent scholars. In conducting the vote, they act in fun and do not pretend to be officially inducting words into the English language. Instead, they are highlighting that language change is normal, ongoing, and entertaining.

In a companion vote, sibling organization the American Name Society voted "*Caitlyn Jenner*" as Name of the Year for 2015 in its eleventh annual name-of-the-year contest, to recognize issues relating to naming conventions in the transgender community.

POINTS TO CONSIDER

1. What would you pick as the Word of the Year for this year? Why?

2. Some people claim a grammatical reason for keeping *they* plural — good style, they assert, demands a distinction between singular and plural pronouns. What arguments can you see on their side? Do you agree? Why or why not?

3. Many activists claim that pronoun inclusivity needs to go further and that all people should be able to choose their own unique pronouns. What do you think? Are there limits to how specialized pronouns should be in order to make everyone feel comfortable?

Katie Davis (student essay)

Gender-Neutral Bathrooms: Why They Matter

[*The Red and Black*, University of Georgia, April 11, 2016]

BEFORE YOU READ

Do state or federal governments have the right to mandate which bathrooms people must use? Do you think people who don't feel defined by their biological sex should have to use the bathroom of a particular gender?

WORDS TO LEARN

legitimacy (para. 1): the state or quality of being lawful (noun)

inherently (para. 1): intrinsically (adverb)

implication (para. 6): something implied (noun)

assertion (para. 9): statement (noun)

perpetuate (para. 10): to continue (verb)

North Carolina passed a law, House Bill 2, requiring individuals to use public restrooms in accordance with the sex indicated on their birth certificate — completely denying the legitimacy of an individual's gender identity. This bill is inherently discriminatory toward transgender people and it is unacceptable.   1

I have been concerned with the way bathrooms perpetuate the idea that people necessarily must choose a gender or sex and it must be their "biological sex" — according to the law, the sex an individual was born as. This definition creates problems in itself. HB2, commonly referred to as the "bathroom bill," has brought the issue to the public eye and brought more people than social justice activists into the discussion. Moments after this bill came into existence, my Facebook friends shared their opinions and divided themselves into two camps: those who think it is completely repulsive that people should use the same bathrooms and those who think people are all just people, so it should not matter which bathroom they use.   2

I pitch my tent in that second, more inclusive, camp. I have supported gender-neutral bathrooms for years and I will continue to support them.   3

Katie Davis is a philosophy and sociology major at the University of Georgia.

I am not alone in my support for gender-neutral bathrooms. Celeb- 4
rities, such as Bruce Springsteen, have canceled shows in North Carolina
in protest of the bill, and out-of-state companies have forbidden travel to
North Carolina unless it is absolutely necessary.

> Nothing will ever convince me that money matters more than people.

A common argument against more in- 5
clusive social policies is that they do not
matter as much as economic policies. I
have never agreed with such an argument
because nothing will ever convince me that
money matters more than people. However,
avoiding travel to North Carolina as a result
of the "bathroom bill" will have economic consequences for the state;
this is fascinating because it demonstrates how this absurd social policy
can affect the economic welfare of North Carolina. Perhaps crises like
these will convince individuals concerned more with economics than
people that social policies are just as important as, and arguably more
important than, economic policies.

The "bathroom bill" is now most relevant to North Carolina, but it 6
has implications for everyone, in all states. For example, this discriminatory bill has the potential to become law in other states as well.

Offering only divided bathrooms for males and females and perpetu- 7
ating the idea that sex and gender are purely biological obviously leads to
problems not just within trans communities but also for intersex people.
If someone is not defined as either male or female, how do we expect this
individual to use the public restrooms? And why does society even think
it is its business to police matters as private as going to the bathroom?

Of course, there is the misconception that bathrooms are segregated 8
for safety, but discriminatory laws do not make the bathroom any safer
for anyone. Someone who wants to harm another person in a public restroom is clearly not the type of person to be stopped by a simple law.

People also seem to believe that sharing public restrooms with all 9
other people would result in dirtier restrooms. However, I have never
been particularly impressed by the cleanliness of public restrooms in
general, so I do not think sharing them with other people would make
the situation worse. Those who believe bathrooms would be dirtier if we
all shared them tend to believe males are the ones who make public restrooms dirty. This argument is as sexist as a "boys will be boys" argument;
that is to say, men are not necessarily dirtier than women in a bathroom
and such an assertion is unfair to males.

Several students and organizations created campaigns at the Univer- 10
sity of Georgia Athens in support of gender-neutral bathrooms on campus, but as you have probably noticed, these campaigns have not been

particularly successful: Our campus bathrooms continue to perpetuate the idea that a gender binary exists and should be socially enforced.
People should be allowed to use the restroom based on their gender
identities.

VOCABULARY/USING A DICTIONARY

1. What does the prefix *trans* mean in *transgender* (para. 1)?

2. What is a *gender-neutral* (para. 4) bathroom?

3. What is the definition of *binary* (para. 10)?

RESPONDING TO WORDS IN CONTEXT

1. If someone is *perpetuating* (para. 2) an idea, what is happening to that idea?

2. What is another way of saying "this bill came into *existence*" (para. 2)?

3. What part of speech is *police* in paragraph 7? What does it mean in this context?

DISCUSSING MAIN POINT AND MEANING

1. How, according to Davis, did people respond when HB2 was introduced?

2. What are some of the reasons people offer for why transgender bathrooms
   aren't a good idea?

3. How does Davis respond to the arguments against transgender bathrooms?

EXAMINING SENTENCES, PARAGRAPHS, AND ORGANIZATION

1. Davis writes, "Of course, there is the misconception that bathrooms are segregated for safety, but discriminatory laws do not make the bathroom any
   safer for anyone" (para. 8). How does Davis use language in this sentence to
   express the problems with HB2?

2. Does Davis sum up her argument in the concluding paragraph? Which
   sentence states her position?

3. Davis wrote this essay from a first-person perspective. Do you think this
   essay benefits from this perspective? Why might Davis have chosen to use
   first person?

THINKING CRITICALLY

1. Is there a difference between trans people and intersex people (para. 7)?
   If so, what is it?

2. Do you think protests by celebrities will have an effect on the reception of
   HB2? Why or why not?

3. If the "bathroom bill" can pass in North Carolina, it can also pass in other states.
   Which states are more likely to pass such a bill? Which are less likely, and why?

WRITING ACTIVITIES

1. In a brief essay, discuss your reaction to HB2 and at the same time put yourself in one of the camps Davis describes: those who think it is completely repulsive for people to use the same bathrooms and those who think people are just people, so it should not matter which bathroom they use. It doesn't matter if you have different reasons than Davis does for why you are for or against HB2 — based on whether you are for or against, try to write partly from the perspective of your "camp."

2. Arguments about gender fall into three basic categories. Some argue that there are two inherent genders, male and female. Others argue that gender falls along a spectrum. And others argue that gender is imposed by society. In small groups, discuss the rigidity versus the fluidity of gender. Have one member of the group create a chart on a piece of paper, using the three categories listed here as column headings, and then take notes about the group's discussion (noting under each category when a point is raised or questioned in the group).

3. Identify some of the rationales for or against gender-neutral bathrooms that are mentioned in this essay. Using one statement as a starting point, respond to that statement and bring in examples to support what you say. Examples can be personal or based on research (if they are based on research, be sure to cite your sources).

LOOKING CLOSELY

Effective Persuasion: Expressing an Opinion Clearly and Emphatically

Although we should try to arrive at our opinions by openly exposing ourselves to conflicting or opposing opinions, that does not mean that once we have formed an opinion we cannot express it forcefully and passionately. Often, as many orators and political figures have learned, persuasion may require a direct, personal, and unambiguous declaration of where we stand on an issue. Observe how University of Georgia student Katie Davis opens her essay on a recent and controversial North Carolina law requiring that people must use public restrooms in accordance with their biological sex. In "Gender-Neutral Bathrooms: Why They Matter," Davis begins by summarizing the new law and immediately voicing a strong objection to it. Without using the first person (*I*), her opening paragraph makes it clear at once where she stands. She will use the rest of the essay to explain why she believes what she does, but she wants her opening to be clear and emphatic.

1 Effective summary of law	(1) North Carolina passed a law, House Bill 2, requiring individuals to use public restrooms in accordance with the sex indicated on their birth certificate — (2) completely
2 What the law denies	denying the legitimacy of an individual's gender identity. (3) This bill is inherently discriminatory toward transgen-
3 Emphatic declaration of objection	der people and it is unacceptable.

Brett Arends

The Idea of the "Gender Pay Gap" Is Mostly Bogus

[*MarketWatch*, April 14, 2016]

BEFORE YOU READ

What do you think explains the difference in average pay between men and women? Are there reasons besides gender that might cause one person to earn less than another?

WORDS TO LEARN

patrol (para. 3): the act of walking around, checking an area for safety (noun)

indulgent (para. 3): permissive (adjective)

obnoxious (para. 6): offensive (adjective)

depreciation (para. 6): a decrease in value (in this case, of money) (noun)

trump (para. 8): to outdo (verb)

consultancy (para. 10): a firm that offers consulting services (noun)

constitute (para. 12): to form (verb)

physique (para. 18): the appearance of one's body (noun)

residual (para. 19): remaining (adjective)

C an everyone please stop talking complete nonsense about the "gender pay gap"?

The recent "Equal Pay Day" has produced, once again, the tedious and predictable flood of half-truths and untruths about the relative pay of men and women.

1

2

Brett Arends is a writer and journalist who reports especially on finance, markets, and economics.

But repeating something over and over doesn't make it correct. A 3
million angry tweets do not rebut a single fact. And while it's terrific that
we are on patrol against unfair discrimination, it's terrible that we are
nationally so indulgent about lazy thinking.

No, women don't get paid 79 cents on the dollar for doing the same 4
work as men. Nothing like it. Nothing close.

Sorry, folks. But that's not what the data say. 5

Most of that gap is explained by personal choices being made by 6
millions of individual women and men — about whether to major in literature or economics in college, about whether to pursue a career at a nonprofit or a bank, and about whether you'd rather find yourself at 7 p.m. on
a Wednesday night in February sitting at home reading a bedtime story
to your children or sitting in a windowless conference room in Cleveland
arguing with an obnoxious client about depreciation schedules.

Most of the choices being made are being made freely. Indeed, the 7
gaps get bigger as you move up the socioeconomic scale, which is precisely where individuals have more power to choose.

> Who is to say
> someone has
> been "disadvan-
> taged" because
> they chose quality
> of life over more
> money?

When we focus on this 79-cents fig- 8
ure, we are actually being the opposite of
feminist. We are embracing a traditionally
"male" perspective, where money trumps
everything else. Who is to say someone has
been "disadvantaged" because they chose
quality of life over more money? On the
contrary, pretty much all psychological
research and historical wisdom point the
other way.

So why are we not instead talking about a male "gender gap" in qual- 9
ity of life?

When I was young, I worked for a blue-chip management consul- 10
tancy, stacked with Type-A MBAs. Most of the people at the top were
men. Yes, they earned a fortune. They also spent most of their time living
out of suitcases and flying around the world to meetings.

That's fun at 28. Not at 48. I didn't envy them at all. (Missing, too, is 11
any math on how money is spent, not just earned. If a wife owns 50% of a
couple's assets and spends 50% of the money, what is her real economic
share of the partnership?)

We are also forgetting to factor in one of the effects of the "glass ceil- 12
ing." Super-high earners, the "0.01%," are mostly men. But those earners constitute just a tiny share of the overall population, male or female.
Including billionaire hedge fund managers in the data boosts the "average
male income." But it doesn't mean one extra nickel to the typical male.

Meanwhile, we have to watch the female members of this tiny elite 13
wagging their fingers at the rest of us. A woman pockets tens of millions
by exploiting, underpaying or laying off thousands of ordinary workers.
If most of them are men, does that make her a feminist hero? Really?

Ma'am, if you think Arianna Huffington or Marissa Mayer is your 14
"sister," I have a used car to sell you. And a bridge.

Strip out all the personal choices and the data actually say that the 15
real apples-for-apples pay gap between men and women is in single
digits — maybe 5% to 8%.

Yes, that's still discrimination. Yes, that's unjust. Yes, that matters. 16
No, I'm neither justifying it nor dismissing it.

But here's what you don't hear: Much of that gap may actually be 17
accounted for by height.

No kidding. Research conducted in multiple countries has found 18
that shorter people earn less than taller people. Actually, a lot less. The
height penalty (or shortness penalty) is believed to be somewhere
between 1.5% to 6% per inch. It's astonishing, and bizarre. Some of the
explanations are rational (such as the advantages of a bigger physique in
some circumstances). Many of them aren't. People just give more respect
to taller people. Taller kids get more attention at school, in the classroom
and on the playground. They develop more confidence. Taller adults are
more likely to get promoted. And so on.

So the main residual issue may be height discrimination rather than 19
specific gender discrimination.

The "average" woman is about five inches shorter than the average 20
man. When you adjust for everything, including height, choices and so
on, a typical woman of 5 foot 5 inches may not earn much less than a
man of the same height doing exactly the same job. She might even earn
the same.

Sorry, folks. 21

Bring on the angry tweets . . . 22

VOCABULARY/USING A DICTIONARY

1. How might you feel if you had to do a job that was *tedious* (para. 2)?

2. What part of speech is *rebut* (para. 3)? What does it mean? If you don't know
   the definition, can you think of any words that share its root?

3. If someone is *exploiting* (para. 13) someone, what is he or she doing?

RESPONDING TO WORDS IN CONTEXT

1. Is the word *data* (para. 5) singular or plural?

2. What do you think Arends means by the term *socioeconomic scale* (para. 7)?

3. When Arends says he is neither *justifying* nor *dismissing* discrimination (para. 16), what does he mean?

DISCUSSING MAIN POINT AND MEANING

1. What explains the pay gap, according to Arends?
2. In response to the focus on the pay gap, what does he think men should be complaining about?
3. Who is the "tiny elite" he mentions in paragraph 13? What does Arends accuse its female members of?

EXAMINING SENTENCES, PARAGRAPHS, AND ORGANIZATION

1. How would you describe the diction Arends uses? How would you describe his tone?
2. Look at your answer to question 1 in this section. Why do you think Arends is choosing to write this way? How might a reader respond to his choice?
3. What rhetorical device is Arends using in paragraph 4? Does he use anything like it elsewhere in the essay?

THINKING CRITICALLY

1. Do you think a difference in pay is fair? Why? When is it not fair?
2. How do you respond to Arends's arguments about the idea of the "gender pay gap"? Has he provided enough evidence to convince you of his position?
3. Do you think the pay gap has more to do with a widening gap between the very rich and the very poor (or the very rich and the not-so-rich), or do you think it has more to do with gender? Why might women receive less money for the work they do?

WRITING ACTIVITIES

1. Write a response to Arends's essay. When you conclude your response, end with a sentence that imitates the style of his sentences in paragraph 14: "Ma'am, if you think Arianna Huffington or Marissa Mayer is your 'sister,' I have a used car to sell you. And a bridge."
2. In memo form, write a bulleted response to the main points raised by Arends to discount the "gender pay gap."
3. Write a brief essay that argues that one group of people should earn less than another group. What is the difference between the two groups of people? Why should one group earn more (or less) than the other? Develop arguments that explain why the disparity exists (even if your essay is satirical).

Christina Cauterucci

Should Women Be Required to Register for the Draft?

[*Slate*, February 3, 2016]

BEFORE YOU READ

In order for men and women to be truly equal, is it important that both sexes be required to sign up for the military draft? Why were women excluded from the draft for so long?

WORDS TO LEARN

scrap (para. 4): to discard (verb)

fundamentally (para. 5): basically (adverb)

dilemma (para. 5): a situation in which there are no good choices (noun)

chivalry (para. 6): the action of gallant gentlemen (noun)

conserver (para. 7): one who conserves or preserves (noun)

reinstate (para. 8): to put back (verb)

provisions (para. 8): stipulations (noun)

stipulate (para. 8): to require specifically (verb)

imprimatur (para. 9): support (noun)

canards (para. 9): unfounded reports or beliefs (noun)

deferment (para. 11): postponement (noun)

align (para. 11): to bring into line (verb)

W omen should be required to register for the draft along with men, top-ranking military representatives said on Tuesday [February 2, 2016]. At a Senate Armed Services Committee hearing, Army chief of staff Gen. Mark Milley and Marine Corps commandant Gen. Robert Neller testified that since the Department of Defense struck down all military restrictions based on gender in January, and women are now serving in combat roles, there's no reason to exclude them from Selective Service[1] requirements. 1

Current Selective Service law requires all "male persons" to register within 30 days of their 18th birthday. The U.S. military has been an all-volunteer force since the '70s, but the draft still includes all men up 2

---

[1] Selective Service (para.1): The Selective Service Act, enacted in 1917, gave the federal government the power to raise a national army through compulsory enlistment.

Christina Cauterucci is a staff writer for Slate *magazine.*

to age 25 as "a very, very, very inexpensive insurance policy," Selective Service system director Larry Romo told KPCC in October.

The U.S. has only seriously considered drafting women once in its   3 history.

When Defense Secretary Ash Carter announced in December 2015   4 that the department would end all gender-based exclusions, the chairmen of the Senate and House Armed Services Committees gave Congress 30 days to consider the decision's impact on Selective Service law. It renewed a debate that began in January 2013, when then–Defense Secretary Leon Panetta broadcast his plan to end the military's ban on women in combat roles, a recommendation made unanimously by the Joint Chiefs of Staff. Back then, some argued that lifting of the ban might legally force Congress to either include women in the draft or scrap it altogether for good. In fact, some activists, like Elaine Donnelly, president of the Center for Military Readiness, opposed lifting the combat-roles ban precisely *because* it could affect civilian women, who'd be forced to sign up for the draft.

In the '70s and '80s, though polls indicated that more than 70 per-   5 cent of the country supported the Equal Rights Amendment, some people opposed it because they believed it would require women to serve in the same military roles as men, including combat units, and to register for the draft. Feminists were divided on the issue — though the vast majority agreed that women were physically able to serve in any military capacity, pacifist feminists could not support the expansion of an institution they believed was fundamentally destructive and immoral. "The dilemma for many feminists became trying to deny that the intention of the ERA would be diluted by gender considerations in military service, while not recommending the extension of conscription for another segment of the population," wrote Swarthmore College Peace Collection curator Wendy Chmielewski in 1989.

The U.S. has only seriously considered drafting women once in its   6 history: during a military-nurse shortage in World War II. In response, a group of activists formed the Women's Committee to Oppose Conscription. "Objection to the conscription of women . . . ought not to proceed from the assumption that chivalry requires the shielding of women from hardship," WCOC chairwoman Georgia Harkness wrote at the time. "There is no reason for objecting to it either on the basis of special privilege of sex or of the exemption of anybody from the hard requirements of our time." Instead, the group opposed women's inclusion in the draft because it would roll back the independence won by first-wave feminists. "Women have fought for years for the right to be free from the domination of men — the right to be educated, to vote, to marry or not to marry as they want, to work," wrote WCOC director Mildred Scott Olmsted. "The army gives [women] . . . opportunity to do only minor jobs. They would have no real influence in the army, and no freedom, and they know it."

Still, Olmsted's argument rested on a traditional view of women's roles in society: "Women are naturally and rightly the homemakers, producers, and conservers of life. . . . They play their part during the war by 'keeping the home fires burning until the boys come home' by carrying on the services that hold the community together." 7

In 1980, when President Carter requested that Congress reinstate the draft, he also recommended it allow the president to evaluate the military's needs upon possible future conscription and make a decision then about whether and how to include women in the draft. Congress did restore Selective Service registration but did not add any provisions for the inclusion of women, chiefly because the Department of Defense did not allow women to serve in combat roles. Members of Congress also argued that there was no pressing need to widen the draft pool by adding women and that it might harm existing social structures. The National Organization for Women issued a statement opposing the draft, but stipulating that if a draft must exist, it should include women. 8

> The National Organization for Women issued a statement opposing the draft, but stipulating that if a draft must exist, it should include women.

Around the same time, a group of men filed a lawsuit claiming that the exclusion of women from the draft violated their Fifth Amendment right to due process. A 6–3 Supreme Court decision denied their claim in 1981 in *Rostker v. Goldberg*, once again because of the Department of Defense's ban on women serving in combat roles. "The existence of the combat restrictions clearly indicates the basis for Congress' decision to exempt women from registration," Justice William Rehnquist wrote in the majority opinion. "The purpose of registration was to prepare for a draft of combat troops. Since women are excluded from combat, Congress concluded that they would not be needed in the event of a draft, and therefore decided not to register them." Justice Thurgood Marshall issued a compelling dissent, writing that the draft's gender-based exclusion "places its imprimatur on one of the most potent remaining public expressions of 'ancient canards about the proper role of women.'" 9

Throughout the entire modern history of the military draft, each time its exclusion of women has been questioned, government committees 10 have fallen back on *Rostker* and the Department of Defense's ban on women in combat. That ban is no longer. Women compose 15 percent of active troops and 23 percent of new military officers; they've graduated from Army Ranger School and will soon become Navy SEALs. When the military officially began to open all combat jobs to women in December 2015, the *Bloomberg* editorial board argued that women have no more reason not to register for the draft. "The Selective Service requirement remains essential to keeping the U.S. prepared for the unthinkable," the board wrote. "Should a larger military be required, it's important to have a registry of all potentially eligible participants."

Though Congress is highly unlikely to ever resume active conscription, the purpose of a nationwide Selective Service registry is to enforce an equal distribution of the burden of war. Since the Vietnam War, when the wealthy and powerful easily avoided the draft, most easy-to-access deferments have been scrapped. If the draft is to have its desired effect — forcing decision-makers in the federal government to personally grapple with the severity of sending combat troops overseas and lessening the disproportionate consequences of war borne by poor communities and communities of color — women must be implicated by its reach. Military officials can debate how and where drafted women will serve according to their merits when and if the unthinkable comes to pass. For now, it's up to Congress to align one of our country's last remaining discriminatory laws with today's military reality.[2] 11

VOCABULARY/USING A DICTIONARY

1. What does it mean if something is *unanimous*? What does *unanimously* (para. 4) mean?

2. What word is at the root of *expansion* (para. 5)?

3. What is a synonym for *conscription* (para. 5)?

RESPONDING TO WORDS IN CONTEXT

1. What is the difference between *exclude* (para. 1) and *exclusions* (para. 4)?

2. Men are required to *register* (para. 5) for the draft. What happens when they *register*?

3. What substance is usually *diluted*? If the ERA is *diluted* (para. 5) by certain considerations, what happens to it?

---

[2] In June 2016, the U.S. Senate passed a bill requiring women who turn eighteen on or after January 1, 2018, to register with Selective Service. The bill remains controversial.

DISCUSSING MAIN POINT AND MEANING

1. What has the military recently decided to change? How will this change make things different from how they have been in the past?

2. Why were some feminists divided over the Equal Rights Amendment in the 1970s and 1980s, according to Cauterucci?

3. Why did the Supreme Court rule in 1981 that women could be excluded from the draft?

EXAMINING SENTENCES, PARAGRAPHS, AND ORGANIZATION

1. Consider the structure of the first sentence: "Women should be required to register for the draft along with men, top-ranking military representatives said on Tuesday." Why do you think the sentence is structured in this way?

2. Why is paragraph 7 its own paragraph? Why isn't it attached to paragraph 6?

3. Cauterucci quotes different sources at various points throughout the essay. Why do you think she used so many quotations? What is the effect on the essay overall?

THINKING CRITICALLY

1. President Carter wanted to reinstate the draft. Do you think a draft is a good idea? Explain why it is or isn't a good idea, whether the United States includes women in the Selective Service registry or just men.

2. How did WCOC members feel about the idea of drafting women? Why were they against it?

3. Do you think women should be banned from combat? Why or why not? Do you think men *and* women should be registered for the draft?

WRITING ACTIVITIES

1. Ask students to formulate questions and interview each other in pairs about whether or not women should be required to register for the draft. Then have them cowrite a brief article under the headline "Should Women Be Required to Register for the Draft?" The article should be written as a response to the statements Cauterucci begins with, at the Senate Armed Services Committee hearing (para. 1). It should include student opinions and quotations from the interview in its argument.

2. On the topic of women and the draft, the *Bloomberg* editorial board has argued: "The Selective Service requirement remains essential to keeping the U.S. prepared for the unthinkable. Should a larger military be required, it's important to have a registry of all potentially eligible participants" (para. 10). Write a response to this statement. You may respond to it based

on your feelings about women's signing up for the draft, or you may respond based on your feelings about conscription in general.

3. In a freewriting exercise, explore the idea of the draft as "a very, very, very inexpensive insurance policy" (para. 2). As you write, consider the ages of registered individuals. Consider possible scenarios that might make an active or inactive draft seem necessary or worthwhile. Consider any benefits and drawbacks to having to register on your eighteenth birthday, whether you are male or female.

Spotlight on Data and Research

Elizabeth Aura McClintock

The Psychology of Mansplaining

[*Psychology Today*, March 31, 2016]

In 2008, noted author and activist Rebecca Solnit published a now-classic essay, "Men Explain Things to Me." In her 2014 book of that title, she recalls that after the essay appeared, a "website named 'Academic Men Explain Things to Me' arose, and hundreds of university women shared their stories of being patronized, belittled, talked over, and more." She goes on to say that the term mansplaining *was coined soon after, but she "had nothing to do with its actual creation," though her essay "apparently inspired" the coinage. In the following study from* Psychology Today, *Notre Dame professor and gender researcher Elizabeth Aura McClintock takes a close look at the new word and the not-so-new behavior it describes.*

In a recent episode of *Jimmy Kimmel Live*, Kimmel "mansplains" the art   1 of political speech to Hillary Clinton. He begins by mansplaining the concept of mansplaining:

> **JK:** Are you familiar with mansplaining? You know what that is?

> **HC:** That's when a man explains something to a woman in a patronizing way.

> **JK:** Actually, it's when a man explains something to a woman in a condescending way. But you were close.

Kimmel goes on to interrupt Clinton frequently, offering contradictory and sexist advice. Of course, he and Clinton were intentionally parodying the phenomenon of mansplaining, but it reminded me of a conversation I'd actually had the day before:

> **Man:** How do you calculate the area of a rectangle?

Me: Length times width.

Man: No, base times height.

In retrospect, my answer *should* have been that of course I know that—
I've taken several advanced calculus courses and I teach statistics—and
who is he to quiz my basic geometry knowledge anyway?

Taken together, the Kimmel-Clinton skit and my own experi- 2
ence piqued my interest in mansplaining more generally. The term has
only been around since 2008 (Rothman, 2012) but it has attracted a
great deal of popular attention, making the long list as a contender for
Oxford's word of the year (Steinmetz, 2014) and the short list in the
American Dialect Society's "Most Creative" category (Zimmer, 2013).
According to the *Oxford English Dictionary* editors, mansplaining is "to
explain something to someone, typically a man to woman, in a manner regarded as condescending or patronizing" (Steinmetz, 2014).
The American Dialect Society defines it as "when a man condescend-
ingly explains something to female listeners" (Zimmer, 2013). Lily
Rothman, in her "Cultural History of Mansplaining," elaborates it as
"explaining without regard to the fact that the explainee knows more
than the explainer, often done by a man to a woman."

Mansplaining as a portmanteau may be new, but the behavior has 3
been around for centuries (Rothman, 2012). The scholarly literature
has long documented gendered power differences in verbal interaction:
Men are more likely to interrupt, particularly in an intrusive manner
(Anderson and Leaper, 1998). Compared to men, women are more
likely to *be* interrupted, both by men and by other women (Hancock
and Rubin, 2015). Perhaps in part because they are accustomed to
it, women also respond more amenably to interruption than men do,
being more likely to smile, nod, agree, laugh, or otherwise facilitate the
conversation (Farley et al., 2010).

Interruptions matter: They are linked to social power—in dyadic 4
interactions, the more *powerful* partner is more likely to interrupt
(Kollock et al., 1985). Unfortunately, researchers have tended to focus
on easily quantifiable *aspects* of speech, rather than the *content* of speech.
More research is needed to ascertain the extent to which the condescension mansplaining posits is indeed common and gendered (directed
disproportionately by men toward women).

Mansplaining is problematic because the behavior itself reinforces 5
gender inequality. When a man explains something to a woman in a
patronizing or condescending way, he reinforces gender stereotypes
about women's presumed lesser knowledge and intellectual ability. This
is especially true when the woman is in fact *more* knowledgeable on the
subject. This aspect of mansplaining was central to the Kimmel-Clinton

continued

parody — clearly, Clinton has the greater expertise giving political speeches. It is also evident in Rebecca Solnit's tale of a man trying to explain her *own* book to her, despite not having read it himself. It was her essay, "Men Explain Things to Me," and the subsequent book that many credit for sparking the dialogue that ultimately generated the term *mansplaining*. (To my knowledge, Solnit herself did not use the word.) Having had numerous men explain *gender* to me — both in a general sense and as relates to my own research — I can sympathize with Solnit.

But mansplaining is also problematic in the gender-stereotypic 6 assumptions it makes about *men* (see Cookman, 2015). Misandry doesn't promote equality, nor does it undermine misogyny. Yes, mansplaining is sexist and boorish, but the term isn't fair to the many men who support gender equality (and don't mansplain). Moreover, men don't have a monopoly on arrogance or condescension — women are quite capable of both.

Mansplaining has caught the popular imagination because it pro- 7 vides a label for a common and offensive social reality: Women are often assumed to be ignorant and unintelligent, at least compared to men. Having a label for something is useful in that it makes it more visible, potentially working to erode both the behavior and the sexist assumptions that drive it. But it risks becoming a means of trivializing mansplaining as not worthy of real outrage and of degrading men generally (Cookman, 2015).

References

Anderson and Leaper. 1998. "Meta-Analysis of Gender Effects on Conversational Interruption: Who, What, When, Where, and Why." *Sex Roles* 39(3–4):225–252.

Cookman. 2015. "Allow Me to Explain Why We Don't Need Words Like 'Mansplain.'" *The Guardian*.

Farley, Ashcroft, Stasson, and Nusbaum. 2010. "Nonverbal Reactions to Conversational Interruptions: A Test of Complementary Theory and Status/Gender Parallel." *Journal of Nonverbal Behavior* 34(4): 193–206.

Hancock and Rubin. 2015. "Influence of Communication Partner's Gender on Language." *Journal of Language and Social Psychology* 34(1): 46–64.

Jimmy Kimmel Live, March 24, 2016.

Kollock, Blumstein, and Schwartz. 1985. "Sex and Power in Interaction: Conversational Privileges and Duties. *American Sociological Review* 50(1): 34–46.

Rothman. 2012. "A Cultural History of Mansplaining." *The Atlantic*.

Solnit. 2008. "Men Explain Things to Me." *LA Times*.

Steinmetz. 2014. "Clickbait, Normcore, Mansplain: Runners-Up for Oxford's Word of the Year." *Time*.

Zimmer. 2013. "Tag, You're It! 'Hashtag' Wins as 2012 Word of the Year." *Visual Thesaurus*.

DRAWING CONCLUSIONS

1. Does McClintock establish that mansplaining is a real social problem? Do you believe that the examples she gives prove the issue exists? Do you believe in mansplaining? Why or why not?

2. Besides mansplaining, what imbalances do you perceive in the ways men and women communicate? Do men use communication to establish power dynamics? If so, how?

3. McClintock points out that research has focused on the quantifiable aspects of speech, not its content, in studying mansplaining. How would you propose scientifically studying the content of speech to quantify mansplaining, or for that matter "womansplaining," "whitesplaining," and so on? Imagine an experiment you might design.

Judy Brady

I Want a Wife

[Ms., 1972]

If you were a college student taking composition in the 1970s, you would almost certainly have had to read Judy Brady's "I Want a Wife." The short essay appeared in practically every composition anthology available. Published when the contemporary feminist movement was in its early stages and gaining members rapidly (it was then often referred to as "women's liberation" or, in a sometimes heckling tone, "women's lib"), the essay appropriately first appeared in the premier issue of what became the movement's leading magazine, Ms. Although the essay is no longer anthologized to the extent it once was, some books still include it. Over forty years later, with the goals and principles of feminism far more established across the nation, it is interesting to see what this now-classic essay means to today's college generation.

Before the legendary essay appeared in Ms., "I Want a Wife" was delivered aloud for the first time in San Francisco in 1970 at a rally celebrating the fiftieth anniversary of women's right to vote in the United States. Brady (b. 1937) still resides in San Francisco, where she writes and is an activist for women's causes and the environment.

I belong to that classification of people known as wives. I am A Wife. And, not altogether incidentally, I am a mother.

Not too long ago a male friend of mine appeared on the scene fresh from a recent divorce. He had one child, who is, of course, with his ex-wife. He is looking for another wife. As I thought about him while I was ironing one evening, it suddenly occurred to me that I, too, would like to have a wife. Why do I want a wife?

I would like to go back to school so that I can become economically independent, support myself, and, if need be, support those dependent upon me. I want a wife who will work and send me to school. And while I am going to school I want a wife to take care of my children. I want a wife to keep track of the children's doctor and dentist appointments. And to keep track of mine, too. I want a wife to make sure my children eat properly and are kept clean. I want a wife who will wash the children's clothes and keep them mended. I want a wife who is a good nurturant attendant to my children, who arranges for their school-ing, makes sure that they have an adequate social life with their peers, takes them to the park, the zoo, etc. I want a wife who takes care of the children when they are sick, a wife who arranges to be around when the children need special care, because, of course, I cannot miss classes at school. My wife must arrange to lose time at work and not lose the job. It may mean a small cut in my wife's income from time to time, but I guess I can tolerate that. Needless to say, my wife will arrange and pay for the care of the children while my wife is working.

I want a wife who will take care of my physical needs. I want a wife   4
who will keep my house clean. A wife who will pick up after my chil-dren, a wife who will pick up after me. I want a wife who will keep my clothes clean, ironed, mended, replaced when need be, and who will see to it that my personal things are kept in their proper place so that I can find what I need the minute I need it. I want a wife who cooks the meals, a wife who is a *good* cook. I want a wife who will plan the menus, do the necessary grocery shopping, prepare the meals, serve them pleasantly, and then do the cleaning up while I do my studying. I want a wife who will care for me when I am sick and sympathize with my pain and loss of time from school. I want a wife to go along when our family takes vacation so that someone can continue to care for me and my children when I need a rest and change of scene.

I want a wife who will not bother me with rambling complaints   5
about a wife's duties. But I want a wife who will listen to me when I feel the need to explain a rather difficult point I have come across in my course of studies. And I want a wife who will type my papers for me when I have written them.

I want a wife who will take care of the details of my social life.   6
When my wife and I are invited out by my friends, I want a wife who will take care of the babysitting arrangements. When I meet people at school that I like and want to entertain, I want a wife who will have the house clean, will prepare a special meal, serve it to me and my friends, and not interrupt when I talk about things that interest me and my friends. I want a wife who will have arranged that the children are fed and ready for bed before my guests arrive so that the children do not bother us. I want a wife who takes care of the needs of my guests so that they feel comfortable, who makes sure that they have an ashtray, that

they are passed the hors d'oeuvres, that they are offered a second helping of the food, that their wine glasses are replenished when necessary,
that their coffee is served to them as they like it. And I want a wife who
knows that sometimes I need a night out by myself.

I want a wife who is sensitive to my sexual needs, a wife who makes   7
love passionately and eagerly when I feel like it, a wife who makes sure
that I am satisfied. And, of course, I want a wife who will not demand
sexual attention when I am not in the mood for it. I want a wife who
assumes the complete responsibility for birth control, because I do not
want more children. I want a wife who will remain sexually faithful to
me so that I do not have to clutter up my intellectual life with jealousies.
And I want a wife who understands that my sexual needs may entail
more than strict adherence to monogamy. I must, after all, be able to
relate to people as fully as possible.

If, by chance, I find another person more suitable as a wife than the   8
wife I already have, I want the liberty to replace my present wife with
another one. Naturally, I will expect a fresh, new life; my wife will take
the children and be solely responsible for them so that I am left free.

When I am through with school and have a job, I want my wife to   9
quit working and remain at home so that my wife can more fully and
completely take care of a wife's duties.

My God, who *wouldn't* want a wife?   10

BACKGROUND AND CONTEXT

1. In your opinion, what stereotypes about husbands and wives does Brady
   rely on in her essay? Do you think she exaggerates? Do you think these
   stereotypes still apply to marriages today? Explain why or why not.

2. Note that at the opening of her essay Brady wishes for a wife because she
   "would like to go back to school" (para. 3). How is this significant? What does
   it tell you about the era in which the essay was written? What does school
   have to do with her main goal in the essay? How does her behavior change
   toward her "wife" once she imagines herself being in school?

STRATEGY, STRUCTURE, AND STYLE

1. In rhetoric, the repetition of the opening words in a sentence is known as
   anaphora. Note how often Brady starts her sentences with "I want a wife."
   That repetition is clearly the dominant stylistic element of the essay. Why do
   you think she repeats the words so often, and what effect do you think it is
   intended to have on a reader?

2. Writers often use humor to make a serious point. How would you briefly summarize the point of Brady's essay? In what ways does humor contribute to that point?

COMPARISONS AND CONNECTIONS

1. In an essay that refers to at least one of the selections in this chapter, discuss how relevant you feel this forty-plus-year-old essay is. Try to explain what parts you think still matter to women today. Do you think she raises any issues that don't matter any longer? If she wrote the same essay today, how might she need to adjust to the existence of gay marriage?

2. In a brief essay, describe the "logic" of the essay. The "I" of the essay is already a "wife," so what does she become when she has a wife? Explain how Brady suggests what a "husband" is like. What advantages does her argument gain in setting up the differences in this indirect fashion instead of complaining directly about the behavior of husbands?

Discussing the Unit

SUGGESTED TOPIC FOR DISCUSSION

Gender identity, once limited to categories of "male" or "female," is now seen by many as more fluid. The embrace of the word *they* as a generic singular pronoun is evidence of a growing rejection of a traditional gender binary. And yet, many of the characteristics presumed of someone who is "male" or "female" continue to stereotype gender. Women still struggle for equality in light of their history as second-class citizens based on gender, and the debate continues about whether or not men and women are treated equally in American society. How do you think the newly expanded and more fluid concept of gender will affect the future of feminism and its goals?

PREPARING FOR CLASS DISCUSSION

1. In the past, men and women were viewed and treated very differently. Do you think those same biases and differences still exist today? If not, what happened to them? If so, why do you think they still exist?

2. When you think about gender, what traits do you think are particularly male? What traits are particularly female? Are there traits that you would consider "gender neutral"? If so, what are they?

FROM DISCUSSION TO WRITING

1. How do men and women treat each other as "other"? Using examples from at least three essays in this chapter, analyze the ways in which men and women respond to each other differently.

2. Which of the essays in this chapter advocate for gender equality, and which state that divisions between men and women simply exist? Write a short comparison of how the authors in at least three of these essays view gender.

TOPICS FOR CROSS-CULTURAL DISCUSSION

1. Do you think of yourself as specifically male or specifically female? Would it bother you if someone referred to you as *he* instead of *she* or vice versa depending on your gender identification? Using two essays from this chapter, write an essay in which you consider your gender identification and explore how these essays support your perception of gender.

2. How have gender roles and stereotypes developed and changed since "I Want a Wife" (p. 390) was written? Do wives or women still fill the roles mentioned in that essay? Do any of the other essays in this chapter offer an argument that things have changed?

12

The Climate Crisis: Have We Reached the Point of No Return?

The United Nations Intergovernmental Panel on Climate Change recently concluded that (1) the past three decades have almost certainly been the hottest in nearly one thousand years and (2) humans — through their insatiable appetite for the burned carbon that lights their cities and powers their vehicles — are almost certainly to blame. The report is nothing all that new, but headlines like it throw us now and then into a frenzy: What can we do to stem rising temperatures and the global calamities that might accompany them? Vociferous proposals ranging from a tax on carbon to a complete rewiring of the nation's power infrastructure speak to the urgency with which some people greet climate-change facts and figures.

A large part of the debate revolves around how "settled" the science behind climate change actually is. The science part may be hard enough for the average person to follow — with its computer models, statistics, and frequent references to CO_2 ppm (carbon dioxide parts per million) — but the issue is made even more difficult because it has grown so politicized. Before we explore some of the science, this chapter's "In Brief" feature looks at the ways different political viewpoints affect attitudes toward climate change, regardless of what scientists report. In "People's Views on Climate Change

Go Hand in Hand with Their Politics," the *Economist* cites a survey that found "70% of Democratic voters saw evidence of man-made climate change in recent weather patterns, whereas only 19% of Republican voters did." As we move forward, will discussion of climate change be less about irreversible events occurring at the earth's poles and more about what voters say at the nation's polls?

Where does the scientific community stand on climate change? Is there an overwhelming consensus of opinion, as some say? Or, as others say, are there many reputable scientists who remain skeptical about both the reality and catastrophic impact of climate change? It's significant to note, moreover, that some climate-change skeptics do agree that the earth is getting warmer, but they believe this change is the result of natural causes rather than emissions produced by a carbon-dependent human population. They do not believe sufficient data exist to claim the warming is man-made. As Patrick Moore, one of the cofounders of Greenpeace, maintains in "Why I Am a Climate Change Skeptic," "We don't understand the natural causes of climate change any more than we know if humans are part of the cause at present." Yet in "Why Climate Skeptics Are Wrong," Michael Shermer makes the case for "anthropogenic global warming (AGW)," the scientists' term for man-made warming of the earth. Shermer has no doubt that a consensus of scientists firmly accepts man-made climate change, and he argues that the skeptics have no coherent body of evidence to support their position. He cites a leading researcher who succinctly makes this point: "There is no cohesive, consistent alternative theory to human-caused global warming."

Not an authority on the subject herself, San Diego State student Maddy Perello weighs in on the scientific debate by citing articles and studies that demonstrate not just that the earth is growing warmer, but that a majority of people are insufficiently aware of the fact. In "Climate Change: A Serious Threat," she quotes a recent study by the Yale School of Forestry and Environmental Studies that grades Americans on their knowledge of climate change and concludes that only 8 percent "have knowledge equivalent to an A or B, 40 percent would receive a C or D, and 52 percent would get an F."

If the planet is growing warmer, why is that a bad thing? Can there be beneficial effects of global warming? Despite forecasts that an increasingly warmer earth will cause catastrophes, many people, especially Americans, have been enjoying a long spell of improved weather. In the abstract to their scientific article "Recent Improvement and Projected Worsening of Weather in the United States," Patrick J. Egan and Megan Mullin claim that "virtually all Americans are now experiencing the much milder winters that they typically prefer, and these mild winters have not been offset by markedly more uncomfortable summers or other negative changes." This situation is only temporary, the authors warn, but the improved weather throughout large parts of the nation has been "a poor source of motivation for Americans to demand a policy response to climate change."

At the height of the Cold War, a best seller appeared that convincingly showed Americans that they had more to fear than a Soviet nuclear attack. This was Rachel Carson's 1962 classic *Silent Spring*, a book some call the foundational text of the environmentalist movement. This chapter's "America Then" comes from her introductory chapter, "A Fable for Tomorrow." Carson imagines a bleak future, many years after we have neglected our environment and overexploited our natural resources. "No witchcraft, no enemy action had silenced the rebirth of new life in this stricken world," she writes. "The people had done it themselves." As you read, consider whether you agree, over fifty years later, that this kind of future could await us on our current path. What can we do to swerve out of its way?

The Economist

People's Views on Climate Change Go Hand in Hand with Their Politics

[*The Economist*, November 28, 2015]

*I*n November 2015, the Economist, one of the world's leading periodicals, put out a special report on climate change in anticipation of a major international conference in Paris. Skeptical of several popular solutions to the problem — such as "existing solar and wind technologies" — the Economist warned that mankind will "have to think much more boldly about how to live under skies containing high concentrations of greenhouse gasses." Along with various articles, the editors included a brief sidebar, reprinted below, pointing out that, based on the number of Google searches, Kim Kardashian receives more public attention than climate change and that since the late 1990s the issue has been characterized by a persistent "partisan divide."

For all the torrent of scientific reports, books and television documen-   1
taries on the subject, climate change commands a good deal less public attention than Kim Kardashian, a reality-TV star. Early in 2007 Google searches for Ms. Kardashian's name overtook searches for "climate change." She has never fallen behind since. Even Bangladeshis Google her more than they do the forces that threaten their country — in English, at least.

The rich are more concerned about climate change than the poor, who   2
have many other things to worry about. A giant opinion-gathering exercise carried out by the United Nations finds that people in highly developed countries view climate change as the tenth most important issue out of a list of 16 that includes health care, phone and Internet access, jobs, political freedom and reliable energy. In poor countries — and indeed in the world as a whole — climate change comes 16th out of 16.

Even in the rich world, interest flagged for a few years following   3
the financial crisis of 2007. It is now recovering a little. But in America, another psephological[1] trend is plain: attitudes to climate change have become sharply polarized along political lines.

---

[1] psephological (para. 3): Relating to the analysis of voting patterns and elections

"The partisan divide started in 1997," says Jon Krosnick of Stanford   4
University. That was when a Democratic president, Bill Clinton, threw
his weight behind the UN effort to introduce mandatory caps for
greenhouse-gas emissions. It has since widened. YouGov, a pollster,
found in 2013 that 70% of Democratic voters saw evidence of man-
made climate change in recent weather patterns, whereas only 19% of
Republican voters did. A similar, though smaller, divide was found in
Britain.

It is not that conservatives are ignorant. Knowledge of science   5
makes little difference to people's beliefs about climate change, except
that it makes them more certain about what they believe. Republicans
with a good knowledge of science are more skeptical about global warming than less knowledgeable Republicans.

The best explanation for the gap is that people's beliefs about climate   6
change have become determined by feelings of identification with cultural and political groups. When people are asked for their views on climate change, says Dan Kahan of Yale University, they translate this into a
broader question: Whose side are you on? The issue has become associated with left-wing urbanites, causing conservatives to dig in against it.
The divide will probably outlive Ms. Kardashian's fame.

POINTS TO CONSIDER

1. What do you think is the point of starting and ending this brief report with
   the celebrity Kim Kardashian? What purpose does this serve?

2. "Knowledge of science makes little difference to people's beliefs about
   climate change, except that it makes them more certain about what they
   believe." Consider this statement from paragraph 5 carefully and explain
   what you think it means.

3. Why do you think Democrats are more likely to be seriously concerned
   about climate change than are Republicans? How does the last paragraph
   attempt to explain this divide? Do you agree?

Patrick Moore

Why I Am a Climate Change Skeptic

[*Heartland*, March 20, 2015]

Michael Shermer

Why Climate Skeptics Are Wrong

[*Scientific American*, December 1, 2015]

BEFORE YOU READ

What is your understanding of the debate over climate change? What information about climate change do you believe or disbelieve, and why?

WORDS TO LEARN

preposterous (Moore, para. 4): absurd (adjective)

apocalypse (Moore, para. 6): a time of destruction and disaster (noun)

convergence (Moore, para. 9): meeting point (noun)

stoke (Moore, para. 9): to increase the strength of something (verb)

curtail (Moore, para. 10): to limit or reduce (verb)

emit (Moore, para. 13): to send forth (verb)

consilience (Shermer, para. 2): concurrence (noun)

induction (Shermer, para. 2): an inference made from particular information (noun)

consensus (Shermer, para. 3): general agreement (noun)

anthropogenic (Shermer, para. 3): having to do with the influence of human beings on nature (adjective)

anomaly (Shermer, para. 4): a deviation or exception (noun)

incongruity (Shermer, para. 4): something out of place (noun)

gainsay (Shermer, para. 4): to contradict (verb)

deceptive (Shermer, para. 7): misleading (adjective)

integral (Shermer, para. 7): necessary (adjective)

Patrick Moore is a cofounder of the environmental activist organization Greenpeace and has been an important leading figure in the environmental field for over forty years. Michael Shermer is the publisher of Skeptic *magazine, which focuses on skeptical inquiry and science, and the author of* The Moral Arc *(2015).*

Patrick Moore

Why I Am a Climate Change Skeptic

[*Heartland*, March 20, 2015]

I am skeptical humans are the main cause of climate change and that it   1
will be catastrophic in the near future. There is no scientific proof of
this hypothesis, yet we are told "the debate is over" and "the science
is settled."

My skepticism begins with the believers' certainty they can predict   2
the global climate with a computer model. The entire basis for the dooms-
day climate change scenario is the hypothesis that increased atmospheric
carbon dioxide due to fossil fuel emissions will heat the Earth to unliv-
able temperatures.

In fact, the Earth has been warming very gradually for 300 years,   3
since the Little Ice Age ended, long before heavy use of fossil fuels. Prior
to the Little Ice Age, during the Medieval Warm Period, Vikings colo-
nized Greenland and Newfoundland, when it was warmer there than
today. And during Roman times, it was warmer, long before fossil fuels
revolutionized civilization.

The idea it would be catastrophic if carbon dioxide were to increase   4
and average global temperature were to rise a few degrees is preposterous.

Recently, the Intergovernmental Panel on Climate Change (IPCC)   5
announced for the umpteenth time we are doomed unless we reduce
carbon dioxide emissions to zero. Effectively this means either reducing
the population to zero, or going back 10,000 years before humans began
clearing forests for agriculture. This proposed cure is far worse than
adapting to a warmer world, if it actually comes about.

IPCC CONFLICT OF INTEREST

By its constitution, the IPCC has a hopeless conflict of interest. Its   6
mandate is to consider only the human causes of global warming, not
the many natural causes changing the climate for billions of years. We
don't understand the natural causes of climate change any more than
we know if humans are part of the cause at present. If the IPCC did not
find humans were the cause of warming, or if it found warming would be
more positive than negative, there would be no need for the IPCC under
its present mandate. To survive, it must find on the side of the apocalypse.

The IPCC should either have its mandate expanded to include all   7
causes of climate change, or it should be dismantled.

POLITICAL POWERHOUSE

Climate change has become a powerful political force for many reasons. 8
First, it is universal; we are told everything on Earth is threatened.
Second, it invokes the two most powerful human motivators: fear and guilt. We fear driving our car will kill our grandchildren, and we feel guilty for doing it.

> Climate change has become a powerful political force for many reasons.

Third, there is a powerful convergence 9
of interests among key elites that support
the climate "narrative." Environmentalists
spread fear and raise donations; politicians
appear to be saving the Earth from doom; the media has a field day with
sensation and conflict; science institutions raise billions in grants, create
whole new departments, and stoke a feeding frenzy of scary scenarios;
business wants to look green, and get huge public subsidies for projects
that would otherwise be economic losers, such as wind farms and solar
arrays. Fourth, the Left sees climate change as a perfect means to redis-
tribute wealth from industrial countries to the developing world and the
UN bureaucracy.

So we are told carbon dioxide is a "toxic" "pollutant" that must be 10
curtailed, when in fact it is a colorless, odorless, tasteless gas and the
most important food for life on earth. Without carbon dioxide above
150 parts per million, all plants would die.

HUMAN EMISSIONS SAVED PLANET

Over the past 150 million years, carbon dioxide had been drawn down 11
steadily (by plants) from about 3,000 parts per million to about 280 parts
per million before the Industrial Revolution. If this trend continued,
the carbon dioxide level would have become too low to support life on
Earth. Human fossil fuel use and clearing land for crops have boosted
carbon dioxide from its lowest level in the history of the Earth back to
400 parts per million today.

At 400 parts per million, all our food crops, forests, and natural eco- 12
systems are still on a starvation diet for carbon dioxide. The optimum
level of carbon dioxide for plant growth, given enough water and nutri-
ents, is about 1,500 parts per million, nearly four times higher than today.
Greenhouse growers inject carbon dioxide to increase yields. Farms and
forests will produce more if carbon dioxide keeps rising.

We have no proof increased carbon dioxide is responsible for the 13
earth's slight warming over the past 300 years. There has been no significant warming for 18 years while we have emitted 25 percent of all the

carbon dioxide ever emitted. Carbon dioxide is vital for life on Earth and plants would like more of it. Which should we emphasize to our children?

CELEBRATE CARBON DIOXIDE

The IPCC's followers have given us a vision of a world dying because of   14
carbon dioxide emissions. I say the Earth would be a lot deader with no carbon dioxide, and more of it will be a very positive factor in feeding the world. Let's celebrate carbon dioxide.

Michael Shermer

Why Climate Skeptics Are Wrong

[*Scientific American*, December 1, 2015]

A t some point in the history of all scientific theories, only a minor-   1
ity of scientists — or even just one — supported them, before evidence accumulated to the point of general acceptance. The Copernican model, germ theory, the vaccination principle, evolutionary theory, plate tectonics and the big bang theory were all once heretical ideas that became consensus science. How did this happen?

An answer may be found in what 19th-century philosopher of sci-   2
ence William Whewell called a "consilience of inductions." For a theory to be accepted, Whewell argued, it must be based on more than one induction — or a single generalization drawn from specific facts. It must have multiple inductions that converge on one another, independently but in conjunction. "Accordingly the cases in which inductions from classes of facts altogether different have thus *jumped together*," he wrote in his 1840 book *The Philosophy of the Inductive Sciences*, "belong only to the best established theories which the history of science contains." Call it a "convergence of evidence."

Consensus science is a phrase often heard today in conjunction with   3
anthropogenic global warming (AGW). Is there a consensus on AGW? There is. The tens of thousands of scientists who belong to the American Association for the Advancement of Science, the American Chemical Society, the American Geophysical Union, the American Medical Association, the American Meteorological Society, the American Physical Society, the Geological Society of America, the U.S. National Academy of Sciences and, most notably, the Intergovernmental Panel on Climate Change all concur that AGW is in fact real. Why?

It is not because of the sheer number of scientists. After all, science   4
is not conducted by poll. As Albert Einstein said in response to a 1931
book skeptical of relativity theory entitled *100 Authors against Einstein*,
"Why 100? If I were wrong, one would
have been enough." The answer is that there

| After all, science
| is not conducted
| by poll.

is a convergence of evidence from multiple lines of inquiry—pollen, tree rings,
ice cores, corals, glacial and polar ice-cap
melt, sea-level rise, ecological shifts, carbon
dioxide increases, the unprecedented rate of temperature increase—
that all converge to a singular conclusion. AGW doubters point to the
occasional anomaly in a particular data set, as if one incongruity gainsays
all the other lines of evidence. But that is not how consilience science
works. For AGW skeptics to overturn the consensus, they would need to
find flaws with all the lines of supportive evidence *and* show a consistent
convergence of evidence toward a different theory that explains the data.
(Creationists have the same problem overturning evolutionary theory.)
This they have not done.

A 2013 study published in *Environmental Research Letters* by Austra-   5
lian researchers John Cook, Dana Nuccitelli and their colleagues examined 11,944 climate paper abstracts published from 1991 to 2011. Of
those papers that stated a position on AGW, about 97 percent concluded
that climate change is real and caused by humans. What about the remaining 3 percent or so of studies? What if they're right? In a 2015 paper
published in *Theoretical and Applied Climatology*, Rasmus Benestad of
the Norwegian Meteorological Institute, Nuccitelli and their colleagues
examined the 3 percent and found "a number of methodological flaws
and a pattern of common mistakes." That is, instead of the 3 percent
of papers converging to a better explanation than that provided by the
97 percent, they failed to converge to anything.

"There is no cohesive, consistent alternative theory to human-caused   6
global warming," Nuccitelli concluded in an August 25, 2015, commen-
tary in the *Guardian*. "Some blame global warming on the sun, others on
orbital cycles of other planets, others on ocean cycles, and so on. There
is a 97% expert consensus on a cohesive theory that's overwhelmingly
supported by the scientific evidence, but the 2–3% of papers that reject
that consensus are all over the map, even contradicting each other. The
one thing they seem to have in common is methodological flaws like
cherry picking, curve fitting, ignoring inconvenient data, and disregard-
ing known physics." For example, one skeptical paper attributed climate
change to lunar or solar cycles, but to make these models work for the

4,000-year period that the authors considered, they had to throw out 6,000 years' worth of earlier data.

Such practices are deceptive and fail to further climate science when exposed by skeptical scrutiny, an integral element to the scientific process.   7

VOCABULARY/USING A DICTIONARY

1. From what language does the word *skepticism* (Moore, para. 2) derive? What does it mean?

2. What is a *mandate* (Moore, para. 6)?

3. What part of speech is *heretical* (Shermer, para. 1)? What does it mean?

RESPONDING TO WORDS IN CONTEXT

1. What does Moore mean when he refers to the *umpteenth* (para. 5) time? Why does he choose that "number"?

2. What is a *constitution*? How is the word used in paragraph 6 of Moore's essay?

3. Shermer uses the phrase *in conjunction* twice — once in paragraph 2 and again in paragraph 3. How might you explain what it means, based on context?

DISCUSSING MAIN POINT AND MEANING

1. What reasons does Moore give for his skepticism of climate change?

2. What is the "convergence of evidence" (para. 4) that Shermer says confirms the idea of anthropogenic global warming?

3. What have climate-change skeptics *not* done in order to disprove AGW theory, according to Shermer?

EXAMINING SENTENCES, PARAGRAPHS, AND ORGANIZATION

1. Choose a handful of words to describe the opening paragraphs of both essays. Which one states a thesis from the outset? What do you think of the authors' approaches?

2. Choose a handful of words to describe the organization of both essays. What are some of the main differences between them?

3. What does Shermer's first sentence suggest about science and scientific theories? How does he get this idea across at the sentence level?

THINKING CRITICALLY

1. Do you agree with Moore's insistence that the IPCC should be dismantled? Explain why you agree or disagree.

2. As an AGW skeptic, does Moore make an argument against man-made climate change that meets the criteria for overturning the consensus (as outlined in Shermer's essay)?

3. What do you think of the evidence Shermer offers in support of the theory of AGW? Is it convincing? Why or why not?

WRITING ACTIVITIES

1. Create an outline of both essays. Compare the outlines. How has each writer crafted his argument? What are the main similarities and differences?

2. Write a brief response to the essayist whose ideas you disagree with. With what points in his argument do you take issue? Are there points you think are valid? Once you respond to his argument, state your own position clearly.

3. Write a brief response to the essayist whose ideas you agree with. On which points do you agree? Is there anything you find weak about his argument? What would you add to it, if it were your essay?

Maddy Perello (student essay)

Climate Change: A Serious Threat

[*The Daily Aztec*, San Diego State University, September 16, 2015]

BEFORE YOU READ

Can you explain the different causes of climate change? How much do you know about it?

WORDS TO LEARN

species (para. 2): a category of biological classification in which certain characteristics are shared (noun)

spur (para. 3): to urge on (verb)

polarization (para. 3): a division into two opposing factions (noun)

fluctuation (para. 7): a change from one condition to another (noun)

excessive (para. 7): going beyond the usual (adjective)

deforestation (para. 8): the clearing of forests (noun)

multifaceted (para. 10): having many parts (adjective)

replenish (para. 11): to build something up again (verb)

overview (para. 14): a description that encapsulates or summarizes a situation (noun)

Maddy Perello is a student at San Diego State University.

Human use of natural resources coal, oil and gas could melt all the ice on the planet in as little as 5,000 years, according to *National Geographic*'s interactive "Rising Sea Levels" map.

When that happens, San Diego, the Central Valley, and the entire Eastern Seaboard of the U.S. will be underwater, and the average global temperature will go from 58 to 80 degrees Fahrenheit. Luckily for us, it is doubtful that most species will survive that long, anyway. As a *National Geographic* article by Nadia Drake estimates, "As many as three-quarters of animal species could be extinct within several human lifetimes."

We are facing constant threats of climate change all over the world. Human carbon dioxide emissions are contributing to ocean acidification, global warming, extreme weather, sea-level rise, species extinction and disease. That sentence alone should be enough to spur action toward change. Instead, climate change has fallen victim to political polarization and doubt.

> Human carbon dioxide emissions are contributing to ocean acidification, global warming, extreme weather, sea-level rise, species extinction and disease.

A recent study by the Yale School of Forestry and Environmental Studies reports that 63 percent of Americans know that climate change is happening, but only 8 percent "have knowledge equivalent to an A or B, 40 percent would receive a C or D, and 52 percent would get an F."

Everyone, but college students especially, should have an understanding of the problems we are going to inherit from older generations and pass on to younger ones.

The basics of climate change are as follows: The sun radiates heat to Earth, and Earth radiates heat back into outer space. Greenhouse gasses in the atmosphere trap some of that heat and it warms up the planet. This is known as the greenhouse effect and is largely natural and precisely balanced.

In fact, without the greenhouse effect, Earth would be too cold to sustain life. Fluctuations in this balance are also natural and have happened throughout the planet's 4.6-billion-year history (think ice ages and periods of extreme heat). Humans are disrupting the balance with excessive carbon dioxide emissions.

CO_2 accounts for 0.035 percent of Earth's atmosphere naturally. Between the constant burning of fossil fuels, agriculture and deforestation, humans emit seven gigatons of CO_2 per year (about the weight of 1 billion elephants), and have brought this number up to 0.04 percent, according to a Teachers TV video.

It is estimated that the average temperature of the planet will be 2–6   9
degrees warmer by the end of the century. In all of the planet's recorded
history, the temperature has never changed by more than 2 degrees in
100 years, so there is no doubt that humans are accelerating the global
warming process.

Anthropogenic climate change has environmental, social and eco-   10
nomic implications. It is a vast and multifaceted issue that will affect
all life on the planet. This is the world that today's college students are
graduating into.

August 13 was Overshoot Day — the day on which humans have   11
used the amount of natural resources Earth can produce in 12 months —
according to the World Wildlife Fund. That means we are using more
than the planet can support and replenish.

There is a famous anonymous quote, "We do not inherit the Earth   12
from our ancestors; we borrow it from our children."

People have an obligation to limit the damage done to the Earth   13
because it provides every essential resource that humans and all other
living things need to survive.

This is merely an overview of the huge, all-encompassing fields of   14
environmental science and sustainability. Amongst many complex problems, one thing is clear: Something needs to change. Since less than half
of the population of the U.S. is knowledgeable about climate change,
education is step one.

VOCABULARY/USING A DICTIONARY

1. Can you define *sustainability* (para. 14) even if you don't know the meaning
   of the word? What clues are in the word itself?

2. What kind of force is a *gigaton* (para. 8)?

3. If something is *anonymous* (para. 12), what do we know about it?

RESPONDING TO WORDS IN CONTEXT

1. What part of speech is *estimates* in paragraph 2? What does it mean in this
   context?

2. What is *ocean acidification* (para. 3)?

3. What happens in a *greenhouse* (para. 6)?

DISCUSSING MAIN POINT AND MEANING

1. What is the benefit of the greenhouse effect?

2. How informed are Americans about climate change, according to Perello?

3. What specific change does Perello point to as the main indication that humans are responsible for accelerated global warming?

EXAMINING SENTENCES, PARAGRAPHS, AND ORGANIZATION

1. How does Perello begin her essay? Do you find her beginning effective or ineffective? Explain your answer.

2. Why does Perello include a sentence that begins with *we* in paragraph 3? Does she do this anywhere else in the essay?

3. Many people argue that climate change is the result of human activity. Others argue that climate change is a completely natural occurrence. What position does Perello take on climate change?

THINKING CRITICALLY

1. What grade would you give yourself for your knowledge of climate change? Why did you choose the grade you chose?

2. Perello quotes a *National Geographic* article that suggests "as many as three quarters of animal species could be extinct within several human lifetimes" (para. 2). Does this statistic surprise or concern you? Why or why not?

3. Did any of the information in Perello's essay convince you that climate change is an urgent issue we need to address? What in particular did you find convincing, even if you disagree with any parts of her essay?

WRITING ACTIVITIES

1. Perello includes a famous quotation: "We do not inherit the Earth from our ancestors; we borrow it from our children" (para. 12). With this quote in mind, write briefly about how the earth was returned to you. In what condition do you believe you will return it to your or others' children in the future?

2. How might Americans become more knowledgeable about climate change? Why are so many people informed, but not well informed? What is missing? In small groups, discuss the ways in which we can become more informed. Do you agree with Perello's statement that "education is step one" (para. 14)?

3. Take notes on this essay, grouping Perello's ideas into a list or outline. How does her argument progress? Are there points she returns to, or does she move from one idea to the next? Discuss your lists and outlines as a class and try, in a large group, to identify the basic movement and structure of her essay.

Supporting Opinions Using Experts and Authorities

"The Persuasive Writer" section at the beginning of this book discusses various ways of supporting opinions, one of which is using the findings of experts and authorities on a particular subject (see p. 15). Such support is especially important when writing on scientific topics, such as climate change, that normally demand substantive and quantitative evidence. Note how San Diego State student Maddy Perello bolsters her argument with such citations in "Climate Change: A Serious Threat," a column she wrote for the school paper, the *Daily Aztec*. Note, too, how she offers multiple sources of evidence. As a writing strategy, this is more persuasive than relying on a single expert or authority.

1 *Opens with an authoritative source*	(1) Human use of natural resources coal, oil and gas could melt all the ice on the planet in as little as 5,000 years, according to *National Geographic*'s interactive "Rising Sea Levels" map.
2 *Quotes an authoritative article*	(2) As a *National Geographic* article by Nadia Drake estimates, "As many as three-quarters of animal species could be extinct within several human lifetimes."
3 *Cites a prestigious study*	(3) A recent study by the Yale School of Forestry and Environmental Studies reports that 63 percent of Americans know that climate change is happening, but only 8 percent "have knowledge equivalent to an A or B, 40 percent would receive a C or D, and 52 percent would get an F."
4 *Includes information from a video*	(4) Between the constant burning of fossil fuels, agriculture and deforestation, humans emit seven gigatons of CO_2 per year (about the weight of 1 billion elephants), and have brought this number up to 0.04 percent, according to a Teachers TV video.

STUDENT WRITER AT WORK
Maddy Perello

R.A. What inspired you to write this essay? And publish it?

M.P. I started realizing that many people don't know about the climate-change crisis, and if you don't understand it, can you really care? I decided to start writing short, to-the-point articles about all things sustainable in order to get people interested.

R.A. What was your main purpose in writing this piece?

M.P. I truly believe if people learn about climate change and understand what a pressing problem it is, they will want to do their part.

R.A. What response have you received to this piece?

M.P. The response to this article and my entire sustainability column has been great. I've been interviewed for other publications, motivated to write more and spread more knowledge, and I'm being published in a textbook!

R.A. Have you written on this topic since? Have you read or seen other work on the topic that has interested you?

M.P. I have written on many related topics: fish farms, agriculture, the sale of *National Geographic*. I read about climate change all the time. The most recent book I read was *This Changes Everything: Capitalism vs. the Climate*, by Naomi Klein.

R.A. Do you generally show your writing to friends before submitting it? Do you collaborate or bounce your ideas off others?

M.P. I talk to my friends about my articles if they're interested. I love bouncing ideas off of my editors, who generally aren't sustainability majors. They help me gear my writing toward the interest of the general public.

R.A. What topics most interest you as a writer?

M.P. Sustainability, oceanography, climate change, agriculture, and current events.

R.A. What advice do you have for other student writers?

M.P. Write about what you're passionate about — it will show in your writing.

Spotlight on Data and Research

Patrick J. Egan and Megan Mullin

Recent Improvement and Projected Worsening of Weather in the United States

[*Nature*, April 21, 2016]

Attitudes toward climate change, as everyone knows, are often based on immediate experience: While shoveling a car out of two feet of heavily impacted snow, an individual may well consider global warming something to look forward to. In the following abstract of their report in the prominent science journal Nature, *Patrick J. Egan and Megan Mullin discuss a fact that helps explain why the American public may not take the problems of a warming planet urgently: In recent years, climate change has caused weather patterns in the United States to be generally more pleasant than in earlier decades. They find "that 80% of Americans live in counties that are experiencing more pleasant weather than they did four decades ago," with milder winters and less uncomfortable summers. But, they point out, these improved conditions are merely temporary.*

As climate change unfolds, weather systems in the United States have   1
been shifting in patterns that vary across regions and seasons. Climate
science research typically assesses these changes by examining individual weather indicators, such as temperature or precipitation, in
isolation, and averaging their values across the spatial surface. As a
result, little is known about population exposure to changes in weather
and how people experience and evaluate these changes considered
together. Here we show that in the United States from 1974 to 2013, the
weather conditions experienced by the vast majority of the population
improved. Using previous research on how weather affects local population growth to develop an index of people's weather preferences, we find
that 80% of Americans live in counties that are experiencing more pleasant weather than they did four decades ago. Virtually all Americans are
now experiencing the much milder winters that they typically prefer,
and these mild winters have not been offset by markedly more uncomfortable summers or other negative changes. Climate change models
predict that this trend is temporary, however, because U.S. summers
will eventually warm more than winters. Under a scenario in which
greenhouse gas emissions proceed at an unabated rate (Representative
Concentration Pathway 8.5), we estimate that 88% of the U.S. public
will experience weather at the end of the century that is less preferable than weather in the recent past. Our results have implications
for the public's understanding of the climate change problem, which
is shaped in part by experiences with local weather. Whereas weather

patterns in recent decades have served as a poor source of motivation for Americans to demand a policy response to climate change, public concern may rise once people's everyday experiences of climate change effects start to become less pleasant.

DRAWING CONCLUSIONS

1. Many scientific and academic articles contain an abstract, a summary of the article's contents. Note that the passage above is not the article itself. What do you think is missing from the abstract?

2. Note that the abstract does not refer to catastrophic weather-related events such as hurricanes, flooding, tornadoes, wildfires, or drought. Do you think these are unrelated to the public's view of improving weather? Explain why or why not.

3. What is the implication of the United States' experiencing worse weather conditions in the future? How will it affect the public motivation for "a policy response to climate change"?

Rachel Carson

A Fable for Tomorrow

[*Silent Spring*, 1962]

In the early summer of 1962, a series of articles began appearing in the
New Yorker *that would help transform the way the American public*
understood the toxic impact of synthetic chemicals in the form of pesticides
on humans, animal life, and the natural environment. Later that year, the
articles were collected, expanded, and published in a best-selling book, Silent
Spring. *Written by Rachel Carson, a marine biologist and the author of*
several highly successful books on nature, the book achieved an enormous
influence; in fact, it is credited with initiating the modern environmental
movement. Celebrating the book's fiftieth anniversary in 2012, the Atlantic
reported: "Reading Silent Spring *today, it is disquieting to realize how much*
was already known in 1962 about the environmental health impacts of
petrochemicals. Even more shocking is to recognize how little our regulatory
response to these chemicals' effects has changed, despite the past five decades'
great advances in scientific understanding." The lyrical opening chapter of
the book included here, "A Fable for Tomorrow," was written last and served
as a prologue to alert readers to the impending environmental disasters her
book would describe and explain.

After receiving a master's degree in zoology at Johns Hopkins University,
Rachel Carson (1907–1964) spent a few years teaching and then took a
position in marine biology with the U.S. Department of Fisheries. In the
1930s, she partly realized her early ambition to be a poet when she began
publishing literary essays on the sea that would lead to a best-selling trilogy:
Under the Sea-Wind *(1941),* The Sea Around Us *(1951), and* The Edge
of the Sea *(1955). While writing* Silent Spring, *Carson was battling breast*
cancer, and she died within two years of the book's completion.

There was once a town in the heart of America where all life seemed to live   1
in harmony with its surroundings. The town lay in the midst of a check-
erboard of prosperous farms, with fields of grain and hillsides of orchards
where, in spring, white clouds of bloom drifted above the green fields. In

autumn, oak and maple and birch set up a blaze of color that flamed and flickered across a backdrop of pines. Then foxes barked in the hills and deer silently crossed the fields, half hidden in the mists of the fall mornings.

Along the roads, laurel, viburnum and alder, great ferns and wild-   2
flowers delighted the traveler's eye through much of the year. Even in winter the roadsides were places of beauty, where countless birds came to feed on the berries and on the seed heads of the dried weeds rising above the snow. The countryside was, in fact, famous for the abundance and variety of its bird life, and when the flood of migrants was pouring through in spring and fall people traveled from great distances to observe them. Others came to fish the streams, which flowed clear and cold out of the hills and contained shady pools where trout lay. So it had been from the days many years ago when the first settlers raised their houses, sank their wells, and built their barns.

Then a strange blight crept over the area and everything began   3
to change. Some evil spell had settled on the community: mysterious maladies swept the flocks of chickens; the cattle and sheep sickened and died. Everywhere was a shadow of death. The farmers spoke of much illness among their families. In the town the doctors had become more and more puzzled by new kinds of sickness appearing among their patients. There had been several sudden and unexplained deaths, not only among adults but even among children, who would be stricken suddenly while at play and die within a few hours.

There was a strange stillness. The birds, for example — where had   4
they gone? Many people spoke of them, puzzled and disturbed. The feeding stations in the backyards were deserted. The few birds seen anywhere were moribund; they trembled violently and could not fly. It was a spring without voices. On the mornings that had once throbbed with the dawn chorus of robins, catbirds, doves, jays, wrens, and scores of other bird voices there was now no sound; only silence lay over the fields and woods and marsh.

On the farms the hens brooded, but no chicks hatched. The farmers   5
complained that they were unable to raise any pigs — the litters were small and the young survived only a few days. The apple trees were coming into bloom but no bees droned among the blossoms, so there was no pollination and there would be no fruit.

The roadsides, once so attractive, were now lined with browned   6
and withered vegetation as though swept by fire. These, too, were silent,

deserted by all living things. Even the streams were now lifeless. Anglers no longer visited them, for all the fish had died.

In the gutters under the eaves and between the shingles of the roofs, a white granular powder still showed a few patches; some weeks before it had fallen like snow upon the roofs and the lawns, the fields and streams. 7

No witchcraft, no enemy action had silenced the rebirth of new life in this stricken world. The people had done it themselves. 8

This town does not actually exist, but it might easily have a thousand counterparts in America or elsewhere in the world. I know of no community that has experienced all the misfortunes I describe. Yet every one of these disasters has actually happened somewhere, and many real communities have already suffered a substantial number of them. A grim specter has crept upon us almost unnoticed, and this imagined tragedy may easily become a stark reality we all shall know. 9

What has already silenced the voices of spring in countless towns in America? This book is an attempt to explain. 10

BACKGROUND AND CONTEXT

1. When Carson's book appeared, many chemical companies and scientists affiliated with them condemned her approach and professional knowledge. What part of "A Fable for Tomorrow" do you think adversaries of her position would point to critically? Explain what you think they would object to.

2. Consider the book's title, *Silent Spring*. What do you think it refers to specifically? Explain what larger significance the title suggests.

STRATEGY, STRUCTURE, AND STYLE

1. Why do you think Carson begins her short prologue by describing an American town and then ends it by claiming that the "town does not actually exist" (para. 9)? As you read, did you think she was describing a particular town? Why or why not? How did you feel as a reader when you discovered she had imagined this town?

2. How would you explain Carson's decision not to include specific details in the prologue? For example, why do you think she uses expressions such as "a strange blight," "evil spell," and "mysterious maladies" (para. 3)? Identify similar words and expressions that appear in her description. How does this language establish a tone and a mood? How do you think her essay would differ if she mentioned chemicals and pesticides right off?

COMPARISONS AND CONNECTIONS

1. Throughout the chapter, we have seen scientific explanations and statistics used to persuade people to accept or reject the reality of climate change. Although Carson does cite scientific studies in her book, in her short prologue she does not. Explain how effective Carson's prologue is in terms of convincing readers about environmental dangers.

2. Carson's book is specifically about the dangers of pesticides. How might one use her method of writing, as seen in her prologue, to describe the environmental hazards many people worry about today, such as global warming, fracking, pollution, or nuclear energy? In a brief essay, try adopting Carson's style to warn readers about a particular hazard that concerns you.

Discussing the Unit

SUGGESTED TOPIC FOR DISCUSSION

Everyone — scientists, environmentalists, professors, students — has an opinion about climate change. Is it real? Is it our fault? Many who are watching shifting and worsening weather patterns wonder less about what is causing them and more about how we will begin to adapt if our entire ecosystem starts changing. The question we may soon be facing, no matter which side of the debate we fall on, is this — will even those who deny climate change is man-made still need to find explanations for extreme weather?

PREPARING FOR CLASS DISCUSSION

1. Why is there no consensus on global warming? How can there be so much disagreement? What do those who believe in climate change say causes it? What do those who are skeptical say causes climate change? Whom do you believe, and why?

2. What climatic and environmental changes are currently happening that most Americans are aware of? What have scientists and environmentalists noted as different or alarming? What might happen if we ignore climate change? What sort of difference might we be able to make if we pay attention now?

FROM DISCUSSION TO WRITING

1. The writers in this chapter offer scientific data to support their positions. How, then, do their positions conflict? Write an essay that shows that although some of these writers argue with each other, they all use seemingly valid research. Use at least three essays from this chapter in your comparison.

2. What do you think it will take to make more Americans respond to the question of global warming? Why aren't they discussing it more than they are? Do you think the topic is on everyone's mind? Make a case that supports your answers by using information from the *Economist*'s "People's Views on Climate Change Go Hand in Hand with Their Politics" (p. 398), Maddy Perello's "Climate Change: A Serious Threat" (p. 406), and Patrick J. Egan and Megan Mullin's "Recent Improvement and Projected Worsening of Weather in the United States" (p. 412).

TOPICS FOR CROSS-CULTURAL DISCUSSION

1. How have the earth and environmental studies changed from the time Rachel Carson was writing? How are they strikingly similar? Answer these questions by citing material from the essays in this chapter.

2. Consider the anonymous quote Maddy Perello uses in paragraph 12 of her essay (p. 406). Does it sound like a quote from a Western scientist? Why or why not? Draw from at least three of the essays in this chapter to support your position.

Continued from page ii

Patrick J. Egan and Megan Mullin. "Recent Improvement and Projected Worsening of Weather in the United States." Reprinted by permission from Macmillan Publishers Ltd.: *Nature* 532 (April 21, 2016): 357–60. Copyright © 2016.

Sarah Elliott. "Women: Stop Apologizing; Be Confident." From the *Graphic*, October 28, 2015. Copyright © 2015. Reprinted by permission of the *Graphic*, the student newspaper of Pepperdine University.

Susan Estrich. "Modern Family." September 30, 2015. Copyright © 2015 by Creators.com. By permission of Susan Estrich and Creators Syndicate, Inc.

Suzanne Fields. "There's More to Learning Than a Job Search." From the *Washington Times*, September 9, 2015. Copyright © 2015 by Creators.com. By permission of Suzanne Fields and Creators Syndicate, Inc.

Eric Foner. "Birthright Citizenship Is the Good Kind of American Exceptionalism." From *The Nation*, August 27, 2015. Copyright © 2015 The Nation. All rights reserved. Used by permission and protected by the Copyright Laws of the United States. The printing, copying, redistribution, or retransmission of this Content without express written permission is prohibited.

John A. Fry. "Allowing Guns Won't Make Campuses Safer." From *Philadelphia Inquirer*, October 19, 2015. Copyright © 2015. Reprinted by permission of the author.

David Fryxell. "Shooting from the Lip." From *Desert Exposure*, October 2014, http://www.desertexposure.com/201410/201410_ednote.php. Copyright © 2014. Reprinted by permission of *Desert Exposure*.

Ernest B. Furgurson. "The End of History?" From the *American Scholar* 84.4 (Autumn 2015). Copyright © 2015 by the author. Reprinted by permission.

Paul Fussell. "A Well-Regulated Militia." From *Thank God for the Atom Bomb and Other Essays*, by Paul Fussell (Summit Books, 1988). Originally published in the *New Republic* (June 1981). Copyright © 1988 by Paul Fussell. Reprinted by permission.

Andrew Hacker. "83 Seconds: How Fast-Paced Standardized Testing Has Created a New Glass Ceiling" (originally published under the title "Standardized Tests Are a New Glass Ceiling"). From *The Nation*, March 1, 2016. Copyright © 2016 The Nation. All rights reserved. Used by permission and protected by the Copyright Laws of the United States. The printing, copying, redistribution, or retransmission of this Content without express written permission is prohibited.

Adam Hamze. "Removal of the Jefferson Davis Statue Falls Short." From the *Daily Texan*, August 20, 2015. Copyright © 2015. Reprinted by permission.

Langston Hughes. "That Word *Black*." From *The Return of Simple*, by Langston Hughes, edited by Akiba Sullivan Harper. Copyright © 1994 by Ramona Bass and Arnold Rampersad. Reprinted by permission of Farrar, Straus & Giroux, LLC.

Suzanna Hupp. "My Gun Was 100 Yards Away, Completely Useless" (originally published under the title "The Gun-Rights Advocate"). From *Texas Monthly*, April 2016. Copyright © 2016. Reprinted by permission.

Jacksonville Daily News, Staff. "Intolerance Doesn't Belong on Campus." From *Jacksonville Daily News*, June 2, 2015, http://www.jdnews.com/article/20150602/Opinion/306029922. Copyright © 2015. Reprinted by permission.

Tom Jacobs. "Racism in the Kindergarten Classroom." From *Pacific Standard*, February 2, 2016. Copyright © 2016. Republished with permission of the Miller-McCune Center for Research, Media, and Public Policy. Permission conveyed through Copyright Clearance Center, Inc.

Carinn Jade. "Should We Make Our Children Say Sorry? No!" From *Brain, Child: The Thinking Magazine for Mothers*, January 5, 2015. Copyright © 2015. Reprinted by permission.

Wendy Kaminer. "A Civic Duty to Annoy." First published in the *Atlantic* (September 1997). Copyright © 1997 by Wendy Kaminer. Reprinted by permission of the author.

Suzy Khimm. "The New Nuclear Family: What Gay Marriage Means for the Future of Parenthood." From *New Republic*, July 23, 2015. Copyright © 2015 The New Republic. All rights reserved. Used

Index of Authors and Titles